Making
Walt Disney World Vacation
MEMORIES

Making
Walt Disney World Vacation
MEMORIES

Aronda Parks

The Original Press
Summerville, SC

Making Walt Disney World Vacation Memories
By Aronda Parks

All Rights Reserved ©2005 by The Original Press, Dann Hazel and Josh Fippen

No part of this book may be reproduced or transmitted in any form or by any means, graphic, electronic or mechanical, including photocopying, recording, taping, or by any information storage and retrieval system, without the written consent of the publisher.

For information, contact:

**The Original Press
Post Office Box 3466
Summerville, South Carolina 29484-3466**

This book makes reference to various Disney copyrighted characters, trademarks, marks and registered marks owned by The Walt Disney Company and Disney Enterprises, Inc.

Making Memories is not endorsed by, sponsored by, or connected with The Walt Disney Company in any way.

Aronda Parks is a copyrighted character owned by The Original Press. Image of **Aronda Parks** ©2005 www.clipart.com.

**ISBN: 0-9660615-4-3
LCCN: 2004117466**

Printed in the United States of America

Acknowledgements

The author would like to thank the following individuals and organizations for their assistance and support:

Twenty-four Walt Disney World veteran travelers who shared their opinions and experiences; Steve Soares for providing a wonderful Web site designed to keep travelers as up-to-date as possible prior to their arrival; Deb Wills and Deb Kona, AllEarsNet; Mary Waring, Mousesavers; Steve Frearson, WDWMagic; Dave and Jennifer Marx, PassPorter Publishing; Mike Scopa & Staff of MousePlanet; Jim Hill Media; Dave Card & Tagarel; Michelle Baumann, Walt Disney World Media Relations; Steve, Cami, Valerie, Kevin and Marjorie at Central Plains Book Manufacturing; and Walt Disney World Resort cast members, for making memories happen for all of us who love Disney.

Aronda's Memories Team of Experts

Becky Banfield, Downers Grove, IL
Susan and John C., Northern Indiana
Carrie Carney, New Orleans, LA
Chrislette and Jim Cherveny, Streator, IL
Megan Conley, Lehigh Valley, PA
Kathy, Sam & Julianne Cridlin, Indianapolis, IN
Lisa Cubbon, Marietta, GA
Dania Dewese, Texas
Brian Fineberg, Smithfield, RI
Josh Fippen, Charleston, SC
Dann Hazel, Charleston, SC
Sue Holland, Fort Myers, FL
Lindsey Holway & Chuck Smith, St. Louis, MO
Ed Igoe, Millersville, MD
Lynda and John Kutey, Green Island, NY
Melanie McDaniel, Jefferson City, TN
Maribeth and Thomas Moore, Pittsburgh, PA
Amanda Parr, Mandeville, LA
Shelle, Bob & Amanda Scheirer, Allentown, PA
Lauralee and Jason Scott, Green Bay, WI
Nicole Soh, Fort Bragg, NC
Crystal, Linda & Tom Swaim, Nennah, WI
Toni and Jim Veit, Smyrna, DE
David Wells, Pompano Beach, FL

Contents

Preface..1

Introduction..4

Chapter One
A Vacation with Character
Conjuring Your Own Unique Magic
18

Chapter Two
Getting It in Mouse Gear
Navigating the Planning Maze
27

Chapter Three
A Dream, the Wish Your Heart Makes
The Magic Kingdom
56

Chapter Four
Avoiding VABS (Vacation Burnout Syndrome)
The Mellow Vacationer
92

Chapter Five
The "If You Can Dream It, You Can Do It" Park
Epcot
98

Chapter Six
Tale as Old as Time
Falling in Love at Walt Disney World
133

Chapter 7
There's No Business Like Show Business
Disney-MGM Studios
140

Chapter 8
When The Mouse Is Just a Rodent
Turning the Skeptic on to the Magic
164

Chapter 9
A Walk on the Wild Side
Disney's Animal Kingdom
173

Chapter 10
Avoiding the Disney Meltdown
Traveling with Youngsters
195

Chapter 11
Rest for the Weary
Disney's Resort Hotels
214

Chapter 12
When the Touring Gets Tough, the Tough Go Shopping
Walt Disney World's Shopping Venues
245

Chapter 13
Give Me the Soup, the Salad, and the soufflé--and Nobody Gets Hurt
Disney Dining
277

Chapter 14
Shake Your Groove Thang!
Disney's Nightlife
328

Chapter 15
Enough Is Enough Is--Not Enough!
Expanding Your Disney Vacation
344

Chapter 16
Fitness, Fun, and Health
Disney Recreation
372

Chapter 17
Casting Their Spell
Cast Members' Roles in Making Magical Memories
392

Appendices
Disney Resort Hotels FAX and Phone Numbers
398

Index
400

About Aronda Parks

Like Stitch from Disney's *Lilo & Stitch*, Aronda can't be stopped. In fact, she's taken over the entire **Making Memories** project—including a major change to the title! "It was time to lose that stuffy old title," she opines. "You can wrap your mouth around ***Making Walt Disney World Vacation Memories*** much better than you can ***Making Memories on Your Walt Disney World Resort Vacation***." She nods sagely. "It was time for a big change, so I stole the pen from the old authors, and began revising."

You'll see Aronda's love for Disney—as well as her willingness to criticize when criticism is warranted—reflected through all 428 pages. Furthermore, she has redesigned the content pages throughout the book, as well as included more than 150 photos—most of them brand new to this edition.

"I was also determined to enhance the quality of the Resort maps," she explains. "Disney doesn't release its park maps ahead of your vacation, so I thought: What help it would be if we could provide full-color park maps for our readers as they plan their next WDW vacation."

Aronda also packs a bonus CD with each book, which includes vacation-planning extras—like games and coloring activities for the kids, Disney Trivia tests, and more than a hundred full-color photographs of favorite attractions. And for the first time ever, readers may order ***Aronda's Prep Pad***, a pocket-sized planner to help customize their Walt Disney World vacation.

But most of all, Aronda invited twenty-four Walt Disney World vacation veterans to provide their opinions about making the most of a Walt Disney World vacation. "A trip to Orlando is a huge investment of time and money," says Aronda. "So I wanted to make certain my readers enjoyed the benefit of opinions beyond my own."

About Aronda's Worksheets

Throughout *Making Memories 2005*, you'll find references to various worksheets designed to help you prepare for making Walt Disney World vacation memories. Because page size limits your workspace, Aronda has made letter-size editions of the worksheets available to her readers.

Log onto **www.arondaparks.com**, where you'll find full-size worksheets suitable for printing. Using these full-size sheets will make planning more fun and more comfortable. These worksheets are also included on your bonus CD.

Walt Disney World puts on one heck of a show—and ensures there are plenty of ways to involve you, the guest. To get started with your vacation planning, visit Aronda's Web site at **www.arondaparks.com**, the official WDW Web site at **www.disneyworld.com**, or call **1-407-WDISNEY**.

Preface

Thanks for allowing **Making Walt Disney World Vacation Memories 2005** to provide the essential vacation planning information you need for a unique—and magical—Walt Disney World vacation.

Though my Memories Team and I have worked diligently to provide the most accurate, current information possible, please remember that policies, prices and entertainment offerings change frequently at Walt Disney World. That's why it's not only important—but prudent—to call the Resort **(1-407-WDISNEY)** prior to your trip to confirm all details critical to your vacation enjoyment. You may also access lots of planning information on Walt Disney World's Official Internet site, lo-

2 MAKING MEMORIES

cated at **www.disneyworld.com**.

Walt Disney World is a place of grand traditions—one of which is the frequent launching of Resort-wide celebrations. Though it's tough to top the 100 Years of Magic Celebration (which ended in February 2003), The Walt Disney Company recently announced The Happiest Celebration on Earth, which begins in May 2005. Though the Celebration technically honors the fiftieth birthday of Disneyland Resort in Anaheim, California, The Walt Disney Company decided to include all theme parks worldwide in the festivities. **Making Memories** will alert you of special attractions and events to mark the Celebration.

Though Central Florida has many great attractions vying for your travel dollar—like Universal Studios Florida, SeaWorld, Busch Gardens and Kennedy Space Center—Aronda has devoted this entire vacation planning guide solely to Walt Disney World. The Resort comprises an overwhelming array of entertainment, dining, shopping, recreational and educational venues. If you plan to spend time at other Florida attractions, you'll find many excellent guides—and several Internet sites—to help you plan. However, don't make the mistake of allocating insufficient time to fully appreciate all that Walt Disney World offers. As one good friend put it: "I honestly thought that Disney World was merely a collection of amusement parks that I would tire of quickly. Once my family and I arrived, we quickly understood that you can have a first-class, fun-filled vacation without once leaving Disney property. We ended up discarding some of our plans so we'd have time to enjoy Disney attractions that we're certain would never have been surpassed by what we'd planned to do before leaving home."

Let's be very clear about one thing. Walt Disney World puts on one heck of a show. Several members of the Memories Team spent a week in October 2004 taking in many of the International Food and Wine Festival delights as well as Mickey's Not-So-Scary Halloween Party. They returned in December, during MouseFest, to savor the Resort in all its holiday splendor—from gloriously decorated resort hotels, to lavish parades, to concerts and meals fit for royalty. Even after numerous trips to the Resort—hundreds of them when you include all members of the team—since it opened in 1971, the Team still found attractions, shows, exhibits and other eye candy they never noticed before. They also continued to meet many wonderful people, both guests and cast members. Even while visiting old favorites, they found nuances and details missed on earlier trips—heightening their sense of vacation pleasure.

You're holding the 2005 edition of **Making Memories**. What makes this guide distinct from others is its determination to help you customize a Walt Disney World vacation just for you—not one that mimics the vacation that your neighbors, close friends or relatives had. You, your friends and family are unique individuals, with your own idea of magic, with special affinities and dislikes. Your vacation should reflect that individuality.

Toward that goal, make sure that each time you plan an extraordinary Disney vacation, you're using the most current edition of **Making Memories**. Walt Disney World is a dynamic enterprise. It's difficult to keep abreast of its transfigurations and transformations, which occur at a frenetic pace. While this guide will alert you to changes implemented since the previous edition, our companion Internet site, **www.arondaparks.com**, can keep you abreast of current news, along with photos, news, attraction descriptions and Resort "specials."

As you begin your journey through the world's most popular vacation destination, we promise to do our best to make **Making Memories**—and its companion Web site—the most comprehensive unofficial planning guide to be found anywhere. Your insights, comments, and concerns are welcome. Feel free to contact Aronda via e-mail **(disneyguide@arondaparks.com)** or fax **(843-851-2373)**.

Meanwhile, keep wishing upon your lucky star, soak daily in pixie dust, paint with all the colors of the wind, and make your dream vacation a reality—soon!

INTRODUCTION

Discovering The World: The Real Planning Begins!

First Impressions

Whether it's your first time or your one-hundredth, the remarkable sensation—once you envision your Disney vacation, or begin to make your plans, or drive onto the vast Walt Disney World property—is surprisingly similar. You are amazed, delighted and filled with anticipation! Even the most

Introduction/First Impressions

jaded find it hard to resist those impressions. Nor does your age matter. Here, all sensations are related to the experience of youth, of childish delight—and even if you pursue your Disney experience with breath-taking speed and intensity, you'll savor the transcendence of innocence over age and cynicism.

A popular misconception, even after its thirty-four years of welcoming guests, is that Walt Disney World is primarily an amusement park destination for children. Perish the thought! Certainly, rides and attractions abound for children and youth—experiences like Dumbo the Flying Elephant, Rock 'n' Roller Coaster Starring Aerosmith, Triceratop Spin and Playhouse Disney: Live On Stage!—but mature experiences await you, too (if you wish; many Disney guests are seen with new tee-shirt designs promising the wearer never intends to grow up). Even if you're not inspired by the Resort's commitment to superior customer service (something we often find precious little of in our communities), the cleanliness of the parks and resort hotels, environments that can be described as inspiring, and the complexity of the entire Walt Disney World operation, you'll enjoy a dizzying two hundred plus restaurants from which to choose dining experiences, an array of near-Broadway-caliber shows, several thrill rides whose effects rely less on the "barf factor" and more on spectacle and story, and an energetic nightlife. Shopping, too, surpasses the superficial hunt for Disney souvenirs. For the athletic- or fitness-minded, Walt Disney World provides golfing, fishing, hiking, jogging, horseback riding, boating, an auto-racing experience, tennis, swimming and more. In fact, a sports aficionado can easily plan a stay at the Resort and still have a grand time, never setting foot in a theme park.

What separates a Walt Disney World vacation from, say, a trip to New York or San Francisco, or to New Orleans or Las Vegas—or one of the many other marvelous vacation destinations in the world? In a word or two, subtle control. Unapologetically, Disney takes control of your vacation experience, doing its best to ensure that your safety, satisfaction and

6 Making Memories

Walt Disney World's attention to details throughout the Resort makes this vacation destination as appealing to adults as it is to children. In Mickey's Toontown Fair, Minnie has decided that she's had enough of Mickey's self-portrayal as an artist. Here, in Minnie's Country House, she demonstrates her artistic talents, as well.

security (as well as that of your children) are given full attention. Cast members appear to have only your enjoyment as their top priority. If you're not happy with your room, a meal or any part of your vacation experience, Disney wants to know—and that's why Guest Relations and Disney Research are such vital parts of the company's culture. Many of Disney's most popular characters are members of royal families, so it's little wonder that Disney tries to treat you the same way—with the exception of the sometimes long waits in lines. But Disney has even addressed that inconvenience with something called FASTPASS (a system available to park guests which allows you to schedule attractions with minimal wait times). Actually, the Company's allegiance to your vacation satisfaction heightens your enjoyment. While other destinations sometimes take your hard-earned dinero, without even the appearance of appreciation, Walt Disney World is gracious, at the very least, when you sign that charge slip at check-in, or place your cash into Mickey's big gloved hand. And the Company's overarching objective is that you should always feel as though you've gotten more than your money's worth. Yes, a vacation at Walt Disney World is expensive; we'd be the last ones to lie to you about that. But you'll return home feeling confident that you've gotten a first-class, unique and magical vacation experience — as long as you take the precautions you'll read about here! Another first-timer's impression, whether during the planning process or the experience itself, is that Walt Disney World is huge! In fact, in terms of total land area, it's twice the size of Manhattan, or roughly the size of San Francisco. One-third of the property is devoted to Disney's immense entertainment venues, including its theme parks; one-third has been designated as nature preserves; and the remaining one-third awaits future development. (According to Walt Disney World President Al Weiss, the Resort has room for seven major theme parks.) In 1996, The Walt Disney Company incorporated its first planned community called Celebration. Here, in a residential and commercial development that lies just outside Walt Disney World property, about 5,500 people reside in Disney's version of an ideal, idyllic setting committed to social harmony, architectural aesthetics and positive urban planning. Though Celebration, whose population could ultimately reach twenty thousand citizens by the time the project is complete, has been the subject of several hypercritical articles and books, no one can deny the beauty — or the ambition — of the neighborhood. Furthermore, the town has no problem attracting new residents, despite the pricey homes.

FASTPASS distribution center at Magic Kingdom's newest attraction, Stitch's Great Escape.

8 MAKING MEMORIES

A History

In 1955, Walter Elias Disney opened Disneyland in Anaheim, California, after a rigorous one-year construction schedule. After the theme park's opening, a number of dignitaries, from the United States and abroad, approached The Walt Disney Company with offers of free land so Disney could open yet another theme park.

But Walt Disney simply wasn't interested. Besides, he and his staff of Imagineers—his term for designers, artists and builders who breathe life into Disney magic—were busy developing four attractions for the 1964 New York World's Fair: General Electric's "Carousel of Progress," Ford's "Magic Skyway," Pepsi-Cola's "It's a Small World," and the State of Illinois' "Great Moments with Mr. Lincoln." Even with this ambitious slate of projects, Disney found himself preoccupied with expanded aspirations—aspirations that included a theme park similar to Disneyland Park, but with changes bigger and more comprehensive.

For his East Coast Project—its code name was Project X—Disney needed an immense parcel of land. In 1963, even before the opening of the New York World's Fair, Walt sent his brother, Roy, on a number of land-search expeditions across the country. Roy and his team traveled clandestinely, checking into hotels under assumed names, and making anonymous inquiries on available land parcels. Eventually, they settled on a collective tract of land about forty-seven square miles in size (or 27,500 acres) in Central Florida, just outisde Orlando, in Orange and Osceola Counties. Walt purchased the land for $180 per acre, on average. Once word spread that Disney was the mysterious buyer—media had previously speculated that the buyer was Howard Hughes, the Ford Company or perhaps even Walt Disney—the price of land in the area skyrocketed to $80,000 per acre.

Few knew what Walt's aggressive venture was all about. In a large room kept perpetually locked with a key Walt jealously guarded—a room located next to his office at the Studios—he kept preliminary plans for Project X, which called for a city (EPCOT, or the Experimental Prototype Community of Tomorrow), administration buildings, recreation areas, hotels and resorts, and a theme park.

On November 15, 1965—just a year and a month before he died of lung cancer in a California hospital—Walt held a press conference in Orlando with brother Roy and the governor of Florida. He told the global public of his plans for a city of the future, along with a vast vacation retreat—the "Vacation Kingdom of the World"—a retreat that would include theme parks, resort hotels, shopping venues and golf courses.

Unfortunately, Walt never saw his Florida dream come true. He walked the land. He even laid much of the groundwork for his Imagineers, so they could continue without him. When "Disney World" was presented to the world in October 1971, Walt's brother officially changed the name to Walt Disney World so no one would ever forget the man who dreamed the giant, magical dreams that would give us such pleasure. Sadly, Roy died about two months after making this loving gesture to his late brother.

"Partners," a statue in front of Magic Kingdom's Cinderella Castle.

Because Walt felt frustration, helplessness and dismay as he watched the rapid commercialization of the streets surrounding Disneyland, he was determined to maintain control of Walt Disney World's development. He had enough land to keep the encroaching business district at bay, and through agreements with Florida government officials, the Reedy Creek Improvement District (RCID) was formed. RCID was—and still is—a self-controlled governing district of all areas of Walt Disney World. Not only would Florida taxpayers not have to spend money on Disney construction, Disney would also need no state agency approval of any of its construction projects. It could grow as big—and as quickly—as it wished.

The first phase—consisting of the Contemporary Resort (originally dubbed the Tempo Bay Resort Hotel), the Polynesian Village Resort, Fort Wilderness Campground (later to be renamed Fort Wilderness Resort and Campground), and the Magic Kingdom—began in April 1969, and was completed in just two years. The resort hotels and Magic Kingdom were situ-

A Walt Disney World Resort Timeline

1971--Walt Disney World Resort opens on October 1.
1972--Carousel of Progress & If You Had Wings open.
1973--Pirates of the Caribbean, Richard F. Irvin River Boats, The Walt Disney Story and Tom Sawyer Island open in Magic Kingdom.
1974--Star Jets opens in Magic Kingdom.
1976--River Country, a water park at Fort Wilderness, opens.
1977--Main Street Electrical Parade opens in Magic Kingdom.
1980--Big Thunder Mountain Railroad opens in Magic Kingdom.
1982--EPCOT Center opens October 1.
1983--Journey Into Imagination, New World Fantasy Show, Horizons and Epcot Outreach and Teachers Center open in Epcot.
1984--Morocco opens in Epcot; American Journeys opens in Magic Kingdom.
1986--Captain EO and The Living Seas open in Epcot.
1988--Wonders of Life, Norway and IllumiNations open in Epcot.
1989--Disney-MGM Studios opens. Body Wars & Cranium Command open in Epcot.
1990--Star Tours opens at Disney-MGM Studios.
1991--SpectroMagic debuts in Magic Kingdom. Jim Henson's Muppet*Vision 3-D & Beauty and the Beast Stage Show open at Disney-MGM Studios.
1992--Splash Mountain opens in Magic Kingdom. Voyage of The Little Mermaid opens in Disney-MGM Studios.

Introduction / Disney History

ated around the Disney-created 172-acre Seven Seas Lagoon, connected by a narrow canal (called a "water bridge" since it flows above automobile traffic) close to the Contemporary Resort to Bay Lake, the only naturally-occurring body of water on property. Contemporary Resort was an "extension" of Tomorrowland in the Magic Kingdom—you can even see the resort from Tomorrowland Transit Authority, Astro Orbiters, the Indy Speedway and the Walt Disney World Railroad. Though not visible from inside the Magic Kingdom, the Polynesian Village Resort complemented Adventureland, and

A Walt Disney World Resort Timeline

1993--Backlot Theater opens in Disney-MGM Studios.
1994--Legend of the Lion King & The Timekeeper open in Magic Kingdom. Innoventions replaces Communicore, and Honey, I Shrunk the Audience replaces Captain EO in Epcot; Twilight Zone Tower of Terror opens in Disney-MGM Studios.
1995--Alien Encounter opens in Magic Kingdom.
1996--Ellen's Energy Adventure opens in Epcot; Disney's The Hunchback of Notre Dame--A Musical Adventure opens at Studios.
1998--Disney's Animal Kingdom opens. Disney Cruise Line opens.
1999--Test Track opens in Epcot.
2000--The Many Adventures of Winnie the Pooh and Buzz Lightyear's Space Ranger Spin open at Magic Kingdom; Rock 'n' Roller Coaster opens at Disney-MGM Studios.
2001--Disney's Animal Kingdom Lodge opens; Magic Carpets of Aladdin opens in Magic Kingdom; Who Wants to Be a Millionaire: Play It!, Walt Disney: One Man's Dream open in Disney-MGM Studios; Dinorama & Triceratop Spin open in Disney's Animal Kingdom.
2003--Mission: SPACE & new China film open in Epcot; Mickey's PhilharMagic & "Wishes" Fireworks open at Magic Kingdom; Disney's Pop Century Resort opens. Magical Gatherings debuts.
2004--Stitch's Great Escape opens to replace Alien Encounter in MK.
2005--Light, Motors, Action! Extreme Stunt Show opens in Studios; Soarin' opens in Epcot; Cinderellabration premieres in MK.

12 Making Memories

Fort Wilderness was a direct reference to the fort on Tom Sawyer Island in Disneyland. Though the construction of Epcot was years away, the planned community's progressive concepts were implemented from the beginning. The Resort built its own laundry, energy plants (to compensate for power outages during Florida's frequent thunderstorms), maintenance shops, a food center, and a wastewater treatment plant. Highly advanced computer systems were installed on property to control essentially the entire show, from power distribution, to resort and dining bookings, to room assignments and show execution.

Home gardeners are particularly intrigued by the "plant show" at Walt Disney World. On property, Disney's horticulturists run their own nurseries and tree farm. Originally, the inventory of trees numbered more than eight thousand — a number that has surely increased — with exotic plant life coming from as far away as Asia, Australia, the Pacific Islands and Africa, among many other locales. In fact, for every three trees you see in Walt Disney World parks, a duplicate tree is kept backstage, to replace onstage trees that may be destroyed in a storm, during a hurricane, or by disease. It's Disney's way of ensuring a consistent show from day to day.

Disney's awesome "Highway in the Sky" always attracts massive guest attention — as well as speculation about future monorail expansion. Walt Disney was avidly interested in science and technology; it's little wonder that The Walt Disney

An impressive sight is one of the sleek, swift monorails transporting guests. Propelled by electricity, with top speeds of 40 mph, the monorail is Disney's cleanest and most efficient mode of transportation.

Company was the first to utilize a monorail system, with the stated intent to showcase the impact such a transportation system might have on major cities. Initially, two monorail tracks circled the Seven Seas Lagoon, as they do today. One track belongs to an Express monorail from the Transportation and Ticket

Vacation-Planning Mistakes to Avoid

Don't be one of many Disney guests who sabotage their vacations by neglecting important components of the planning process. Take note of the following critical pointers.

Don't underestimate the expense of your vacation. (Budget planning sheets are provided on your Bonus CD and at www.arondaparks.com.)

Don't underappreciate the complexity of the Walt Disney World experience, thereby inadequately preparing for your vacation.

Don't forget to include rest times throughout each day to recharge batteries— your kids', and your digital camera's.

If you can't stand the heat, for heaven's sake, don't go during the summer!

Be sure to make Priority Seating arrangements at the most popular table-service restaurants before you leave home.

Study (and comprehend) Disney's complicated ticket pricing structure to get the best bang for your buck.

Know the intricacies of all resort hotels. All have unique features and amenities. Be sure to investigate before you make your selection from among the many accommodations.

Utilize FASTPASS whenever possible. It's the best time-saving device at your disposal--and it's included in your theme park admission.

Be sure to research all Disney entertainment opportunities beyond the four major theme parks. Otherwise, you're likely to cheat yourself of some wonderful experiences!

Center directly to the Magic Kingdom. The other monorail stops at all resorts (Polynesian, Contemporary, and Grand Floridian) situated around the Seven Seas Lagoon. (Few sights at Walt Disney World are more impressive than the sleek monorail gliding through the center of the Contemporary Resort.) Originally, plans called for a monorail extension to Lake Buena Vista, and the hotels at the Disney Village Resort (now, Downtown Disney Resorts), but this route has never made it past the planning stages. When EPCOT Center opened in 1982, another monorail line was extended 2.5 miles to connect the Transportation and Ticket Center (TTC) to EPCOT Center.

As construction workers excavated the great hole that was to become the Seven Seas Lagoon, sand and soil were piled onto finished service structures, which look like giant hallways leading into warehouse-size rooms. Then, the Magic Kingdom was built atop these structures which comprised a nine-acre tunnel system, called "Utilidors," providing easy backstage access to utility system offices, storage areas and passages to cast member work locations (to avoid costumed performers showing up in the land innappropriate to their attire). Essentially, Magic Kingdom guests play on the second story, while beneath them, the nerve center for the park's computer systems controls virtually everything in the park. These computers direct all projection systems, fireworks, parade operations — and park cash registers.

Vertical construction of Magic Kingdom began in early 1970, starting with Main Street, U.S.A. and Cinderella Castle, which towers 189 feet above the park. Walt Disney Imagineers took eighteen months to complete the Castle — though some of the interior areas were never finished, including an apartment intended for the Disney family. After Roy died, no other Disney family member was as directly involved with Walt Disney World, and the apartment was never completed. (By the way, don't be tempted to think the structure is made of stone. Cinderella Castle consists mostly of steel and fiberglass.) During the construction of the Castle, early-hired cast members hosted the Walt Disney World Preview Center at Lake Buena

Introduction/Bottom Line 15

Vista. More than one million guests dropped in even before Magic Kingdom opened to gaze at artists' renderings, slides and film designed to heighten guest anticipation of the grand opening. On October 25, 1971—opening day—only ten thousand guests showed up. The following month—one day after Thanksgiving, in fact—all parking lots filled to capacity, and staff closed the gates. Cars were backed up on the four-lane Interstate highway for miles. Now, it's not unusual for Magic Kingdom alone to welcome more than fifteen million guests through its turnstiles per year. When attendance at Epcot, Disney-MGM Studios and Disney's Animal Kingdom is added to the mix, between forty and forty-five million guests visit Walt Disney World yearly.

The Bottom Line

Making Memories 2005 intends to demonstrate that a Walt Disney World vacation can be not only magical and exciting, but also *one that can be tailored to each traveler's unique interests and aspirations.*

The Orlando Magicard

If you're planning to venture out of Mickey's kingdom, we recommend the Orlando Magicard, sponsored by the Orlando/Orange County Convention Visitors Bureau, Inc.

Armed with this free card, you're entitled to discounts at many attractions, accommodations, restaurants and shops. You'll find a tremendous array of hotel discounts throughout the Orlando/Disney area, often including Disney resorts, along with discounts at Univeral Studios Florida. Each card issued is valid for up to six people.

You can request the card online at www.orlandoinfo.com, or call **1-407-363-5872**. Better yet, you can download a printable discount card from the Internet site. You'll find good deals at area attractions—including SeaWorld, Universal Studios Florida, Busch Gardens and Kennedy Space Center, to name just a few. Other discounts that are often available include outlet malls and car rental establishments. Keep checking the website, as deals change frequently.

16 Making Memories

Despite the fact that many Walt Disney World guests tackle the parks in commando mode, your vacation can be customized exclusively for you, your friends and family, without falling victim to Disney burnout, fatigue, stress and sensory overload (unless that's your cup of tea). Yes, Walt Disney World is enormous; it has hundreds of shows, attractions, rides and exhibits. Performers frequently regale you at every turn in all four major theme parks. But you owe it to yourself and your travel companions to make your vacation one that's tailored to your notion of what makes a wonderful vacation—one that captures the magic, the delight, the happiness and the energy that is Disney.

What you can expect from **Making Memories 2005** is candor and honesty—honesty about the expense, honesty about the fun factors, honesty about the quality of Disney attractions. When, in our view, Disney fails—when it shortchanges the guest in some way, large or small—we'll point that out, too, so you can determine the risk before you decide whether to subject yourself to the experience. But most of all, we'll spotlight those attractions and experiences which tap into the magic, the smiles, the refreshing sense of fun—commodities often in short supply in our everyday lives.

But there are some things we can't—or won't—do. For one, we won't provide a play-by-play account of all of Disney's quirks, idiosyncrasies, and even slips in logic—though we'll cover quite a few of them. We won't sample every appetizer in every restaurant, though we'll point out the ones we like best. Nor will we devise tedious touring plans to which few are able to commit. (It's not *your* vacation if we're telling you what to do, when, and in what sequence.) We're also uncomfortable providing a rating system for each attraction—like stars, or thumbs-up—since we feel you should try everything at least once, if possible. However, if your time is limited, pick what's best for you and skip the rest. Otherwise, you'll need another vacation just to recover from the one you're planning now.

If you want thorough, concise menus for most of Walt

Disney World's restaurants, check out the wonderful All Ears Net, the brainchild of Deb Wills, located at www.AllEarsNet.com. We'll provide menu samples most of the time, but Deb—thanks to guests who frequently return home with menus to share (as well as Deb's own experiences)—has comprehensive coverage of Disney cuisines. Most Memories Team members never plan a vacation without several visits to her site.

If you'd rather stay at a resort hotel off Disney property—with daily (and usually inconvenient) treks back to Walt Disney World—you may wish to do a little research on the Internet. Orlando Magicard has a number of great hotel specials always going on. In our chapter on resort hotels, we presume the reader's desire to stay in a Disney resort or hotel. Still, we've provided convenient lists of off-property establishments, with contact information and sample rates, though they are likely to change with the travel seasons. Likewise, Central Florida has plenty of other worthwhile attractions to visit, but they won't be reviewed here. Our focus will remain exclusively on the Mouse.

We promise to tell it the way we see it in terms of resort quality, dining opportunities and food palatability, shopping variety, and entertainment experiences. Still, a lousy meal for us may very well tantalize your taste buds. Or, we may hate a room that fits your needs perfectly. Perhaps we'll love a show that you find tediously boring. In short, use our observations as a guide, not as a "final word" in your vacation planning.

Despite the subjectivity of taste, we pledge never to lose sight of the magic of making memories, of living the dreams of make-believe, of tapping our inner child on the shoulder and winking when he or she looks around.

In the end, you alone must determine how Walt Disney World can give your vacation meaning—how it can inject magic, memories and uniqueness that defy imitation. Our guide will help you accomplish just that.

Chapter 1

A VACATION WITH CHARACTER
Conjuring Your Own Unique Magic

You can definitely count on *one* thing during your vacation at Walt Disney World. At least once during your stay, you'll experience a "magical moment"—a point in time that will forever linger in your most cherished memory, tapping into your own distinction as an individual, a family or group of friends. This moment—honestly, though, there will be more than one—will contribute to the building of your unique vacation, set apart from any other. To encounter a magical moment, you have to make friends with your inner child, ready for the delight of fresh experience, like discovering a shell on the beach for the first time, or wishing on your first falling star, or waking up to the surprise of your first bike on Christmas morning. If you're traveling with children, establish a link to them, their joys and delights; they'll show you what it's like if you've become too jaded to understand.

A Walt Disney World vacation isn't for the hopelessly cynical, the sourpuss who finds the world full of only worry, tedium and vulgarity. You should abandon your frustrations, your vexation with the world, and let Tinker Bell have her way with you (so to speak). Let yourself experience the delight of your first (or hundredth, if you're so lucky) glance at Cinderella Castle. Let a tear fall when Beauty's love resurrects the Beast. Succumb to the temptation to purchase a Mickey Mouse-shaped ice cream bar, and eat it with delight as you stroll through a park. Hold your Pal Mickey close as he whispers park touring tips in your ear. Don't hold back in expressing your awe as Mickey battles the forces of evil in Fantasmic! Forget the numbing theme park rush when Streetmosphere characters stop to play with you; join in the improvisation, and build a magical moment that no

Suggestions for a Unique Vacation

1. Pick a theme for your vacation--like Relaxation, Family Quality Time, A Disney Romp, Buffing Up, or Wining and Dining.
2. Prioritize the types of activities that support your vacation theme.
3. Develop an itinerary with built-in flexibility.
4. Allow your family or other travel companions to have input into your planning.
5. Plan at least two activities which get you out of the parks for awhile, to enjoy a taste of other Disney offerings.
6. Budget for souvenirs that provide a tangible connection to your theme--a golf shirt, for example, if you've planned a golfing vacation.
7. Get in the spirit prior to your trip by ordering some Disney attire or accessories from DisneyDirect.com.

20 Making Memories

To enhance your vacation relaxation, don't overlook quiet spots that can be found in all of Disney's parks. These fussy parrots make their home on Discovery Island in Disney's Animal Kingdom.

one else can claim.

Sam, Kathy and Julianne enjoy their first-day ritual at the Magic Kingdom. "We buy hot dogs from Casey's Corner, then sit on the curb waiting for the parade. Then, after we finish our hot dogs, one of us goes to the ice cream shop for floats. Then, the Share a Dream Come True or SpectroMagic parade begins. At that time, we have left the real world to live in Walt's."

As you surrender to the magic, that's the feeling you may initially experience—a feeling that you've entered the magical world of every Disney fan's favorite uncle, Walt Disney. Fortunately, it's a feeling that lingers as you recognize that the only social gaffe here is a refusal to wave at the Disney characters.

Another gaffe about which the Memories Team agrees is a negligence to plan. "Reading as much available information as you can about the parks pays off immeasurably," says Ed. "I am always astounded by guests who are wandering along Main Street, U.S.A., looking for an attraction that's over at Epcot, simply because they didn't take a few minutes to read about the parks. You don't have to become an expert. But with the size of Walt Disney World, with so much to see and do, you really need some idea of what you're gettting into, and where things are. That doesn't mean planning exactly where you're going to be, or what you're going to do, every hour of the day. This is supposed to be a vacation (or 'holiday,' to you Brits). It's supposed to be fun." Ed heightens his vacation enjoyment by "sending a postcard back to myself from Walt Disney World so it's sure to get home before I do."

Often, building magical moments doesn't involve you specifically, but someone else in your party—particularly if your original intention was to provide a little Disney magic for someone you care deeply about. "Several years ago, my son and I were at Superstar Television [Editor's Note: a discontinued attraction at Disney-MGM Studios] with my grandmother, who was around eighty at the time," says Sue. "She was selected to be the wife in the soap opera scene. She is someone who likes to stay in the background, so I had to push her backstage to go with the cast member. She ended up being absolutely wonderful on stage—a cute little white-haired lady (all one hundred pounds of her) waving a gun at her cheating forty-year-old husband, and talking to her hunky lover on the phone. It was hysterical, and the audience loved her. She had never done anything like that before, and I'll never forget it. She has since passed away, and although we had many won-

---

What is a Pal Mickey?

Pal Mickey is a plush on steroids. The product, available only for purchase (WDW discontinued the rental option) looks like a plush Mickey Mouse character toy, but when you turn him on, he tells you everything you always wanted to know about the parks--and then some! Sensors in the parks trigger the program that's embedded in Pal Mickey, cuing him to let you know things like the best vantage point for watching fireworks, imminent showtimes, and tidbits of info about the attractions. If you're a first-timer, or a big Disney fanatic, then Pal Mickey is a must. Otherwise, he's more of a curiosity. Some have even said he's a burden--because once you get him started, Pal Mickey doesn't want to stop talking!

derful trips together to Walt Disney World, that memory is very special."

For Walt Disney World veterans, it's important to keep encore vacations fresh. Thomas and Maribeth "always try to do something that we've not done before. We always try to eat at one or two new (to us) restaurants." Considering the sheer number of dining venues available to you, there's really no way to try every restaurant—unless you've booked a Disney vacation that lasts more than two months!

Speaking of dining, Crystal and her parents, Tom and Linda, feel it's essential to "have Priority Seatings arranged for the best-quality dining experiences such as the California Grill (atop Disney's Contemporary Resort), O'Hana at Disney's Polynesian Resort, the Hoop-Dee-Doo Musical Revue at Disney's Fort Wilderness or the Spirit of Aloha, also at Disney's Polynesian Resort. We always book them eight months in advance, and always have front-middle seating."

Kids find themselves the center of Disney's attention—a phenomenon that makes wonderful memories for both parents and children. However, it's important to ensure that expectations are clear before you leave for your Walt Disney World vacation. "Get feedback from your entire party regarding things they want to do, and things they don't really care about," says Amanda. "Check and make sure everyone has the same assumptions about wake-up times, bedtimes, meal times and types of meals they are expecting to enjoy."

One of the best ways to touch your inner child is to find a way to produce a magical moment for a child—even if he or she isn't your own. "During a dinner at Boma at Disney's Animal Kingdom Lodge, a family of four sat at a table next to us," says Dann. "I was wearing a pin featuring Mickey Mouse as a fireman. The older brother, I noticed, was pointing at my lanyard and whispering to his father. Clearly interested in buying one for his son, the boy's father asked me where I had gotten the pin. Since I had purchased an extra pin for trading, I took the pin from my lanyard and gave it to the young man. Though the youngster's parents offered to buy me a drink,

Little princesses accompanying you can find the most interesting ways to showcase their membership in royal circles. At Disney's Pop Century Resort, one youngster decorated her family's room window with Tinkerbell, who welcomed her back each night after playing in the parks.

the look on the boy's face was sufficient reward for my 'good deed'."

Jason and Lauralee share a unique ritual when they arrive at Walt Disney World that sets the tone for a relaxing trip. "One of the things we always like to do is to play a game of checkers outside the Shootin' Gallery in Frontierland in the Magic Kingdom. We grab a couple of sodas, and sit on the wooden barrels, playing checkers and watching the people go by."

Toni and Jim enjoy a unique ritual that "gets us in the mood for a Disney vacation. On our first evening, we usually enjoy a character meal, like Chef Mickey's. The characters are always so much fun—even for adults!"

Disney's unique resort hotels offer memorable breaks from the parks, once your vacation is fully underway. Resort-hopping makes for an enjoyable afternoon, and can take the stress off park-hopping as you spend the afternoon looking at different resorts, and maybe even trying a different type of cuisine in some of the resort restaurants. And, if you make dinner priority seating at one of the restaurants around the Magic Kingdom, make it for twenty minutes prior to the Wishes Nighttime Spectacular fireworks display. Viewing the fireworks while you're dining is a nice extra.

Often, when the parks are particularly crowded, other people become objects of resistance rather than fellow members of the human race. Competition for the best place in line happens more frequently than adult guests would like to ad-

"Your Key to the World," or your Resort ID and room key, identifies you as a guest on Walt Disney World property. You may also link a credit card (or cash) to the key, which can then be used to charge meals and purchases throughout the Resort. This "Key" is arguably the most important piece of plastic in your wallet or purse during a Disney vacation.

mit. Rather than entering that particular race, why not strike up conversations with other people in the same line? Several Memories Team members "have always enjoyed talking to other guests." Some members have had conversations with strangers while in line for rides, waiting for IllumiNations, even in a buffet line at a restaurant. You may find hearing about other guests' experiences to be enjoyable or beneficial to your own plans.

However, special moments also occur in the absence of the typical Disney crowds. "My most memorable experience at the Magic Kingdom was when Maribeth and I were waiting for our Keys to the Kingdom tour," says Tom. "We were in the park prior to the gates opening and hardly anyone else was in the park. Main Street, U.S.A. was empty. We were able to get pictures of Cinderella Castle without anyone else in the picture. It was so peaceful and quiet, and we were able to wander around without any distractions."

Adult travelers without children often muse that touring the Magic Kingdom would be more enjoyable for them if there were fewer kids. John and Lynda "always come down for three weeks during the month of September. We wish Disney would do E-Ride Nights during September. It's so wonderful to be in the Magic Kingdom at night. There are so many strollers during the day, that it's often very difficult to move. At least with an E-Ride Night, there aren't as many kids."

Another complaint, with no solution, is that "getting out of the parks after the nighttime parade or fireworks is a horrible affair," according to Jason. "Leaving the Magic Kingdom after Wishes, I found the line for the monorail went all the way down the ramps. So, we decided to try the ferryboat. A couple of thousand people packed onto the boat like sardines in the hot, humid weather was NOT a good way to end the day. We had to wait for three boats before finally boarding one. This was the only time we regretted using our car and not the resort bus." Some guests suggest strolling around the park until at least half an hour past closing; that way, you're more likely to find the lines to Disney Transportation have shortened. Epcot's World Showcase is beautiful at night, and relaxing and romantic to enjoy after closing. However, if you're all worn out, you may be more than a little eager to turn in for the night. The closing cattle rush is, as Jason indicates, a bit of a problem, partially owing to Disney's success as a popular vacation destination.

Sam warns that a party's assigned (or self-assigned) photographer may get the short end of the stick. "Guests recording the party's vacation should take care not to spend their vacation behind a viewfinder. It's important to watch things in real time. If you want to film fireworks or a show, see it twice. And put your loved ones in the photo. Cinderella Castle is much prettier with my daughter in front."

All Disney cast members have the capacity to spread pixie dust—even Disney Housekeeping. "It is amazing how people, in a job which is largely ignored in most of the civilized world, can actually be part of the Disney magic," Ed says. "Ask any family with a lot of kids about coming back to their rooms to find stuffed animals and other room objects arrnaged in a comical manner. These folks go way beyond the norm to try and make guests' stays more special."

Finally, Nicole shares practical advice for heightening the Disney Magic. "Purchasing an Annual Pass has changed my whole Walt Disney World experience," she says. "Now I don't have to worry about wasting a Park-Hopper day when I arrive at the Resort in the late afternoon. I can just go the the Magic Kingdom, for instance, to watch Wishes, or go to Epcot for dinner. Also on the day we leave, we can stop at one of the parks for a couple of hours before we begin the drive home. The AP discounts on Disney hotels are great and have allowed us to stay on property either at a higher level resort or for more nights for less money than we would have spent without the Annual Pass." Annual Passes (AP, for short) also entitle guests to discounts at a number of restaurants, Downtown Disney shops, and the occasional Cirque du Soleil performance. Other perks include discounts on recreation, special previews only for Passholders, and special merchandise available only to AP holders.

Chapter 2

Getting It in Mouse Gear

Navigating the Planning Maze

Twice the geographical size of Manhattan, Walt Disney World covers forty-seven square miles of what was formerly Florida farmland and orange groves—though you'd never know it now! Lest the size of this phenomenal place overwhelm you, bear in mind that only one-third of the property has been developed, another one-third is designated as a wildlife preserve, and one-third awaits authorization from the Burbank brass for future expansion. Still, with four major theme parks, more than two dozen resorts, two water parks (River Country closed "until further notice" more than two years ago), three shopping/entertainment areas, six golf courses, and one sports complex, you can't pack a duffel bag and head out with no advance planning and expect your vacation to fall into place. Planning is essential for a unique Walt

28 Making Memories

Disney World vacation. Indeed, it is part of the fun, as long as you don't fall into the trap of eliminating any chance of spontaneity. Some of the best Walt Disney World experiences are those which pop up out of the blue—defying the schedule, but pleasing like nobody's business. "Some families we know tend to over-plan for their trip, particularly if they haven't been to Walt Disney World often," say Lindsey and Chuck. "Our

Online Vacation Planning Resources

Official Walt Disney World Resort Site
www.disneyworld.com

All Ears Net, Deb Wills' extremely thorough site, including trip info, menus and weekly updates
www.AllEarsNet.com

Great photos, park hours, updates and more
www.themeparks.com

Park entertainment schedules for all parks, updated every Saturday night. Check it out right before your trip.
pages.prodigy.net/stevesoares

Companion site to this guidebook.
www.arondaparks.com

Discussion boards and Trip Reports catering to avid Disney fans.
www.tagrel.com

Usually updated nightly, a great place to review media coverage
www.laughingplace.com

Lots of inside info for fans of all Disney theme parks
www.mouseplanet.com

advice would be to resist temptation to try and do everything. There are so many attractions and activities, stick to what really matters to you. Before each trip, we make a list of must-see attractions. Those are the things that really matter to us and anything else we get to see or do is an added bonus." And Dania cautions guests to "allow time for the unexpected. Do not plan your days down to the minute. Disney doesn't have to be done commando-style."

As planning begins, you and your traveling companions need to **determine your best time of year to travel**. Holidays can be oppressively crowded, while late summer is always oppressively hot. Unfortunately, if you have kids in school—particularly in middle or high school grades—you may have no other choice. Not to worry. We'll help you navigate through the crowds and have just as magical a time as someone who travels during off-season. However, Becky says "the single best piece of advice I can give is go during the off-season. Go in the autumn, or in January or February. Do

Extra Magic Hour

As part of the "Magic Your Way" ticket program, Walt Disney World announced yet another feature for guests staying on property. Morning Extra Magic Hour means the designated theme park opens one hour earlier than published opening time. Evening Extra Magic Hours extend three hours beyond the designated park's scheduled closing time. This means that you'll be able to enjoy more time playing with Disney characters and "riding the rides" than ever before. When the hours extend a park's closing, you'll delight in the ambience that Disney parks after dark produce. As Jiminy Cricket says in his introduction to Wishes Nighttime Spectacular, the evening was Walt Disney's favorite time in the park.

Morning Extra Magic Hour
Monday—Epcot
Tuesday—Disney-MGM Studios
Friday—Magic Kingdom
Saturday—Animal Kingdom

Evening Extra Magic Hours
Sunday—Disney-MGM Studios
Tuesday—Animal Kingdom
Wednesday—Magic Kingdom
Thursday—Epcot

30 MAKING MEMORIES

not go at Christmas, during college spring breaks, or in the summer. If you go at peak time, you'll spend too much time standing in line for rides, buses, shows and more. You won't spend enough time enjoying the attractions. The past two times I've visited have been in September, and there were virtually no lines anywhere! I watched log after log after log go down the Splash Mountain hill empty! I rode Splash Moun-

Walt Disney World "Magic Your Way" Tickets

Ticket	7-Day	6-Day	5-Day
Base Ticket	$199 $28.43/day	$196 $32.67/day	$193 $38.60/day
Add Park Hopper	$35 $5/day	$35 $5.83/day	$35 $7/day
Add Plus Pack	$45 5 visits	$45 4 visits	$45 3 visits
Premium Ticket	$279	$276	$273

Tickets	4-Day	3-Day	2-Day
Base Ticket	$185 $46.25/day	$171 $57/day	$119 $59.50/day
Add Park Hopper	$35 $8.75/day	$35 $11.67/day	$35 $17.50/day
Add Plus Pack	$45 3 visits	$45 2 visits	$45 2 visits
Premium Ticket	$265	$251	$199

All prices quoted for the new "Magic Your Way" ticket program do not include tax. Guests under the age of 10 will enjoy lower ticket rates. Please call 1-407-W-DISNEY, or inquire online (www.disneyworld.com) for more information.

tain twice in row, and Buzz Lightyear three times with no waiting at all. And I didn't have to get up at the crack of dawn to hit the parks, either."

Now, you must decide how many days you want—and can afford—to stay. If you're a Disney Virgin, at least a week's stay is highly recommended. Even then, you'll probably have to save a few attractions for a future visit. Certainly, before

Walt Disney World Tickets & Passes

Type of Ticket	Adult	Child (3-9)
Annual Pass**	$403.64	$342.93
Premium Annual Pass **	531.44	451.56
One-Day, Water Parks	33.02	26.63
Water Parks Annual Pass	106.45	85.73
One-Night Pleasure Island	21.84	21.84
Pleasure Island Annual Pass	58.52	58.52
Wide World of Sports	9.69	7.46
One-Day DisneyQuest	33.02	26.63
DisneyQuest Annual Pass	84.14	67.10
DisneyQuest + Water Parks	137.39	105.44
Cirque du Soleil	Tiered at 90.53, 77.75, or 62.84	Tiered at 62.84, 52.19, or 41.54
Special Seasonal Events	Call/Check Online	Call/Check Online

All prices quoted above include tax, and were correct at press time.

**New Annual Pass. Discounts apply for timely renewals.
***Tip: If you choose the No Expiration option, you may return on a future visit and use any days left on your tickets. However, this option will cost between $10 and $55, depending on the number of days your ticket includes.

32 Making Memories

you even begin planning in earnest, you should order a free vacation video from Walt Disney World. Visit the official Web

Walt Disney World Tickets & Passes
Ultimate Park Hopper Passes

Ultimate Park Hopper Passes are linked to your reservation for your vacation duration. Admission includes all major theme parks, water parks, Pleasure Island, DisneyQuest and Disney's Wide World of Sports. Discounts are available for advance purchases online.

Length of Stay	Adult	Child (3-9)
Three Nights	$260.94	$208.75
Four Nights	311.00	249.23
Five Nights	348.27	277.99
Six Nights	384.48	307.81
Seven Nights	422.82	338.69
Eight Nights	466.90	366.38
Nine Nights	492.06	394.06
Ten Nights	521.88	418.55
Eleven Nights	544.23	436.66

Theme park parking is $8.00 for non-Resort guests. Disney resort guests do not pay for parking, nor do Annual Passholders or Disney Vacation Club (DVC) members. Park passes, except Unlimited Park Hoppers and others as noted, may also be purchased via mail, but always call 1-407-W-DISNEY to verify prices. Be sure to include $3.00 for shipping and handling. Send payment to:

Walt Disney World
Attention: Ticket Mail Order
PO Box 10140
Lake Buena Vista, FL 32830-0030

In the Memories Team's opinion, nothing beats staying with the Mouse. Disney's Wilderness Lodge, quiet and elegant as they come, is nestled in a dense forest just minutes from the Magic Kingdom.

site **(www.disneyworld.com)**, then click on "Order Your Vacation Planning Kit Today." You'll be instructed on how to obtain your planning video, which provides an excellent overview of what to expect. You can also order the video by calling **1-407-W-DISNEY**.

Once you've selected your travel dates, it's time to place your call to the Central Reservations Office (CRO) to **book hotel accommodations** — if you've decided to stay on property. You may also reserve Disney accommodations online, as long as you have no discount codes. CRO's number is **407-934-7639**. (The toll-free listing is **800-511-9777**.) Though we highly recommend staying on-site in a Disney-owned hotel, some travelers prefer off-site accommodations — to enjoy a respite from Mickey and the gang for awhile. In the Orlando-Kissimmee area, there is no shortage of hotel accommodations. When you stay on property, not only does the magic — and impeccable Disney service — continue after you've left the parks, but Disney also throws in a few perks to its hotel guests — like Extra Magic Hours, both morning and evening, free transportation to all Disney destinations, and guaranteed park entry even when the parks are full and closed to the general public. So, if you're sold on the idea of sleeping in one of the Mouse's more than 27,000 rooms—an experience you'll never forget—your next decision is to determine the kind of accommodations you require. Chapter Eleven outlines your choices.

Now, **determine the type of tickets you wish to purchase.** On December 2, 2004, Disney announced "Magic Your Way," an innovative ticket plan that allows guests to create their own tickets for a customized vacation. The more you play, the less you pay, per day. Though a single-day ticket increased to almost $60.00, guests who add days to their Disney vacations will experience unprecedented savings. First, guests choose the number of days they want on a base ticket that allows them to visit one theme park each day. Then, they can select from a menu of ticket options that includes other features. The Park Hopper Option allows guests to come and go as they please through all four theme parks each day for the length of their ticket. Extra cost to the base-price ticket is $35.00. The Magic Plus Pack Option provides for Disney fun beyond the four theme parks, including Disney's water parks, DisneyQuest, Downtown Disney Pleasure Island or Disney's Wide World of Sports Complex. Extra cost to the base-price ticket is $45.00 (which includes 2-5 visits to these other attractions, depending on the number of base ticket days purchased). Magic Your Way Premium Option combines the benefits of Park Hopper and Magic Plus Pack options, and is priced ac-

Walt Disney World is a popular destination for newlyweds. Not only do they honeymoon here, but they often book their weddings at Disney's Grand Wedding Pavilion.

Chapter 2/Customizing Your Vacation

Walt Disney World offers more than 200 choices of dining experiences throughout its entertainment and resort venues. Hollywood & Vine at Disney-MGM Studios is a moderately-priced eat-til-you-pop buffet. Kids particularly love the dessert bar. Shield their eyes as you enter the restaurant, since the desserts are featured prominently just inside the front door.

cording to the number of days you elect to stay. Magic Your Way tickets expire fourteen days after first use. If you elect the No Expiration Option, you may come back and take advantage of unused ticket entitlements at any time. Extra cost for this Option ranges from $10.00 to $55.00. The savings get even sweeter when you purchase 5-, 6-, or 7-day Magic Your Way tickets with the Park Hopper or Magic Plus Pack Options—or both—before leaving home. When we went to press, Disney had just announced this new program, so information continued to be updated until the official launch date of January 2, 2005. Check with Aronda's Web site to get current children's ticket prices.

Unless fast food and counter service will satisfy throughout your trip, you'll need to **consider the wide variety of dining opportunities available at Walt Disney World**. For table service restaurants—particularly the very popular ones—you should attempt to plan your meals in advance. Instead of reservations, however, Disney utilizes a procedure known as

Disney Weddings

So you want to tie the knot at Walt Disney World?

Since 1991, over fifteen thousand couples have taken their vows either at Walt Disney World Resort's Wedding Pavilion, located adjacent to Disney's Grand Floridian Resort & Spa, or at other Resort locales--including ceremonies in front of Cinderella Castle. And while these weddings aren't cheap--they can set you back from three to fifty thousand dollars, depending on whether you choose an Intimate, Classic, Premium or Lavish wedding--they *will* create memories of your special day that you'll treasure for the rest of your life. Wedding specialists work with you every step of the way, with plans for a "sky's the limit" celebration, or a small, intimate ceremony.

Your wedding guests will love you, too, when they discover the magical setting for your wedding. Disney will work with the bride and groom to provide select accommodations for both wedding party and guests--usually at a discount.

A Disney wedding is not your cup of tea? Perhaps you'd enjoy a honeymoon at this magical place. Specialists can help you plan the most spectacular honeymoon on the planet.

Even couples who want to renew their vows can arrange a ceremony.

For more info about Fairy Tale Weddings and Honeymoons, contact a planning specialist at 321-939-4610 (or your travel agent). Additional information can be found at **disneyweddings.disney.go.com/disneyworldweddings/**.

Priority Seating (PS). Here's how it works. Once you call **Disney Dining (1-407-WDW-DINE, or 1-407-939-3463; dial 55 from your resort room phone)** to set up a meal time, you'll be given a PS number. Rather than holding a specific table for you and your party, Disney, upon your arrival and check-in at the restaurant at the designated time, seats you when the next table appropriate for the size of your party becomes available. That way, the "walk-ups" (i.e., guests without Priority Seating) must wait until you've been accommodated. Of course, some of us like a bit more spontaneity in choosing restaurants. If you're

CHAPTER 2/CUSTOMIZING YOUR VACATION 37

Even if you feel worn out at the end of massive park touring, the Pleasure Island AMC Theater offers a relaxing way to wind down in the evening. And don't think it shows only Disney films. All the hot new releases make appearances here.

willing to dine between the standard meal times, you can be seated fairly quickly, even without a PS number. During off-season, you're more likely able to let your appetite guide you. During Disney's busiest seasons, however, even lunch as late as 2:30 p.m. may still be difficult to arrange without a long wait because of the crush of hungry people. An alternative to dining inside the parks—if those restaurants are just too crowded for you—is to select one at a nearby Disney resort hotel. Many resort restaurants offer even better fare than those in the parks—and often are much less crowded. A meal at one of the resort establishments not only affords a sampling of a unique menu unavailable in the four parks; it also provides a refreshing escape from the throngs. John and Lynda advise that you "plan as far in advance as possible. Know what you want to see and do each day. When the first day to call for a Priority Seating arrives, call first thing in the morning at seven o'clock."

For more than a decade, Walt Disney World has transcended its reputation as a showcase of world-class theme parks, delightful hotels, unique shopping venues, a diversity of sports and fitness activities and well-planned development. It now offers quite an array of sizzling nighttime entertainment. Keep in mind, though, you may wish to leave the kids behind. Finding more kid-appropriate activities won't be a problem. Disney provides in-room babysitting service (for a

Tips for Guests with Special Needs

Guests with special needs should remember several important facts as they plan for their Disney vacation.

First, always communicate with cast members whenever you have questions or concerns about accessibility. Secondly, make sure you acquire the *Guidebook for Guests with Disabilities*, a cornucopia of information about Disney's conscientious effort to provide a great show for everyone. Get your copy from Guest Relations, or call Disabled Guests Special Requests at 1-407-939-7807.

In Spring 2005, PassPorter Travel Press will release *PassPorter's Walt Disney World for Your Special Needs*, co-authored by Deb Wills and Debra Martin Koma. Check www.AllEarsNet.com for order opportunities.

Transportation. Most Disney transportation can accommodate various types of wheelchairs, though the wheelchair must fit the lifts on the buses. Boats and monorails are perhaps the "friendliest" modes of transport.

Wheelchairs & ECV. You can bring your own, or rent one at the four parks. Electric Convenience Vehicles (ECVs) are also available. Deposits are required, and wheelchairs and ECVs may be used only in the park where they were rented.

Attractions. Most attractions are accessible, so specific instructions are too detailed to include here. Refer to your *Guidebook* for all the details.

Annual Pass Benefits

Your best value for stays in excess of eight days at the Resort is an investment in the Annual Pass (four major theme parks only) or the Premium Annual Pass (which adds water parks, DisneyQuest, Pleasure Island and Disney's Wide World of Sports to the mix). While you may balk at the idea of having a ticket that's good for 365 days when you can visit only once this year, keep in mind that you'll probably save money (or at least break even) over the Magic Your Way tickets. Besides, you'll receive a few benefits as a Passholder that could save you even *more* money, depending on your vacation plans.

- ☑ *Mickey Monitor*, a quarterly newsletter that keeps you in touch with the Mouse and special offers, too
- ☑ 10% off Leave a Legacy at Epcot
- ☑ Emails about special Passholder events when you register online.
- ☑ Occasional discount rates at resort hotels
- ☑ Discounts at Pleasure Island for up to three guests
- ☑ Discounts at DisneyQuest for up to three guests
- ☑ Discounts at water parks for up to three guests
- ☑ 10% off food and beverages at lunch Monday through Friday at many hotel table service restaurants
- ☑ 10% off food and non-alchoholic beverages at lunch Monday through Friday at most Epcot full-service restaurants
- ☑ Restaurant discounts at other locations often apply
- ☑ 10% off merchandise at several of the Downtown Disney shops
- ☑ 15% off most Backstage Tours
- ☑ A variety of discounts for recreational activities, including golf, miniature golf, Grand Floridian Spa, boat rentals

You must present your AP or PAP at the time of purchase for discounts to apply. While benefits were correct at press time, Disney frequently amends perks.

fee) as well as several children's programs that allow your precious little ones to socialize with other kids of similar ages. So, before you arrive to begin your vacation, you'll want to consider ways to **make your evenings as fabulously invigorating as your days**. Even after the parks close, the show continues. Disney offers several dinner shows at various locations within the Resort, as well as a wide variety of lounges and

Disney Gives You a Little Credit

Now, in partnership with Bank One, Disney offers an opportunity to receive its new VISA card, an attractive card sporting images of the Mouse and the Disney logo. Among the "rewards" for owning the card are 1% back on card purchases in Disney Dream Reward Dollars, no interest for six months on vacation packages, and enhanced VISA Platinum benefits.

For more information, check out the offical Web site at **disney.go.com/visa/**. Or, just wait until you get to Walt Disney World; no matter how hard you try, you can't avoid encountering VISA kiosks.

Word of warning: Some card applicants have stated that Disney/Bank One makes it sound easier to qualify than it is in reality.

---

nightclubs at Pleasure Island and Disney's BoardWalk. If you crave a quiet evening, why not catch a film at the AMC-24 Theatre at Downtown Disney? With so many screens, you're bound to find flicks that all members of your family or party are dying to see. The state-of-the-art sound system at AMC-24 was designed by George Lucas of *Star Wars* fame. A favorite nighttime attraction is Cirque du Soleil at Downtown Disney West Side, where *La Nouba* defies all perceptions of nighttime entertainment. (If a clown offers to show you to your seat, humor him. With your cooperation, your evening could become a Fellini-esque experience.) "Cirque du Soleil's *La Nouba* was incredible and beautiful," says one guest. "Any guide should definitely point visitors to that attraction—an attraction whose quality is far and away above anything else that exists in any of the parks."

Customizing Your Vacation

CHAPTER 2/CUSTOMIZING YOUR VACATION 41

Now that some of the decisions about the essentials for your trip are out of the way, you have other important issues to consider. If you're traveling with children, you'll certainly want to consider their experiences carefully. Compromise often works. "Okay, sweetheart, we'll ride Dumbo the Flying Elephant with you if you'll be a little princess while we have a nice meal at the California Grill." Disney also offers, for a fee, in-room babysitting services—a great option if you and you spouse or significant other wish to enjoy a romantic evening alone, or a night on the town. "The main thing that's great about Disney—in contrast to many, many other resorts, especially high-end ones—is that they go out of their way to treat your children with respect. In my experience, that respect is extended to our full, non-traditional family. Frequently, here

---

Disney Without Pawning Your Valuables

The singular, economic realization when planning for a Walt Disney World vacation is quite simple.

You'll never have enough money to spend!

Disney generates a compulsion to spend, spend, spend--from cool gifts and collectibles to delectable snacks. So don't expect an extravagant purchase to satisfy--at least, not completely. However, the wise and frugal traveler will--before leaving home--determine the amount that can be spared without decimating the household budget. The challege is to stick to that limit. Otherwise, you'll come home overwhelmed with guilt that you spent next month's grocery money.

Our recommendation? Use the worksheets found on our Bonus CD (or online at **www.arondaparks.com**) to calculate what you can expect to spend, then increase that figure by at least fifteen percent. That way, you'll have no ugly surprises--nor a heart filled with remorse by the prospect of pinching pennies for the next six months to recover from a week's vacation!

in New York, or in 'nice' resorts, people look at your children as if you'd brought your pet snake or pit bull with you," says one guest.

If you and your spouse crave a romantic vacation setting, Walt Disney World is a great place to be. Your delightful regression to a time of innocence actually nurtures the affection you already feel for each other. More than likely, you'll view your spouse or significant other with new eyes as he or she succumbs to the magic surrounding you both. Perhaps you'll even find a new depth to your relationship that just wasn't apparent in your day-to-day routine. Most couples agree: Walt Disney World is *good* for a relationship.

Traveling with platonic friends? No problem! People you care about heighten the magic. In fact, why not get everyone in your party involved in the pre-trip planning? Have a barbecue or a dinner party at your house, then pull out all the information you've gathered on making the most of your Walt Disney World vacation. Pop in the complimentary planning video you ordered earlier to build some excitement—and to help you with many of the practicalities. Use this guide—and its complementary Web site at **www.arondaparks.com**—to help you come up with an itinerary and a budget. Just don't forget to leave plenty of room for spontaneity! "Visit at least a few Disney planning Web sites—like Intercot, AllEarsNet, MousePlanet and ArondaParks—and possibly buy a book or two like Birnbaum's official guide and *Making Memories*. Or don't. The World is huge. On our fifth trip we finally felt that we 'got' World Showcase. Read trip reports, but know that positive reports are the norm, and negative reports are the exception. Negative reports are usually more exaggerated than the positive ones, but the positive ones tend to be written by the WDW equivalent of Amway distributors," says Sam.

Need to get away from it all—and don't want any company? Consider "doing Disney" solo. Many have reported feeling quite comfortable traveling alone—though they tend to be the independent sort. After all, Disney's guests remain in their own little worlds—as will you—so there's no need to feel out

Packaging a Walt Disney World Vacation

Let's get one thing straight. Vacation packages don't save you any bucks.

So why are these customized vacation packages so popular? In a word--convenience. And, perhaps, vanity. Because Disney's package perks make you feel more special than the Big Cheese himself.

Though you should call 407-WDW-MAGIC to inquire about current offerings--or check the official Web site--here are examples of several popular package deals.

Disney's Magic Your Way Package
Includes accommodations at an on-site Disney-owned resort hotel, and Magic Your Way base tickets.

Disney's Magic Your Way Package Plus Dining
Includes accommodations at an on-site Disney-owned resort hotel, Magic Your Way Base tickets, and dining plan that offers two meals and a snack per person, per package night.

Disney's Magic Your Way Premium Package
Includes everything found in the Disney's Magic Your Way Package, as well as breakfast, lunch and dinner per person per package night and other options: unlimited use of recreation, tours, admission to Cirque du Soleil, admission to Disney Children's Activity Centers, unlimited admission to theme park tours, and admission to Grand Gathering experiences (if you have a minimum of 8 in your party.

How Much?
For a family of four staying six nights/seven days, packages start at $1,500 for Value resorts, $1,800 for Moderate resorts, and $2,500 for Deluxe resorts.

of place because you don't have a hand to hold, children to tend, or someone with whom to joke around. Cast members are almost always friendly, though they're usually too busy to buddy up to for long. If you're single and looking for a meangful but temporary interlude, however, Walt Disney World may not be the best

A Disney Rolodex

CRO (Central Reservations)
407-WDISNEY (934-7639)

WDW Dining
407-WDW-DINE (939-3463)

Walt Disney Travel Company
407-939-7806

WDW Attraction Merchandise Mail Order
407-363-6200

Downtown Disney Tonight Info Line
407-939-2648

Disney Dining Experience (Florida Residents Only)
407-566-5858

WDW General Information
407-824-4321

Hair Care
Contemporary--407-824-3411
Dolphin--407-934-4250
Grand Floridian--407-824-3000
Yacht & Beach--407-934-3260

Car Care Center
407-824-0976

choice. Still, there are many opportunities for people-watching—and guests frequently report finding someone to hang out with for an evening.

If, like some of us, a little gray is beginning to show, but you're convinced that Walt Disney World is for kids, think again! At last count, three times as many adults as kids travel to Walt Disney World. After all, a Disney vacation costs money—a lot of it—and children have to rely on parental generosity in doling out allowances or providing opportunities for earning a little extra spending money. If you take a look around, you'll notice what we mean. Many of Disney's fans grew up with Mickey Mouse back in the Fifties, and remain loyal to this cute little Mouse and his Gang—and Walt Disney's legacy, as memorialized by Walt Disney World and its sister resorts. A growing phenomenon at the Resort, too, is the number of grandparents who travel with their grandchildren, creating special, magical times while the kids' parents, who don't have the time just now to travel, stay at home to work. In fact, Disney has a series of ads targeting grandparents—not to mention the fact that often, children have a special experience with Grandma and Grandpa that they couldn't have with their parents because—well, after all, grandparents are *supposed* to spoil their grandchildren. Right? If you're an individual for whom physical mobility is limited, no vacation destination is better equipped than Walt Disney World for accessibility to shows, restaurants and attractions. While you may not be able to enjoy *every* ride, the Disney folks have ensured that you'll still have a great time. Most Walt Disney World attractions have been tooled so that your special needs won't separate you from the fun. Furthermore, Disney resort hotels have a number of rooms to accommodate a variety of physical challenges, including king size beds and barrier-free showers. All parks and resort hotels have wheelchairs for rent (about $7.00 per day) while the parks make ECVs available (about $30.00 per day per park, with a ten-dollar refundable deposit). Call Disabled Guests Special Requests at **1-407-939-7807** to make arrangements or to inquire for more details. Each park also publishes a *Guidebook for Guests with Disabilities*, filled

A Disney Rolodex

WDW Florist
407-827-3505

Group Reservations (10+)
800-327-2989

Disney-MGM Studios Production Info
407-560-7299

Disney Weather
407-824-4104

WDW Kennels
407-824-6568

AMC Pleasure Island Cinemas
407-298-4488

Cirque du Soleil
407-939-7600

DisneyQuest
407-828-4600

Lost & Found
407-824-4245

Disney's Wide World of Sports
407-939-1500

Guided Tours
407-WDW-TOUR

If all else fails, dial 407-824-2222; the Operator can direct your call.

with useful information about navigation, accessibility and services Disney provides to help you enjoy the show.

Seasons at the Parks

While it's impossible to predict when the crowds will make for long lines at Disney's four major theme parks, certain trends help you prepare for park congestion.

Grating On Your Last Nerve
Christmas Day through New Year's Day
Two weeks straddling Easter Sunday
Week of Fourth of July
Thanksgiving Day and the following Weekend

Just a Little Too Cozy
Presidents Week in February
Memorial Day Weekend
Gay Day (First Saturday in June)
Mid-June through Labor Day

Laid Back, But Festive
After Presidents Week in February through Early March
Late April through Early June (except for Memorial Day Weekend)
First part of Thanksgiving Week (prior to Turkey Day)

It's All About Me--Light Crowds
January 2 through the week prior to Presidents Week
Week following Labor Day through week prior to Thanksgiving
Week following Thanksgiving until mid-December

(Special Events and promotions can influence theme park attendance, so find out if anything special is happening during your vacation.)

Avoiding a Direct Hit in the Wallet

While some folks are convinced visiting Walt Disney World on a budget is next to impossible, we believe that you can be frugal while still enjoying yourself. Nevertheless, we must be clear. A vacation at Walt Disney World is expensive. With The Walt Disney Company struggling to be more accountable to its stockholders, finding discounts has become more challenging. We cannot stress enough the importance of asking directly if discounts are available—particularly when reserving your accommodations. Furthermore, checking your local newspaper's travel section, as well as national and regional magazines, will occasionally result in the discovery of a special vacation offer directly from Walt Disney World. Annual Passholders, Premium Annual Passholders and Disney Vacation Club members also receive substantial discounts on vacation components. The Mousesavers Web site, operated by Mary Waring and located at **www.mousesavers.com**, often provides details of special discounts happening at the Florida Resort.

Dining offerings may not always be haute cuisine at Disney, but most will find them "haute enough." The Coral Reef chef shapes a chocolate dessert to look like The Living Seas pavilion.

The cost of Disney's resort hotels can add a bundle to your vacation budget. If you're an Annual Passholder or Disney Vacation Club member—or you've scheduled a vacation utilizing an advertised discount—you may be able to book reservations at significant savings. An important fact to remember about Disney resort hotels is that they are priced on several levels: Value, Moderate, Deluxe and Home Away From Home. The Value resorts will set you back from $77.00-$124.00 per night (a little less during certain seasons and with certain discounts). The Moderate resorts weigh in between

$133.00 and $219.00 per night. The Deluxe accommodations — well, the sky's the limit. Deluxe rooms start at a little more than $200.00 per night, while certain exclusive suites can set you back by the thousands. And Home Away From Home resorts, which offer kitchen facilities and more spacious digs, range from $224.00 to $990.00 per night. (In all

Guest Relations: Cast Members with Answers

Don't cheat yourself out of a peak Disney experience because you are unaware of the services that the Resort's top-notch Guest Relations department (or Guest Services) provides.

Boldly queue up at any Guest Relations desk in full knowledge that your satisfaction is this department's primary concern.

At least one Guest Relations office is located within each park, water park, Downtown Disney and Disney resort hotel. Any time you have a question that requires a quick, reliable answer, a concern to air, or a complaint to register, Guest Relations is the place to go.

What can Guest Relations do for you?

- Answer almost any question related to Walt Disney World. If your question stumps them, they'll research the answer.
- Recommend time-saving strategies for park-touring.
- Provide a "house phone" to make calls within the vast Resort.
- Make Priority Seating meal arrangements for you.
- Handle security breaches or complaints about service, ticket value, or even other guests.
- Make reservations for Behind-the-Scenes tours.
- Provide information on services for guests with special needs.
- Help locate hard-to-find merchandise in Resort shops.

resort hotels—except Home Away From Home—each extra adult in the room is charged an additional fee. Published rates include up to two adults.) Of course, prices reflect level of service and number of amenities, but we can guarantee that all resort hotels offer unique Disney experiences. And there's nothing like waking up with Mickey each morning. Sometimes, arranging for a wake-up call in a Disney-owned resort means you'll enjoy a special greeting from Disney's biggest star— something that hotels and inns off-site cannot offer.

The prudent traveler will also do a little meal planning before leaving home. Until Michael Eisner took over as CEO in 1984, Walt Disney World's food fell short of guest expectations. Invariably, the offerings were fast food—except for a few resort hotel restaurants, and the table service restaurants in Epcot's World Showcase. But the World has changed—for the better. Fast food and counter service still have a pervasive presence at Walt Disney World, but the food quality and variety have increased tremendously. Even most counter service restaurants have "diet-sensitive" menu items—like salads, soups, deli sandwiches and "veggie burgers"—along with standard hamburgers, tacos, French fries, pizza, hot dogs and chicken fingers. However, you will do yourself and your traveling companions a disservice if you pass up a chance to dine at a few of Disney's table service restaurants. Not only are these venues great fun—the Disney theming is often as interesting as anything you'll see anywhere on property—but some of the entrees are acclaimed as among the best in the Southeast. And all table service restaurants can accommodate a vegetarian diet. We strongly encourage you to budget for meals— because we're convinced that the bucks you pay for food can add up faster than any other expense at the World. (Deb Wills' All Ears Net, located at **www.AllEarsNet.com**, provides sample menus with current pricing at most Walt Disney World restaurants.) Keep in mind that lunch menus often mirror those at dinner, but with lower prices (and sometimes, a greater selection). And don't try to bring picnics into the parks; they're strictly forbidden. (Picnic tables are often located outside park

Disney's parks stay prepared for the onslaught of toddlers in need of their own wheels. If you're traveling with young royalty, you should know where to procure their coach in each park.

gates, as well as Disney's Fort Wilderness Resort and Campground and both water parks.)

Understanding Disney's ticket pricing structure is a formidable task. A one-day, one park pass costs about sixty bucks for an adult, about forty-eight for children 3-9—but unless you're just passing through, a single-day, one-park pass just won't cut it. As part of its Magic Your Way ticket program, Disney offers a Park Hopper Option, which entitles the bearer not only mutiple-day access to all four of Walt Disney World's major theme parks, but also capability to "hop" from one park to the other as often as you wish during the course of the day. Despite this feature, park-hopping can be an immense waste of time for guests who have not planned well. Only two of Disney's parks are linked via monorail, the most efficient mode of transport. To get to the Disney-MGM Studios or to Disney's Animal Kingdom, you have to board the buses—or, in a few cases, the even slower water taxis. So, it's conceivable that you could spend more time in transit from one park to the other than on the rides and attractions you're pursuing. The best use of the park-hopping option is to enjoy a late-closing park after leaving another one. For example, you might travel to Epcot to enjoy dinner and IllumiNations after Disney's Animal Kingdom, which usually keeps banker's hours, has closed

for the day.
Depending on the length of your stay, your ticket could cost a few hundred dollars. Bear in mind, though, that if you plan to extend your vacation beyond the eight-day mark, be sure to compare prices for the Magic Your Way tickets to the prices for Disney's Annual Pass or Premium Annual Pass. An Annual Pass (or Premium Annual Pass if you wish to enjoy the water parks, DisneyQuest and Pleasure Island in addition to the major parks) may be your best bet if you plan to stay more than eight days. The Annual Pass or Premium Annual Pass not only possesses the same features as the Park Hopper option, but includes some cool perks, too. Though the Annual Pass and Premium Annual Pass are valid for an entire year (making it even harder to resist repeat visits to Walt Disney World), you'll still save money if you plan for an extended stay. But beware. Annual Passes and Premium Annual Passes are issued only to the guest for whom they are activated. If you give your Pass to a friend or relative—or allow children to "share" tickets—rough waters lie ahead, matey. A biometric reader checks the bearer's fingerprints against those encoded on the Pass, and Disney is perfectly within its right to ask for a photo ID if a match isn't found. Not only will your "partner in crime" have to pay full price to be admitted, but Disney may very well revoke your Pass for attempting to

> **Disney for the Dogs**
>
> If you'd rather not say goodbye to Spot or Fluffy when you're vacationing, keep in mind that Walt Disney World has several topnotch kennel facilities that are members of the American Boarding Kennel Association. Each kennel can watch out for your pets by day, as well as overnight. Fees range from $6 to $11, depending on whether you're staying on property. Here's a list of the kennels:
> **Magic Kingdom: 407.824.6568**
> **Epcot: 407.560.6229**
> **Fort Wilderness: 407.824.2735**
> **Disney-MGM Studios: 407.560.4282**
> **Animal Kingdom: 407.938.2100**

beat the system. Mickey doesn't like cheaters.

Frequent visitors to Walt Disney World will attest, with sheepish embarrassment, that Tinker Bell's pixie dust compels you to hand over your cash and credit cards to the Mouse for purchases you'd never dream of making at home. Under the narcotic of Disney Magic, Mickey beanie hats with propellers look cool, Goofy ears are essential fashion accessories, Mickey gloves would certainly spiff up that new tuxedo, and a princess tiara tops it all off. But what looks great in Orlando and environs may incur the wrath (or certainly the laughter) of the fashion police back home. Sure, many souvenirs can't be found anywhere else. But what kind of fashion statement can you make wearing Minnie Mouse flip-flops, Pluto sunglasses and a glow-in-the-dark night shirt?

An even bigger seduction is the fact that many of Walt Disney World's souvenirs are of such high quality. Often, they are one-of-a-kind. Frequently, what you see today won't be in the shops six months later. (Actually, Aronda has seen popular items disappear in an hour, never to be restocked.) Take a peek at that gorgeous, hand-blown Cinderella Castle located in a Main Street, U.S.A. shop. Gotta have it? Well, it can be yours — for about $20,000! Of course, less expensive, but equally seductive souvenirs can be

> **Disney's PhotoPass**
>
> Remember when that cast member shot a picture of you posing in front of Cinderella Castle?
> And remember how you didn't have time to procure your photo at the end of the day?
> No worries now, my friend. Walt Disney World has introduced PhotoPass, an online service allowing you to purchase that missed photo package up to a year after your vacation ends!
> Just keep up with the tracking card provided by the Disney photographer. The card provides a web address (disneyphotopass.com) and an ID code. All park photos will be available for purchase online. By early 2005, you'll even be able to choose action sequences to enhance your photos!

Chapter 2/Disney On a Budget

For guests who wish to get the most out of their Walt Disney World vacation, FASTPASS is just what the doctor ordered. With this feature, included in your ticket price, you can legally go to the front of the line!

found all over the Resort—including clothes for men and women, collectible lapel pins, animation cels and figurines by Disney artists, housewares, gourmet foods, timepieces, jewelry—even furniture. If you forget to make an important purchase during your vacation, you can place a telephone order for park merchandise from home—by calling 1-407-363-6200. You may also opt to e-mail **wdw.mail.order @disneyworld.com**.

Not too long ago, guests often complained about the long waits for "E-Ticket" rides and attractions. ("E-Ticket" refers to gate-buster attractions that draw the biggest crowds. The allusion hails back to a time when Walt Disney World priced all attractions separately, placing them into categories A-E, with E-Ticket rides being the most expensive.) In fact, surveys indicated a significant degree of guest dissatisfaction when, at closing, they had not seen all they wished to see because of so much time wasted in line. Walt Disney World has responded admirably. The award-winning FASTPASS is offered at no additional charge to park guests. Many popular attractions have been granted FASTPASS status. While our chapters devoted specifically to the four major theme parks list attractions which offered FASTPASS at press time, keep in mind that Disney continues to add this feature to various rides and shows as guest demand warrants. Your park guidemap—available at check-in at your official Disney-owned resort hotel, or at each park's main entrance—will indicate the latest list of attractions that offer FASTPASS.

Here's how the system works. Find the FASTPASS distribution area for the attraction you wish to experience—they're usually located close to the "Stand-By" entrance (for guests enduring the regular wait)—and insert your ticket (or plastic resort ID, if your ticket is linked to your room). The dispenser will, in turn, issue a small ticket labeled "FASTPASS," informing you of the window of time during which you can return to the ride or show with essentially no wait. When you return—you must relinquish your FASTPASS to the designated cast member—queue up in the FASTPASS line—*not* the Stand-By line. Before you know it, you'll be whisked into the attraction ahead of guests who didn't take advantage of the system for this attraction. A caveat, however. Sometimes, even with FASTPASS, you may encounter a ten- or fifteen-minute wait—but that's not so bad, really, when many of the popular rides ordinarily have wait times of seventy-five or ninety minutes—or even two hours during busy season. (Once, Josh noticed a three-hour Stand-By wait for Test Track. He purports that he doesn't "wait longer than thirty minutes to ride anything.") The system has its limitations, however. You can't stock up on FASTPASSes and whip through a Disney park in short order. (For one thing, you'll miss some of the most delightful and professional live shows, improvisations and parades.) You must

Disney's professional transportation team gets tens of thousands of guests around the Resort quite efficiently, even if you have to rely on Disney buses.

wait until the time designated on your FASTPASS before you obtain your next one.

If you plan to devote your entire Florida vacation to Mickey, the need for a car is negligible. Many Memories Team members drive, but usually park their cars in the resort lot for their entire stay. Other guests swear by their cars, while swearing *at* Disney's transportation system; they much prefer driving from hotel to park rather than relying on Disney buses and boats. Park closing translates into the typical hordes of traffic congestion for either Disney transportation or your own—so why not let Disney foot the bill? The monorail is, by far, the fastest and most efficient way of transporting the tens of thousands who show up daily, but the monorail connects only two parks and three resort hotels. The bulk of the Walt Disney World transportation system consists of a bus fleet and a navy of boats—both of which do an amazing job of transporting guests across the massive piece of real estate, considering the overwhelming number of guests who show up. Still, Disney's transportation system has become overtaxed—particularly because of its over-reliance on bus transportation—and this "transportation stress" occasionally translates into guest frustration.

"The best way to enjoy Walt Disney World is to relax," say Jason and Lauralee. "You have to realize that not only can you *not* see it all in one trip, but you don't want to! You want to be able to keep coming back over and over, and keep seeing new things. We always pick two or three things that we each want to do, no matter what, and then play the rest by ear. Finally, let yourself act like a kid again. Never be too serious at The World!"

Chapter 3

A Dream, the Wish Your Heart Makes

The Magic Kingdom

What is it about the Magic Kingdom at Walt Disney World that brightens the faces of tens of thousands of men and women, boys and girls, regardless of how skeptical they were of Disney's abilities to delight? "There are so many magical, memorable experiences to be found in the Magic Kingdom," says Carrie. "I suppose my favorite would be going into Town Hall with my daughter, Rachel, who was then only thirteen monhts old. We had been having a nice time and were heading back to the hotel for a nap. The place was pretty deserted, except for several characters who were smitten with her. Dopey sat on the floor with her, trying to teach her to walk. Pinocchio carried her over to a bench and played with her. It was great, a truly magical moment."

In many ways, the Magic Kingdom transports us back to a simpler era in America's history—the flip of the page when the nineteenth century segued into the twentieth—when change was slower, standards firm and clear, and sex was something kept in the bedroom, not the topic of nightly television shows. And yet, not everything was rosy. Prejudices were abundant; sexual inhibitions were commonplace; and oppression of women, minorities and people perceived as "different" occurred, both subtly and overtly. Yet, the Magic Kingdom has whitewashed—okay, let's be honest; it has eliminated—all allusion to the negatives that typified American society. When you hear the music from the turn of the twentieth century—or admire the reassuring architecture of the same historical period—or stroll through a land evoking the Old West—you scarcely associate the frivolous elements here with political and social characteristics of the same milieus. Nothing here seems to offend—unless it's shameless capitalism at its most infectious. And cast members, costumed to match the theme of their respective "lands," go out of their way to make you feel welcome.

Magic Kingdom FASTPASS Attractions

Fantasyland
Peter Pan's Flight
The Many Adventures of Winnie the Pooh
Mickey's PhilharMagic

Tomorrowland
Buzz Lightyear's Space Ranger Spin
Space Mountain
Stitch's Great Escape

Frontierland
Splash Mountain
Big Thunder Mountain Railroad

Adventureland
Jungle Cruise

Liberty Square
The Haunted Mansion

Part of the Magic Kingdom's appeal to adults is that it frees them to become a kid again—and if those same adults are parents, to experience their own inner child through the eyes of their offspring. Laugh. Play. Skip down Main Street, U.S.A. Race other guests for that perfect spot from which to view the afternoon parade, Share a Dream Come True. No one will care if you honor the lost child inside. "Only once have we managed to be at the Magic Kingdom for park opening," says Nicole. "To be standing outside the gates and see Mickey Mouse and his friends arriving on the train while the loudspeakers play music and welcome you to the Magic Kingdom was a wonderful, goosebumps moment."

So, buy that Goofy hat, or Cinderella's tiara—or the Mickey Mouse-shaped ice cream bar or ever-popular turkey leg. Have your picture made with your favorite Disney character. Feel the delight of your little ones as you take them on their first Dumbo, The Flying Elephant ride. Then, after embracing your own inner child—and your son or daughter, if you have one—step into the seven lands that comprise a World children dream of best.

The Magic Kingdom is eye candy at its most delectable.

Differences Between the Guidemap and the Times Guide

The Park Guidemap, available in all of Disney's four major theme parks, as well as both water parks and Downtown Disney, is a colorful, illustrated map of each specific venue with pertinent information that doesn't change from day to day or week to week--like where restrooms are located, and all the dining and shopping spots. The Times Guide is a single panel of paper which discloses the schedules for all the live shows and provides info on when specific attractions open late or close early--decisions that are made based on anticipated attendance levels.

Cinderella Castle looms before you, even more magnificent than before with the tall trees that once obstructed its view replaced, its spires reaching into Florida's glorious blue skies. Suddenly, you *know* — even though you thought you knew before — what GRAND is! Like a magnet — or, better yet, a spell — the Castle draws you deeper into the park, and you are locked under an enchantment like no other you've ever experienced — except, perhaps, when you first fell in love. "The most memorable experience at the Magic Kingdom," allege Chrislette and Jim, "is watching your child's light up when seeing a character face to face."

As you drift — and by all means, allow yourself to drift; this is the best way to experience the "first time" — transfixed, toward that magical Castle, try to take note of Main Street, U.S.A. — the street leading to the Castle and the magical lands beyond. The street where the best parades in America are staged. You'll want to return to savor the delights. Far too many discoveries deeper in the park beckon you, and a latent sense of wonder and fascination is kindled. Besides, Main Street, U.S.A., full of bustling atmosphere, is a bit short on attractions — as it was designed to be. On Main Street, U.S.A., you'll find plenty of shops — but save them for later — and the Magic Kingdom Railroad Station from which you can board a train (Walt

---

Character Appearances

Here's where you can find Disney's famous and infamous characters.

Mickey's Toontown Fair
Mickey in Judge's Tent
Mickey's Pals in Toontown Hall of Fame
Main Street, U.S.A.
Disney Pals in Town Square
Disney Characters at Castle Forecourt
Adventureland
Peter Pan Characters at Pirates of the Caribbean
Aladdin Characters near Swiss Family Treehouse
Liberty Square
Woody & Friends at Diamond Horseshoe
Fantasyland
Characters from Alice in Wonderland near Mad Tea Party
Tomorrowland
Buzz Lightyear near Galaxy Palace Theater

Check Times Guides to see when your favorite characters will appear.

Disney himself was fascinated by trains, as evidenced by the numerous photos on display among the lockers beneath the Station) to circumnavigate the entire park—if you're too impatient to walk. Besides, the train ride isn't a bad way to get oriented.

Restroom Locator

Here's where you'll find convenient restroom facilities in the Magic Kingdom:
- Front Gate, far right
- Next to City Hall
- Next to Crystal Palace
- Next to Plaza Pavilion
- Around corner from Diamond Horseshoe
- Next to Pecos Bill
- Around corner from Pirates of the Caribbean
- Between Big Thunder and Splash Mountain
- Around corner from Peter Pan's Flight
- Around corner from it's a small world
- At Fantasyland entrance to Mickey's Toontown Fair
- Next to Fairytale Garden
- Around corner from Stitch's Great Escape
- Between Space Mountain and Tomorrowland Stage

Adventureland

Our first stop as we tour the park in a clockwise direction, Adventureland invites you to participate in five delightful experiences.

The Jungle Cruise, a boat ride (on submerged tracks, though cast member "captains" actually determine the speed) along a river through dense forests and abandoned temples, makes contact with many wild animals from Africa, Asia and other countries. The animals are robots—Disney calls them Audio-Animatronics—but they look amazingly lifelike, were it not for the sometimes comical postures they've assumed. Your captain delights you with corny jokes all the way through the attraction. If time permits, you might take the Jungle Cruise during both daylight and night hours; the Cruise at night feels somewhat menacing, compared to the same ride during the day. While this adventure isn't Disney's best, it has Walt's imprimatur; the Disneyland version was one of his pet projects. Crystal loves the Jungle Cruise because "for as long as I can remember, it has been my dream to become a Jungle Skipper. When I was ten, I was able to be a junior skipper. I will never forget it." Your cruise lasts about ten minutes.

Though Disney has endured occasional criticism for perpetrating some chauvinistic stereotypes through this attraction—and then criticized again for succumbing to demands for political correctness when minor changes were made to address the earlier concern—**Pirates of the Caribbean** still maintains high marks among guests. Certainly, women are depicted as "carnal merchandise"—several pirates shout "We want the redhead," in reference to a seductive villager on the auction slab—but the pirates are caricatured as louts and drunks. These Audio-Animatronics interlopers—some of Disney's most realistic figures—wage war on a village (watch out; your boat is in the path of cannon fire), steal its gold and women, set fire to the town, then bend the elbow a bit before you sail away—and all to a very catchy tune. You'll find yourself singing, "Yo ho, Yo ho, a pirate's life for me," as you exit the attraction. If you're going to raise hell, according to this experience, the locals don't object quite as strongly when you do it with a song. During the summer of 2003, Disney released a film based on the attraction called, *Pirates of the Caribbean: Curse of the Black Pearl,* starring Johnny Depp, Orlando Bloom and Keira Knightley. The film did quite well at the box office,

Hidden Mickeys

Throughout the Resort, you'll find delightful reminders of the Mouse that started it all. Walt Disney Imagineers frequently place Mickey images in attractions. Finding them has become a pasttime for many fans.

- Arrangement of dishes on table at Haunted Mansion's banquet.
- "Wishes" fireworks occasionally form the famous three circles.
- Pink cloud above the Zip-A-Dee Lady paddlewheeler in Splash Mountain looks like the profile of Mickey Mouse lying on his back.

62 Making Memories

Fast-loading, relaxing, yet filled with suspense--particularly when the pirate skull warns that "there be rough waters ahead"--Pirates of the Caribbean is the quintessentially classic Disney attraction that has a good story line and engaging special effects. It's a nice break from the heat, too.

reflecting the huge popularity of this attraction. "Pirates of the Caribbean always makes me feel like a kid again," says Jason. "When we first went to Walt Disney World back in 1995, this was the ride I wanted to ride first, because I remembered it from my trip to Disneyland back in 1985." Your adventure on the high seas takes about ten minutes.

The attraction based on the film, *Swiss Family Robinson*, is certainly a "B-Ticket" attraction. In the **Swiss Family Treehouse**, you climb a tree—but not in the conventional way. Thanks to Robinson ingenuity, instead of scaling bark like a squirrel, you take this house tour via stairs—lots of stairs. (There is no handicapped access to this attraction.) Along the way, you pause briefly to see how the family slept and ate. You visit their study, their family room, the kids' rooms. You keep climbing,

Though certainly not what you'd call an E-Ticket attraction, the Swiss Family Treehouse provides a welcome break from the hordes of park guests, and is a great example of Imagineering creativity.

one stair after another. You wait with anticipation. Nothing happens — but it's a nice, relaxing exercise, and an escape from the masses below. If you're particularly observant, you'll enjoy a quite different perspective of this section of Adventureland from various vantage points. The organ salvaged from the sunken ship actually plays a tune as you tour the treehouse. By the way, the tree was designed by Walt Disney Imagineers, and consists largely of steel, mortar and paint. Expect your climb to last about ten minutes.

Next stop? A cute attraction dubbed **The Enchanted Tiki Room: Under New Management**. The original Disneyland version was showcased during one of Walt Disney's "Wonderful World of Color" television episodes back in the sixties, but Walt Disney World's version has been souped up a bit. (You can still see the original version at Disneyland Park in Anaheim, California.) A bunch of Audio-Animatronics tropi-

The entrance to the Enchanted Tiki Room only hints at the mayhem you encounter inside, though some Disney purists lament the revised attraction.

cal birds—led by Iago from *Aladdin* and Zazu from *The Lion King*—serenade you and try to teach you to sing "like the birdies sing." But things go awry when Iago angers the Tiki gods by suggesting a transformation of the legendary Tiki Bird Room into a huge money-making enterprise. Soon, the audience is subjected to a realistic storm, tempered by singing tree trunks. Their bizarre nature startles at first, then amuses. A couple of campy jokes will tickle your funny bone. Plan to spend about nine minutes with Iago, Zazu and a host of their fine-feathered friends.

Cute, short and definitely "off-the-shelf," **The Magic Carpets of Aladdin** is the last attraction in Adventureland in your quick tour. It's a carnival ride similar to Dumbo the Flying Elephant—only with a twist. You board, then control your own vehicle, shaped like a magic carpet—very cute, admittedly. You can make your carpet go higher or lower, or even

The Magic Carpets of Aladdin are aesthetically pleasing, but the ride is a typical carny ride. Watch out for the added Disney touch of a spitting camel!

swivel front to back. What you can't do is make it stay in the air longer! At the center of the ride is a magic lantern. On one side of the ride is a cocky-looking camel. At first glance, you think it's just a Disney tongue-in-cheek ploy to engage you. Then—watch out! This dromedary spits. Though the kids love this ride—and certainly, Magic Carpets adds to the aesthetic appeal of Adventureland—it's only mildly entertaining to adults. Your carpet completes its tour in about ninety seconds.

Frontierland

This land is a tribute to America's frontier—with a touch of homespun humor thrown in for kicks. It's one of the Magic Kingdom's most popular areas, and considering the entertainment value of its attractions, it's easy to understand why.

Give 'Em a Hand When You Hop

If you've chosen the park-hopping option for Magic Your Way, your park pass will allow you to travel from park to park over the course of the day. When you park hop, though, don't forget to give the cast member at the Exit turnstile a hand.

Either one will do.

As you leave one park for yet another, you must have your hand stamped (unless you're an Annual Passholder). Upon entering your destination park, insert your ticket for admission, then pass your hand beneath the black light. It's Disney's way of making sure you're not sharing your ticket with an "unauthorized" guest.

By the way, don't worry about the invisible ink rubbing off. Even after a swim and a shower, the stamp still magically appears beneath the light.

But please use park-hopping privileges wisely. Without careful planning, hopping can turn into a huge waste of time.

Big Thunder Mountain Railroad is a tame rollercoaster by industry standards, but great fun—and yes, you will experience a rush or two before your experience ends. (If you're trying to desensitize a younger one to thrill rides, it may be best to acclimate him or her to Disney's thrills on Big Thunder prior to Splash Mountain or Space Mountain—the other two attractions that are part of the Magic Kingdom's mountain range.) The theming is tops here; you're in prospectin' country at the height of the Gold Rush. You board an old mine train that quickly loses control, and the next thing you know, you narrowly miss a piercing job—by protruding fossilized bones and stalagmites. In a dark cave at the beginning of the ride, bats head for your belfry (so warn the little ones of that moderately frightening occurrence). If you're brave enough to look away from the track in front of you, you'll notice a burning cabin, across the Rivers of America on Tom Sawyer Island. (The effect is much better at night.) You can have a prolonged view of the cabin along the exit path heading back to the main thoroughfare in Frontierland. Your train isn't brought back under control for about four minutes. **Note**: This experience has a height restriction. Passengers must be at least forty inches tall to board.

Back in bruin country, you'll find **The Country Bear Jamboree**, an attraction on which a 2002 Disney film, *The Country Bears*, was based. The Jamboree is a classic country music hoedown—with an amusing twist. The performers are all Audio-Animatronics bears, with distinct and usually quirky personalities. Don't let a distaste for country music steer you away from this attraction; the songs trend toward comedy, and you'll chuckle at the cornpone humor. Bunny, Bubbles and Beulah will bring a nostalgic tear to many an eye when the trio sings "All the Guys That Turn Me On Turn Me Down." And you'll adore Big Al, who can neither carry a tune nor play a guitar, though he attempts to do both, with ear-shattering, though comic effect. Big Al has something of a cult following—and his own store. Generally, youngsters find the show to be a hoot, too—so it's a nice place for Mom and Dad to relax while the kids "clap their hands and stomp their feet." The mounted heads of a moose, buffalo, and a deer join the audience, and provide comic relief by goading the performers. This classic Disney attraction lasts about fifteen minutes.

Though **Splash Mountain** may strike the casual observer as a typical theme park log flume ride, it's anything but! Terrific show elements are housed inside this fairly long attrac-

Splash Mountain, part of the Walt Disney World mountain range, will have you humming "Zip-a-Dee-Doo-Dah" all day long! The anticipation of this drop is worse than the drop itself--particularly when you encounter two or three shorter falls as you prepare for the plummet to end all plummets. After you see the fear was unwarranted, ride this attraction once more--this time to appreciate the intricate craftsmanship of the Walt Disney Imagineers.

tion (particularly for a mild thrill ride, the likes of which usually end before you know it). The climax of the ride—which is visible from the pathways of Frontierland—looks more frightening than it really is. Your hollowed-out log of a ride vehicle nosedives down a waterfall and into a misty briar patch. If, after witnessing the plunge, you still feel anxious, watch the other thrill-seekers as they disembark. You'll see that most of them exit with smiles of delight on their faces—and a determination to ride it again. The strains of "Zip-a-Dee-Doo-Dah" will linger in your memory for a long time after the experience. This attraction, which has a height requirement of at least forty inches, also takes your picture during the plunge. You'll have an opportunity to purchase the resulting photograph for posterity as you leave the attraction. Once you've boarded, you'll spend about ten minutes meandering through this musical mountain. "This is my favorite ride as an adult," says Becky. "The goofy banjo music, strange visuals, and great length add up to an experience out of one of Jerry Garcia's acid-drenched bluegrass dreams. And remember, most Americans under forty haven't seen *Song of the South*, so the ride just seems like a group of unrelated scenes out of a froggy *Deliverance*. Still, it's pretty good, sure as you're born! Plus, what happens after you get to the bottom of the drop is what separates Disney from Six Flags and Paramount. Those parks would have just taken you straight to the unloading ramp. Disney goes the extra mile."

Tom Sawyer Island is a favorite among the younger set. It's a place to explore dark caves, cross "dangerous" bridges, and defend the Island while stationed at Fort Sam Clemens. Many adults like it, too—if for no other reason than it's a nice place to escape the crowds back on the mainland, and provides the absolute best vantage point for photos of The Haunted Mansion and Big Thunder Railroad. The disadvantage of this attraction is that it's only accessible via slow-loading rafts which cross the Rivers of America. But once ashore, you're free to explore as long as you like—until the Island closes at sunset. You'll find a fort, several air-conditioned caves (go inside with timid children, as the darkness can be a bit intimidating), a snack bar (which sells sandwiches, sodas and desserts), a couple of bridges (including a barrel bridge, which fascinates children), a playground and lots of paths for leisure walks—as well as some great views of Frontierland. Depending on your level of interest (or the line at the rafts, both coming and going), you will spend between ten minutes and forty-five minutes on this Island.

The Diamond Horseshoe Saloon is the setting of a short-lived show called Goofy's Country Dancin' Jamboree. Now, the Saloon is a character meet-and-greet site for **Woody & Friends**. While kids need as many venues in which to meet characters, have photos taken, or procure autographs as possible, to turn a quaint theater into a character meet-and-greet borders on impudence. "I hope Disney mends its ways soon," says Aronda, "and brings us a show worthy of this venue."

Before you leave Frontierland, savor the ambience by walking around and noticing the sights and enjoying the aromas—creosote is a predominant smell here. Occasionally, you can snag a rocking chair on the porch of one of the stores and enjoy a little people-watching. Another **Walt Disney World Railroad** Station is located in Frontierland, with stops at Main Street, U.S.A., and Mickey's Toontown Fair.

Liberty Square

Liberty Square is a refreshing patriotic and supernatural tribute to the American Spirit.

Jaded about what America has become? Enjoy the Disney version! Liberty Square is a spin on history in a (mostly) entertaining way.

You must visit Disney's **Hall of Presidents** at least once. Unfortunately, some guests are convinced that once is enough. The entrance is architecturally patterned in the Federal style, and the attraction is more dignified than you'd ever expect in a theme park. In the pre-show area, a cast member frequently quizzes waiting guests on American history trivia, so you're likely to learn little-known facts about US presidents. Usually, president-related displays set up in the pre-show area engage the audience waiting for the show to begin. (Bill Clinton's saxophone and George W. Bush's boots are two components of recent displays.) Then, you enter a huge

Parent-Swapping Is Perfectly Legal at WDW

Do you have youngsters who are either too young or too short to experience an attraction, but you and your spouse really, really want to?

Then, the parent swap is for you!

First, parents and kids all stand together in the queue for an attraction. Then, one parent rides with older kids (or alone), while the other parent stays with the baby or under-height kids. Then, the rider reverses roles with his or her spouse.

Just tell cast members at the attraction, and they'll make it happen for you.

auditorium where you view a wide-screen movie presentation highlighting United States history—with most of the focus on the Revolutionary War and the Civil War. Finally, the curtain rises on a huge tableaux of all US Presidents, both living and dead. These Audio-Animatronics figures are so lifelike, they whisper, twitch, blink and nod. After the presidential roll call—you're introduced to each President by name—President George W. Bush, whose Audio-Animatronics figure is the most intricate among the current cast of Presidents, delivers an inspiring speech. While the attraction feels a bit monotonous after awhile—some mothers have actually voted the Hall of Presidents as the best place in the Magic Kingdom

Magical MK Photo Spots

You'll get the best shots of:	By taking the photo from:
Cinderella Castle	Town Square; Tomorrowland Transit Authority; Bridge leading to Tomorrowland; Main Street, U.S.A. Railroad loading area
Big Thunder Mountain Railroad	Tom Sawyer Island
Space Mountain	Open area in front of attraction
Haunted Mansion	Riverboat & Tom Sawyer Island
Splash Mountain	In front of drop
Walt & Mickey Statue ("Partners")	In front of Cinderella Castle

to breastfeed—it's enjoyed a spurt of popularity since the terrorist attacks of September 11, 2001. The presidential figures attest to the best of Disney's artistry and technical skills. Walt Disney Imagineers conducted quite a bit of research to ensure historical accuracy in costumes, appearances, stage props— and even the characteristics of each President's voice. When Abraham Lincoln delivers one of his famous speeches, you may experience a chill or two. This attraction lasts about twenty minutes. We've noticed than in this, more than any other attraction in the Magic Kingdom, kids seem to be the most restless. You may wish to include this attraction in your itinerary before they get tired—and have other, more kid-appropriate attractions to look forward to. Also note that Hall of Presidents often closes at 5:00 p.m., regardless of park hours.

Ride with Height Restrictions

Splash Mountain
40 inches

Big Thunder Mountain Railroad
40 inches

Goofy's Barnstormer
35 inches

Tomorrowland Indy Speedway
52 inches (unless accompanied by an adult)

Space Mountain
44 inches

Stitch's Great Escape
35 inches

Upon exiting, you'll notice a huge Mississippi riverboat, called Liberty Belle, docked on the Rivers of America at an attraction called **Liberty Square Riverboat**. If you need to relax, soak up the view, or enjoy a romantic interlude with your spouse or significant other, take the short trip around Tom Sawyer Island. Beware of the Riverboat during the summer, however. It is one of the hottest places in the World! Josh, who loves to visit Tom Sawyer Island (the view of which is fantastic from the Liberty Belle Riverboat), says, "The Liberty Belle Riverboat is just not worth the investment of valuable

Viewing Spots for "Wishes" Fireworks Display

You'll find several great spots from which to view "Wishes". Main Street, U.S.A. always provides a grand view, better now that the once-tall trees in front of the Castle have been replaced with shorter ones. The Hub around the Partners statue in front of Cinderella Castle, too, makes for a great spot. Others include the bridge leading into Tomorrowland, the Main Street, U.S.A. Railroad Station, and the "rose walk" leading from Main Street, U.S.A. to Tomorrowland bridge--but be sure to avoid the light poles and trees.

---

park touring time—particularly when it's a hundred degrees in the shade!" Disney characters sometimes make appearances on board, but mostly, this trip is a way to take a break from the "Disney Dash" throughout the park, or to give your child a chance to take a nap. The journey lasts about sixteen minutes.

Before leaving Liberty Square, stake claim to a "Doom Buggy" in the delightfully ominous **Haunted Mansion**, and socialize with hundreds of "happy haunts." (On November 26, 2003, Disney released the film, *Haunted Mansion*, based on the attraction. Starring Eddie Murphy and Jennifer Tilly, the film features a busy real estate agent determined to sell the haunted mansion for a lavish profit, but the ghosts in the house

If the temperature in the Florida sunshine is sweltering, avoid the Liberty Square Riverboat. Otherwise, you'll be cooked by the time you disembark. If the temps are bearable, the ride is scenic and relaxing.

Chapter 3/Magic Kingdom

The foyer a little ominous, the "stretch room" a hoot, and the ride component humorous and unnerving, the Haunted Mansion is one of the most intricate attractions in the Magic Kingdom.

teach him values that transcend greed and opportunism.) Cast members who work the Mansion consistently stay in character, and often delight in adding a scare or two to the guest's experience. Even if you're generally weak-hearted, don't pass up this great attraction. (But be sensitive to timid youngsters who resist the Haunted Mansion; communicate to them that the scares are only make-believe. And rather than terrify a child, parents should take turns on the ride, utilizing Disney's convenient parent-swap program, if the child still insists on not experiencing the attraction.) Though some of the effects can be a bit unnerving, Disney has thrown in a generous sampling of humor, so even the occasional scream is followed by a guffaw. The weakness of the attraction is the obtuse storyline. With moderate attention, you can detect a strand of a story about a bride who has died — perhaps from grief that her fiance abandoned her. A "soothsayer" called Madame Leota (who now has a creepy tombstone in the Mansion's front lawn; be sure to have a look) summons the spirits in a séance room, but we're not sure why. Our "Ghost Host," his everpresent voice and faux-sinister laugh in our ear, attempts to draw us into the plot, such as it is, by cajoling us to sign up as the one-thousandth ghost. Finally, as a foolish mortal who refused to make that commitment, you're the victim of a wayward hitchhiker close to the attraction's exit. One of the 999 ghosts sneaks into your Doom Buggy, and rides out of the Haunted Mansion with you, a passenger into the world of flesh and blood. This ride — one of Disney's best — lasts about ten minutes.

Fantasyland

Cinderella Castle serves as the official entrance to Fantasyland, while several other paths also lead into it.

Kids rule in this area of Walt Disney World — though adults, whether parents or not, can find plenty of enjoyable attractions, as well. Fairy dust proliferates here! Even if you

Cinderella's Golden Carrousel is a beautiful attraction just behind Cinderella Castle. Children always love to ride; adults, too, if the wait isn't too long.

don't have a kid of your own, try a few of Fantasyland's offerings through the eyes of your inner child.

Cinderella's Golden Carrousel is the first ride you encounter as you enter Fantasyland through the arched portal of the Castle. Don't expect a typical carnival ride, as this gorgeous, restored antique carousel has its own cast member assigned to keep the horses in top shape. Youngsters love this ride; it provides marvelous views of Fantasyland—especially, Cinderella Castle. The arrival of dusk makes the ride even more magical. The parental pay-off for accompanying your children is the delight in their eyes. Bear in mind that the wait is usually fairly long for this three-minute experience; lines may be shorter in the evening.

Though **Dumbo the Flying Elephant** is one of the most photographed rides in the park, it's a simple carny ride, with a few Disney touches. (The ride mechanism is the same as in The Magic Carpets of Aladdin.) Up and down vertical motion is controlled independently in each ride vehicle. Long lines can form here—it's at least as popular with youngsters as the Carrousel—and you may be put off a bit when you remain in the air for about ninety seconds after waiting thirty minutes to board. Again, this attraction has shorter lines after dark—a compelling argument for taking the kids back to the resort for an afternoon nap before returning to the parks. This way, they'll have a second burst of energy and, well-rested, they'll enjoy their Disney experiences a bit more.

it's a small world not only has the World's most addictive song, but also Walt Disney's signature on it, since he personally directed the development of this attraction for the New York World's Fair in 1964-65. It has its moments—particularly moments when the boats are trapped in a traffic jam, and you're stuck—forced to listen to "it's a small world after all" over and over and over again. Small children find the attraction a delight—particularly kids who enjoy dolls—but once in elementary school, they're likely to be a bit more cynical in their tastes. Certainly, everyone should ride because of its historical significance to The Walt Disney Company—and be-

In Disney's "it's a small world," you'll see dolls, dolls, and more dolls! And we're not talking Broadway dolls, either. An adorable attraction, expect a sparkling new treat in the spring of 2005, when its refurbishment will be complete.

cause the show building is a cool retreat from the heat. The attraction will be closed for refurbishment until the spring of 2005, during which a new entrance, a new soundtrack, and complete retooling of attraction components will occur. The ride lasts about eleven minutes—barring a "boat jam." "I cried in this attraction, with my husband, on our honeymoon trip in 1996," says Amanda. "The attraction is just so pure and innocent and sweet, it really touched me. Now I've had the chance to take our son on it and share it with him, which is wonderful."

The Mad Tea Party is a dizzying carnival ride which places you in spinning cups and saucers—and if you have a low tolerance for spinning, or more seriously, vertigo, then you may wish to avoid this attraction. The kids seem to tolerate this ride, based on Disney's animated feature, *Alice in Wonderland*, better than adults—and some teens get a big thrill in seeing how fast they can get their ride vehicle to spin. (Aronda has witnessed several teens stagger off the ride, only to reboard right away. Ah, youth!) Since each vehicle has its own "spinning wheel," you control the intensity. It can be made to go very fast indeed. Another short ride—it lasts about ninety seconds—Mad Tea Party is best enjoyed when crowds have dissipated, and you don't have to stand in a long line. And, oh yes, make sure your stomach is empty. David quips: "Who

A short but delightful attraction, Peter Pan's Flight features a breath-taking aerial view of London. You can view the working model of the attraction in "Walt Disney: One Man's Dream" at the Disney-MGM Studios Theme Park.

doesn't have fun spinning themselves into total dizziness?" Are you a big fan of Winnie the Pooh and Friends? Then, Disney has just the attraction for you. In **The Many Adventures of Winnie the Pooh**, you're deposited into a "hunny pot" and sent through a storybookland. The attraction, which replaced Mr. Toad's Wild Ride after it closed in 1998, is extremely popular—so popular, in fact, waits in excess of forty-five minutes often occur. Fortunately, Disney added its FASTPASS feature in 2002. Most children—and all Pooh fans—adore this delightful little ride, which encourages reading since the backdrops are oversized pages from a Pooh book. When Tigger comes on the scene, your hunny pot goes bouncing along with him. Despite a light, fleeting "scary" spot in the ride, you'll find the five-minute Pooh will delight most kids.

Peter Pan's Flight is visually stunning—particularly the cityscape of London. But anyone who's not already familiar with the tale will be lost—so make sure any kids (or adults, for that matter) you're treating to a Disney vacation have brushed up on the adventures of Peter Pan, Tinker Bell and the Little Lost Boys. Ride vehicles shaped like sailboats soar above three-dimensional scenes from the movie, *Peter Pan*. Even adults find this panorama spectacular. Peter Pan's journey lasts about three minutes.

Disney magic meets Disney music in a new 3-D film spectacular which debuted in October 2003. **Mickey's PhilharMagic** stars Mickey Mouse, Donald Duck and other

Mickey's PhilharMagic is one of the Disney's most delightful offerings. Though the show belongs to Donald Duck, you'll see a smorgasboard of Disney characters on one 3-D screen.

favorite Disney characters animated in a way they've never before been seen: grand, glorious, in-your-face three dimensions. The PhilharMagic cast includes Mickey and Donald, as well as Ariel from *The Little Mermaid*, Aladdin and Jasmine from *Aladdin* and Simba from *The Lion King*. Set in the PhilharMagic Concert Hall, which replaced "Legend of the Lion King" in Fantasyland, the eye-popping 3-D experience unfolds on one of the largest screens ever created for a 3-D film, a 150-foot-wide canvas. Complete with in-theater special effects—such as bursts of wind and light water spritzes—the attraction immerses guests in the richly animated world of the Disney characters. The story begins with Donald insult-

Snow White's Scary Adventure has been known to scare a child or two, but overall, the storyline is pretty tame--and it has a happy ending.

ing a flute. The rest of the orchestra rallies to her defense, and sends Donald—and Mickey's hat—into a flight featuring encounters with many Disney characters. The 3-D effects are spectacular from any vantage point, but best from the center of the rows. Guests often neglect to follow Donald's "flight" from the screen to the rear of the theater at the film's end. The attraction lasts about twelve minutes. "We love Mickey's PhilharMagic because it gives Donald Duck a time to shine," say Lindsey and Chuck. "It is by far the best 3-D show we've ever seen. PhilharMagic combines sights, sounds and smells to make for a very memorable experience." Ed considers the film an even better version of 3-D films than MuppetVision 3-D over at Disney-MGM Studios. "It's very entertaining, and I noticed a lot of small children totally enjoying themselves." John and Lynda caution guests to try and sit approximately in the fourth row from the back for the best viewing. Other guests suggest close-to-the-front vantage points work best.

Snow White's Scary Adventure is a dark ride—meaning it relies on bright colors illuminated by black light—which promises to be scary, but generally fails for adults. Perhaps that's as it should be in Fantasyland. However, youngsters intimidated by the dark may be somewhat apprehensive, so comfort them before boarding and during the ride. There's a wicked Witch enticing us with a poisoned apple, but the familiar story has already warned us not to bite. In 1994, the ride received a make-over to include an appearance by Show White who had been conspicuously absent until then. The ride lasts about three minutes.

Ariel's Grotto is a picturesque character meet-and-greet, designed for the famous "Little Mermaid." Personally, Aronda has a difficult time overlooking this big waste of prime theme park real estate (Disney can find another nook from which Ariel could entertain) which once housed 20,000 Leagues Under the Sea (1971-1994), a submarine adventure during which guests escaped a sea monster and experienced the fairly realistic sensations of a submarine descent. (A derivative is found at Tokyo DisneySea, which opened September 4, 2002.) In

2004, Disney began the lengthy task of removing the Lagoon and props, and hints have recently surfaced that the area may become a Winnie the Pooh Play area. In late 2004, the Times Guide stated that Ariel's Grotto was "temporarily closed," it is unlikely that this attraction will be resurrected. However, Ariel fans may visit with their heroine in other venues.

Mickey's Toontown Fair

This land began as Mickey's Birthdayland in 1988 to honor the Big Cheese's sixtieth birthday. The kid-sized attractions here remain essentially the same, with a few enhancements. The Fair is the best place to meet the Fabulous Five — Mickey, Minnie, Pluto, Donald and Goofy. Though designed primarily for children, adults, too, will appreciate the creativity thrown into the place, and it's good for at least a walk-through, even if you don't have children accompanying you.

Goofy's Barnstormer, a cute, whimsical roller coaster for youngsters, is located at Goofy's Wiseacre Farm, which is worth a short tour before boarding the ride. The seats are a bit smaller than those found in adult-size roller coasters, but guests of any age will fit, albeit some more comfortably than others. Expect to crash through a barn and disrupt a few chickens (the feathered kind). Passengers must be at least thirty-five inches tall to ride.

Donald's Boat is a toddler's delight. Essentially, it's a fountain for kids to cool off a bit. It seems that Donald's boat, named for his girlfriend, Daisy, has sprung a few leaks. Kids love trying to avoid getting squirted — love it even more when the boat doesn't miss!

Ever want to see Mickey Mouse's Magic Kindgom estate? Well, you can, at **Mickey's Country House**. You're invited to take a quick tour through the Mouse House itself on your way to the Judge's Tent, where Mickey is busy greeting guests under the incessant flashes of a photo op. And that's the reason Mickey's not at home — just in case the kids ask. The rooms are filled with cute furnishings both kids and adults

Disney's Magic Music Days

On many days, Magic Kingdom--in addition to the other major theme parks--provides a sensational performance venue for talented young musicians from all around the world. However, groups and ensembles don't merely sign up and hit the park streets, or file onto the stage beneath the band shell. These performers have to meet certain Disney standards for selection. Visiting groups--who perform in parades and on stages throughout the Resort--work with a Disney Guest Talent Coordinator to fine-tune their performances. In fact, Disney even offers these young talents a chance to enjoy hands-on workshops dedicated to their particular performance skills.

So, when you see a group of "guest" performers participating in Magic Music Days, extend to them an enthusiastic ovation of appreciation.

---

will enjoy — and you can engage your children in a contest to see who can find the most Hidden Mickeys! (The House is filled with them.)

If you have your heart set on meeting other Disney characters, too, then head on over to the **Toontown Hall of Fame** — the best place to meet many of the characters in Disney's "stable." Characters rotate here, so it's impossible to predict which characters you'll see, but signs above the queue areas leading into each room will indicate which characters await an audience with none other than — you!

Minnie Mouse is such a tease — and nothing demonstrates this personality trait better than **Minnie's Country House**. Youngsters love Minnie's house because she obviously decorated with them in mind. Here, it's okay for the kids to climb all over the furniture, listen to other people's messages on

Minnie's answering machine, and try to raid Minnie's fridge.

You'll also find another **Walt Disney World Railroad Station** located here. Boarding in Toontown will take you around the park—or you can disembark at either Main Street, U.S.A. or Frontierland. Also note that a pathway connects Mickey's Toontown Fair with Tomorrowland, and provides a great photo spot as the Walt Disney World Railroad passes by.

Tomorrowland

Nothing pleased Walt Disney more during his lifetime than the promise and possibilities of the future—and Tomorrowland is proper homage to his fascination. Besides, it contains some of the Magic Kingdom's most popular—and most thrilling—attractions.

Though Space Mountain vehicles scurry along their track at a rather tame rate of speed, the fact that they do so in star-studded darkness makes the ride appear to go faster. Waits are often substantial here, so utilize Disney's FASTPASS system.

CHAPTER 3/MAGIC KINGDOM 83

Space Mountain, a roller coaster in the futuristic, mountain-shaped building (and part of the Magic Kingdom's three-peak mountain range), travels about twenty-eight miles per hour; however, it feels wilder and faster than it really is. Why? You're traveling through a darkened building in rocket ships. Projections cast on the ceiling, blacklights and sound effects give this attraction its appeal—and its perceived higher speed. Hundreds of guests hurry after the morning rope drop (when Disney allows guests to leave Main Street, U.S.A., and head to all the other lands) to get in line for Space Mountain. The ride feels shaky and jerky—don't expect a smooth flight at all. In fact, it's a typical Wild Mouse coaster, if you could peel the show building away. The seats are positioned fairly high in the vehicle, a design feature that doesn't make you feel very secure—but who's supposed to feel secure in outer space? For parents exposing their youngsters to this ride for the first time, keep in mind that passengers cannot sit side-by-side; rather, guests are positioned one behind the other. And, there is a height restriction that must be met before boarding; passengers must be at least forty-four inches tall. Your flight lasts about three minutes. "Finally, at age 39, I worked up the courage to try Space Mountain for the first time," says Sue. "And now, it's one of my favorite attractions."

Feeling a little competitive? Try your hand at ***Buzz Lightyear's Space Ranger Spin***, where you shoot lasers from your moving vehicle at the evil Emperor Zurg, who's stealing all the batteries for toys to power his weapon of mass destruction. As you hit each "Z" positioned within the sets throughout the ride, your vehicle computer tabulates your score in your training to be a Space Ranger. Spin ranks as a wonderful ride which parents can enjoy with their children. Though there's no tangible prize, you can enjoy the assurance that your shots helped save the world. And now, you can purchase a photo of your five-minute battle with Zurg after you disembark. Be sure to smile when the bright flashes commence, and check out your photo as you exit. Spin is Brian's favorite attraction in Magic Kingdom "because I am always totally fo-

Before Hawaii. Before Lilo. There was a troublesome little alien. Experiment 626. Intelligent? Highly. Difficult? Certainly! Mischievous? You betcha! This is Disney's description of the star of the Magic Kingdom's newest attraction called Stitch's Great Escape, which replaced the less kid-friendly ExtraTERRORestrial: Alien Encounter.

cused on getting points." Shelle says that Buzz Lightyear brings out the inner child in her entire family — husband Bob and daughter Amanda. "We become very competitive. In fact, we kept going back because my husband would win. So, Amanda and I made him go back in for a do-over, three times in a row."

Gloating about your high score on Buzz Lightyear's Space Ranger Spin is not so easy when an alien has escaped just across the street. In **Stitch's Great Escape**, mischief abounds, as you might imagine, considering the source. The Academy-Award nominated film, *Lilo & Stitch*, inspired the new attraction that's really a "pre-quel" to the film. This venue once housed Alien Encounter (some fans will miss it terribly; few Disney attractions featured such outrageous camp), but

Tomorrowland Indy Speedway attracts guests by the hundreds, resulting in some rather formidable lines. Though certainly not "speedy," the small roadsters offer some scenic views of Tomorrowland.

Stitch's Great Escape is a family-friendly adventure showcasing the mayhem caused by the mischievous "Experiment 626" — a.k.a. Stitch — when first discovered in the Galactic Federation. Entering Stitch's Great Escape, guests are recruited by the Galactic Federation Grand Councilwoman to provide additional security for a captured alien whose reputation for being extremely "difficult" has preceded him. Even so, authorities underestimate Stitch's capacity for playful disobedience, causing havoc to erupt with guests caught in the middle of the fun. The attraction features some of the most sophisticated Audio-Animatronics technology developed by Walt Disney Imagineering, along with sensory elements that appeal to the eyes, ears — and nose! Disgustingly funny is the aroma of chili dog after Stitch belches. The Stitch character is 39 inches tall, with more than 350 detailed, hand-machined parts and more than 40 separate functions. Dann thinks the show is a huge compromise compared to Alien Encounter. "I didn't have a problem with Disney's decision to replace an older show that lost its popularity," he says. "But shouldn't replacements be of higher caliber than their predecessors? Honestly, guests are quite capable of detecting inferiority." However, Josh views the show "as basically the same as Alien Encounter. I liked the idea of giving Stitch his own attraction. But Disney doesn't really capitalize on Stitch's personality to the degree the com-

Astro Orbiter is a ride similar to Magic Carpets of Aladdin and Dumbo The Flying Elephant. The difference is significant. Your rocket vehicles are perched on one of Tomorrowland's rooftops.

pany could." The show lasts about 15 minutes.

Tomorrowland Indy Speedway is frequently populated with parents in the passenger seats of these little race cars while their son or daughter steers. Keep in mind, though, you have to step on the gas, which takes you nowhere near racing speeds, and you have to actually steer the car. However, a steel guard on the track keeps you from passing into someone else's lane. For particularly young children, Mom or Dad may have to depress the accelerator when their kids cannot reach the pedal. For the most part, though, adults will find little that appeals to them in this attraction. (Some have never understood its placement in Tomorrowland.) Still, it offers several nice vantage points for views of scenic areas in the park—a wonderful view of Cinderella Castle, for example, and of Disney's Contemporary Resort. Your noisy "race" lasts about five minutes, but beware: Long lines often form at this attraction because of slow loading and the length of the ride. Keep in mind that, while children of all heights can enjoy this attraction with a parent, they must be at least fifty-two inches tall to ride alone.

Tomorrowland also features the **Astro Orbiter**, a souped-up version of Dumbo the Flying Elephant in Fantasyland. As with Dumbo, you control the up-and-down motion of the vehicle. However, if you're afraid of heights, you may wish to skip this ride, since it's constructed on the roof of Tomorrowland Transit Authority, and travels a bit faster than Dumbo. (You reach the boarding area via an elevator. Frequently, lines grow fairly long.) Still, if you can keep your eyes open, this ride offers some gorgeous views of Cinderella Castle. Your flight above Tomorrowland lasts about two minutes.

Robin Williams, Jeremy Irons and Michael Piccoli make appearances in **The Timekeeper**, a CircleVision 360 production (the screen completely surrounds you in a seat-less theater) enhanced by a few special effects and a couple of endearing Audio-Animatronics figures—one of which is the droid version of a delightful Robin Williams with wild, silver hair. The Timekeeper sends his co-hort, yet another droid, named 9-Eye (voiced by Rhea Perlman of *Cheers*), into history, where she meets Jules Verne and H.G. Wells—but *not* before she disrupts a recital by Mozart, and distracts Michelangelo as he paints the Mona Lisa. Jules gets carried away with this "proof" that time travel really works, and that's where the drama heightens. Jules confronts the present (his future) as he experiments with fairly commonplace transportation in unusual ways. You'll spend about twenty minutes in your time travel capsule—when it's available. Since May 2001, The Timekeeper has opened only periodically, usually during peak attendance periods. So, guests who travel during off-peak seasons may not be able to experience this attraction—too bad, really, since it's a highly creative show with off-the-wall Robin Williams' humor. (When you travel over glacial formations, Timekeeper deadpans, "Daiquiris for everyone!") A drawback for the children who experience The Timekeeper is their difficulty seeing above the heads of any adults who may be standing in front of them. We suggest guests with youngsters head toward the front of the theater to enjoy the show, since Dad will annoy guests behind him when he places his kid on his shoulders.

Walt Disney's Carousel of Progress opens only during limited hours and peak seasons. Unfortunately, its popularity has waned over the years, despite having enjoyed Walt's personal touch. (Disney designed the attraction for the 1964-65 New York World's Fair.) However, the implementation of FASTPASS at Buzz Lightyear's Space Ranger Spin and Space Mountain has afforded many guests a little extra time in Tomorrowland, so they frequently squeeze a Carousel show into their itineraries. The show, once sponsored by General Electric, has been updated at least once to reflect something more than the evolution of electricity. The unique aspect of this attraction is the revolution of the theater around several stages constructed in the center axis. Uniquely, Carousel becomes both a ride *and* a show. The problem for some guests is that the plot relies heavily on the traditional June-and-Ward Cleaver type of family — not that there's anything wrong with that, except that we're subjected to several rather sexist views of women. The "little woman" is essentially portrayed as a "house maid" determined to keep her family happy — even if it takes her five days to finish the family's laundry! However, the last scene has Grandma competing with her grandson as they play a virtual reality game set in space. And Grandma wins! Dad also fills a nontraditional role as a cook for the Christmas holidays — though not a fully competent one. Aronda has heard that Carousel of Progress may be scheduled for a major, much-needed refurbishment in 2005. Walt Disney's Carousel of Progress lasts about twenty minutes.

For a relaxing ride through Tomorrowland — and an overview of many of Tomorrowland's attractions — take the **Tomorrowland Transit Authority** (formerly known as the WEDway People Mover — WED stands for Walter Elias Disney). This unique journey above the rooftops of many shops and attractions is powered by magnetic conduction, transporting your vehicle at varying speeds about twelve feet above this part of the Magic Kingdom. If you chickened out before boarding Space Mountain, and wonder what it's like, here's a way to see inside the attraction without subjecting yourself to the trauma. A very relaxing attraction, and a great way to keep an eye on the crowds below, Tomorrowland Transit Authority is also a way to get a few great camera shots. You'll particularly enjoy several wonderful views of Cinderella Castle. Your tour of Tomorrowland takes about ten minutes.

Beyond the Rides

Even after consuming all the major fare at the Magic Kingdom, you still have other tasty treats to enjoy. Parades and other live entertainment by talented performers complete the menu of Walt Disney World's oldest, most seasoned park.

The **Dapper Dans**, a barbershop quartet, performs several times daily on Main Street, U.S.A. Complete musical sets last about twenty minutes, though you're free to wander away at will. You'll also enjoy the **pianist at Casey's Corner** who tickles the ivories on a white, upright piano. Daily, usually about 5:00 p.m., you can appreciate the dignity of a **Flag Retreat**. Several times a week, the **Main Street Philharmonic** adds its talents to the Retreat. The Philharmonic, a twelve-piece brass and percussion ensemble, plays its own concert several times a week in Town Square. **Poet Laureate Penelope Prose**, a Streetmosphere character on Main Street, U.S.A., joins **Mayor Weaver**, **"Scoop" Sanderson** and **Dewey Cheatem**, among other performers who interact personally with shoppers and diners. Guest Relations, located in Town Square at City Hall, can assist you in finding performance locations, since schedules are not always printed in your Times Guide.

In Fantasyland, kids will adore **Cinderella's Surprise Celebration**, when Cinderella invites friends to her castle and shares her dream of giving the special gifts of Romance, Laughter, Courage and Friendship. The Evil Queen appears and calls on several of her henchmen to spoil the party, causing an evil transformation of the castle. But Cinderella's gift of Courage brings some very special heroes to save the day. After the performance, a huge character greeting occurs, and kids can meet their favorites as well as acquire their autographs. This show will be replaced by **Cinderellabration** in May 2005, a "gift" from Tokyo Disneyland which is part of "The Happiest Celebration on Earth." Filled with sparkling pageantry, luxurious costumes, romantic choreography and a lush musical score incorporating new compositions and several classic Disney songs, "Cinderellabration" welcomes a who's-who of Disney princesses to join in the gala coronation ceremony in which Cinderella is at last crowned a princess.

In Frontierland, you're likely to encounter the **Notorious Banjo Brothers and Bob**, a hilarious traveling trio of musicians—two banjo players and a tuba player. Several actors in Frontierland schmooze with guests, as well, always remaining in appropriate character—like **Prospector "Gold Dust" Gus**. You can also enjoy brief sets of the **Frontierland Hoedown** five days a week.

Before you take an afternoon break, be sure to view the daytime parade, **Share a Dream Come True**, which features spectacular snowglobes and one hundred Disney characters depicting some of the greatest scenes from Disney animation history. Eight larger-than-life-size snowglobe floats, designed to illustrate Walt's Dream, and a "flurry of classic Disney moments frozen in time," pass by. At different intervals during the parade, lights twinkle and snow begins to swirl inside the giant globes. As a music box-style soundtrack swells, the floats stop while the characters inside each snowglobe strike a new pose. You'll see Aladdin rise up on his magic carpet in "A Thousand Dreams to See" float, and the Queen from *Snow White and the Seven Dwarfs* turns into the crone with her poison apple in the unit entitled "Face the Darkest Fears." This parade begins each afternoon around 3:00 p.m., but always confirm show times when you arrive, as Disney frequently amends its schedules. This parade is a gorgeous menagerie of floats. The Villains float is a stellar display of evil. You may even find yourself cowering beneath Maleficent's withering glare. She's a creature in serious need of therapy. Though the parade lasts about twenty minutes, expect to devote about forty-five minutes to the waiting this event requires.

And when the Magic Kingdom stays open past dusk, treat yourself to **Wishes Nighttime Spectacular**. Wishes is a twelve-minute pyrotechnics extravaganza (Fantasy lasted only five

Chapter 3/Magic Kingdom 91

minutes) which ignites eight hundred shells per show. The musical score is set to the children's song, "Starlight, Starbright," with Jiminy Cricket as the narrator. Story elements include Ariel wishing to be on land, Aladdin wishing on the lamp, and Pinocchio wishing to be a boy. It's an extraordinary display, with an inspiring theme to all guests to pursue their dreams as "Fate jumps in to see you through." Tinker Bell's Flight remains part of the show, but this time, she's all aglow. You'll have to see her to believe her!

SpectroMagic — the only nighttime parade in any of the parks — is an edgy cavalcade of floats illuminated by lights and fiber optics depicting famous Disney characters in a variety of scenarios. The music — which is almost as exciting as the visuals — is contemporary and driving, and the characters' costumes are powered by heavy energy packs unobtrusively attached to their bodies. The enthusiasm of the performers pervades the night, and guests find themselves moving their bodies to the catchy tunes. SpectroMagic lasts about thirty minutes — and though performed only "on special nights," it absolutely *must* be seen.

King Triton's Electrical Water Pageant is a short but exciting parade, in lights and synthesized music, with a delightful twist. The whole thing floats on all-but-invisible barges around Seven Seas Lagoon and Bay Lake. The parade, which features King Triton and a number of sea creatures, begins its route about 9:00 p.m. Your best viewing areas are on the docks of Disney's Grand Floridian Resort & Spa, Disney's Polynesian Resort, Disney's Contemporary Resort or Disney's Wilderness Lodge — or at Disney's Fort Wilderness Resort and Campground. (You can't see King Triton's Electrical Water Pageant from inside the Magic Kingdom, though you may catch a glimpse outside the park's front entrance.) This unique parade is a great opportunity to enjoy a nightcap purchased from a resort lounge after spending a busy day in the parks — particularly the "dry" Magic Kingdom. Ask resort hotel cast members for specific times and best locations for viewing.

Chapter 4

Avoiding VABS

The Mellow Vacationer

What's VABS? you ask. It's the Vacation Burnout Syndrome, a low-grade infection you're likely to contract if you don't leave time for a little relaxation during your exciting Walt Disney World vacation.

The key to ensuring a relaxing, mellow vacation for yourself and your loved ones is the recognition right away that you *may* have to skip some attractions, shows and experiences, particularly if you're visiting during a crowded season, or your vacation lasts only a few days. This fact is relatively easy to accept if you know you'll be able to take future (and hopefully frequent) vacations for your periodic Disney fix. But for individuals who live far, far away — or for whom budget considerations preclude frequent Disney trips — the next adventure may be years away. Then, your dilemma's only solu-

Chapter 4/The Mellow Vacationer

tion is to make certain you've planned a vacation long enough to include everything on your "must-do" list while maintaining a pace that leaves you refreshed and rejuvenated when you return home. In other words, you want to leave the World feeling that you've had a vacation, rather than having competed in some grueling endurance test (though you'll find plenty of opportunities for that at Walt Disney World). During your preliminary planning, prioritize your Disney experiences by determining which attractions should come first. If time (and FASTPASS) allows you to get ahead of schedule, then consider those lower-priority attractions as icing on the cake. And for heaven's sake, whatever you do, don't belly up to a queue whose wait time is more than forty-five minutes (unless it's spring break or the week preceding New Year's Day, when you won't have much choice). Either use FASTPASS or try again later. Wait times fluctuate enormously during the day—except perhaps for Test Track, Tower of Terror, Kilimanjaro Safaris and Splash Mountain (whose lines grow longer during Florida's intense heat). We always recommend FASTPASS for those attractions—or the single rider line, if available.

One of the most exasperating experiences for several members of our Memories Team has been the sight of children who are obviously frazzled by parents who have succumbed to the Disney Dash Syndrome—"We're gonna have a good time, damn it, even if it kills us." Part of that attitude can, understandably, be attributed to the fact that an investment in a Walt Disney World vacation is a substantial one—and parents, equally understandably, want to get their money's worth. But you must ask yourself: "Do I want my family to cherish and value this vacation for years to come—or regret the trip because I was such a pushy jerk?" If you aren't sensitive to that question, you may discover that your family and friends have a horrible time, and they may even vow never again to return to Walt Disney World—or, at least, not with you!

So, with the assumption that you want to incorporate

some time for relaxation, our Memories Team offers suggestions for kicking back, mellowing out, and recharging.

Sue isn't the kind of person who schedules long hours in Disney's theme parks. And while she's not your typical Disney guest, it's true, knowledge of her favorite things might help you tailor a few relaxing activities for your party. "I relax in many ways," Sue explains. "I lie beside a pool, or at Typhoon Lagoon. I may ride a bike through Fort Wilderness, or ride a boat on one of many Disney waterways. Or, I might have a nice lunch in the mid-afternoon, meeting friends just to sit around and chat. Or maybe I'll watch a soap opera in my resort room. Just sitting on the porch with a cold drink and a good book often does it for me. Basically, I do things that could be done anywhere; it's just that doing them at Walt Disney World makes them extra nice just because the surroundings are so pleasant." Sue also cautions not to wear brand new shoes; they should be broken in before you arrive.

Jason and Lauralee avoid tiring out by never waiting long in line. "If a wait is more than thirty minutes or so," they explain, "we get a FASTPASS and move on. Of course, we try to visit during the off-season whenever possible. When it's so busy that all the rides have long waits, we watch the street performers, do a little shopping, or head back to the hotel for a swim."

A nice meal can help calm the frayed nerves that often result from fighting the park crowds. "We like to have at least one nice sitdown meal a day, which gets you out of the hustle and bustle, and makes you feel you've had a nice break from the theme parks," Melanie says. "It's also nice to go to a resort hotel near the park you're visiting, and take in the sights there, perhaps have a meal, and relax a bit. Taking the time to just soak up the atmosphere helps, too. Get an ice cream cone, sit on a bench and people-watch." Melanie warns that many people try to cram too much into a short period of time. "Make sure your trip is long enough to get everything you want done," she continues. "If you can only take a short trip, then make priorities. Don't have a commando-type plan, but do

*Pausing for attractions that are not thrill-oriented will heighten vacation enjoyment. At the American Film Institute Showcase, you may see Johnny Depp's costume from **Pirates of the Caribbean**.*

have an idea of what you want to do."

Ed concurs with other members of the Memories Team that it's important to take your time. "It is such a common error to rush back and forth between attractions, trying to fit everything in," he warns. "Plan your days for the most efficient times to see the attractions, allow plenty of time, and enjoy the ones you *do* get to see. But don't fret over what you *don't* see."

Crystal and her parents, Tom and Linda, usually spend a couple of evenings just hanging out at the pool or beach. "Sometimes guests tend to wake up as early as possible and stay at the parks as late as possible. There is always time to take a break in the middle of the day and come back at night — especially during peak seasons when the parks are open later."

Dania recommends the perennial pastime of people-watching. "Or perhaps you can take in a show," she says. "Personally, I love to just sit and relax and not rush through everything."

Carrie warns that a common mistake is to stay in the parks from open to close. "That's enough to cause exhaustion, and make for increasingly tired days for the duration of your vacation." Then she offers a meaningful adage: "Seeing it all in one day means you only get glimpses!"

Susan and John take a systematic approach to relaxing at Walt Disney World. "We love to take the paper with us to Extra Magic Hour. After we've ridden a few rides, we get coffee, sit on a bench, watch the people and read the paper. Or, we may go back to the resort after noon, when most people seem to be just arriving and the parks start getting really crowded, take an adult beverage and our books, sit by the quiet pool, and soak up the sun." The couple cautions that getting too far off your regular schedule — like staying up much later than normal, not eating anything healthy, or trying to do everything without regard to rest or nourishment — can really diminish the quality of your vacation.

Becky, however, scoffs at the idea of relaxing at Walt Disney World. "Walt Disney World isn't for relaxing!" she says. "However, I will advise that the most tiring park is Epcot. There is so much walking that even a person in reasonably good shape will be exhausted. A guest should not try to do all of

Epcot in one day."

For Amanda, relaxation translates into personal indulgence. "I like to spend a couple of evenings away from the parks, sampling resort restaurants," she says. "California Grill and Boma are two of my favorites. I also make time for the resort hot tub, if there's one, and book at least one massage during my stay. Another wonderful break from the parks is renting a watercraft from one of the Magic Kingdom resort area marinas and just tooling around the lakes."

Thomas and Maribeth often eat at a table service restaurant for lunch, or return to their hotel. "If you have smaller children, returning to the hotel is especially helpful," they advise. "Usually, halfway through the day, you see people carrying their children around. Both the parents and the children look exhausted. The biggest mistake that we have seen is people trying to do everything all in one visit. Take your time; don't rush. Disney is going to be around for quite some time. Besides, some of the parks just cannot be seen in one day."

If, like Toni and Jim, you can spend two weeks, finding time to relax is even easier. "We have days in between so that we just sit by the pool, or maybe go to Typhoon Lagoon," they explain. "Believe it or not, we'll take a nap. We also like Downtown Disney. Other times, we just sit and people-watch."

Sam, Kathy, and Julianne relax by hitting the hotel pool. "Or, we may sleep in and eat breakfast from room service, or the hotel food court or restaurant instead of doing Extra Magic Hour," they say. "It's just exhausting to go morning to midnight all the time. Yes, you want to do as much as you can, but enjoy fewer attractions and shows more, instead of more attractions and shows that you enjoy less."

Lindsey and Chuck find it most relaxing to "play it by ear. We will plan which park to go to each day, but other than that, leave the day open. By doing that, we allow ourselves to slow down and take everything in."

Chapter 5

The "If You Can Dream It, You Can Do It" Park
Epcot

During the monorail trek from the Transportation and Ticket Center to Epcot, the narrator over the public address system sometimes speaks of "The Spirit of Epcot" driving all facets of Walt Disney World—from the development of new shows and attractions, to showcasing new approaches to agriculture, to implementing principles of psychology in crowd management and customer satisfaction. Aronda's understanding of this phrase is "participation in discovery," a homage to Walt Disney's oft-quoted sentiment: "If we can dream it, we can do it." While Future World underscores the reality that the past is actually the foundation of our future, it dramatically depicts the challenges and rewards of human progress. It's difficult not to visit this portion of Epcot, and not be amazed at how technology can change our lives. However, not everyone shares this sense of awe. "I don't care for Epcot in general," says Becky. "The science pavilions really aren't much different from anything I can see in a big-city science museum and the international pavilions are basically just shops and very badly overpriced restaurants. Except for Figment, 'Honey, I Shrunk the Audience,' and Test Track, I can experience almost everything in Epcot somewhere in the Chicago area." Josh, however, feels that Epcot's atomsphere is evocative "of a huge urban festival. I enjoy just wandering around Epcot, dining and watching the live performances, even when I'm in no mood for rides."

World Showcase, positioned around World Showcase Lagoon, pays tribute to cultural, economic, and artistic diversity as represented throughout its eleven international pavilions. The cultural sophistication represented here by nations much older than ours will make you feel as though you've left the United States for a whirlwind tour of exotic, romantic lands. In this part of the park, ambassadors from host countries — young people in the United States on a special visa status of one year (actually, a status that The Walt Disney Company petitioned the Immigration Office to implement specifically for this program) — often feel comfortable engaging you in conversation, sometimes practicing their language skills (or helping you with yours), and are almost always forthcoming with responses to your questions about their countries. Because World Showcase — indeed, most of Epcot — is more of a "cognitive park," children often find warming up to its venues difficult. For that reason, make sure you stop for character encounters as well as Kidcot experiences in World Showcase. Kidcot Fun Stops, sponsored by *Family Fun* magazine, allow children to participate in crafts and build anticipation for the evening events, while learning a little about the country they are visiting.

Future World

Spaceship Earth is the towering silver "golf ball" that's often visible from commercial airplanes as they fly across Central Florida — and the first true attraction you encounter after entering the front gate turnstiles. Inside, you're treated first to the history of communication, then projected into a putative future. Though the communication tour — told largely through Audio-Animatronics figures — sounds a bit pedantic for children, Disney frequently includes children as characters, along with lively scenes — and the anticipation of what lies around the next bend as you travel toward the top of the sphere. From your Time Machine — Disney's nomenclature for your ride vehicle — you'll bump into a supine Michelangelo painting the ceiling of the Sistine Chapel; actors in the ancient Greek theatre, performing lines of the plays of antiquity in their native tongues; telephone operators attempting to connect impatient

Spaceship Earth is Epcot's "trademark" attraction. Disney veterans as well as Disney virgins find the show inside this geosphere relaxing, educational and inspiring.

phone customers during the early days of telephone communication; a monk on a snooze break from illuminating a manuscript; and a paper boy barking his enticement to busy business folk to "read all about it." During the descent of this slow-moving ride, whose original script was penned by science fiction author Ray Bradbury, you may wonder if Walt Disney Imagineers ran out of inspiration. Instead of portraying the future with the past's level of artistry and sophistication, they illustrated future possibilities with strands of multi-colored lights and strategically-placed wide-screen television sets that can be found in many a living room. Regardless, the narration by Jeremy Irons is moving, though brooding; it's a great sensation to realize you're traversing to the peak of the park's official icon. The combination of delightful scenes and the excitement of being inside this widely-recognized icon makes this attraction a favorite of many on the Memories Team. Spaceship Earth is a continuously-loading ride; your journey through time lasts about fifteen minutes. "Spaceship Earth has that definitive Epcot touch to it," says Crystal. "I always feel like I'm 'home' when we're on that ride. It also provides so

Innoventions, located in Future World, can provide tired kids as well as adults a way to relax without leaving the park. In the Disney Interactive exhibit, you can try your hand at Disney-themed computer games at no extra charge.

Engage Your Kids at Kidcot Fun Stops

Many parents report that an antidote for kiddie burnout in the culture-oriented World Showcase is a stop at each Kidcot Fun Stop located strategically throughout this section of the park. Enjoy your children's broad smiles as they "travel the world" discovering these activity-filled craft areas to draw, write, stamp and create. At every Pavilion, their personal visions come to life in the form of vibrant masks, colored and cut to personal perfection. Additionally, kids often learn words in languages native to each respective country. Kidcot Fun Stops are sponsored by *Family Fun* magazine.

---

much hope for me at the very end with all the lights and the breathtaking music. It reassures me that everyone truly shares the common bonds of hope, sorrow, dreams and joy. Sometimes you need to be reassured that there are other people in the world, wondering why things have to be the way they are. Then you go on Spaceship Earth, and life seems a little easier."

Though not a ride, **Innoventions**, housed in two buildings, treats guests to high-tech displays from some of the biggest and most innovative companies in Corporate America. (By the way, Innoventions East and Innoventions West flank the Fountain of Nations, an attraction in its own right—particularly when it "performs" to music. Be sure to catch its colorful beauty in the evening.) If you're a technology nut, you can visit the House of Innoventions, which sports a television set in the shower, a heated toilet seat, an ergonomic wheelchair that will ultimately revolutionize the mobility prowess of handicapped individuals, and a computer that fully automates the home. The short (fifteen-minute) walking tour of the exhibit reflects the newest technology for your home. Recent additions include Home Automated Living (HAL), a system which allows you to control everything in your home via voice commands, new products from Kitchenaid and Whirlpool, and the LaScala Bathing and Entertaining Center from Jacuzzi, a whilrpool bath with surround sound and a 43-inch plasma high-definition television monitor. The Whirlpool washer and dryer duet can accommodate 22 bath size towels at one time! The Ultimate Home Theater will knock your socks off with state-of-the-art sounds and images, while Tom Morrow 2.0's Playground provides an interactive play area for the whole family, featuring video games with larger-than-life digital screens, an advanced sound system and state-of-the-art technology. Guests can compete in a digital "dance marathon" with Mickey and friends, or become a character in a video game, controlling movement by jumping on a giant floor mat. If you haven't had a chance to check out the Segway Human Transport System, one of Innoventions' newest exhibits will demonstrate its technology. In fact, an increasing number of Epcot cast members are frequently seen sporting about on these unique devices. Where's the Fire?, a new exhibit for 2005, features an interactive game house that challenges guest teams to find and eliminate fire hazards. And Fantastic Plastic Works offers three areas showing how plastics have enhanced daily life, from basic bottles and bags to medical breakthroughs. Though exhibits taken in succession can grow a bit academic and time-consuming, they are executed in an imaginative way. "I suggest interspersing Innoventions stops throughout your day," Aronda says. During these breaks, kids will love the overload of interactive computers and other hands-on exhibits. Follow the Innoventions Highway, designed to look like an Interstate Highway, throughout the buildings. Depending on your level of interest and willingness to interact with both humans and machines, expect to spend anywhere from thirty minutes to two hours in Innoventions. Word of warning: If you have limited time to

Epcot's Hottest Photo Spots

Spaceship Earth
Inside front gate; Fountain of Nations (for dramatic photo, shoot through water)
Imagination Fountains
Front of Imagination Pavilion
Mexico
Front of Pavilion
Norway
Front of Pavilion
China
Front and various locations within Pavilion
Germany
Front of Pavilion; in Courtyard
Italy
Front and locations within Pavilion
America
Front of Pavilion; foyer inside
Japan
Front of Pavilion; gardens in back
Morocco
Full of photo ops throughout
France
Front of Pavilion; courtyard
United Kingdom
Several spots, including gardens in back
Canada
Front of Pavilion; waterfall; gardens
Panoramic Shots of World Showcase
From Friendship launches and locations around World Showcase
Mission: SPACE
Front of Pavilion; queue area

enjoy Epcot, put Innoventions lower on your priority list of things to see. While interesting and entertaining, Innoventions is not an E-Ticket attraction.

In the *Universe of Energy*, which features Ellen DeGeneres, Bill Nye the Science Guy, Alex Trebeck and Jamie Lee Curtis in "Ellen's Energy Adventure," you're propelled millions of years into the past to come nose-to-snout with dinosaurs. These reptiles aren't likely to pursue you—though one *does* blow his nose on unsuspecting guests, and the steady glare of these life-size Audio-Animatronics creatures can unnerve the sensitive guest. The purpose of the dinosaurs' presence in the show is to dramatize the origin of fossil fuels. After a humorous pre-show film which sets up the ride portion of the pavilion—a *Jeopardy!* contest between Ellen and an

Drinking Around World Showcase

Each country within World Showcase offers its own unique libations, whether beer, wine, saki or specialty cocktails. Many guests regularly sample spirits in each country, only to find themselves a little tipsy by the time they reach Mexico. (Starting from Canada is, for some reason, highly recommended.) A delicious Margarita seems to hit the spot after traversing eleven countries. A derivation of Drinking Around World Showcase is sampling each country's special pastries and candies—basically, Getting Sweeter by the Nation! The best time for food sampling is during Epcot's International Food & Wine Festival, but you have to travel from mid-October to mid-November.

old school rival, Judy (Jamie Lee Curtis) — you're led into a huge auditorium with unusual metallic-colored seats facing a screen. Once you sit down, Ellen's dream continues with a compelling film during which you experience the "Big Bang" (children may wish to cover their ears), the formation of land areas and the seas, and the origin of the dinosaur. Then, your seat begins to turn toward a small opening in the wall, through which you journey into three-dimensional jungles to confront, with Ellen and Bill Nye, the creatures that are the *real* stars of the show. Bill gives Ellen a quick tour of the origin and development of energy sources, both conventional and unique, so that she can return — in her dream, of course — to her *Jeopardy!* round to defeat Judy and the third contestant, an inexplicably dense Dr. Albert Einstein. Note that the Audio-Animatronics image of Ellen as she's avoiding the sharp teeth of a ferocious "snake-like creature" isn't among Disney's best. Some guests have remarked that this figure looks more like a pre-pubescent boy. The show concludes with the final round of *Jeopardy!*, and an opportunity for Ellen to show everyone what she's learned. Your adventure, largely powered by the two acres of solar panels on the roof of the pavilion, lasts about forty-five minutes. "I love experiencing 'Ellen's Energy Ad-

"Ellen's Energy Adventure," housed in one of Epcot's most unique buildings, owes its popularity, in part, to the appearance of dinosaurs in a prehistoric setting. The attraction's ride vehicles are perhaps the most unique of all at Walt Disney World.

venture'," says Maribeth. "I never miss it. I love the smell in there. It's one of my Disney smells. Disney has so many wonderful smells!"

The **Wonders of Life** pavilion, which opened October 19, 1989, is often closed in 2005, due to its loss of corporate sponsorship and dwindling popularity. However, during peak seasons, you may have an opportunity to visit. Though an impressive 72-foot tall DNA molecule marks its entrance, the building itself looks like a big, domed tent spray-painted gold. The pavilion houses several attractions — **Body Wars**, **Cranium Command** and **The Making of Me**.

First off, there's **Body Wars**, a motion simulator which takes guests through the arteries of a man whose splinter is being removed by a miniaturized scientist injected into the patient's body. In the set-up for this thrill ride, guests are dispatched in a special vehicle to perform a routine probe of the body — until a white blood cell attacks the scientist removing the splinter. Now, it's up to us to rescue her. Though theme park ride technology has advanced significantly since the premiere of Body Wars, this attraction still provides the occasional rush—particularly if you're an aficionado of old sci-fi films from the 1950s. Color is about the only thing that differentiates this film from those B-grade classics. If you're squeamish about blood, guts or motion, skip this one. Also, when compared to Star Tours—also a motion simulator experience, located at Disney-MGM Studios—Body Wars tends to be a bit more violent—particularly as you're pumped through the patient's heart. Youngsters seem to handle Star Tours better, since humor is a significant show element. Body Wars is, largely, a somber affair. From the audience's miniaturization to its extraction from the patient, the journey lasts about five minutes. Adventurers, prior to size reduction, must be at least forty inches tall.

Cranium Command's pre-show is an absolute hoot. The Cranium Commander, General Knowledge—seemingly styled after Gomer Pyle's Sergeant Vince Carter in the old TV series, *Gomer Pyle, USMC* ("So what if I'm showing my age?" quips Aronda. "It was a cool show!")—barks orders to recruits whose assignment is to pilot new brains that have recently come off the assembly line. Occasionally, the General even barks orders in *your* face, as you stand in the pre-show area, before he directs you into the main theater, designed as the inside of a pre-adolescent boy's head. As a member of the audience, you peer into small, circular screens placed strategically where the eyes, nose and mouth are located, and you view what Buzzy, the pilot of the "cranium" of Bobby, a twelve-year-old boy, is experiencing. The hypothalamus gland makes an appearance, and plays straight man to the antics of the stomach, the adrenal gland, the heart and the left and right brain. The show is a unique, entertaining way to teach us how the brain controls the functioning of many parts of our body—including those parts affected by physical attraction. Enter Jennifer, Bobby's new classmate. The drama begins as Bobby's brain tries to interface all the emotional and physiological sensations he feels as a result of the attention she pays to him. Children respond enthusiastically to this show, which lasts

By now, you've seen the show building for Mission: SPACE. Here's what you see as you approach your Mars shuttle simulator—a narrow door leading into your craft.

about seventeen minutes. The cast includes Dana Carvey and Kevin Nealson (reprising their Hans & Franz roles from classic *Saturday Night Live* episodes), Charles Grodin, John Lovitz, Bobcat Goldthwait and George Wendt.

The Making of Me created quite a stir when the Wonders of Life pavilion first opened. Some purists lamented what they perceived to be the beginning of the end for Disney, who should never include s-e-x so overtly in its attractions. Basically, the movie, located inside a small theater in the center of the pavilion, is designed as a pedestrian sex education film for children, incorporating both live actors—Martin Short is the narrator who, via flashback, actually witnesses his own birth—and animated images representing sperm and eggs. The film follows the patterns and experiences of attraction, courtship, marriage and procreation, and the sexual elements will definitely elicit a hearty laugh, hence keeping the subject light for children. The Mae West imitation of an impatient egg as she waits for one good man—er, sperm—receives a pretty hearty chuckle among adults. By the time the subject of the film comes screaming from his mother's birth canal—a touching moment for the audience— expect to have spent about fourteen minutes in the theater.

In the most technologically advanced attraction ever created by Disney, **Mission: SPACE** takes guests straight up in simulated space flight—right on up to Mars. The setting for the attraction, sponsored by Compaq, is the not-so-distant future at the International Space Training Center (ISTC). As the crew selected for this ultimate space mission, guests head to the dispatch area and then move to the Ready Room where they receive a history of astronaut training and are given the role they will assume during the mission—as the commander, pilot, navigator or engineer. Then, the flight crew—that's you, in case you aren't keeping up—moves along the pre-flight corridor to load into the spacecraft. After final briefings from Gary Sinise at the CapCom and a countdown filled with anticipation, liftoff occurs. It's the most unique and exhilarating ride launch you'll ever experience. The earth begins to rumble, white clouds of exhaust start to stir as the ascent toward the sky starts, and guests are rocketed into the solar system. CapCom then asks you to perform vital tasks that will land your spacecraft safely on Mars. The mission comes with a few twists, turns and challenges that test every astronaut. Quick thinking and fast reactions are needed by each guest to successfully complete the mission. "Mission: SPACE is an amazing ride," says Megan. "Imagineers did a wonderful job, taking you into a real space flight. The feeling of weightlessness is incredible. This ride is unlike anything I've ever experienced." After the capsule safely lands, guests proceed to Mission: SPACE's postshow. In this Advanced Training Lab, guests of all ages have an opportunity to explore several interactive space experiences. In Space Race, two teams compete against each other in a race to send their rocket from Mars back to Earth. In Space Base—for junior astronauts—fun, interactive crawl space allows the youngsters some degree of involvement in the attraction. A joystick and a jetpack button help guests explore the Martian surface in Expedition: Mars. And finally, guests can e-mail to friends back home a video of themselves with one of the space-themed backgrounds and create a great souvenir of their Mission: SPACE experience. Though the actual ride portion of the attraction lasts about four minutes, you may spend as long as an hour if you choose to enjoy the Post Show activities. Please note that astronauts-in-training must be at least 44 inches tall to fly. "It really feels like you go into space," says Sam. "My wife, Kathy, would only do it once, and my daughter Julianne got freaked out by all the warnings. I believe the rumor that when the Imagineers didn't tell guests it spun, nobody got motion sickness. I get woozy on the Teacups, but had no problem. Kathy doesn't have an issue with the Teacups, but got woozy on Mission: SPACE."

Inside the General Motors pavilion, you'll find *Test Track*, where you'll survive the longest (in distance, not duration) thrill ride at Walt Disney World. This high-tech, high-speed sports car ride—which takes you through many of the maneuvers a test dummy would experience at a bona fide General Motors test track—zips you around hairpin curves and steep grades at about sixty-five miles per hour. Test Track is thrilling, without being all that frightening, as it propels you along a track high above the pavilion's backstage cast member parking lot. Imagine a life-size version of a slot car set, with lots of curves and hills, and hand the controls over to a devilish hobbyist, and you have a good idea of what's in store. Some highlights include a heat and cold endurance test (supposedly for the car, but you bear the brunt of it), an acid test (*maybe* it's only colored water), and the threat of a collision test. Each vehicle comes equipped with a computer on board, whose dashboard display (in both front and back seats) discloses your speed and other critical informa-

---

Future World Live Entertainment

Kristos
Exterrestrial Ballet
Innoventions Logo Plaza

JAMMitors
Loud, funny "trashcan" band
Mission: SPACE, Test Track

Robot
Various Locations

Figment
Character Greeting at Imagination

Mission: SPACE Character Greeting
Innoventions East Breezeway

Finding Nemo
Character Greeting at Living Seas

Test Track is one of the most intricate attractions at Epcot—and the fastest! When you enter the speed and handling test, your vehicle approaches speeds of 65 mph, though Test Track hardly relies solely on thrills for its impact. A not-to-be-missed experience!

tion about your specific car. Unfortunately, the attraction closes once a rain cloud bursts, since rain drops falling on your head at sixty-plus miles an hour wouldn't feel so great. A spin on Test Track takes about five minutes—but General Motors has other Post Show activities to regale you, including a display of brand new cars, trucks and SUVs hot off the assembly line. A virtual reality Post Show attraction, called **Dream Chasers**, is worth a pause if the line isn't enormous. However, in all fairness, Dream Chasers gets mixed reviews from guests who've tried it. Waits for Test Track trend toward the lengthy unless you utilize FASTPASS—though the opening of Mission: SPACE has relieved the excessive wait times. If you prefer, you can queue up in the Singles line which places you in empty seats as they become available when parties in the regular line do not fill up a car. The drawback to the Singles line is that your party will not be seated together. Test Track was developed by a team of both Disney and General Motors scientists and technicians. Please note that drivers under seven must be accompanied by an adult, and all drivers must be at least forty inches tall to board.

The biggest draw at the **IMAGINATION** pavilion, sponsored by Kodak, is **Honey, I Shrunk the Audience**—and Dr.

Own a Piece of the Rock—Leave a Legacy

When you enter Epcot through the front entrance, you'll encounter a large forest of granite sculptures--some cynical guests call them tombstones--through which you must trek to reach the park's rides and attractions. A closer look will reveal laser-etched images of guests on small tiles--originally a tribute to those Disney fans who visited during Walt Disney World's Millennium Celebration.

Though the Millennium tribute is over, you can still purchase a spot among the "Leave a Legacy" obelisks. Find a Photo Capture Station (there are several within Epcot), then fork over your fee (about $35.00). Then, take your position before the camera, think of Mickey, and say "Cheese."

Wayne Szalinski, played by actor Rick Moranis, does just that. In this wild romp of a 3-D movie, Dr. Szalinski accidentally shrinks the theater to the size of a shoebox—a very humbling experience indeed! Once the reduction process is complete, you are subjected to a number of humiliations—including a dog who sneezes on the audience, fugitive lab mice that scurry across your feet and up your legs, and the ever-present possibility of being trampled to pancake thinness by the principal players. It's a hoot—and it's not-to-be-missed. Parents need to be sensitive to their children's tolerance for loud noises and various scares. A very intense scene in the film involves a snake that strikes out at the audience. Make sure youngsters understand completely that everything in the attraction is make-believe. The movie lasts about twenty minutes, and is preceded by a Pre-Show attraction to enjoy while you wait for entry to the

CHAPTER 5/EPCOT 113

The Imagination Institute is an inviting pavilion with two delightful attractions and ImageWorks, the Kodak "What If" Labs, an enticing array of hands-on attractions and unique photo-oriented gifts.

theater.

The ride in the **IMAGINATION** pavilion, *Journey Into Imagination With Figment*, pleased Figment fans who had criticized Disney for removing the purple dragon from the original several years ago. Additionally, the popular tune, "One Little Spark," returns from the Pavilion's original ride, but with a few different lyrics. Dr. Nigel Channing introduces guests — who experience the attraction on slow-moving vehicles — to an Imagination Institute "Open House," intended to be organized, structured and controlled — that is, until Figment takes over. Then, the ride

Height Restrictions in Future World

Body Wars
40 inches

Test Track
40 inches

Mission: SPACE
44 inches

Soarin'
42 inches

becomes pretty wild, with several campy elements and a series of "scientific" demonstrations which subject guests to startling sounds and (slightly) repulsive odors. It's not up to the old show's standards, but you can depend on it to provide a short break from the crowds and heat. Expect to spend about five minutes in pursuit of "one little spark of imagination."

In **THE LAND** pavilion, Epcot's largest attraction, sponsored by Nestlé, not only can you sample some tasty food grown in the pavilion's greenhouses—by purchasing meals or snacks at the Sunshine Season Food Fair and the Garden Grill — but you can also enjoy three different shows. By far, the most popular is the **Living With the Land** boat tour, a thirteen and one-half minute boat ride through greenhouses, a research laboratory, fish and alligator "harvest areas," and a solarium. If you have a green thumb, you'll be fascinated. And even if you prefer a good game of football and surfing the 'Net to communing with nature, you'll still find the ride interesting, if not fascinating. Watch for a Hidden Mickey made of test tubes in one of the research labs. If you want a closer look at Disney's greenhouses and growing areas, take a one-hour backstage tour for only eight bucks ($6.00 for children 3-9), called "Behind the Seeds." Many of the veggies and fish grown here are served in restaurants located in The Land. The alligators are spared, though—at least for awhile. Once they reach a certain size, they're relocated to other facilities to be harvested. Be sure to take note of the research partnership between NASA and Disney. Note that "Behind the Seeds" has been discontinued until Soarin' opens in May 2005.

Soarin' is an exhilarating flight over California's diverse terrain, including mountains, deserts, and the ocean. Because the experience involves flight, the entry to the attraction, located where the *Food Rocks!* attraction used to be, is designed as an airport hangar. Using amazing cinematic artistry and state-of-the-art motion base technology, Soarin' literally lifts 87 guests at a time 40 feet aloft inside a giant projection screen dome. From all sides, your field of vision is completely surrounded and filled with the beauty and wonder of California as your flying theater seats take you on an unforgettable journey. Among the many sights you'll see are the Golden Gate Bridge, the Redwood forests, Napa Valley, Palm Springs, Yosemite, and San Diego. The experience is intensified as you feel the sweeping winds and smell the fragrance of orange blossoms and pine trees all around you. Jerry Goldsmith composed the orchestral score. The experience lasts about five minutes. Passengers must be at least 42 inches tall to soar!

Epcot FASTPASS

Future World

Test Track

Living With the Land

Soarin'

Honey, I Shrunk the Audience

Mission: SPACE

World Showcase

Maelstrom

The Lion King cast participates in **Circle of Life: An Environmental Fable**, a film about how the human disregard of environmental issues has impacted our planet. Some of the scenes of nature's destruction are disturbingly graphic, and at times, the film's often pedantic tone annoys. But overall, the impact is dramatic enough to make the guest seriously consider the message. Pumbaa and Timon provide occasional comic relief as they plan to build a money-making resort, while Simba shows them reasons why they should think carefully before exploiting the jungle's natural resources. This film, part of **THE LAND** pavilion's repertoire, lasts about twenty minutes. *Please Note:* The Land will be closed for awhile in early 2005 during a major refurbishment.

The Living Seas, which opened in 1986, is the remaining pavilion in Future World. From a ride perspective, it can be a bit disappointing. But the ride is just a set-up for the real attraction. You take a Hydrolator (an elevator floating through water) to Sea Base Alpha after watching a film whose most

Tom's favorite Epcot attraction is The Living Seas. "I'm all about anything that deals with water," he says. Disney has been slowly but surely placing Finding Nemo overlays in the attraction, making the tone less pendantic. Some of us just wish the Sea Cabs would return.

overly-dramatic lines are: "And then the clouds came. And they rained. And rained. And rained. Rained upon that planet Earth. The deluge." Finally, the theater exits to the Hydrolators, then you move a few feet into the glass-enclosed tanks — and here are the real thrills! Inside the 5.7 million gallon aquarium, the largest facility of its kind in the world, you will view more than sixty species of sea life — a total of some two thousand creatures. You may see divers conducting research — this is, after all, a bona fide research facility in partnership with a Florida university — or an even more unique spectacle. Mickey Mouse himself has been sighted underwater, in specially outfitted scuba gear. Also, be sure to check postings for scheduled feedings of the marine life, when divers descend into the aquascape. View dolphins, sharks, manatees and thousands of tropical fish as you explore an amazing coral reef environment. Try out wet suits, join marine mammal researchers, or check out cutting-edge dolphin communication activities. Discover how the resources of the sea hold answers to our past and keys to our future. Kids will particularly love the brand new Turtle Talk with Crush, where guests engage in live, unrehearsed conversations with the animated sea turtle from *Finding Nemo*. From his digital world under the sea, Crush chats, plays, and jokes with guests, even recognizing them and asking them questions about themselves and the human world. Using digital projection and voice-activated animation, Imagineering created a way for guests to personally interact. "This is an amazing attraction," says Dann. "Crush is outrageously funny, and knows how to relate to youngsters." Guests will also encounter Bruce's Shark World, where photo ops and lots of fun facts about sharks abound. In the queue area, note the eleven-foot long model of the Nautilus from *20,000 Leagues Under the Sea*. Depending on your level of interest, you can easily spend anywhere from forty minutes to an hour in this pavilion, which is also host to a wonderful restaurant, the Coral Reef Café. Guest diving programs are also available; check out Chapter 13 for specific information. Melanie loves The Living Seas. "I could spend hours at the tanks, watching the marine life," she says.

Epcot Restroom Locator

- Outside and to the left of the front gate entrance
- Inside front gate, parallel to Spaceship Earth, both sides
- Directly in front of The Land
- Adjacent to the Imagination Pavilion, in back
- Inside building where Ice Station Cool is located
- In front of Test Track
- Between Mexico and Norway
- Between Germany and Italy
- Adjacent and to the rear of American Adventure
- Between Morocco and France
- Adjacent to the United Kingdom
- Next to Canada, side closer to Future World
- International Gateway (just outside the park's rear entrance)

World Showcase

Don't expect too much in the way of Disney show technology or thrilling rides in Epcot's World Showcase—which usually opens at 11:00 a.m., some two hours after Future World's opening. But you can find some of the best live entertainment anywhere in Walt Disney World—a feature that many guests often miss in their quest to experience every ride. These acts— ranging from mime, to comedy, to music and dance—along with shopping and superb dining opportunities, are the *real* attractions in this area of the park. If you can't globetrot this year, World Showcase with its eleven international pavilions is not a bad substitute.

"I can't help shopping my way through World Showcase," says Amanda. "Frankly, the items in each country's shop are marked way up over their normal retail price, but they are so unique and hard to find in America, I always end up spending money here."

MEXICO has its own version of "it's a small world" called *El Rio del Tiempo*. In this adventure, your boat first passes

Best Views of IllumiNations

There is no *great* viewing area for IllumiNations: Reflections of Earth--unless you're with a group who's rented space for an exclusive viewing. Even then, the show is so huge as to be monstrous--there's no way you can see everything. Still, you can find a few good viewing spots. If you can snag a late Priority Seating at Rose and Crown on the patio, that's an excellent place. Other good vantage points can be found in front of Italy (though that location is often reserved), Mexico, and an area close to Harry Ramsden's Fish & Chips in the UK, and from the restaurant level of the Japan pavilion. Regardless of your space, be certain there are no trees or light posts blocking your view--not always an easy task, since some of the light rigging actually telescopes from the ground shortly before the show starts. Oh, and *never, never* watch from near the America pavilion--the absolute worst vantage point!

CHAPTER 5/EPCOT 119

Mexico is one of World Showcase's liveliest pavilions--and one of only three with either rides or Disney's popular Audio-Animatronics shows. New guests often make the mistake of rushing through pavilions, never realizing that each building is full of surprises.

between a Mayan temple, a smoking volcano and a restaurant, then journeys through canals where you witness scenes designed to give you a taste of life in various Mexican locales. You'll pass Acapulco, a Festival of the Dead celebration, and a marketplace where vendors try to sell their wares. But the most enjoyable component of this pavilion is the great care taken to re-create a Mexican plaza at night. Here, you can shop for inexpensive items as well as elegant crystal, masks and sculpture—all imported from Mexico. A wonderful restaurant—San Angel Inn—is located here, too, beneath a Disney-created night sky at the foot of a smoking volcano. The restaurant is situated on the bank of the river and diners can gaze out upon the ride vehicles as they sail leisurely into the show areas. Check the Times Guide, provided with your official Guidemap, for showtimes for Los Carnales, traditional Mexico Tejano music performed inside the pavilion. Also, a mariachi band, called Mariachi Cobre, periodically performs both inside and outside the pavilion, and provides mellow mood music while you shop, dine or people-watch. Before you leave, be sure to spend a few minutes in the museum

Norway's Stave Church isn't just a landmark for Disney's intricate theming. There's actually an exhibit inside. Unfortunately, many guests, as they hurry toward Maelstrom, don't pause for this glimpse into a little-known history.

located inside the pavilion, just as you enter. Unfortunately, many guests pass right by. A recent exhibition featured exquisitely-executed, colorfully vibrant animal sculptures. Remember, to feel immersed in each culture represented in World Showcase, you *must* slow your touring pace.

In **NORWAY**, you'll enjoy a short boat ride called **Maelstrom**. Here, the Audio-Animatronics figures are very believable — particularly the polar bears and the trolls. You'll even encounter a mild thrill or two — when the trolls cast you out of their territory and your boat *almost* careens out of the show building and into the courtyard below. During your journey — even sensitive children should be able to handle Maelstrom without being traumatized — you'll also pass by oil rigs as you head into a Norwegian village, where you unload into an area where you must wait for the next showing of a Norway tourism film before exiting. Many guests speed through the theater and out of the attraction without seeing the film, but we suggest viewing the film at least once. You may wish to experience the ride multiple times, however. While the five-minute film is moderately entertaining, with beautiful footage from Norway, it's not a necessary part of the show. If you're into high-quality sweaters, ski jackets and toboggans by Helly Hansen and other designers, you can find plenty of them in the Norway shops. In Puffin's Roost, kids love to pose for family photos with the huge troll in the center of the store. You'll also find a wonderful gallery inside the Stave Church reproduction at the front of the pavilion, which provides insight into the cultural impact of stave churches throughout Norwegian history. "Stave" refers to the posts which provide the architectural foundation for these unique structures. In fact, Stave churches mark a historical connection between the Viking and Christian eras. A live performance occurs in Norway, as well. Spelmanns Gledje, a musical ensemble featuring a violinist,

Find Epcot's Hidden Mickeys

⇨ Check out the mural above the queue line for Maelstrom in Norway. You may be able to spot Mouse ears on a Viking explorer.

⇨ In Spaceship Earth, Mickey hides in the constellation just beyond the loading area.

⇨ In the mural above the entrance to Body Wars, you may be able to spot a "cellular Mickey"--i.e., he's formed by the inner structure of cells and corpuscles. This one is very difficult to find.

⇨ In Mouse Gear, you can find Mouse images in the cogs and gears that decorate the store.

China's majestic architecture invites guests along the World Showcase promenade to drop in, see a Circlevision 360 film, and browse in its shops.

saxophonist, bassist and guitarist, plays folkloric Norwegian music influenced by other cultures, as well.

CHINA boasts a CircleVision 360 film entitled **Reflections of China**, which lasts about twenty minutes, shown in Disney's reproduction of the Beijing's Temple of Heaven. Explore China as never before in this stirring film that puts you in the center of the action. Sweep from Beijing to Shanghai, from inner Mongolia to the Forbidden City, from the distant lands of the Hunan province to the Great Wall, discovering all the brilliant

Germany is an intricately designed pavilion, though some feel Disney should offer entertainment accessible to everyone. Most live entertainment is part of Oktoberfest in Biergarten, the pavilion's restaurant.

facets of this Land of Many Faces. The film (formerly called "Wonders of China") was recently updated to include scenes of a fast-paced, modern China as well as traditional scenes. The attention to architectural detail in the China pavilion will amaze and delight you, as will the exhibits in the small museum that most guests miss. (A recent exhibit focused on the Chinese contributions to baseball.) A short stroll through the gardens outside the theater is also relaxing. Don't forget to view China's live shows, consisting of Si Xian, folk music from the Shanghai region of China, and the Dragon Legend Acrobats, a variety of thrilling acts direct from China.

In festive **GERMANY**, the Oktoberfest dinner show grows pretty spirited with singers and other musicians who create a rollicking atmosphere while you sample authentic German cuisine—and German beer. Be sure to visit Volkshunst, a shop which stocks cuckoo clocks, both large and small, along with other German products. Germany is an intricately designed pavilion that delights, rather than bombards, the senses. The statue in the center courtyard honors St. George, the patron saint of soldiers. It's a pity such an architecturally interesting pavilion doesn't boast at least one attraction.

Like its neighbor Germany, **ITALY** does not have a per-

Character Encounters

Want to put a little character into your vacation?

Disney Princesses
Innoventions West

Disney Characters on Holiday
Find the bus around
World Showcase

Aladdin Characters
Morocco

Beauty & the Beast
Hunchback of Notre Dame
France

Various Characters
International Gateway

Winnie the Pooh
Mary Poppins
United Kingdom

124 Making Memories

Ah, romantic Italy. Here, guests are treated to one of Epcot's most popular World Showcase live acts, Imaginum: A Statue Act. An actress in costume as a classical statue strikes humorous poses with guests who don't mind being in front of the audience this performance always draws.

manent attraction, movie or otherwise—though several exclusive shops are located here along with one of Disney's most popular restaurants. However, you'll find some very interesting entertainment if you linger long enough. Imaginum: A Statue Act regales guests with very realistic poseurs, decked out in costumes and make-up to look exactly like marble statues—until they move when you least expect it. Some very entertaining—and hilarious—moments often result. Accordion Artiste performs frequently in Italy, but only in the table-service restaurant located there. Oh, and don't forget to try some of the wonderful chocolate!

Architecturally, **AMERICA** is the least interesting pavilion in World Showcase, yet it boasts the most compelling attraction called **The American Adventure**. Presented as a stage show, this thirty-minute presentation meshes Audio-

The American Adventure is a patriotic, but hardly a rose-colored, tribute to history. Adventure is the first Disney-produced show which tackles, in a thoughtfully sensitive way, the nuances of American democracy.

Animatronics, music, cinema, special effects, historical authenticity and lighting into an inspiring tribute to the United States. In The American Adventure, Benjamin Franklin and Mark Twain (watch smoke actually come from Twain's cigar, while Franklin climbs laboriously up several stairs — the first time a Disney Audio-Animatronics figure has accomplished this task) are our narrators who, through dramatizations of historical milestones, establish that the "American Experiment" will remain in a stage of perpetual evolution. In a moving film montage played against an equally compelling song, "Golden Dreams," you'll experience a number of sentimental — and sometimes bittersweet — moments. Martin Luther King, Jr., delivers part of his "I have a dream" speech; John F. Kennedy advises us to ask what "you can do for America;" Eleanor Roosevelt waves to the crowd; Elvis' hips gyrate to screaming fans; Walt Disney smiles as Tinker Bell flies across the "Wonderful World of Disney" set; and Judy Garland's big smile appears, though fleetingly, on the giant screen. A particularly

Jason and Lauralee relate a memorable experience in Japan. "We bought pearls in Japan where they crack open the oyster in front of you. All the cast members were extremely pleasant, and genuinely excited for us when we got a very large pearl."

moving segment occurs when vocalists sing "On a Beautiful Morning," which captures the sadness and tragedy of the division that occurred in the United States during the Civil War — a division which, in this case, destroys a family. At the end of the presentation, which always elicits applause and more than a few tears, Ben Franklin reminds us all that the success of the American Adventure relies on "people's right to be themselves" — and then, one by one, statues representing the "Spirit of America" are illuminated. Other inspiring — and live — entertainment also occurs frequently in and around the America Pavilion. Several times during the day, you can enjoy the Spirit of America Fife and Drum Corps as the ensemble marches and plays along the promenade in front of the pavilion. The Voices of Liberty, an ensemble which has been part of the Epcot experience since the park opened, performs folk songs and patriotic music a cappella. They are excellent, personable performers, with sparkling, captivating voices. Recently, The American Adventure opened a brand new American Heritage Gallery. The inaugural exhibition explores the connection between historical African art objects and their influence and significance as interpreted by contemporary African-American artists.

The resounding drums you hear probably come from the pagoda in **JAPAN**, where Matsuriza performs the sounds of the traditional Japanese Taiko drums. Though you won't find a ride or movie in this imposing pavilion, you can easily spend thirty minutes viewing exhibits in its museum, the Bijutsu-Kan Gallery, often overlooked by guests, located in the back. The gardens of Japan provide a relaxing, beautiful stroll. And before you move on to the next pavilion, be sure to spend some time in the recently-remodeled Mitsukoshi Department Store, where you can sample saki, browse among authentic Japanese clothing, and purchase tasty Japanese snacks. On most days, you can also witness Miyuki, the art of Japanese candy-making. Kids are allowed to sample the final product. "My

One of the most detailed pavilions in World Showcase, Morocco invites guests inside for leisurely strolling and no-pressure shopping.

favorite store is the Mitsukoshi Department store," says Amanda. "They have the best gummy fruit snacks, and the last time I looked there were some amazingly funky, fun handbags." And don't forget to try the roasted peas with your favorite beer. They're yummy!

Now it's on to **MOROCCO**. When this pavilion was constructed in 1984, Moroccan artisans traveled to Epcot to place the decorative tiles within the beautiful architecture. In Aronda's opinion, Morocco, a gift from that country's king, is one of the most impressive and ornate pavilions in World Showcase. Its architecture is its main attraction, and you'll delight in strolling in and out of its many nooks and crannies. You'll discover a unique museum here, with authentic artifacts and pottery, as well as a meditation room that will invite quiet introspection. It's amazing that such a peaceful, humble place is located within a bustling theme park. And don't miss Mo'Rockin, a band of musicians who serve up some very en-

It's easy to spot France as you approach the pavilion. Here you can enjoy French wine and pastries, as well as the comic acrobatics of Serveur Amusant (A Chair Act).

CHAPTER 5/EPCOT **129**

tertaining rock music fare—with a Moroccan flair. Founded in 1998, Mo'Rockin started performing at the Morocco showcase in April 1999; the band blends the music and rhythms of the Maghreb, Middle East, Africa, Spain and America to create a unique high-energy sound. Infectious grooves, soulful vocals, exotic dance and improvisation mixed with traditional and modern instruments make Mo'Rockin an exciting new sound. Moroccan music and belly dancing are treats for diners in the underrated Restaurant Marrakesh, located in the rear of the pavilion. The belly dancer often invites diners to join her in the performance. Occasionally, a free tour of the pavilion, called "Treasures of Morocco," is offered to interested guests. You can sign up for the tour in the tourism office located next to Kidcot Fun Stop. The tour is very informative, with revelations of many Moroccan customs and a surprising connection to the United States dating back to George Washington. The Moroccan cast members are a delight. "It always rains the day we go to Epcot," says Toni. "A man in Morocco was distributing good luck charms, and engaged us in a wonderful conversation. He gave me one of each color. We thought it might make the rain stop. Instead, it rained harder. He

Here, you'll smell the enticing aroma of fish and chips. Get ready to experience the delights of the United Kingdom.

thought that was funny."

Travel now to **FRANCE**, where you can view an inspiring film called *Impressions de France* on a 200-degree screen in an enchanting theater that could easily be located in Paris. The gorgeous scenes and narration are played against a soundtrack background of the music of the greatest French composers, including Debussy. The film lasts about eighteen minutes. Outside the theater, you're likely to encounter a number of live acts, including Le Mime Roland: A Visual Comedy Act. Roland interacts with guests through balloon artistry. It's a hoot to watch his interactions with children and their parents. Serveur Amusant features two very talented acrobats who comically build towers of chairs, then balance on

With a CircleVision 360 film, delightful shops, a stellar restaurant, and two musical groups, Canada is one of the most vigorous of all World Showcase pavilions.

CHAPTER 5/EPCOT

them. The World Showcase Players often perform their comic take on Cyrano de Bergerac called *Cyranose de Bergerac*. Volunteer, if you dare, for a role in the short street spectacle. It's performed in the courtyard with lots of guest interaction, including a male villain dressed in a tutu.

Besides boasting Epcot's best pub—and a restaurant to sample fish and chips—you'll find a wide variety of shops representing various locales and experiences of the **UNITED KINGDOM**. Several times during the afternoon and evening, you can indulge your infatuation with The Beatles as four Beatles impersonators, called The British Invasion, belt out your favorite Beatles classics as well as other top tunes from the sixties by classic British rock groups. These guys may be impersonating the Fab Four (and a very good impersonation, to boot), but their voices are the real thing. And for a different spin on the classics, don't miss the United Kingdom's street theater performance by the World Showcase Players entitled *King Arthur and the Holy Grail*. Don't be shy to volunteer for supporting roles—it'll heighten the fun. Pianist Pam Brody entertains by leading patrons in beer songs in the Rose and Crown Pub. Her big, floppy hats perched on her silver hair make her quite the character in her own right. She's charming, and quite the sport, often singing tunes which are tributes to guests' hometowns. Leon Gregory also appears as a pub pianist.

Final destination? **CANADA**, where the CircleVision 360 film, *O Canada!*, is shown throughout the afternoon and evening. While you'll enjoy the beautiful lyrics that provide the background of the film footage—"O Canada, you're a lifetime of wonder on this planet earth"—the film feels dated and a bit patronizing of Canadians. The show lasts about seventeen minutes. The film criticism notwithstanding, the architecture of this pavilion is spectacularly imposing. Be sure to spend a few minutes enjoying the waterfall, the gardens and shops. Finally, don't miss a performance of Off-Kilter, a progressive band of men-in-skirts playing variations on Celtic tunes on less-than-traditional instruments. Off-Kilter is one of the most popular bands in the park, and band members will happily autograph their newest release, which is available for purchase in the park. A recent addition to Canada's musical offerings is Alberta Bound, a four-member band playing traditional Canadian folk music.

Before leaving World Showcase, be sure to check the schedule for the **America Gardens Theater**, an amphitheater across from the America pavilion bordering World Showcase Lagoon which frequently showcases live performances Now, Disney features its *Eat to the Beat* series, featuring popular rock and disco stars from the sixties, seventies and eighties. During the spring, the Flower & Garden Festival features rock groups from the "hippie era" in its Flower Power concerts.

Recently, a second a capella group, called American Vybe when it performed in the America pavilion, attained its own designated performance venue at Showcase Plaza. In its current incarnation, the same group is called **Epcot Vybe**. These mostly young performers focus on jazz and popular classics, with occasional Broadway show tunes thrown into the mix for good measure. Aronda hopes that Disney soon gives Epcot Vybe performance space they deserve.

Then, at park closing, gather around the World Showcase Lagoon in anticipation of ***IllumiNations: Reflections of Earth***, a spectacular extravaganza of music, lasers, fireworks, flames, fountains and moving vocals. The show begins with the narrator setting the stage for the seventeen-minute story, which begins after he blows out the torches, strategically placed around World Showcase Lagoon, with Chaos, and ends in celebration of the tenacity of the human spirit. You'll feel chills as you listen to the haunting lyrics of "We Go On." At the end of this, one of Disney's most inspiring spectacles, you can still hear chanting from the Millennium Celebration. You can't help but feel grateful to be in this moment as you exit the park to the chant's strains.

Chapter Six

Falling in Love at Walt Disney World

When it's time to pick a great vacation spot, lovebirds, confronted by the challenge of selecting a destination that offers a romantic atmosphere, sometimes eliminate Walt Disney World as such as destination.

Though it might strike some skeptics as unlikely, The World is one of the best places to experience that "tale as old as time." Cast members make a special effort to ensure that you can find plenty of places to be alone with your cherished one, and opportunities to have a few magical moments all to yourselves.

Night falls, and an evening of enchantment begins. Dreamy looks. Warm embraces. A stolen kiss. A honeymoon—first, second or third—in your favorite Disney resort.

Whatever your idea of romance—even if it's dancing the night away—Walt Disney World can probably deliver.

Lindsey and Chuck say "one of the most romantic spots is right in front of Cinderella Castle. We like to sit there to watch **Wishes Nighttime Spectacular**, then wait out the crowds exiting the park at the end of the day. Just sitting there and enjoying the atmosphere is romantic."

The Magic Kingdom offers several wonderful ways to "feel the love tonight." **Dumbo the Flying Elephant, Cinderella's Golden Carrousel, The Magic Carpets of Aladdin** and **Astro Orbiter** are all simple rides which tap into a carefree, childlike innocence that will make the two of you feel closer than ever. Don't be embarrassed; hop on and enjoy. Certainly, holding one another while experiencing **Wishes** will put you in an amorous frame of mind. So will the viewing of the night-time parade called **SpectroMagic**. The delight these shows bring will affirm your happiness to be in love.

"The most romantic evening at the Magic Kingdom," says John, "was when I gave my wife, Lynda, a Mickey-shaped anniversary band for our fifteenth wedding anniversary in front of Cinderella Castle, right after the **Wishes** fireworks display."

Melanie suggests dinner at **Cinderella's Royal Table**, the restaurant inside Cinderella Castle. "It is a beautiful setting, and if you can get a window table and watch the fireworks bursting over Fantasyland, it seems magical."

You don't even have to be *inside* the Magic Kingdom to capture the romance of that park. **California Grill**, the restaurant atop Disney's Contemporary Resort and the most frequently named romantic spot among our Memories Team, offers many tables with a Magic Kingdom view. If your dinner reservation coincides with the evening's fireworks performance, you'll have one of the most unique perspectives possible. (The musical accompaniment to the fireworks plays over the restaurant's sound system.) Susan and John's "most romantic evening occurred on Valentine's Day 2003. We had dinner in the Wine Room at California Grill, sharing everything, except our cocktails. We also enjoyed a quiet, calm, beautiful view of the sunset. Then, we went out on the observation deck [atop the Contemporary Resort], and watched the fireworks. When they concluded, we returned inside for coffee and dessert."

Raves about California Grill don't seem to stop! "During our honeymoon, we arranged a Priority Seating at California Grill," relate Thomas and Maribeth. "We arrived early, and asked for a window seat. We were told that we were probably not going to be able to sit there because of an already lengthy wait list. Surprisingly, about ten minutes later, we were seated at one of the window tables. We had a beautiful seat from which to watch Cinderella Castle change colors. The wait staff was wonderful, and the food outstanding."

If you've booked a room at **Disney's Contemporary Resort**, **Disney's Polynesian Resort** or **Disney's Grand Floridian Resort & Spa**, you may be able to see the pyrotechnics from your own balcony. But even if you don't have a Magic Kingdom view, you should certainly stroll down to the resort's marina and enjoy the fireworks from the dock. "Our favorite romantic spot is at Disney's Polynesian Resort, viewing Cinderella Castle from one of the hammocks on the Polynesian's beach," says Brian.

Melanie, who also regards the Polynesian as one of Disney's top romantic spots, suggests claiming a hammock in time to watch King Triton's Electrical Water Pageant, as well as adding a tropical drink to the mix. From that setting, say

Some couples book Breathless for some Crescent Lake privacy.

Tom and Linda, "the only worries you'll have are hoping there isn't too long of a line for Space Mountain tomorrow." Fireworks tap into something primal in the romantic soul, and easily put a spark into your romance. At Epcot, ***IllumiNations: Reflections of Earth*** is a wonderful show presented in a park that serves alcoholic libations. Lisa suggests finding a bench over by the Odyssey in advance of IllumiNations' beginning. That way, you and your partner can listen to the music before the show begins.

Chrislette and Jim "like to walk around World Showcase after the showing of IllumiNations, as most people are rushing to get to the exits. We stroll around World Showcase — nothing is open, but you can appreciate the architecture of the buildings, the landscaping of the countries. It's also quiet, with low lighting, and very romantic for about thirty minutes following the show." Lingering awhile will also give you a chance to hear the Millennium Chant from the now-defunct 2000 Tapestry of Nations parade.

While Disney-MGM Studios offers ***Fantasmic!***, the other two fireworks displays are more romantic — though Fantasmic! is still a must-see. During the show's finale, the power of love and romance is showcased through Disney's famous character couples. However, with seven thousand other guests sitting on bleachers all around you, Mickey's battle against villainous forces just doesn't allow a couple to feel alone in the magic as the other shows do. Still, you can't help but be moved when the showboats appear during the show's finale, and Beauty and Beast, Snow White and her Prince Charming, Ariel and Prince Eric, Minnie and Mickey Mouse, and many other famous Disney couples begin to waltz the night away.

Pleasure Island and ***West Side*** at Downtown Disney also provide several romantic escapes — though you and your companion must, by nature, enjoy a vigorous party scene. At West Side, be sure to acquire tickets to see ***La Nouba***, performed by Cirque du Soleil. Like little else, this experience will draw you and your companion even closer together as you enjoy an extravaganza that is indescribable. The show will spark conversation for hours! You'll also be drawn together by the comedy at the **Adventurers Club** and **Comedy Warehouse**, both located on Pleasure Island. Each club takes a distinct path to your funny bone. In Adventurer's Club, you'll enjoy more frequent opportunities for participation than Comedy Warehouse, with quite hilarious results. Whether you're learning bawdy beer songs from a frisky puppet in the drawing room, or relishing some good-natured ribbing about your relationship in the Library, or participating in the Club's bizarre initiation ceremony, you won't leave this place in sober spirits, even if you don't buy a single cocktail. The same can be said for Comedy Warehouse, where you'll discover a very talented troupe of improvisational comics who concoct skits and routines based on audience suggestions. "What's more romantic than laughing together?" asks Sue. "Comedy Warehouse is my spot. Holding hands and sharing a great show can be very romantic."

If dancing is your bag, head for Pleasure Island's **Mannequins Dance Palace**. Usually crowded after ten o'clock, the Palace's music of choice is techno-pop, and the clientele is fairly young. **8-TRAX**, **Rock n Roll Beach Club**, **Motion** and **BET Soundstage** are other dance clubs whose music pulls couples to the dance floor. Check them all out to find your favorite. If you haven't bar-hopped in awhile, Pleasure Island offers the best way to get re-initiated to the party scene!

If you're feeling a little mellow, try the **Pleasure Island Jazz Company**, where live jazz and blues bands and soloists perform nightly. The club looks like a nice jazz joint in New Orleans; in fact, bartenders serve a mean Hurricane that compares favorably to the original cocktail at the famous Pat O'Brien's. Small, round tables invite intimate conversation and the rapport between musicians and audience often grows intimate. If you just want to hang out and soak up the music (instead of the liquor), go for it. Frequently, lovebirds dance cheek-to-cheek on the smallish dance floor close to the stage.

No romantic evening at Pleasure Island is complete without witnessing the **New Year's Countdown** at the West End

Stage. With gigantic television screens providing close-ups of both the audience and music video stars (and sometimes live bands), you and your companion will be seduced into making a new set of New Year's resolutions — one of which may well be to "do Disney" whenever your romantic life needs "one little spark." At about 11:45 p.m., fireworks explode in the night sky, and the crowd grows just a little wilder.

When couples put their minds to it, they can think of unique ways to put a little magic into their romance. "My fiancé and I took a carriage ride through Fort Wilderness Campground," says Lindsey. "It was a little colder than usual that day, so our driver had a blanket in the carriage. We were offered champagne and snacks upon boarding. Riding through the Campgrounds and cuddling together to keep warm was a very romantic experience for me."

According to Sue, "key ingredients are quiet and a beautiful setting. Perhaps with lights twinkling and reflecting on the water. Strolling around any body of water, walking hand in hand is very romantic — like walking behind Disney's Beach Club Resort or along the waterfront at Pleasure Island."

Walt Disney World offers a number of romantic dining opportunities, not only in the resort hotels, but also in the parks. At Epcot, you'll enjoy **Les Chefs de France** (with great window seats), **San Angel Inn** (in a darkened plaza in Mexico), and **Restaurant Marrakesh** (in an ornately-styled building in Morocco). All three are excellent places to dine in a relaxing atmosphere while getting to know each other all over again. At Disney-MGM Studios, **Sci-Fi Dine-In Drive-In** is romantic enough, with you and your honey sitting in a convertible watching silly, B-grade science fiction movie excerpts, but the food barely passes with a C+. If elegance and refinement characterize your relationship, by all means, show up for **High Tea at the Garden View Lounge**, located on the ground floor of Disney's Grand Floridian Resort & Spa. Tom and Linda "love going to Citricos at the Grand Floridian. There is something about Disney's Grand Floridian that just screams romance."

If you have extra disposable vacation dollars, you and your companion may also wish to book an *IllumiNations Cruise*. For about $180.00, you can rent Breathless (named for a *Dick Tracy* character), a 24-foot Chris Craft reproduction of a 1930 runabout boat. The price includes your own personal driver — and guaranteed privacy. (If desired, the boat holds up to seven guests.) Or, if you want a few friends to celebrate a special occasion, you may also rent a pontoon, which seats up to ten passengers comfortably, for about $120.00. Booking a Birthday Fireworks Cruise will cost about $220.00. Both boats depart from Disney's Yacht and Beach Club Bayside Marina about thirty minutes before IllumiNations begins. During the show, the boats anchor beneath the International Gateway Bridge (located toward the rear of Epcot), providing a wonderful view of the water, the colorful fountains, the "laser ball" in the shape of Earth, and the riveting fireworks and flames. You also enjoy partial views of many of the World Showcase pavilions (which are also part of the show), except Canada and Japan. Though the fireworks explode all around you, you are far away from the throngs craning their necks for only a fraction of the view you have. Reservations for these popular experiences can be made ninety days in advance by calling **407-WDW-PLAY**. These cruises are very popular, so you'll need to book as quickly as possible within the ninety-day window. Some experienced guests suggest that, to avoid disappointment, your efforts should begin in early morning (preferably 7:00 a.m.) *exactly* ninety days before you want to schedule.

For some, there is no one certain place at Walt Disney World that captures the spirit of romance. "Simply spending time together in the room, knowing all of Walt Disney World is out there, waiting for us, but nothing is more important at that moment than being together," says Sue. "Some wine, good food, great company, beautiful accommodations — that's all we need or want in terms of romance."

And Walt Disney World has plenty of all that — and so much more!

Chapter 7

There's No Business Like Show Business

Disney-MGM Studios

A lesson in Disney animation. An exploding oil tanker. A beast's love for a village beauty. An elevator plummeting thirteen stories. A thrilling limo ride through Los Angeles. A 122-foot tall Sorcerer Mickey hat. The adrenalin-pumping antics of stunt cars. An exploration of a visionary's career. A Mouse's magnificent imagination.

You'll experience all these things, and more, at Disney-MGM Studios, Walt Disney World's whimsical, yet enlightening, tribute to Hollywood. Since its premier in 1989, this park evolved quickly into one of Disney's most exciting entertainment venues, with several thrill rides and a generous sampling of Broadway-style shows. However, Aronda feels the theme park is suffering a bit of an identity crisis as it tries to recapture the glitter it once had. Becky also feels "Disney-MGM Studios is a park in trouble. It alternates between kiddie attractions that have no adult appeal at all, and Six Flags-style thrill rides that have only a tangential connection to the movies." Still, it offers one of Disney's best-themed rides, and a roller-coaster that thrills every teen's heart. Unfortunately, you won't find much in the way of Audio-Animatronics here (except in The Great Movie Ride and MuppetVision 3-D); instead, the emphasis is on live performers—and transforming you into a star.

One of the most entertaining features of this park?

Disney-MGM Studios FASTPASS Attractions

Indiana Jones Epic Stunt Spectacular

Who Wants to Be a Millionaire: Play It!

Rock 'n' Roller Coaster Starring Aerosmith

Twilight Zone Tower of Terror

Jim Henson's MuppetVision 3-D

The Voyage of The Little Mermaid

Star Tours

Lights, Motors, Action! Extreme Stunt Show

The **Streetmosphere** performers, comic actors all dressed up—and behaving—as wannabe stars and starlets looking for their big, Hollywood break. Other showbiz "types," like waitresses who'd rather primp than serve, Tinsel Town gossip columnists, shop proprietors whose customers are allegedly big stars, garbage collectors struck by all the Hollywood glitter, bellhops who turn luggage into stage props, cops trying to clean up the city, and the Sunset Boulevard Glee Club also seize the streets. Don't hesitate to interact with them. Through participation, you'll find yourself part of an evolving, improvisational street happening. These Streetmosphere performers have taken camp to a new level—and you'll love them. Sometimes, however, the performers can be hard to find, so ask Guest Relations for the Streetmosphere schedule and locations. (Mostly, they appear on Hollywood Boulevard and

Sunset Boulevard, often wandering into souvenir shops, restaurants and even attraction queue areas.) You owe it to yourself to catch at least *one* performance during your vacation. "These performers give the whole feel of old Hollywood in Disney-MGM Studios," says Shelle. "The performers are very corny, but the performances are enjoyable."

After soaking up a little Streetmosphere, head on down Hollywood Boulevard to **The Great Movie Ride**. Generally, this attraction is easy to find; just look for the building fashioned after Grumman's Chinese Theater in Hollywood, located just behind the 122-foot tall Sorcerer Mickey's Hat. Inside the tremendous show building, its unique queue area changing exhibits from classic movies and segments from some of the films featured on the ride portion of the attraction, you'll board trams designed to look like sections of a movie auditorium; the difference is that the auditorium is on wheels to enable you to travel into the movies, from one film set to the next. Audio-Animatronics action is juxtaposed with live action, and the transitions are often seamless—depending on the acting skills of your guide (who doubles as the driver of your vehicle). As your vehicle slowly takes you into the movies, watch out for a slimy *Alien* (and a tough Sigourney Weaver bravely protecting you from attack), a violent cowboy or gangster (depending on which route your vehicle takes) who hi-jacks your

Finding Hidden Mickeys in Disney-MGM Studios

❍Though obscured by the Hat, the Hollywood Plaza area and surrounding buildings in front of the Grumman's Chinese Theater form a huge Mickey Mouse face--but only when viewed from the sky.
❍Several characters are hidden among the hieroglyphics in the Indiana Jones Well of Souls' scene in The Great Movie Ride.
❍In the Tower of Terror preshow, check out the plush in the little girl's hand in the televised "Twilight Zone" sequence. You'll recognize a familiar form. But look fast; the figure isn't there for long.

Once guests board The Great Movie Ride vehicles, the marquee lights up, a cast member yells, "Action!", and an entertaining journey into the movies begins.

ride vehicle, and snakes which scared the dickens out of Indiana Jones ("Snakes! Why'd they have to be snakes?" They're so close to your vehicle that you'll ponder the same question). You'll also see Gene Kelly "Singin' in the Rain," Clint Eastwood and John Wayne looking to settle scores, and Mary Poppins flying over London—you'll have to look extra hard to see how Disney created the illusion of flight. A delightful tribute to Judy Garland occurs on the *Wizard of Oz* set as we "follow the yellow brick road" toward the attraction's grand finale, which regales you with short takes from last century's most notable movies. (It's time for an update, fellas!) Your cinemagical journey lasts about twenty-two minutes, and as Bette Davis says in the attraction's finale: "Fasten your seatbelt, fellas. It's going to be a bumpy night." Most children handle this attraction fairly well—as long as they are warned about the moderately creepy *Alien* scares and the Audio-Animatronics snakes. "This attraction," says Tom, "transports you back into the middle of the time when Hollywood was in its prime. It is a great tribute to the productions and actors of the day." Jason and Lauralee share Tom's enthusiasm. "Experiencing all the scenes from your favorite movies is great. Of course, for the ride to be really good, you need a great cast member [as your tour guide], which is hit or miss."

Down the street, you'll find **Drew Carey's Sounds Dangerous**, a sound effects show executed mostly in total darkness while you wear headphones to access those effects. The show barely passes as a novelty; few guests will admit they enjoy it. Disney's sound effects demonstration won't impress, but you'll find that Drew Carey is witty with puns and sound gags. The story involves a criminal smuggling diamonds in snow globes, and Drew is the detective assigned to stop him. Watch out for an elephant blowing its "nose" toward the end of the show — and the sensation of a barber giving a shave may unnerve you. Even with the cute presentation, the show simply doesn't deliver. Parents should beware: With the darkness and the occasional loud noise over the headphones, children often become frightened. Fortunately, the experience lasts only about twelve minutes. As you exit the show, you'll find a number of kiosks and sound booths where you're placed in the role of sound technician. One interesting activity — more interesting than the one inside — allows you to experiment with background music for *Star Wars*. It's a dramatic demonstration of the role music plays in heightening tension or setting mood. "Maybe Disney should consider that the production of sound effects doesn't make a good topic for an attraction," Josh muses.

Certainly *not* a disappointment is an attraction you'll find just across the street called **The Indiana Jones Epic Stunt Spectacular!** — and this show delivers just what it promises. With lots of heart-pounding stunts and explosions so intense that those sitting closest to the stage will definitely feel the heat, this presentation dramatically examines the dynamics of stunt performing from some of the most famous scenes in the Indiana Jones films. Before the performance, volunteers (no children, though) to play "extras" are enlisted from the audience. The demonstration begins with Indy's narrow escape from a huge boulder—you know the one—and ends with the famous plane scene where a Nazi mechanic has an unfortunate encounter with the propellers of an airplane. (All visual references to Nazis and swastikas have been removed from the performance.) This show is riveting, and often humorous—particularly when the director unfairly picks on one of the volunteers. A thoroughly engrossing thirty minutes with enough slapstick, action, suspense and special effects to keep all age groups spellbound. This show utilizes FASTPASS in a unique way. It provides tickets for a particular show time, and it's the best way to ensure a seat. Rather than waiting in a long line, you claim your seat about ten minutes before the show starts. Lighting effects are more dramatic after dark,

Hot Photo Spots at Disney-MGM Studios

To get excellent shots of:	Take your photo from:
Art Deco Entrance Front Gate	Outside Park Entrance
Sorcerer Mickey Hat	Several vantage points around and along Hollywood Boulevard
Entrance to working Studios	To right of The Great Movie Ride
Facade of Magic of Animation	Front of attraction
Echo Lake	Front of Indiana Jones Epic Stunt Spectacular
Muppet Fountain	Front of MuppetVision 3-D
Big City Skyline	Streets of America Backlot
Star Wars' movie props	Front of Star Tours
Hollywood Tower of Terror	Sunset Boulevard
Rock 'n' Roller Coaster Starring Aerosmith	Facade of attraction and entrance gate (upside-down limo)

Disney-MGM Studios Attractions with Height Restrictions

Star Tours
40 inches

Rock 'n' Roller Coaster Starring Aerosmith
48 inches

Twilight Zone Tower of Terror
40 inches

but Disney only schedules late performances during busy seasons.

Around the corner and down the street, you'll find **Star Tours**, a motion-simulator ride which puts you into the spacecraft of an inexperienced droid pilot just now earning his wings—and at your expense. Predictably, the situation grows sour, and you're left at the novice droid's mercy. You hurtle through the vast reaches of space—actually, footage recycled from early *Star Wars* films—longing for terra firma, with a few extraterrestrials in hot pursuit. This show is a must for any *Star Wars*' fan—and is much more kid-friendly than Body

Though the ride technology is outdated—particularly with the opening of Mission: SPACE in sister park, Epcot—Star Tours continues to entertain. Kids even find the mild turbulence tolerable, and the appearance of the amusingly incompetent droid pilot is sure to bring laughs.

Wars over at Epcot's Wonders of Life pavilion. Still, it's a turbulent ride, and parents must assess their children's tolerance level for this kind of experience. Each tour lasts about seven minutes, and star travelers must be at least forty inches tall to ride. During May — and sometimes extending until early June — this attraction becomes the centerpiece for *Star Wars* Weekends, when actors from all *Star Wars* films show up for autograph and Q&A sessions. You can also expect a street party, updates about the continuing saga from LucasFilms, and plenty of chances to have your photo made with famous *Star Wars*' characters. In fact, it's almost impossible not to have an encounter with all manner of alien life in this area of the park. The lovable but attitude-laden Chewbacca is a particularly popular celebrity. For the Disney collector, *Star Wars* Weekends feature special limited edition lapel pins and other treasures released every weekend.

Though a bit dated now, **Jim Henson's MuppetVision 3-D** is still tremendous fun. Kids love the show, but adults will also be thoroughly delighted by subtle jokes and innuendo the kids won't appreciate. In this 3-D movie (the effects are achieved only by wearing special glasses distributed as you enter the theater) — with another dimension thrown in by those zany Muppets at Muppet Labs — the best-laid plans of Kermit, Miss Piggy and Fozzie go hilariously awry. You'll laugh uproariously at Sam

Restroom Locator

- Outside Main Entrance, to the left
- Beside Oscar's Service Station
- Adjacent to ABC Theater
- Between Star Tours and Radio Disney Studios
- Across courtyard from MuppetVision 3-D
- Adjacent to Entrance of Backlot Tour
- Between Millionaire and Mermaid
- Adjacent to Magic of Disney Animation
- Halfway down Sunset Blvd. toward Tower of Terror
- Fantasmic! Amphitheater
- Entrance to Lights, Motors, Action! Extreme Stunt Show

148 MAKING MEMORIES

You'll know you've reached your destination for MuppetVision 3-D when you see the fountainous tribute to Miss Piggy. In fact, you may encounter the real McCoy in the theatre's courtyard. But be nice; this is one pig with attitude. If Miss Piggy ain't happy, ain't nobody happy!

Eagle's abbreviated, but "glorious two-hour finale, a tribute to all nations—but mostly America." You'll consider yourself lucky once you escape from the rubble of a theater that has exploded under duress of cannon and musket fire. Two of the three Audio-Animatronics figures in the show with the balcony seats are Statler and Waldorf—and they deliver several of the funniest (though admittedly corny) lines in this attraction. Prepare to have your funny bone tickled for thirteen minutes. <u>**Insider's Tip:**</u> Look for Razzo's outrageous impersonation of Mickey Mouse during the preshow.

Now it's time to queue up for the **Backlot Tour**, where heroes from the audience can volunteer to be enlisted soldiers in a short battle scene based on Touchstone Pictures' 2001 hit, *Pearl Harbor*. The first portion of the show unfolds on a miniature set designed to depict a battleship. If you're selected as one of the volunteer crew members, you'll be assigned to several watery details, but you *should* remain dry through it all, since cast members drape you in a heavy-duty raincoat and provide a few cues when it's time to duck and cover. (If you get wet, cast members have access to a bin full of towels! Isn't *that* reassuring?) Audience members standing closest to the demonstration may get splashed as guns are fired and torpedoes race through the water toward their target. This portion of the attraction gives Disney a chance to showcase some of the sophisticated (and in some cases, not-so-sophisticated, though undeniably clever) techniques used to create the dazzling special effects seen in film. Your guide also demonstrates how digital imagery is interfaced with live action in the final cut of the film. After enjoying the special effects tank, you pass through another queue that winds through a prop warehouse where short takes play on TV sets on your way to board a tram transporting you through Disney's backlot. Here, you'll catch a peek at the world's largest costume shop and some of the props used in Disney films, including the Touchstone,

Fantasmic! Dinner Package

Disney-MGM Studios often offers a Fantasmic! dinner package to interested guests staying at Disney resorts. If you'd rather not spend an hour (or more) waiting in line to be admitted into the amphitheater, this may be a great option, since dinner package holders are allowed through a backstage entrance twenty to thirty minutes before showtime. However, keep in mind that the seating, while definitely close to the action, is located on the far right side of the stage, so if you're obsessive about center seating, you'll be disappointed. Also keep in mind that you must now pay for the meal ahead of time--and that includes appetizer, entree and dessert. Each of the five participating restaurants, including Hollywood Brown Derby, Hollywood & Vine, Mama Melrose's Ristorannte Italiano, Sci-Fi Drive-In Dine-In, and 50s Prime Time Cafe, is priced according to how "haute" its cuisine.

To enhance your Backlot Tour, volunteer for "bit" parts in the special effects demonstration. Though torpedos come dangerously close, you'll be all right. Honest.

Hollywood, Miramax, Walt Disney Pictures and Buena Vista film divisions. Though the tour is interesting, it's not particularly exciting—until you arrive on the "hot set" for Catastrophe Canyon. Here, a conniving director gets you in on the action. The bridge on which your tram stops suddenly quakes, an oil tanker explodes and a deluge threatens to drench you. (Indeed, guests sitting on the left side of the tram, facing the driver, will get a little wet.) If you survive all that, the tram driver takes you behind the set to explain how the Catastrophe happened. *Once Lights, Motors, Action! Extreme Stunt Show* opens, expect some major changes to the Backlot Tour's route. This tour lasts about forty minutes.

In the Lights! Camera! Action! Theater, you'll find **Walt Disney: One Man's Dream**, sponsored by Hallmark. This compelling attraction, which opened as a feature of the 100 Years of Magic Celebration in October 2001, is a walk-through exhibition showcasing the life and career of the creator of the Mouse who started it all. After viewing exhibits that include never-before-heard audio clips of Walt talking about his most meaningful and emotional moments, guests will also view several displays never before seen from the Walt Disney Archives. CEO Michael Eisner (retiring in June 2005) narrates a short film about the life and career of Walt Disney. In this largest collection of archival Walt Disney material ever displayed in

Even if you have mild interest in the founder of the Disney empire, you'll be glad you stopped for a visit at One Man's Dream. True fans will be moved and inspired by the exhibit.

public—a display whose creation was supervised by Dave Smith, Archives Director for The Walt Disney Company—you'll find costumes from the Mickey Mouse Club, concept art from films and parks, as well as collectibles dating back to the thirties. As you pass through the decade-by-decade timeline of Walt Disney's life on your way to the fifteen-minute film, you'll hear Walt discussing such accomplishments as drawing Mickey Mouse for the first time, his relationship with his wife, Lillian, and daughters, and building Disneyland, whose streets Walt, wearing his bathrobe, once walked when he couldn't fall asleep in his fire station apartment overlooking Main Street, U.S.A. (Today, in his memory, Disneyland Park keeps a single light always burning in the window of Walt's apartment.) Also in the exhibit, you'll see Walt's elementary school desk with his initials carved into it, his working office as it was at the time of his death in 1966, and the famous "dancing man" model that was the prototype for Audio-Animatronics figures. (The "dancing man" was none other than Buddy Ebsen, whose dance steps Walt emulated in the movements of the small-scale Audio-Animatronics device.) The chances are good that, unless you are totally turned off to the Disney mystique, you'll have at least one or two tearful moments—especially when you chance upon the *New York Times'* image of a tearful Mickey Mouse mourning the death of his creator. Expect to spend forty-five to sixty minutes in this marvelous attraction.

Despite its namesake's overexposure and subsequent cancellation on ABC-TV, **Who Wants to Be a Millionaire: Play It!**, occupying two soundstages, is still very popular among Walt Disney World guests. It allows guests to play for points which can be redeemed for various prizes, like trading pins, hats and jackets. While you can never expect to win a million bucks, each million-point prize winner gets a four-day cruise for four aboard the Disney Cruise Line. Each host does an excellent job, and often gets as excited as the player in the hot seat. When a player is asked a question, the audience answers on the keypad in front of their seats. If you're the fastest accurate responder—and the player in the hot seat bungles the answer—you could find yourself taking his or her place. Each show lasts an invigorating thirty-five minutes. Lindsey and Chuck feel "this attraction truly captures the theme of the park. Each experience is unique. Seeing this show makes you feel like a part of show business. The lights are bright, the stage reminds you exactly of the TV show, and you get to participate, just like the real version!"

A highly creative, energetic puppet show performed in dramatic blacklight, **Voyage of The Little Mermaid** may be targeted to a children's audience, yet it is so delightful and artistically rendered that adults adore it, too. The theater is

---

Finding Disney Characters at Disney-MGM Studios

❀ Along Mickey Avenue, you'll encounter several characters who've emerged from their location trailers
❀ Animation Courtyard
❀ Character Prop Shop near Washington Square
❀ Al's Toy Barn (but only *Toy Story* characters)

CHAPTER 7/DISNEY-MGM STUDIOS 153

Though difficult to accomplish, Who Wants to Be a Millionaire? Play It! offers an opportunity to win a Disney Cruise Line vacation for four. Even though Disney turns most guests into losers, playing along from your seat still affords enjoyment if you aren't too competitive.

one of the most beautiful in the entire Resort. A very fine mist—so unobtrusive it will not get you wet—floats above you during the short opening moments of the show, creating the illusion that you've plunged beneath the sea. Ariel's lament that she has been shut out of the world's experiences resonates with anyone who has ever felt ostracized in their lives. The show is a lovely dramatization of the insights that ostracism can inspire, no matter how painful; it is also the jubilant celebration of a soul that's finally understood. "You've got to let children be who they are," Sebastian the Crab says, and it's a great message to parents, educators and other caregivers. When Ursula the Sea Witch takes Ariel's beautiful voice in exchange for "normalcy," the message is strong that all worthwhile gains involve sacrifice—another example of Disney's penchant for wholesome messages to children (and adults, too). Your Voyage with Ariel and her family "un-

The Little Mermaid has her own beautiful show, and it's not to be missed. With a fine mist hovering above you, and beautiful music and expert puppetry, this quarter hour will pass quickly.

der the sea" lasts about fifteen minutes.

Across the courtyard from Voyage of The Little Mermaid, you'll find **Playhouse Disney—Live On Stage!** It's a cute musical extravaganza catering to youngsters, with seating on the carpeted floor—great for your kids, but not-so-great for parents. The show isn't one you'll likely enjoy if you're an adult traveling solo, or with only other adults in your party—but you'll love the show through your children's eyes. The musical, based on several Disney Channel children's programs, invites the audience to sing, dance and play with characters like Bear in the Big Blue House, Rolie Polie Olie, Winnie the Pooh,

and Stanley. It's amazing to see how enticing the show is for the little ones in the audience. They laugh, dance and sing along with all the characters in the show. So, if you're a Mom, Dad or grandparent—or if a youngster is in tow during your Walt Disney World vacation—make sure to treat your kids to this experience. They'll adore you for it. The musical lasts about twenty minutes.

Once upon a time, you couldn't possibly have a complete Studios experience without spending the required commitment of thirty-five minutes participating in the Disney Animation Studios Tour called **The Magic of Disney Animation**. Now, with two revamps since the Florida Animation unit closed, the hybrid tour has become nothing short of a mess. It starts entertainingly enough, with a cast member portraying a role as animator talking to Mushu about the making of *Mulan*. It's hardly necessary to say that Eddie Murphy as Mushu is hysterical. Then, guests are invited to gaze at posters of movies soon to be released from Disney, and participate in interactive computer experiences. For example, by inputting certain components of your personality, one kiosk will tell you

With the recent closure of Disney's Florida Animation unit, The Magic of Disney Animation isn't quite as magical. The tour has been revamped, with imported components from Disney's California Adventure. But with no professional animators to talk to guests about their craft, the tour is a disappointment.

which Disney character you resemble. You can also try your hand at drawing Mickey Mouse in a classroom setting (okay, this is *moderately* interesting). When Aronda test-piloted the attraction in the fall of 2004, characters from *The Incredibles* appeared for photo ops and autographs. Kids will find the experience somewhat entertaining, but adults will be more than moderately bored. Expect to spend between twenty and thirty minutes in this attraction. "The Magic of Disney Animation as it used to be was one of my favorite parts of the Studios," says Melanie. "I once loved to watch the animators and dream that I could reinvent my life and become a Disney animator." Unfortunately, the attraction no longer has that magical appeal.

Head on over now to Sunset Boulevard where some high-speed thrills and spine-tingling chills await you, along with a short musical production and a nighttime fireworks extravaganza. **Beauty and the Beast—Live On Stage** sparkles with great dancers and a tight script. Though kids will love it, certainly, it has the kind of appeal any stage musical connoisseur would expect. Since the show is staged in an outside arena, some of the effects, which would be more engaging in the dark, are lost—unless you're lucky enough to visit when the performances are scheduled into the evening. The park has been home to this production since its opening in 1989, though on a smaller stage (on whose site several shops have been constructed). In *Beauty,* Disney dramatizes the theme that everyone, regardless of their uniqueness, can find happiness, with persistence, personal insight and determination. This show lasts about twenty minutes. To warm up the audience, an a cappella all-male singing group called Four for a Dollar sings a number of familiar pop tunes on select days. The guys' voices are awesome, with a crowd-pleasing rendition of "Love Potion Number Nine."

It would be a cardinal sin to miss **The Twilight Zone Tower of Terror**, a riveting combination of superb show effects and thrills, located appropriately at the dead end of Sunset Boulevard. Everything is over the edge in this attraction, which establishes the creepy story in the hotel's concierge li-

The moment of truth has arrived! Guests board an elevator that will plummet thirteen stories during a dimensionalized episode of "The Twilight Zone." Besides the thrill factor, the Twilight Zone Tower of Terror is arguably one of Disney's best-themed attractions, with incredible attention to detail, story--and let's not forget--thrill!.

brary via a TV set mysteriously "channeling" Rod Serling. This ride is all good, scary fun, and that's the level on which it is best enjoyed. The set-up? The exclusive Hollywood Tower Hotel was once the scene of a horrible accident of nature — an entire family, father, daughter, mother and nanny, disappeared while riding the hotel elevator during a thunderstorm — which caused the Hollywood Tower Hotel to lose most of its business. Finally, the resultant negative cash flow forced it to close. But you, Rod Serling's unwitting guest, are invited to take the service elevator to tour this fascinating landmark from Hollywood's glorious past. (Glorious, indeed. Many of the furnishings throughout the lobby and library were acquired at estate sales and auctions unloading the possessions of some very famous celebrities.) Supposedly, the service elevator is the safe way to ascend to the top. Alas, Mr. Serling has misled you, even from the grave. Circumstances go horribly awry, and you take not one, not two, but several thirteen-story plum-

In a synergistic stroke, Disney erected a faded billboard on the upper part of Sunset Boulevard, setting the tone for riders as they approach the boulevard's "dead end," where the Hollywood Tower Hotel, and its infamous elevator, are located.

---

mets before the elevator doors open and you disembark. "The next time you're getting onto an elevator on a stormy night," Serling tells us as the experience ends, "be sure you know just what kind of vacancy you're filling." There are four possible "programs" to experience, some of which include new visuals and other sensory stimuli. If you are wary of heights or falling sensations, keep in mind that while you're in an elevator containing about twenty-four fellow passengers, and have the added security of a seat belt, the elevator doors open several times to give you a glorious (some might say terrifying) aerial view of the theme park. If you wish to see how you looked during your drop — (it probably isn't pretty) — take a peek at the photograph Disney obligingly snaps during your ride. If you like what you see — or need proof that you "did the drop" — you may purchase a copy at the gift shop through

Chapter 7 / Disney-MGM Studios

which you must exit. The delightful aspect of this ride is that the drop becomes (well, almost) secondary to the superb special effects, which are among Disney's best. At least, terror in the Hollywood Tower Hotel lasts only about four minutes. If you get cold feet at the last minute, ask the cast members to show you to the chicken elevator (marked "Express Elevator"), which will take you to the bottom floor at a more comforting pace. Susan and John "took our niece back to Walt Disney World in May 2004. It was a graduation surprise for her. For the first time, we rode the Tower of Terror at night. This is our all-time favorite; we just love it."

The other popular thrill ride at the Studios is **Rock 'n' Roller Coaster Starring Aerosmith**, located to the left of the Tower of Terror's entrance. Though the attraction is essentially a roller coaster, Disney's creative touches make it so much more. During the pre-show, Aerosmith recognizes you as some of the band's most cherished fans, and insists that backstage passes are provided for everyone. However, you're running late to the show, so a huge superstretch limo is beckoned to an alley—a limo that takes you through the treacherous highways of Los Angeles, even turning you upside down via a loop and a corkscrew to get you to the concert on time. Fans of Aerosmith will especially enjoy the limo's sound system

To rev things up around Rock 'n' Roller Coaster, rock band Mulch, Sweat 'n' Shears recently appeared. The musicians, who enter the performance area in their work truck, are funny and talented.

Disney-MGM Studios pulls no punches about your experience on Rock 'n' Roller Coaster Starring Aerosmith. As you enter the Coaster's courtyard, you pass beneath a car that seems to be speeding, upside down and above your head—a fair-enough warning. Aronda thinks.

---

with five high-performance speakers at each seat. Prepare to sing along on "Dude Looks Like a Lady" and "Love on a Roller Coaster." (We guess Aerosmith had to adapt this song, since "Love in an Elevator" refers to their next-door neighbor—Tower of Terror—and not to the Rock 'n' Roller Coaster.) The coaster, housed inside G-Force Records Recording Studio, launches with screaming tires (and passengers) from 0-60 miles per hour in just 2.5 seconds. The glow-in-the-dark LA landmarks are well-done—if you're brave enough to keep your eyes open for the scenery. In a blink of an eye, your limo loops through an "O" in the famous Hollywood sign. Ironically, Josh, who took a while to warm up to Tower of Terror, liked this one from the beginning, though Dann still panics at

CHAPTER 7/DISNEY-MGM STUDIOS 161

the unnerving launch. Nevertheless, this is one baby not to be missed! By the way, you arrive at the concert in about two minutes, where you can purchase a photo of your launch. Let's just say the band photographer has a knack for capturing the "surprise" on your face at take-off. Parents, bear in mind that children are often frightened of this coaster more than any other at Walt Disney World—and there is a height restriction of forty-eight inches before a passenger may board. Be sure to level with children before enticing them to experience the LA freeway as it's never been experienced before!

However, an attraction sure to delight the little ones is the **Honey, I Shrunk the Kids Movie Set Adventure**, a soft-surface playground experience from an ant's perspective. Blades of grass are about thirty feet high, and paper clips are as tall as "real" trees. Kids love the huge Lego toys, and the Lego caves in which to explore. Climbing opportunities include spider webs. Other cool activities range from crawling into a discarded film canister to sliding out of the canister along an oversized piece of film. If your kids love this kind of playground experience, you may find it difficult coaxing them to explore other areas of the park.

High-octane energy explodes on one of the largest stages at Walt Disney World beginning in May 2005. Inspired by a similar attraction at Disneyland Resort Paris, **Lights, Motors, Action! Extreme Stunt Show** features high-flying, gravity-defying automobile, motorcycle and high-speed watercraft stunts. It's one of several high-profile attractions being imported in 2005 to Walt Disney World from Disney theme parks around the world as the Florida Resort honors "The Happiest Celebration on Earth." When the stunt show opens, a cast of more than fifty will thrill audiences with pulse-pounding chases featuring customized and modified automobiles, motorcycles and watercraft. The arena for the experience is a 177,000-foot facility featuring a Mediterranean village set; the stadium seats five thousand guests. The premise of the exciting new show centers around the filming of a spy thriller, with production crew members, stunt managers, and a director and assistant director on the "live" set. The show will feature more than forty vehicles on stage and inside the pre-show garage area. You'll also see several "surprise" vehicles, including one designed to drive backwards and another designed to split in half. At press time, the length of show had not been determined.

Disney Stars and Motor Cars is a daily parade of customized vintage cars loaded with Disney character stars — like Mickey and Minnie Mouse, Aladdin and Jasmine, Mary Poppins and Bert, Lilo and Stitch, Sully and Mike, and more. The afternoon parade evokes a star-studded motorcade of classic Hollywood, with Disney characters getting the red carpet treatment other stars like Garland, Hoffman and Tracy have received in the past. Aladdin arrives in a 1951 Mercury sporting a huge Genie head. Disney movie villains roll down Hollywood Boulevard in a 1934 limo decked out like a hearse, while Buzz, Woody and Jessie ride a vehicle shaped like Andy's bed. Streetmosphere performers provide amusing narrative as the parade units pass by. Expect to spend at least thirty

CHAPTER 7/DISNEY-MGM STUDIOS 163

minutes enjoying this unique parade.

As the grand finale for your day at Disney-MGM Studios, each star-studded evening is a "wrap" with **Fantasmic!** at the Hollywood Hills Amphitheater. The theater seats about seven thousand people—and it usually fills up, so make sure to claim your seat early. Otherwise, you may wind up in the "Standing Room Only" area. (Check with a cast member in the area to see how soon you should queue up.) This show, which features live action, fireworks, lasers, music, fire and fountains, defies description. The setting is Mickey Mouse's imagination, where his inherent benevolence is threatened by Disney's most notorious villains. There's almost always a warm-up act before the show begins, so even if you have to take your seat early, you will still be entertained. But be forewarned. If you sit close to the lagoon, you may get a little moist, since some of the animated sequences are beautifully projected against water mists. If the wind is blowing in your direction, some of that mist may come your way. Also, Maleficent gets you hot by setting the entire lagoon afire—and while that may be soothing during Florida's two months of "winter" (a relative term in the Sunshine State), it can be downright uncomfortable during the warm summer nights. Mickey's goodness, of course, prevails, but only after a spectacular show that puts chills in the hearts of even the biggest Disney Disparagers. When the show ends, you're likely to agree with Mickey when he asks the audience: "Some imagination, huh?" It takes Mickey about twenty-five minutes to defeat the villains and to restore order in our universe. It'll take you much longer to get out of the amphitheater and back to your resort or car. Fantasmic! is Maribeth's favorite attraction at Disney-MGM Studios. "It combines almost every aspect of showbiz. The great effects, the music, the story. It's so energetic. It truly captures you into the story. It is a do-not-miss event." John and Lynda view this experience as "seeing the history of Disney Animation, past and present, in a way you've never seen it before."

And that's a very important point, considering the unfortunate decimation of The Magic of Disney Animation.

Chapter 8

When the Mouse is Just a Rodent

Turning the Skeptic on to the Magic

Most members of the Memories Team are diehard Disney fans. We border on the evangelical in our commitment to Disney, and in our love for Walt Disney World. We don't need any convincing to leap at the chance to spend yet another vacation in Orlando. We've visited the Resort often enough to cultivate vacation plans that transcend the traditional impressions of Walt Disney World as a place often hotter than hell, a den of whining children, and the location of the World's longest lines. More than likely, we know how to circumvent Walt Disney World's worst vices, and to see the intricacies that lie beneath the gleaming facade.

Obviously, we don't know where your view of a Disney vacation lies on the scale that starts with diehard fanatic and ends with all-but-incurable skeptic. Perhaps you are planning your first Walt Disney World vacation, and have little idea what to expect. Or, you may be a seasoned veteran who will readily admit that nothing is published about Disney that you don't read. We pride ourselves on providing a planning guide that is beneficial and enjoyable to both types of traveler. In essence, you'll find all the information you need to plan your first vacation, and you'll also discover countless pointers and tips that will help you formulate an even richer Disney experience.

With that said, most of our Memories Team have suffered some degree of bruising over their Disney affinity. Our friends and family often make fun of us because it seems as though every time they visit—or we visit them—we're planning yet another rendezvous with The Mouse. And others are stringently critical, complaining that we are fools to be turning over our hard-earned bucks to a greedy little rodent. So, naturally, we've developed some insights into our pathology, and most of us can give some darn good reasons why our lives simply wouldn't be worth living if our Walt Disney World habit was taken away from us.

If someone in your travel party (it's probably not you, since you acquired this book) is pressing you to reconsider your vacation choice, the Memories Team offers some viable reasons for visiting The World. Perhaps you can use some of them to convince your naysayer to give Walt Disney World a shot.

"Friends and colleagues often ask me why I keep returning to Walt Disney World," says Dann. "They think I should

Often, skeptics complain that Walt Disney World is for kids, so why on earth would they want to invest in an Orlando vacation? Your reply? If Disney's Animal Kingdom is for kids alone, why does Dawa Bar offer some fairly spirited libations?

certainly be tired of it now. But the older I get, the more appreciative I am of the quality of a Disney vacation. For one thing, I am reminded of my childhood and the many times my father and I sat in front of the tube, watching 'The Mickey Mouse Club.' So that level of enjoyment takes me back to a more innocent time. Secondly, to be honest, I don't know of another travel destination where employees at least *pretend* to derive pleasure at my being their guest. And who knows? Maybe that pleasure *is* genuine. I know Disney is a business. I'm not naïve. But so is my local grocery store, clothing store, barbershop, and hardware store. Often, what I get at those places is bad attitude. Sometimes, I don't even get a 'thanks' for forking over my hard-earned dollars. Disney is tantamount to quality service, and I miss that in most businesses. Still, I have to admit, I always get excited the minute I drive onto property and see the official Walt Disney World entrance."

Nicole doesn't encounter really diehard skeptics, but she has found herself in the position of explaining to people why she goes to Walt Disney World as often as she can. "It's hard to tell someone about the total escape that being at Walt Disney World becomes," she says. "When you are at the Resort, and caught up in the Magic, it's really easy to forget about the responsibilities and stresses in your everyday life."

John and Lynda agree that going to Walt Disney World is like leaving the rest of the world behind. But they are willing to substantiate their point of view with skeptical friends. "Often, we help them plan their own vacations, telling them where to eat, what to do, where to stay, and more."

Lisa takes another approach to spreading the good news. When friends are trying to decide whether to take a Disney vacation, "I come back with stories of wonderful food and sunshine."

Susan and John admit that sometimes, a Disney fan must accept defeat. "We have a friend who's been to Walt Disney World once," they relate. "She traveled with her husband and us to a conference. We took her to Disney-MGM Studios for the day. All of us had a good time. Still, she just can't understand why we go back again and again. Finally, we figured it out. She's looking for adventure and new things on vacation. We're going for familiarity, plus excitement, plus relaxation."

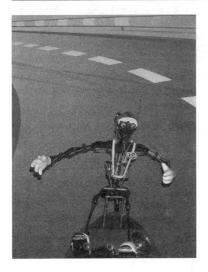

Some naysayers are concerned that a Disney vacation means putting your brain in neutral. Au contraire! Besides being a technological marvel in its own right, Walt Disney World showcases technologies that you can play with — and learn from! Tom Morrow, a robot at Epcot's Innoventions, isn't your typical Disney character. And he doesn't sign autographs. But he does show you what "innoventions" are on the horizon.

But for most diehard skeptics (translation: our families), our attitude is just fine, because some people just don't get it. Talking and cajoling won't make them get it — and that's fine, too."

Even Memories Team members admit that a Walt Disney World vacation, while exciting and entertaining, is expensive. "I have heard people complaining about prices, but I always just say nobody does it like Disney, so don't expect a bargain," says Melanie.

And Carrie points out that "value" has myriad meanings. "If you're talking value as it relates to money, well, I'm afraid I find [a Disney vacation] awfully expensive, too," she admits. "If you're talking value as why Disney is such a worthwhile destination, I have convinced a few skeptics in my day. It is the only place in the world where you can choose to es-

You know planning Disney daytime activities is easy with four theme parks, two water parks, and all kinds of recreational activities. But what can Disney offer to the incurable nightowl? Try Pleasure Island. At 7:00 p.m., the gates open to a Disney world you never expected!

Some of the most frequent Disney criticism comes from skeptics who are convinced that Walt Disney World is only about kids. Even Disney clothing designers know that perception isn't totally true. If children are compelled to ask about the double entendre on this tee-shirt found in several Resort shops, well, then they know too much already!

cape reality entirely. You can be in the jungles of Africa and a bistro in Paris in one day. You can meet people from all over the world, and run into familiar faces. You can feel safe, comfortable, welcome, and childlike."

That "childlike" quality is a recurrent theme when veterans explain why they keep going back. "My fiancé and I enjoy Walt Disney World because it is one of the few places where you can act like a kid, regardless of whether or not you are one," says Lindsey. "Everything is so carefree when you are at Disney; all the problems and stresses of life back home seem to go away whenever we visit. The magic of Disney is everywhere and that magic brings us back each year."

If you have the resources to treat a skeptic to a Disney vacation, you have an even greater chance of "conversion." Years ago, Sue's friend, Tom, "felt Walt Disney World was a day trip. When he felt forced by his wife to go there (and that was very rarely), they'd either drive five hours round trip in a day, or spend one night in some off-site motel. He hated Walt Disney World—no wonder, doing it that way! His wife loved the Resort and wished he was more agreeable to going." Well, Sue was able to help her friend achieve that goal. "I booked a grand villa (three bedrooms, four baths, 2400 square feet) at Disney's Old Key West Resort, and invited this

Don't think for a moment that Disney resorts compromise on amenities and comfort. You'll find resort hotels to fit every budget, as well as those—like Disney's Beach Club Resort—that cater to guests who wish to spare no expense for comfort.

---

couple as two of my guests. At the time, park passes were included with the Disney Vacation Club (DVC) membership, so they had five nights free lodging and five days free park access. Tom saw that there was a right way and a wrong way to 'do' Walt Disney World, and he'd been doing it the wrong way! Imagine my surprise when a few months later, he told me they'd joined the DVC! They now visit for at least a few nights at a time at least three to four times a year. They supplement their DVC nights with nights at other Disney resorts."

Recently, Ed was taken by surprise when someone "asked me why I spend so much money on a company that doesn't give a damn about anything but the bottom line. After lifting my jaw up off the floor, I went through the 'Keys to the Kingdom' which I had learned on a recent backstage tour: Safety, Courtesy, Show, and Efficiency. Once I explained those four

CHAPTER 8/DISNEY SKEPTICS   171

components of Disney's business principles, and how they interact, the guy had no response."

Several years ago, Megan went out on a limb with a skeptic near and dear to her heart. "When I took my boyfriend to Walt Disney World three years ago, he initially complained that he didn't want to go to a 'children's park'," she explains. "I forced him to come with my family to Walt Disney World. After one day of being there, he commented: 'We have to come back next time for two weeks!' After experiencing Walt Disney World, he loved it."

Crystal admits that her father (Tom) has always been a little skeptical, "but I just tell him to look around at all the different people you see walking down Main Street, U.S.A. They all have one thing in common. They are all very happy, and living in a Fantasyland for as long as they possibly can. It is the only place where families can come together and kids can be kids, and the young at heart can relive their childhood. It is truly a place of making memories for a lifetime, and that right there is worth every penny."

Chrislette and Jim confess that people question them about

Are you a collector? If so, Walt Disney World offers an opportunity at almost every turn to start a new obsession: pin collecting and trading. It's the hottest craze at Walt Disney World — and it can become addictive.

their Disney passion all the time. "They always ask, 'WHY???' Walt Disney World is a place that satisfies the needs and desires of kids of all ages. There is no lack of anything to do. Plus, it's a place that makes you feel like a kid, too, regardless of your age. It's like walking out of reality, and into a world of fantasy for a few days — out of your life, really. We do not leave any forwarding numbers, we put our newspapers on hold — we go to get away from the stresses of daily life and devote that time to our kids. Pure family fun!"

So if the skeptic in your travel party — or the skeptic in you — questions the decision to vacation at Walt Disney World, tell him or her to "get real!" With good planning that includes time to relax, recreate, and unwind — along with the traditional options that come to mind when you think of Walt Disney World — you'll have a fresh outlook on life when you return. Even a skeptic shouldn't scoff at that possibility.

Chapter 9

Disney's Animal Kingdom

Disney's Animal Kingdom is Walt Disney World's most controversial park—not because of its theme or content, but because veterans are divided in their opinions of it. Touted by some guests as Walt Disney World's most beautiful—and most sophisticated—theme park, others say quite bluntly that there's not enough to do. "I think the complaints are justified to some

FASTPASS Attractions in Disney's Animal Kingdom

Dinosaur

Kali River Rapids

Kilimanjaro Safaris

It's Tough to Be a Bug! (when crowds warrant)

Primeval Whirl

degree," says Ed, "but the future is right around the corner with the new coaster attraction, Expedition: EVEREST (opening in 2006). Disney may have rushed to open before fully developing the property, but I see that as a temporary situation." Chrislette and Jim feel Disney's Animal Kingdom is great, "but it does not create the same magical feeling as shared in the other three theme parks."

By far Disney's largest theme park—it stretches to a massive five hundred acres—Disney's Animal Kingdom honors the creatures of the wild by encouraging humans to live harmoniously with them. However, Disney's Animal Kingdom cannot realistically be described as a zoo—though it *is* certified by the American Zoological Association. In how many zoos can you encounter freely roaming animals while taking an African safari, or trekking through the jungles of Asia, or following winding trails at the base of the Tree of Life on your way to an exciting 3-D movie, or chase a dinosaur in an attempt to rescue him from an imminent apocalypse?

Because Disney took so much care to become a first-class home to the thousands of animals who reside here, the park is playing "catch-up" in adding more shows and attractions so that guests don't leave the park before mid-afternoon, convinced they have been cheated of a full day of Disney entertainment. Unless the park is extremely crowded, you can finish your tour of it in less than a day. In fact, a major criticism is that Disney frequently closes the park at 5:00 p.m.—though during extremely crowded seasons, the park has remained open past sunset, usually during the winter holiday season.

The subtle lighting makes the park all the more beautiful. In 2001, Disney's Animal Kingdom began its second expansion — the first was Asia in 1999 — with more rides and other attractions in DinoLand U.S.A., and the park's second attempt to stage a parade. (The first, The March of the Artimals, was just a bit too surreal for most guests' tastes, and did not feature Disney's stock of famous characters.) Additionally, the possible construction of Beastly Kingdom continues to be the source of speculation and rumor — its on-again-off-again status maddens many Disney groupies. If it ever opens, Beastly Kingdom will be Disney's Animal Kingdom's tribute to animals that existed in mythology — like unicorns and dragons. Though positioned in Asia, a coaster-styled ride, called Expedition: EVEREST, that features a mythical creature — the Yeti, or Abominable Snowman — will open in 2006, an occurrence that creates hope that the park will be revitalized.

Even though Disney's Animal Kingdom is not yet the park it was meant to be, you'll forfeit a marvelous experience if you choose not to visit. The attractions — even the tones, colors and moods — are dramatically different from the other three parks. Here, you'll experience a pervasive feeling, untapped in our computerized world, that we, too, as human beings, are part of this "wild, animal kingdom." As a result, we look to our co-habitants with new respect, affection — even humility. Getting to know the animals is like your first encounter with someone from another culture. "Disney's Animal Kingdom has some of the most innovative attractions and shows of any theme park, and is also one of the best zoological parks in the world," says Amanda. "If you want to learn something about animals, the Pangani Forest Exploration Trail especially offers opportunities to talk with some true experts. Rafiki's Planet Watch has wonderful educational programs; and for younger children, the Education Stations scattered around the park are excellent fun. Add to this some of the prettiest landscaping at Walt Disney World, and beautiful ambient music, and the stunning Tree of Life, and what's not to like? If people would stop rushing around and slow

Though not friendly to photographers because of the unsteady ride, Kilimanjaro Safaris offers many close animal views. Knowledgeable drivers can even describe the animals' personalities. It's not unusual to see a giraffe standing just a few feet away from your vehicle.

down, they might enjoy themselves more."

You'll definitely need to use your Guidemap and Times Guide in this park, the most confusing of the four major parks to navigate. We suggest you start with **Kilimanjaro Safaris**, an expedition in Jeep-like Safari vehicles that bring you nose-to-nose with the wild animals of Africa. This is one trip you won't tire of taking, since along the safari trail, the animals' behaviors, dispositions and "hangouts" often change. An animal that was somewhat hidden the first time you "booked" the safari might venture out very close to the vehicle the next time around. During one safari, an entire vehicle full of guests gasped at the sight of a lion, up on his haunches, sharpening his claws against a tree. And a giraffe with attitude didn't want to move out of the safari trail to allow a vehicle through. When the park first opened, guests criticized Disney over the infrequency of the animals' appearances. But with typical Disney aplomb, exhibit areas were reconfigured so that you can be sure of dramatic views each time you tour. The elephants are always a majestic sight; in fact, the attraction's back story revolves around poachers who are willing to kill these pachyderms in order to acquire the ivory from elephant tusks. If you feel the inclination for a good "joggle," sit in the back of your safari vehicle, where the ride is rougher. Each safari lasts about twenty minutes—and is usually a big hit for younger children. "Kilimanjaro Safaris is hands-down the most memorable ride at Disney's Animal Kingdom," says Lindsey. "Chuck and I try to ride twice during every visit because each safari is unique. You can go on the safari and get right back in line and ride again, and I guarantee you will see different animals each time. A favorite memory of Kilimanjaro Safaris is one ride when an ostrich's face was little less than a foot away from mine!"

After disembarking from your Safari vehicle, be sure to stroll along the **Pangani Forest Exploration Trail**, a walking tour during which your most memorable encounter will involve ten gorillas, several of which are silverbacks. (If you wish to bypass the Safari, there is a dedicated entrance to the Trail.)

Arguably the most popular animal with guests is the gorilla, located along Pangani Forest Exploration Trail. Though this fellow is impressive enough, he's not the only primate. You can usually spot young gorillas, as well as several adult males and females. The habitats are huge and dramatic. Crowds often congregate to watch their antics.

These primates have flourished in Disney's Animal Kingdom's environment, and if you're lucky, you'll get to see the most recent additions to the family. The youngsters are the cutest, and often behave in ways quite distinct from the oldsters, who have become set in their ways. The large male silverback has been dubbed "Gus" by several guests (and cast members), and he is a majestic sight to behold. Gorilla behavior is fascinating, to say the least. Some guests spend thirty minutes or more, intrigued by their antics. The similarity between human behavior and gorilla behavior is uncanny—and often unnerving. One of Melanie's most vivid memories of Disney's Animal Kingdom occured when she saw "a gorilla carry a head of lettuce on his head." Moving close to the animals—these gorillas are not intimidated by human spectators—will renew your appreciation of their size and power. Since Disney's gorillas were purchased or borrowed from other zoos, they are somewhat domesticated. Occasionally, in their nighttime cages, they become playful with cast members, poking them gently through the bars. Another interesting fact is that zoological organizations keep a "family tree" of all the animals to prevent inbreeding. By referring to this database, zoos can ensure the purity of primate bloodlines. Other fascinating stops along the trail are an exhibit of mole rats (discovered only a few decades ago, since their habitats are deep below ground level), a meerkat habitat (a graceful and photogenic creature popularized by *The Lion King*), an underwater view of hippopotami, and a Colobus monkey habitat. Frequently, knowledgeable cast members will be on hand to provide more detailed information about the animals on exhibit, as well as to answer your questions. Expect to spend anywhere from ten to forty-five minutes here, depending on your level of interest. Wheelchair access is excellent. Younger children may get a bit restless after a few minutes, so make sure you keep pointing out animals they might miss because of their height or attention span.

    For guests who are interested in zoological research, **Rafiki's Planet Watch** is a themed area not too far from

Chapter 9/Disney's Animal Kingdom

You'll know you've arrived at Conservation Station, located at Rafiki's Planet Watch, when you see this impressive mural arching into the sky. Guest reaction is mixed for this particular area of the park because of its heavy emphasis on zoological science.

Pangani Forest Exploration Trail, but accessible only by train, the **Wildlife Express**, which takes you through a small portion of Disney's Animal Kingdom's backstage area. (If you're seated along the back rows, peek through the wooden slats behind your seat for a slightly expanded view of backstage.) Though many guests are none too keen on this area—it alternately seems excessively pedantic and humorless, or needlessly sophomoric and childish—presentations by zoologists about various animals in the midst of guests are interesting but alas, seldom exciting. Still, these close encounters are beyond what you'd expect from the garden variety of zoo—and kids usually love to be up-close-and-personal with the animals. Via remote cameras, you may view animals in their backstage "dorms" (if they're not on stage), as well as in their habitats on the Safari. Occasionally, if there are new parents in the park, you may be able to spot the baby animals in the nursery. A number of interactive, computerized exhibits are located at **Conservation Station**—the only permanent structure located at Rafiki's Planet Watch—and with a little patience and technological savvy, you can add significant information to your knowledge base about animals, their behaviors and habitats. Additionally, a number of the "cyber-centers" are designed to keep the kids entertained. Be sure to check out the displays of diet and nutrition supplements of various animals; they're fascinating—particularly those diets which include insects, worms and other creepy crawlers. Children enjoy **Affection Section**—a petting zoo—which provides gentle goats, sheep and llama for more personal interaction. Many guests feel Rafiki's Planet Watch isn't a particularly inspired section of the park—it needs a show!—but it does possess some educational value if you leave a little time for it. Pipa, the Talking Trash Can, is an enormous draw for the kids; in a nutshell, Pipa is your garden variety, industrial green trash can, with the ability to move and talk of its own free will. Last year, Aronda was fascinated by a group of kids who chatted with Pipa, asking it questions, and actually getting responses! You'll also encounter some of Disney's characters in this section of the park. The round trip on the Wildlife Express, together with the visit to Planet Watch, lasts from thirty to sixty minutes, depending on your level of interest, and the loading time

Animal Kingdom's Environmental Emphasis

While visiting Walt Disney World's newest theme park, you'll notice some unique restrictions and opportunities, such as:

✿ Because of concerns for the safety of the animals, you will find no drinking straws in this park.
✿ When you see the Disney Wildlife Conservation Fund seal, you're welcome to make a contribution which will help ensure the survival of wildlife and wild places. You'll also receive a cool button!
✿ Coins should not be thrown into the water here, where animals are likely to mistake the objects for food. (Other Disney theme parks accumulate coins from fountains, then donate the proceeds to charities.)

Chapter 9/Disney's Animal Kingdom 181

for the train. Guests with limited mobility will find touring this section of the park to provide few obstacles.

At the park's center, on Discovery Island, towers a 145-foot icon called **The Tree of Life**, boasting more than 325 hand-carved animals among its cement branches, trunks and roots. You can easily spend an hour trying to locate these works of art which comprise Disney's most ambitious park icon to date—and you'll never find them all. This is the Disney version of a real tree; it's largely constructed of steel and cement, but the illusion of reality is very, very convincing. As you follow the circuitous paths around its base, you'll encounter small animal exhibits along Safari Village Trails. This communion with artistry and wildlife—as refreshing and uplifting as it is—culminates with an adrenaline-pumping 3-D movie called **It's Tough to Be a Bug!** This film is screened inside The Tree of Life—but it is not for the squeamish. Occasionally, terrified children have to be taken out of the auditorium. So, parents, be wary of subjecting your kids to this movie if they're afraid of spiders and bugs. The stars of this flick (Flik, by the way, of *A Bug's Life* fame, is your host) all belong to the bug family. While their performances are comical, lively and campy, they can also be frightening to guests who get the heebie-jeebies at the sight (or sensations) of creepy crawlers. (Apologies to the show's cast, who wouldn't appreciate that epithet.) When the cockroaches march into the audience, the auditorium is reduced to bedlam, then laughter, as guests realize they haven't been attacked by the real filthy thing, but by Disney's convincing special effects. And by all means, hold your nose when the stinkbug gets into position to fire. As you enter the theater, pay attention to the posters along the wall. They are wonderful take-offs on famous Broadway and movie posters. The movie lasts about eight minutes. "I like It's Tough to Be a Bug mainly for the guest reaction," says Crystal, who could be said to have a unique sense of humor. "I think that's fun. I always like to place bets on how many families will walk out of the theater because of their little kids being freaked out."

Located in Camp Minnie-Mickey, **Festival of the Lion**

Sure, Camp Minnie-Mickey offers character-greeting opportunities. But you also find one of Walt Disney World's best musical shows here: Festival of the Lion King. During December, this area of the park is festooned with all kinds of decorations, making it even more festive.

King is a rollicking musical extravaganza staged in an enclosed, air-conditioned amphitheatre with bleacher seating. We applaud Disney's approach of not merely recycling a storyline from its animated films, but creating a stage event around the film that transcends a re-telling of the story. The characters from *The Lion King* gather in the auditorium to participate in a festival to honor Simba, The Lion King, and the performers do their best to enlist audience participation — including a delightful sing-along to the song, "The Lion Sleeps Tonight." The show is all high-energy with great music and several incredible voices. You'll witness gravity-defying acrobatic Tumble Monkeys, huge floats (recycled from a past Disneyland Park parade) displaying your favorite *Lion King* characters, and some clever word games with the audience. By the time the show concludes, you, too, will feel part of the great Circle of Life. This show lasts about thirty minutes, but you'll wish it would last much longer. "Festival of the Lion King is beyond compare," enthuses Shelle.

Pocahontas and Her Forest Friends, located next door to *Festival of the Lion King* in Camp Minnie-Mickey, is a fairly pedestrian display of animal tricks, with an animal handler performing the title role. Actually, her job is to provide musical transition from animal trick to animal trick. The music is canned, and Pocahontas lip-synchs. Several special effects—like the blowing leaves during the movie's theme song, "Colors of the Wind"—will mildly impress you. Adults will quickly tire of the musical animal exhibition, which is mercifully short. Kids, however, seem to enjoy seeing the animals up close and personal—though bear in mind that Pocahontas handles a harmless but large snake during the course of the show. Grandmother Willow is a nice Audio-Animatronics touch, as well as Twig, but mostly, this show provides a relaxing and, at best, marginally entertaining break if your feet are tired. If the weather is hot, please note that this theater provides little protection. Expect to spend about twelve minutes with Pocahontas and her friends.

Restroom Locator

- Outside and to the left of the Front Gate
- Just inside and to the left of the front gate
- Opposite main entrance to Discovery Island Trails
- Camp Minnie-Mickey, opposite main entrance to Character Greeting Trails
- In Harambe, Africa, next door to Ziwani Traders
- Rafiki's Planet Watch, adjacent to Conservation Station
- In Asia, opposite entrance to Maharajah Jungle Trek
- In Asia, in the new village constructed for the opening of Expedition: EVEREST
- In DinoLand, just opposite Tarzan™ Rocks! Amphitheater
- In DinoLand, next to Chester and Hester's Dinosaur Treasures

Now, it's on to Asia, the newest continent in Disney's Animal Kingdom. You'll find only one ride here (for now—Expedition: EVEREST is slated to open in 2006), called **Kali River Rapids**, whose thrill is a short "plummet" down a waterfall which brings with it the unavoidable propensity to get wet—really wet. Pack your poncho, or you'll have to rush back to your room to change into something dry. During this raft ride, which is superbly themed, but too short to have much of an impact, you'll witness wanton destruction of the rainforest by the logging industry. You see and smell the smoldering wood in the forest, but the theme of environmentalism would have been significantly more dramatic with a stronger storyline, more deliberate pacing and *time* for guests to get involved. The attraction simply does not make sufficient effort to build suspense; instead, guests spend most of their time on the ride wondering if they're going to get drenched again. Close to the unloading dock, beware of mischievous guests standing on the bridge above you. In reality, the elephant sculptures, positioned on a platform along your raft's path, are fountains which these guests "squirt" at you as you pass beneath. Kali River

Say "Nahtazu!" Photo Ops at Disney's Animal Kingdom

◆ Characters in character huts along Camp Minnie-Mickey trails
◆ Scores of animal shots in large variety of exhibits throughout the park--particularly along the Pangani Forest Expedition Trail, Maharajah Jungle Trek, Discovery Island Trails and the Oasis
◆ The Tree of Life--both close-ups and panoramic shots--angles too numerous to name
◆ Animals along the trail of Kilimanjaro Safaris
◆ Do not attempt to take photos while riding the Kali River Rapids, unless you have a waterproof camera. Otherwise, you'll ruin your equipment.
◆ Wonderful bird shots during--and after--Flights of Wonder.
◆ Dino Sue--the largest, most complete Tyrannosaurus Rex ever found--in front of Dinosaur. Although a reconstruction of the real thing, it's still quite impressive
◆ Live performers in Harambe, as well as numerous architectural delights.

Usually, one or two guests will remain relatively dry during your Kali River Rapids trek, but because of the circuitous motion of the vehicle, it's impossible to know in advance who the lucky ones will be. Great fun, but you may wish to bring a change of clothes with you to the park. "Supersonic" hand dryers are located in the restrooms close by.

Rapids, another ride with much promise, could have delivered so much more. The queue area is much more intricate than the ride scenes — which is a shame, considering the possibilities. Children, who must be thirty-eight inches tall to ride, should have no problem with this attraction, as long as you honestly tell them about the drenching they're likely to get, and the single waterfall over which your raft will take a spill. This water-logged adventure lasts about five minutes. "We saved Kali River Rapids for the last stop of our day, because we knew we'd get soaking wet," Nicole relates. "We were able to ride four times in a row without getting off."

Flights of Wonder, a live bird show also offered in Asia, can be found just outside the entrance to Maharajah Jungle Trek. This show isn't the typical "bird trick" show you once found in the largely-defunct Florida roadside attractions; instead, it capitalizes on the natural behaviors of birds with demonstrations of what these creatures do to survive in their natural habitats. If there is a gimmick in this presentation, it's the

Where Did They Hide the Mickeys?

🎞 Pebbles in the shape of Mickey's ears around a small manhole cover. Location: Cross bridge from Safari Village to Harambe, and follow remnants of old fort to the right.

🎞 Three round leaves in a jungle mural in the Tiger Exhibit. Location: Maharajah Jungle Trek; painted on wall on the right side of trail.

🎞 Two hard hats and a circular fan in a fenced storage area form a Hidden Mickey. Location: The Boneyard Playground.

---

several incidences of large birds flying just inches above the audience's heads—quite a rush for Dann, who feels the show "is engaging. What it lacks in originality, it makes up for in its ability to really showcase these magnificent birds." The main character is a seasoned tour guide—perhaps a little *too* seasoned—who has not only lost her tour group (that's us, by the way), but also suffers from a bird phobia. By the end of the show, her phobia is miraculously cured through education and exposure, and she has birds eating out of her hand. Bird handlers in Flights of Wonder do an amazing job of enticing the

This owl is one of many magnificent birds showcased in Flights of Wonder, located in Asia. Though the birds do "tricks" of a sort, all demonstrate abilities they possess in the wild.

The Maharajah Jungle Trek is probably about as close as you'd like to get to this cat! Not to worry. You're protected from this tiger and his comrades by thick plexiglass, which allows you to see that tigers are as beautiful as they are ferocious.

birds to show off for the audience; you'll get very close views of creatures you have probably never seen before. This show will entertain you for about twenty minutes. And have your cameras ready. Cast members ask the birds to pose for photos after the show.

Dann's favorite offering in Asia is not a ride at all, but a walk-through series of animal habitats called **Maharajah Jungle Trek**. Here, during your walk among temple ruins, you'll encounter the imposing Kimodo dragon, a host of tigers, gentle tapirs, and huge fruit bats. The habitats showcasing these animals are intricately detailed; you can easily suspend your disbelief to experience the sensation of hiking through the mystical wilds of Asia. The tigers, you'll notice, have invaded the temple ruins — and who'll try to reclaim them? You view these magnificent felines through the rem-

Finding the Characters

⊙ Camp Minnie-Mickey. Four character greeting huts.

⊙ Next door to Wonders of Life gift shop, on Discovery Island.

⊙ Conservation Station

⊙ The Adventure Begins, at park's entrance and The Oasis in early morning

nants of windows on slowly-decaying walls. Often, it's impossible to discern how Disney designed barriers to protect you from the animals you're observing—a mystery which adds to the pleasure and the tension of this tour. You can expect to spend between fifteen and forty-five minutes on this trek, depending on your level of interest and the activity levels of the animals.

In the recently-expanded Dinoland U.S.A., Disney's Animal Kingdom becomes more whimsical and festive. But don't expect any live animals in residence here; this very popular area of the park is devoted solely to a celebration of the revered (and, in one particular attraction, feared) dinosaur. Dinoland U.S.A.'s popularity isn't at all surprising when you consider many people's maniacal obsession with dinosaurs. At Chester and Hester's Dinorama, you'll find a couple of typical carnival rides, suitable for young and old alike. (According to the back story, Chester and Hester are a paleontologist husband-and-wife team who finance their passion for dino study by "exploiting" curiosity seekers like you. In fact, you'll find it hard to resist some of the cool carnival games offered

here, for a nominal extra charge. With marginal skill, you can win some pretty cool prizes.) Both the **Triceratop Spin** and **Primeval Whirl**

Chapter 9 / Disney's Animal Kingdom

Does this ride look a little familiar? Triceratop Spin is the same kind of attraction as Dumbo The Flying Elephant and The Magic Carpets of Aladdin. Adults may find Spin a yawn, but youngsters love it!

would be fairly typical carnival rides but for the added flair of Disney theming. Both rides are a hoot for both kids and adults, though they were added in response to guest criticism that Disney's Animal Kingdom needed more activities and attractions for youngsters. However, some Memories Team members feel Dinoland U.S.A. does not maintain Disney's usually high standards. "My only criticism is the games in Dinoland," says Dania. "They detract from the area, and make it look more

You Have to Be *This* Tall!

The following attractions have height restrictions:

Primeval Whirl
48 inches

Kali River Rapids
38 inches

Dinosaur
40 inches

A Full Day in the Jungle? Surely You Jest!

Many guests are tempted to plan only a half-day at Disney's Animal Kingdom, but our Memories Team cautions against it. The theme park has several topnotch shows, a wonderful 3-D movie, and several innovative thrill rides. The parade may be Disney's best yet--and it happens shortly before park closing. So allow until about 5:00 p.m. to stay here, then trek on over to one of the other parks that stays open later if you're still in touring mode. Consider doing Disney's Animal Kingdom, then schlepping over to Epcot for a meal in World Showcase, followed by IllumiNations. Or, if you've had your fill of parks for the day, what a great opportunity to try out one of Disney's excellent resort hotel restaurants, or rest up for a night out at Pleasure Island.

---

carnival than Disney quality."

Primeval Whirl is a typical Wild Mouse-styled roller coaster (were it not for Disney's rollicking soundtrack) whose vehicles spin as they maneuver up and down hills, with a surprising entry into the mouth of a hungry dinosaur. With Chester and Hester's limited funds, they wished to emulate as much as possible the ever-popular dark ride, *Dinosaur;* Primeval Whirl is the humorous parody of their short-on-cash efforts. The ride lasts about three minutes, and looks more exciting than the experience proves to be.

Triceratop Spin is a spinning ride a la *Dumbo the Flying Elephant* or *The Magic Carpets of Aladdin* over in the Magic Kingdom. Each ride vehicle is shaped like a baby dinosaur, and during the course of the experience, a baby triceratop pops out from the fulcrum of the ride. Each vehicle has individual controls operating the tilt and height of the journey. You'll spend about ninety seconds on the ride. With the addition of these two attractions, along with the games, Dinorama has become a bright, vigorous area that gives new life to Dinoland U.S.A. Josh, however, feels Dinorama "should be bulldozed,

CHAPTER 9 DISNEY'S ANIMAL KINGDOM 191

so that Disney Imagineers can be given more creative freedom." In Dinoland U.S.A., you'll find the only place where the "Lord of the Apes" has been transformed into the star of a rock concert. *Tarzan*™ *Rocks!* features songs from the animated Disney film, *Tarzan*. While some guests complain that the show — which features inline skating, a live rock band, fine voices and some acrobatics — is much too loud for their tastes, their complaints make it obvious that they've either (a) spent little time in a disco or (b) not attended a rock concert lately. If you can deal with the volume, then by all means enjoy this wonderful show. It's much different from anything Disney has ever done before. To introduce the show, two children are selected to give their best Tarzan yells; sitting close to the center horizontal aisle offers the best chance for your kids to be selected. Terk, always popular among youngsters, makes an appearance for a singalong toward the end of the show. The male and female lead singers belt out your favorite Phil Collins' tunes from the movie, and the thematic emphasis is on love, acceptance and family. The acrobatic monkeys are a delight to watch, and often interact with the audience, occasionally searching for snacks in guests' hair. A short, moving aerial ballet performed by Tarzan and Jane is sure to make you smile.

However, you may wish to warn your older kids not to try some of the "monkey business" they see on stage—i.e., the flips and leaps of the monkeys on skates. As you exit this delightful show, you'll feel as though you share "one heart" with the human race; perhaps even the long lines will bother you a little less. The show lasts about thirty minutes, but it will seem much shorter.

For real adult thrills in Dinoland U.S.A., don't pass up an opportunity to experience **Dinosaur**, sponsored by McDonald's. This ride takes you back in time to capture an iguanadon, strictly against the orders of Dr. Marsh, played by Phylicia Rashad, whose delightful presence during the preshow sets the stage for a rollicking ride. The audience is placed squarely between Phylicia's warning to "play it safe" and Dr. Seeker, her miscreant colleague's desire to bring back his dinosaur, no matter the cost. The tension builds as you're propelled back in time to just a few moments before the asteroid ending the dinosaur's reign makes impact. Your ride

Chapter 9 Disney's Animal Kingdom 193

vehicle is pursued by several hungry carnivores, with a couple of them lurching dangerously close to your vehicle. Combined with full-range motion ride technology, and the rough terrain you cover—well, you're in for one heck of a ride. Don't neglect to view the black-and-white monitors suspended from the ceiling above you as you head toward the gift shop after exiting. The story's amusing denouement is shown there. Your narrow brush with extinction—captured in a photo available at the gift shop—lasts about four minutes. "I love this ride," enthuses Josh. "If you can concentrate on Seeker's dialog, you'll be treated to some really witty lines."

Premiering during the 100 Years of Magic Celebration, **Mickey's Jammin' Jungle Parade** rolls out to the percussion of four drum sculptures. Presented as a "traveling, interactive street party," this parade features an expedition of Disney characters and abstract animals. Mickey, Minnie, Goofy and the Gang travel in their own special safari jeeps, while larger-than-life animal puppets, designed by Broadway costume designer Michael Curry, accompany them. The drum sculptures are shaped like an elephant, a camel and a kangaroo, and feature energetic percussionists who accompany the parade's soundtrack. Then, for a special treat, rickshaw taxis appear, carved from tree branches into the shapes of alligators and hippos, and carry lucky guests randomly selected from the crowd prior to the start of the parade. The fifteen-minute parade boasting sixty talented, energetic performers is great. You won't be able to keep your feet still, or your voice from singing along. It's Disney's most innovative parade on property. The parade usually starts at 4 p.m. each afternoon, but always check your current Times Guide for confirmation, since Disney often makes "adjustments" to its schedule.

Depending on the day you tour Disney's Animal Kingdom, you may encounter several impromptu performers. On Discovery Island—where the Tree of Life is located (Discovery Island was once the name of an island where a game preserve was located just a short sail away from Disney's Wilderness Lodge)—the **Beatniks** perform percussion-based music which emulates the sounds of nature. Beginning fifteen minutes prior to park opening until around 11:00 a.m., you can witness *The Adventure Begins*, featuring a few Disney characters. Cast members also appear, carrying live animals to provide close encounters with guests. Usually on weekdays, look for *DeVine*—though that task is easier issued than accomplished. Performance artist Priscilla Blight conceals herself in a towering, hand-made foliage costume; guests gradually realize that they are not really looking at an overgrown vine, but at DeVine, only when Priscilla begins to move, ever-so-subtly. Look for her green, grease-painted face; that's the giveaway. Her message? Only by taking a closer look at nature will you really appreciate what you see.

Finally, in the African village of Harambe, expect to find intriguing storytellers as well as a few live bands whose sounds will have you undulating to the beat. (Conveniently, Dawa Bar, which serves wine, beer and cocktails, is located close to the entertainment. *Dawa*, in Swahili, means medicine.) *Wassalou* is a particularly invigorating band of musicians who manage to entice guests to work on some unusual dance moves. And be sure to catch *Karuka*, a troupe of Kenyan acrobats whose agility will amaze you. The audience is even invited to participate in a few "Limbo Rock" sessions. Remember those?

Before you discount Disney's Animal Kingdom in favor of other venues, Nicole explains why many underestimate this park. "I think Disney's Animal Kingdom is one of the best-kept secrets at the Resort," she says. "I've heard that it's a half-day park and absolutely disagree. I have never been able to experience all the things I want to in a single day. For those whose main goal is thrill rides, then yes, I can see that this park might not seem as fun as the others, but if you take the time to see the attention to detail and the fabulous animal exhibits, it can become a highlight of any Walt Disney World vacation. We especially enjoyed Conservation Station, where there are so many fascinating exhibits and knowledgeable cast members to answer any questions you or your kids may have."

Chapter 10

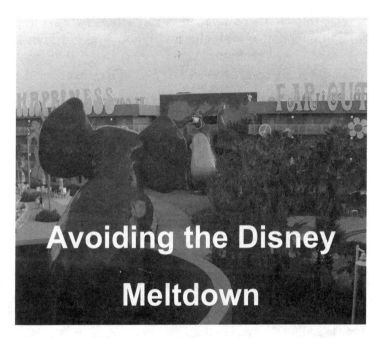

Avoiding the Disney Meltdown

Traveling with Youngsters

At Walt Disney World, a most frustrating sight — unfortunately, a fairly frequent sight — is a weeping, unhappy child who is totally unresponsive to parental supplication to have fun. How, one wonders, is it possible for kids to suffer this kind of meltdown in a place so exquisitely tailored to their entertainment needs?

Often, the answer is that, no matter how well-meaning, parents or other caregivers have failed to recognize their child's limitations, or their tolerance for nonstop stimulation. Like Mom and Dad, or Grandma and Grandpa, the little ones need to be able to relax, wind down or just slip into "Neutral" while their batteries are recharged.

196 Making Memories

Fortunately, Walt Disney World provides a number of ways to ensure that kids keep smiling—and, by extension, their parents or other adults accompanying them. In this chapter, we focus primarily on younger children. If you have teens traveling with you, you'll find the Re-

Children's Programs at Disney's Resort Hotels

Note: Reservations are usually made by calling 1-407-WDW-DINE, though you may also be able to make them directly by using the numbers listed.

Disney's Contemporary Resort
Mousketeer Clubhouse. 4:30-midnight. Potty-trained kids 4-12 years old. $10 per hour. Reservations 407-824-1000 (ext. 3038)

Disney's Polynesian Resort
Neverland Club. 4:00-midnight. Includes kids' buffet from 6-8 p.m. $10 per hour. Reservations 407-824-2000 (ext. 2184).

Disney's Grand Floridian Resort & Spa
Mouseketeer Club. 4:30-midnight. 4-12 years old. $10 per hour. Reservations 407-824-1666.
Pirate Cruise. 3-10 years old. Search for treasure for 90 minutes. $30.01 per child. Reservations 407-WDW-DINE (939-3463).

Disney's Wilderness Lodge
Cubs' Den. 4-12 years old. 4:00-midnight. Dinner from 6:30-8:00 p.m. $10.00 per hour. Reservations 407-824-1083.

Disney's Yacht & Beach Club Resort
Sandcastle Club. 4-12 years old. 4:00-midnight. $10.00 per hour. Dinner from 6:00-8:00 p.m. Reservations 407-934-7000 (ext. 6191).

Disney's Animal Kingdom Lodge
Simba's Cub House. 4-12 years old. 4:30 - Midnight. Call 407-938-4785

Walt Disney World Swan & Dolphin
Camp Dolphin. 4-12 years old. 5:30 until midnight. $10 per hour per child. Includes dinner, activities, trip to Game Room, Disney movies and more. Call 407-934-4000.

sort to be sufficiently safe to provide them the autonomy to enjoy the parks without parents in tow. Certainly, you may want to insist on some quality family time, even with the big kids; consider hooking up for a nice dinner or dinner show, or enjoying a performance of Cirque du Soleil's *La Nouba*.

So, settle back to consider a few suggestions on how to keep your youngsters in the Disney spirit.

Special Programs

Do you and your spouse or platonic companions need some quality adult time together? Chances are, the children *may* enjoy dumping Mom and Dad or even the indulgent grandparents for awhile, too. Walt Disney World offers a number of special programs to keep kids entertained while you're enjoying Pleasure Island at night, or a romantic dinner, or just a stroll along the BoardWalk.

Disney's Pirate Adventure. Kids age three to ten may participate in the popular Pirate Adventure, which leaves from Disney's Grand Floridian Resort & Spa. For $30.01 per child, a pirate ship takes kids to what was formerly known as Discovery Island to search for treasure. Lunch is provided. The Cruise lasts about ninety minutes, and begins at 9:30 a.m. on select days. Call 407.WDW.DINE for reservations.

Resort Fun. All Deluxe resorts offer various Children's Programs (see opposite page), which include activities like watching movies, participating in arts and crafts, learning about wildlife, and computer games. Dinner can often be added for a nominal fee. Most resort programs mandate a minimum four-hour stay; expect to pay around $10 per hour. The programs usually begin around 4 p.m., and end at midnight.

Kids Nite Out. You may also arrange for private, in-room child care at a per-hour rate through your resort's Guest Relations desk. Kids Night Out (407-828-0920) provides professional staff to give individual attention to your kids, while encurging the playing of fun-filled activities. Kids Nite Out

Grand Adventures in Cooking & Wonderland Tea Party

Both activities occur at Disney's Grand Floridian Resort & Spa, and are offered to children ages 3-10. Grand Adventures in Cooking provides kids a wonderful opportunity to be chefs. Not only do they decorate their own aprons and chef hats, they also listen to a children's story before the cooking begins. Don't worry, though. They're closely supervised, and are not allowed to participate in dangerous kitchen duties. After prepping their tasty palatables, they roll carts out into the resort's grand lobby to offer samples to guests. It costs about $25 to participate.

The Wonderland Tea Party, hosted by Alice in Wonderland characters, provides lunch, a chance to make (and eat) cupcakes, have tea with characters and make flower bouquets. The cost is about $30. Be sure to send a camera with your kids to each event. Call 407-WDW-DINE for more information.

---

rates begin at $13.50 per hour.

Downtown Disney

If your kids are tagging along on your journey to Downtown Disney, you'll need to be aware of the kid-friendly stops along the way. While visiting, intersperse activities and attractions which give you pleasure with those possessing child-resonance. Most of **Pleasure Island** will be a big turn-off for youngsters. In fact, many Memories Team members feel Pleasure Island is an inappropriate destination for kids. There's an abundance of drinking (and sometimes, an abundance of inebriated revelers), two dance clubs restricted to guests over twenty-one (at least on some nights), and bawdy humor that will either go over the kids' heads, or teach them new ways to get in trouble once they return to school. Do yourself, your kids, and other Pleasure Island guests a favor. Make arrange-

CHAPTER 10 TRAVELING WITH YOUNGSTERS 199

ments for other activities for your kids while you go clubbing. **Marketplace** should delight younger children—particularly if you've given them a spending allowance for souvenirs. (Some parents suggest allowing kids to earn Disney Dollars for shopping before they leave for their vacation.) The World of Disney has rooms full of toys, clothes, plush and other collectibles, while Pooh Corner will entice anyone who loves the Bear into this, his commercial lair. There's also a shop called Lego Imagination Center with sculpture displays both outside and inside, and Ghiradelli's for a sweet treat—a great reward for a child who's been a trooper about shopping. Once Upon a Toy is a relatively new shopping venue with a huge collection of toys, both classic and new, including a special display of princess dolls and accessories in the back of the store. You'll also discover a carousel that children enjoy, along with Disney's famous, always-popular squirt fountains.

West Side is definitely a mixed bag for kids. DisneyQuest has many games and activities the younger set will enjoy, but most of the offerings tend to be teen-oriented. (Teens, remember, will probably prefer some time here without their parents' watchful eye.) Cirque du Soleil's *La Nouba* is perhaps a bit too sophisticated until your offspring reaches middle school. West Side shopping appeals more to adults; even the restaurants cater to more cultivated taste buds, though Wetzel's Pretzels offers a number of popular snacks for both kids and adults.

Disney's Water Parks

The simple fact is, kids *love* water—and they love water games. You'll be *the bomb* if you treat them to an afternoon at Typhoon Lagoon or Blizzard Beach. Both water parks provide children's play areas, so don't be put off by all the watery thrill rides towering around you. (For those of you who're die-hard Disneyites, please note that River Country has been closed for quite some time, with no reopening date on the horizon.)

At Typhoon Lagoon, **Ketchakiddee Creek** entices chil-

One way to keep your children's attention invested in your vacation is to provide them a tangible souvenir whenever possible. Kids love to hang onto a toy or balloon they've gotten while enjoying their days, and usually, a character-driven gift will bring a smile to their faces — and yours!

---

dren four feet and under with "slides, fountains, waterfalls, squirting whales and seals, a mini-rapids slide, an interactive tugboat, and a grotto with a veil of water kids like to run through." And at Blizzard Beach, **Tike's Peak**, while not as intricately detailed as Typhoon Lagoon, offers a miniature version of Blizzard Beach water thrills, along with a snow-castle fountain play area. Keep in mind that children must be accompanied by an adult, even in these areas.

Disney's Theme Parks

Nothing thrills a child more than an exclusive audience with Disney's famous characters, so make sure you seek out the spots in each park where your children can meet them.

Chapter 10 Traveling with Youngsters

(Each park-specific chapter enumerates meet-and-greet opportunities.) They particularly enjoy collecting autographs of all the characters they meet. And don't forget your camera. A record of these moments will provide cheerful, nostalgic reminiscences for years to come. Cast members are usually happy to take the photo if you want the whole family in on the act, so don't be shy to ask (though they usually appreciate an easy-to-use camera).

At the major theme parks, realize that some attractions appeal more to adults than children, so be sure to mix 'em up on your touring plan to avoid boring your kids. Commando mode in a park will almost guarantee a worn-out, cranky kid long before the day is over. Most Memories Team members strongly suggest breaks from the parks in the middle of day — particularly if they're open late and your kids wish to enjoy the nighttime fireworks or parade.

What follows is a park-by-park review of attractions and activities which kids are sure to get a kick out of — and which generally re-energizes them.

Magic Kingdom

It's almost pointless to say that spending time in Fantasyland will certainly keep smiles on children's faces. This land most dynamically has a kid's touch, from **Dumbo the Flying Elephant** to a ride through the Hundred Acre Woods in **The Many Adventures of Winnie the Pooh**. With Cinderella Castle towering above them, your kids will feel as though they've stepped out of real life and into the pages of a delightful storybook. **Mickey's PhilharMagic** provides a rollicking, multi-sensory 3-D experience featuring the temperamental Donald Duck that is sure to delight the kids — and you as well.

When the kids need a snack, Magic Kingdom more than any other Disney park offers the kinds of yummies kids like — from Mickey Mouse-shaped ice cream bars to popcorn and soda. There's also a candy shop on Main Street, U.S.A., along with a bakery and an ice cream parlor. Your kids are on vacation, too. You can wean them off the junk food once you return home. Another "land" that's a favorite with children is **Mickey's Toontown Fair**—the Magic Kingdom's solution to satisfying kids' demands for more character encounters. There's a youngster's roller coaster, along with a squirt fountain. Kids can also visit the homes of their favorite characters; both Minnie and Mickey have taken up residence here. And in the Judge's Tent, be sure to have your kids queue up for meet-and-greets with many Disney characters. Parents, beware: It may be difficult getting your kids to leave this particular area of the park!

The afternoon parade—**Share a Dream Come True**—couldn't be more suitable for children. The floats are designed as snow globes, each one containing a famous Disney character waving to spectators along the parade route. (When kids express concern that the characters have no air, let them know the snowglobes are air-conditioned.) In the evenings, your children will fall in love with **SpectroMagic**. Not only are its floats the "edgiest" among all that Disney has designed, but the characters have never been seen quite like this. Children's eyes sparkle once this parade begins! But be sure to claim your spot at least half an hour before the parade starts. Otherwise, your child may have a lousy view.

Finally, shame on you if you don't make certain your children get to see **Wishes Nighttime Spectacular**, featuring Tinker Bell's Flight. This awesome display of innovative fireworks explodes for twelve minutes over Cinderella Castle. Toward the beginning of the show, an illuminated Tinker Bell actually flies the night sky from a parapet at the top of the Castle to the roof of Tomorrowland Terrace Restaurant. Children—unless they are timid and easily frightened by fireworks—will adore this Disney extravaganza.

Epcot

Because Epcot has the reputation of being a park primarily geared to adult tastes, it's easy to overlook the many

Chapter 10 Traveling with Youngsters

In a delightful "How did they do that?" kind of an attraction, Epcot's The Living Seas now features "Turtle Talk with Crush," an interactive performance guaranteed to delight most kids.

attractions and activities that are suitable for kids. However, the fact remains that at Epcot, it's easiest to overwhelm your children with attractions that don't appeal all that much to them, while you wonder, with annoyance, why they've decided to methodically ruin one of the best places of all. If you make sure to mix your personal touring choices with Epcot's kid-friendly venues, you'll find your Epcot visit has been as much fun for your kids as it was for you.

Let's start with the section of Epcot that kids frequently called "boring"—World Showcase. With its eleven pavilions representing a variety of nations and cultures, kids begin to feel they're in the midst of a geography and history lesson rather than a theme park. But Disney, recognizing such a danger, responded with what's called **Kidcot Fun Stops** (sponsored by *Family Fun* magazine). In each nation's pavilion, children can visit this special play and craft area to draw, write, stamp, color and create their own special, personal visions on a mask they get to keep. Cast members may teach them a word or two in their native language.

Close to the bridge connecting Future World to World Showcase, you'll find several squirting fountains in which kids love to play. Even Goofy has been known to join kids in a game of "Dodge the Squirts." Be sure to bring a change of clothes for the kids, though. Also, not too far from these fountains, **Ice Station Cool** beckons. Here, you and your children can sample sodas from around the world—free! Don't let them overindulge, however, or they may find themselves suffering from a tummy ache. Coca-Cola-inspired souvenirs are sold here, as well.

Attractions deserving of kids' high marks range from the Living Seas—not only because they're fascinated by the sights of the marine animals in the huge aquarium, but also because of the new *Finding Nemo* additions, both outside and inside the pavilion—to Ellen's Energy Adventure at World of Energy pavilion. (If your youngsters are prone to fright during dark rides, however, you may want to avoid this one, which is a slow-moving ride through a prehistoric jungle saturated with dinosaurs. However, the dinos are more interested in Ellen than in the guests, so reassure your children that everything will turn out all right.) **El Rio del Tiempo** in Mexico, evocative of "it's a small world" in the Magic Kingdom, though reflective of Mexican culture, is a child's delight. While **Maelstrom** (in Norway) has a few tense moments, most kids do fine on this boat ride. **Journey Into Imagination with Figment** also delights the little ones—primarily because the purple dragon is so cute. **Disney Characters on Holiday** engages the kids, too, as the double-decker bus transports many of the popular Disney characters around the World Showcase promenade and into Future World. Check your Times Guide for showtimes.

And if your children don't find fireworks and loud noises intimidating, by all means treat them to **IllumiNations: Reflections of Earth**, Epcot's inspiring fireworks presentation lasting about thirteen minutes. Some guests feel it's the best fireworks presentation on property. And if you purchase your kids a Light Chaser, they'll feel as though they're part of the show. (Warning: These items are very expensive; more intricate novelties have crept toward twenty dollars!)

Disney-MGM Studios

Many fans feel the best show overall at Walt Disney World may be found in the Disney-MGM Studios' **Fantasmic!**, a dramatic good-versus-evil fireworks, lights, water and live-action show which weighs in at just under half an hour. What do kids love most about the show? The sheer saturation of the Disney characters. Even if they have to stay up past their bedtime, don't deny your children this experience! Just make certain you can keep them entertained for about an hour, since you have to queue up for at least that long to get a good seat.

The Studios also has a marvelous parade called **Disney Stars and Motor Cars**, where more characters appear than in any other parade. The customized vintage cars have been designed to evoke stage sets—and Streetmosphere performers announce each unit as it passes by. Mike and Sully from *Monsters, Inc.*, characters from *Lilo and Stitch*, *The Incredibles*, and *Finding Nemo* are the newest additions to the parade line-up.

Mickey Avenue is the place to find "on-location" trailers where the characters tidy up for their appearances among fans. After a short wait (if you time your arrival wisely), voila! Tigger, or Pooh, or Goofy steps into the Avenue, ready for their photo ops with your kids, or to sign their autograph books. It's a cute way to stage a character meet-and-greet.

If you're traveling with a child, make sure you check your Park Guidemaps for the locations of Baby Care Centers. Here, you'll be able to escape the noise and crowds, and attend to baby's needs.

During the winter holiday season, kids will certainly get a kick out of seeing Santa Claus during one of the parades. In fact, a number of families have reported spending their Christmas at Walt Disney World, and having Santa deliver gifts right to their rooms.

A favorite attraction is **Voyage of The Little Mermaid**, a puppet show performed in blacklight that kids usually adore. The theater is the most unique among Disney venues; it evokes an undersea environment. In fact, as the show begins, a fine mist hovers above guests — and kids are delighted.

If your children like the Muppets, they'll love **Jim Henson's MuppetVision 3-D**. Of course, you'll have to convince them that it's cool to wear those strange glasses. Unlike Epcot's "Honey, I Shrunk the Audience," there's very little in this film which will frighten a child — except perhaps the cannon fire at the audience in the grand finale. Still, they will be thoroughly entertained by the possibility of a pie in the face and the "cheap 3-D trick" of a water pistol pointed at the audience. The giddy Waldo, the spirit of 3-D, is especially appealing to the kids. His antics remind you of a lovable, though incorrigible, child.

Kids are incredibly engaged at **Playhouse Disney: Live on Stage!**, where Bear in the Big Blue House, Ollie, and Pooh, among other Disney Channel stars, appear in an entertaining skit especially for kids. Seating is on the floor—the kids seem to be comfortable, even if the parents often aren't. Tutter is struck with a shy streak, and all his friends try to coax him out of his shyness. Finally, Tutter realizes that everyone feels a little self-conscious from time to time—a great lesson to learn, particularly for those kids who tend to be a bit introverted.

Disney's Animal Kingdom

If your children like zoos, they'll love Disney's Animal Kingdom—though calling it a zoo does this theme park a great disservice. Still, real, live animals are the stars here, and most kids are fascinated by them. Even the wild, dangerous ones often look cuddly, and it's not unusual to see youngsters pointing at lions, giraffes, elephants and tigers with boundless affection in their faces.

So far, no fireworks show has premiered in this park—such a show might frighten the animals—but Disney's best daytime parade appears each afternoon. Dubbed **Mickey's Jammin' Jungle Parade**, the show is filled with characters—and if you're lucky, you and your family could be chosen to ride one of the rickshaws pulled along the parade route. This kind of involvement is a great way for the kids to feel part of the show. The music is drivingly energetic, the cast appears delighted to be performing for you, and several floats have cute "gimmicks" to entertain the kids.

Kilimanjaro Safaris provides an African safari for you and your kids—and because of the number of animals that appear along the trail, children will be thoroughly engaged. On the other hand, the **Maharajah Jungle Trek** in Asia may tax young patience—until they arrive at the tiger exhibit.

DinoLand U.S.A. is another popular area with the

Getting the Kids To Sleep!

If your kids aren't worn out by the end of the day at Walt Disney World, you may wish to change their diet. Seriously, though, some kids *do* get incredibly wired at the Resort, and need something extra soothing to end their insomnia. If you stay in a Walt Disney World hotel, try tuning to Channel 14, which offers bedtime stories. The stories are a great ending to a magical day. If you're staying off-site, perhaps you might read a Disney storybook to the little ones — or print some of the children's activities from the Bonus CD accompanying this guide.

---

kids — particularly those who love dinosaurs — and if you have the bucks to spare, you should purchase your young paleontologist one of the very realistic-looking stuffed dinos found in several DinoLand stores, as well as at the Photo Capture area at the end of Dinosaur. At Chester and Hester's Dinorama, you'll find two rides designed first with kids in mind — along with some games where winners can snag a stuffed critter or two. (Your kids may want you to play for them — after they give it a try — since some games may be a bit difficult for them to master.) Though Mom and Dad may find their hearing a bit impaired after the loud music, the kids will love **Tarzan Rocks!**, where Tarzan and Jane swing to a rock beat, and Terk plays straight to the kids in the audience with "Trashin' the Camp."

Camp Minnie-Mickey is the most popular spot for the kids in Disney's Animal Kingdom. Here, they can meet a number of Disney characters, and see a couple of shows which don't condescend to them. "Festival of the Lion King" is a wonderful musical festival celebrating Simba and the Circle of Life; you will hardly be able to watch the performers because you can't take your eyes off the little entranced face next to you. "Pocahontas and Her Forest Friends" is a cute show for the kids — a couple of notches in quality below "Festival" — with live animals working with the star. It's a small theater, so kids get to see the animals up close and personal.

Parent Pointers from the Memories Team

In a Disney-esque spirit of cooperation, our Memories Team provide insights into keeping kids happy at Walt Disney World. Many of them are parents themselves who have taken their children to the Resort, and often learned the hard way how to ensure their sons and daughters received maximum enjoyment from their vacation. If the kids are enjoying their vacation, their parents or grandparents probably are, too.

"I think building anticipation before a trip helps involve the kids," says Nicole. "We always order the latest Disney Vacation Planning Video and watch that several times. We also let the kids give input on which attractions in each park they are most interested in experiencing, and which restaurants they want to eat in. But the single most important thing to remember to avoid Disney Meltdown is that kids get tired! Adults get tired, too, but kids often don't know how to handle that fatigue. Pace yourself. Don't be so worried about spending every single minute of the day in the park that you're too tired to enjoy any of it. Plan your visit so that you have lots of downtime. Go back to your hotel to nap or swim, or even to let the kids watch some TV. If you don't see everything you wanted to on a single visit, that's okay. If your kids were happy, and everyone had a great time, you'll want to go again. If you are all tired out and cranky, you won't enjoy having seen all those things you sacrificed your good mood for, anyway."

"Julianne (our daughter) has as much input into our trips as my wife and I," says Sam. "But we take breaks when they're needed. We enjoy fewer things more, instead of more things enjoyed less."

Chrislette and Jim also include their children in the planning. "As adults, you have to think like a kid at Disney, then the whole family will stay happy. If the kids are tired of park-hopping, then be flexible. Be creative. Have a miniature golf tournament, rent boats or bikes, take walks, go shopping. If

Though not a venue to keep your kids from getting restless, many parents schedule vacations for a time when youngsters can experience their first haircut. At Harmony Barber Shop in Magic Kingdom, stylists are attuned to ways to help kids handle their trimming well. They can even sprinkle pixie dust in your children's hair after the job is done. The Shop, which usually closes at 5:00, is quite popular, so be prepared to wait in line.

necessary, split up the group. Girls do girl things, like lay out by the pool, get a tan, or go shopping. Guys can do guy things, like golfing, swimming, or playing catch. Or, perhaps put kids with kids, and adults with adults. Satisfy the personal needs of each individual and make them feel their needs are important. Then eat dinner together as a family, share the experiences of the day—and laugh together!"

Susan emphasizes the necessity of establishing a reasonable bedtime and a reasonable out-of-bedtime. "John and I are very clear on our expectations before we even arrive at Walt Disney World. Make sure that the kids eat something other than junk. Consult with them on what to do either that morning or in the evening before setting out. The one time our niece came close to a meltdown, I nearly melted down because I had too much invested of myself (and time and money) in the experience. At some point, I just said, 'It's my vacation, too. I earned the money to do this, and I'm not going to prevent myself from enjoying it.' After that, everyone had a better time (I think)."

Amanda manages to avoid meltdowns with her son, but she cautions about another possible problem. "We have very little melting down," she explains. "Now getting sick is another story. About half of our vacations have had someone getting a stomach virus or infection of some kind, and it's usually the youngest member of the party. I would advise everyone to carry antibacterial hand gel and apply it hourly, and coach kids not to touch their faces or put their hands in their mouths before disinfecting them."

By the same token, Nicole shares how impressed she is by Disney's First Aid Centers. "I had occasion to visit both the Magic Kingdom and Epcot locations," she says. "My daughter was running a fever, and of course the one thing I forgot to take on the trip was a thermometer. The nurses in the First Aid Centers were very friendly and very professional. They have disposable thermometers and took my daughter's temperature. When it turned out that she had a fever, they provided her with a dose of Children's Motrin, at no cost. They also provided a pamphlet for Florida Hospital Centra Care. Although I had a car and didn't use this service, the clinics do provide free transportation to and from the clinic. They also accepted my insurance, so I didn't have to pay for the office visit up front. Of course, I would have preferred that my daughter not get sick during our Disney visit, the way the Disney First Aid Centers assisted us made the whole ordeal much more bearable."

When Becky and her brother were little, "we used to go over to one of the monorail hotels," she explains. "We'd just walk around, get something to eat, and sit down for awhile before going back for a few more hours of Mickey Mayhem. I never felt like I was missing anything, and I enjoyed getting to see these resorts."

Teens sometimes pose a different kind of challenge. "A few years back, we took two of my wife's cousins with us—girls thirteen and fifteen," says Jason. "We made the mistake of trying to show them why we enjoyed Walt Disney World. Only when we backed off and let them lead did they really start to enjoy it."

The Transportation Tousle

The most confusing challenge during your vacation? Understanding the logistics of Walt Disney World's Transportation System. The information below will provide the most convenient way to navigate around the complex--from your resort hotel to almost any destination on property. Bear in mind that, depending on attendance levels, the Resort occasionally revises routes and even hours of operation of its Transportation System. Always check with cast members for clarification.

To the Magic Kingdom
From the **Polynesian**: Monorail or Boat
From the **Contemporary**: Monorail, Boat or Walk
From the **Grand Floridian**: Monorail or Boat
From **Epcot**: Take Monorail to Transportation and Ticket Center (TTC), then transfer to Magic Kingdom Monorail.
From **WaterParks**: Bus
From **Downtown Disney**: Bus
From **Disney-MGM Studios**: Bus
From **Wilderness Lodge/Fort Wilderness**: Boat
From **All Other Resorts**: Bus
(If you're staying at BoardWalk, Yacht & Beach Club, Swan or Dolphin, you may opt to walk through Epcot via the International Gateway, then exit through Epcot's front gate to board the Monorail to the TTC. This strategy takes longer and puts more miles on your sneakers, but particularly during peak seasons, when the Transportation System is overtaxed, it often beats waiting for the bus.)

To the Disney-MGM Studios
From **BoardWalk**: Boat, or Walk (ten to fifteen minutes)
From **Yacht & Beach Club**: Boat, or Walk (fifteen to twenty minutes)
From **Swan & Dolphin**: Boat, or Walk (ten to fifteen minutes)
From **All Other Resorts and Parks**: Bus (though Epcot is accessible by walking via the BoardWalk path)
From **Downtown Disney**: Bus

To Disney's Animal Kingdom
From **All Resorts, Parks and Downtown Disney**: Bus (Note: Though Disney's Animal Kingdom Lodge is located nearby, you still must take the Bus.)

CHAPTER 10 THE TRANSPORTATION TOUSLE 213

To Epcot
From **Polynesian, Contemporary, Grand Floridian**: Monorail to TTC, then make the easy transfer to the Epcot Monorail.
From **BoardWalk** or **Disney-MGM Studios**: Boat, or Walk
From **Yacht & Beach Club**: Boat, or Walk
From **Swan and Dolphin**: Boat, or Walk
From **Magic Kingdom**: Monorail to TTC, then transfer to Epcot Monorail.
From **All Other Resorts**: Bus
From **Downtown Disney and Disney's Animal Kingdom**: Bus

To Downtown Disney and Typhoon Lagoon
From **Most Resorts and All Parks**: Bus
From **Saratoga Springs to Downtown Disney**: Walk or Boat
From **Fort Wilderness**: Bus to TTC, then transfer to Downtown Disney Bus. *(Or, you may ride a bus to any open theme park, then transfer there to a Downtown Disney Bus.)*
Before 4:00 p.m., the rules are different. Read carefully:
From **Polynesian, Contemporary, Grand Floridian**: Monorail to TTC, then transfer to Downtown Disney Bus.
From **Wilderness Lodge**: Bus to TTC, then transfer to Downtown Disney Bus.
From **Any Theme Park**: Bus

To Blizzard Beach & Winter Summerland Golf Course
From **All Resorts**: Bus

To Disney's Wide World of Sports
From **All Resorts**: Take the most convenient transportation to Disney-MGM Studios. Then, switch to the Wide World of Sports Bus, which does not stop at any Disney resort.

To Any Other WDW Resort Hotel from Your WDW Resort Hotel
The official Company line is to transfer to Downtown Disney via Bus, then switch to your destination bus. However, Aronda feels the official route is the least effective one. She recommends taking your resort bus to the nearest open theme park, then from that park, hop on the Bus that goes to the resort hotel you desire. Of course, this procedure will not work if you're traveling from one hotel to the other after park closings.

Chapter 11

Rest for the Weary

Disney's Resort Hotels

Planning for a Walt Disney World vacation must include the selection of a place to lay your weary head after an exhausting day touring the parks. You'll not only need a comfy pillow and a firm mattress at the end of each invigorating day — and in the afternoon, if you choose to take the highly recommended nap, particularly if you're traveling with children — but you'll also need to take into account the extent to which a resort hotel can enhance, or impair, the overall quality of your vacation. However, if you share David's sentiments, perhaps your room won't matter. "I am perfectly happy in the All-Star Resorts. After all, it's a bed and a shower. The rest of the time, I'm in in the parks. I'm not a hang-around-the-pool kind of guy."

Still, Disney resort hotels do a grand job of providing the most comfortable digs anywhere. By sleeping with the Mouse, you don't have to leave the magic behind, even when the parks close, the last dance has been called, and the final purchase of the day has been made. Because most members of the Memories Team believe strongly in staying on site to ensure the most magical Disney experience possible, we will provide extensive reviews only for those resort hotels available on Walt Disney World property. However, if you wish to stay off-property, sidebar lists of other local non-Disney hotels and inns are provided. These are quality resorts that can usually be booked at lower rates than Disney hotels. But what you save in dollars, you lose somewhat in terms of theme and convenience. Let's face it. You may not be so thrilled about driving another five or ten miles to hit the sack after you've stayed up late partying in Disney parks. On the other hand, the bucks you save can be diverted to other niceties, like more table-service meals, more souvenirs, and more "extras" like backstage tours and performances at Cirque du Soleil or House of Blues.

At the end of each resort's description, we'll provide a ballpark guesstimate of room rates to expect. Whether you pay higher or lower rates than those listed within each range depends on the season of your stay. Disney has four categories of seasons. Value Season usually occurs in January/February, mid-August-October, and November through early December. Regular season falls from April through mid-August. Peak and Holiday seasons, the most expensive times to visit—and the most crowded—occur between Valentine's Day and Easter, and from December 20 through New Year's Eve. At press time, Disney's toll-free reservation number was **1-800-511-9777,** though toll-free numbers have a tendency to change frequently. If the toll-free number has been disconnected, the Central Reservations

Office (CRO) may be reached at **407-WDISNEY (934-7639)**.

Roughing It

If that old pioneer spirit still burns in your heart, you might enjoy setting up camp at ***Disney's Fort Wilderness Resort and Campground***. Here, you have two options for accommodations. First, if you just need a campsite on which to park your RV or to set up a tent, Fort Wilderness offers sites with partial hookup in a variety of price ranges. Full hookups are a bit pricier. Keep in mind the Preferred Sites, though the priciest of all, have the best views, including panoramas of Bay Lake. Campsites with partial hookups range from $34.00 to $65.00; full hookups range from $39.00 to $76.00; and Preferred Sites range from $47.00 to $80.00 per night. "One

---

Check Out These Publications at Check-In

Upon check-in at your Disney resort hotel, make sure you have among your materials two very important publications: "World Update," and your resort hotel newsletter. A map of your resort should also be provided.

World Update
This glossy brochure provides useful information about the Resort during your vacation stay. The brochure lists "What's New," "Hours of Operation," mini-features about various Resort offerings, special events listings, and helpful Tips.

Resort Hotel Newsletter
Each resort newsletter clarifies perks and entitlements directly related to your stay at that particular resort. You'll find "Frequently Asked Questions," facts about your Resort Identification Card, and security tips. Dining and shopping opportunities are outlined in the newsletter, along with pool and recreation information and an article on "Environmentality." Guest Relations, from Airport Shuttle Service to Weather and Turndown Service, are also handily enumerated.

of my favorite resorts is Fort Wilderness," says Sam. "My family and I spent our vacation with Mom during her last trip before she died from Alzheimer's. The RV felt like home for her, and everything else was pure Disney."

Cabins, part of Disney's Home Away from Home inventory, are also available at Fort Wilderness — but are a significantly higher investment. Per night costs range from $224.00 to $314.00. Accommodations are cabin-like buildings (actually, modular units) decorated with wilderness accents. They accommodate up to six people comfortably. Furthermore, Fort Wilderness offers a number of entertainment options for guests — a big convenience for campers who are interested in *The Hoop-Dee-Doo Musical Revue*, a nightly campfire program that kids are wild about, a petting zoo, a museum, horseback riding and nature trails. (In fact, one of the trails connects Fort Wilderness to Disney's Wilderness Lodge. It provides a relaxing, scenic stroll.) For a laugh, be sure to take a look at the Lawnmower Tree (where, inexplicably, an antique push mower is embedded in the roots of a tree — a real one, not the Disney version.)

Fort Wilderness is also the only resort on Disney property where you can, for an additional fee, bring your pet with you. If Fido or Fluffy is making the trip, too, be sure to ask the cast member when you make your reservations. Bear in mind, though, only service animals are allowed in any of Disney's parks.

You Can Still Be a Star, Even if the Dollars Are Tight!

If your vacation happens to fall at a time of impeded cash flow — or you're the frugal sort — you might try booking a room at one of the Value Resorts — **Disney's All-Star Movies**, **All-Star Sports**, **All-Star Music** and **Pop Century**. While the rooms are a bit smaller than rooms at the moderate and deluxe Disney resort hotels, they're certainly comfortable enough after a busy day enjoying the parks — or if you're planning to

The World's Most Conventional Spaces

Need to book convention space at one of Walt Disney World's hotels? For information and pricing, call **321-939-7129**, or log onto **www.disneymeetings.com**, where you can enjoy video tours of each facility.

Below, you'll find your site options, which range in size from 20,000 to 200,000 square feet.

Swan & Dolphin
Exhibition Hall & Executive Boardroom
Contemporary
Three ballrooms
Yacht & Beach Club
Convention Center
Grand Floridian
A lavish center with silk brocade walls
BoardWalk
Smaller conference area, but also a unique lakeside gazebo
Coronado Springs
Largest ballroom in the United States

Interested? You and your fellow "conventionEARS" can have access to Disney characters and performers. You can even schedule special events in the parks-- all for a price, of course.

If you're not interested in booking a convention, and just want to avoid the associated crowds, keep in mind that Disney's busiest convention seasons occur in January, May, September and October.

---

spend very little time in your room. The typical hotel amenities are found here, as well, including a television, alarm clock, telephone, and an independently-controlled thermostat. (Note that many of Disney's resort thermostats do not set lower than 68 degrees.) If you anticipate being in the mood for a cocktail, you should note there are no lounges here — except at Disney's Pop Century Resort, but Josh reports that during two of his trips, it was frequently closed — but drinks are available at each of the poolside bars. The pools, by the way, are huge, but keep

Chapter 11 Resort Hotels 219

in mind that the Value Resorts are immensely popular with families, so you'll be sharing pool space with lots of kids and their parents. Because oversized icons relating to each resort's theme adorn the buildings and landscape, some guests consider these resorts to be, well, "overstated." The kids, though, absolutely love the over-the-top theming. But even if gargantuan icons don't appeal to you, the price certainly will. Here's yet another word of caution—not that we're trying to sway you away from this choice, but to ensure you make reservations with full awareness of the perks and pit-

Disney's All-Star Music offers giant icons celebrating many of Disney's best showtunes.

Bossy Donald Duck certainly possesses qualities of some movie directors. And the gift shop at Disney's All-Star Movies places Donald in that role at the entrance.

Disney's All-Star Sports Resort bedazzles guests with huge sports-related icons. Frequently, this resort hosts young athletes competing at Disney's Wide World of Sports.

falls. Many guests find these huge resorts (collectively representing over twenty thousand rooms within Disney's inventory) significantly noisier than Disney's higher-priced resorts, while some

Disney's Pop Century is Walt Disney World's newest Value Resort. Though fifty percent of its rooms remain unfinished, they are located across the lake, and do not detract from the ambience of your section.

adult travelers without children feel somewhat overwhelmed by the number of youngsters scurrying about. Finally, the maximum occupancy for each Value room is four, while other resort rooms accommodate five guests. Several Memories Team members reported excess noise from neighbors in rooms above them. Furthermore, the only transportation provided to the Value Resorts is via bus (the stops are a long distance from many of the rooms). A food court at each resort serves breakfast, lunch and dinner—but no table service restaurant is available here. Refillable mugs are also available, and can save a fortune on beverages. "I usually stay at one of the All-Star Resorts when I vacation," says Ed. "I don't go to Florida to see the hotel rooms, so I don't bother with the Moderate or Deluxe class rooms. The money I save there pays for better meals, and other goodies." Lindsey and Chuck have stayed in all three types of resorts at Walt Disney World, and give high praise to the All-Star Movies. "We stayed in the Toy Story building, with a room overlooking a courtyard with giant Buzz Lightyear and Woody statues. The Fantasia pool is so much fun!"

Disney's Pop Century Resort highlights the toys, fads, technological breakthroughs, dance crazes and catch phrases that characterized each decade of the twentieth century. Huge building icons like Big Wheel, Play-Doh and Rubik's Cube loom close to the door of your room, while pools are shaped like a bowling pin, a flower, a computer, a crossword puzzle, a soda bottle and a highway sign. Pop Century is located close to Disney's Caribbean Beach Resort, and fairly close to Epcot—though you must take a bus to get there. Be sure to check out all the "pop" memorabilia on display in the unique lobby area. The gift shop and food court share a huge space called All Things Pop. Be sure to try one of the specialties called "Mom's Night Out," which are served a la TV dinner in an aluminum tray. "My favorite resort is Pop Century," says Dania. "The dining hall doesn't have the crowded feel as the All-Stars do. I stayed in the 70s section during the grand opening week and loved it. I never felt that it was overcrowded."

Downtown Disney Resorts

Located on Disney property, although not owned by The Walt Disney Company, the Downtown Disney resort hotels offer clean, appealing accommodations, usually for a bit less than the Disney-owned resorts. These facilities feel more urban than many Disney accommodations--which makes them favorites of guests who like short escapes from the infusion of Disney fantasy during their vacation. While these hotels do provide bus service, pickups occur only once every half hour--often longer for Disney's Animal Kingdom. Point your browser to **www.downtowndisneyhotels.com** for more information.

Perks have traditionally included:

◆ Guests can rent cars on premises.
◆ Free bus service to Disney's four major theme parks, as well as water parks and Downtown Disney. Several hotels are located within comfortable walking distance of Downtown Disney.
◆ Preferred access to Disney golf courses.
◆ Twenty percent (20%) discount on Pleasure Island admission with dinner at a Downtown Disney hotel restaurant.

Per night rates for all Value Resorts range from $77.00 to $124.00, though keep checking on **www.mousesavers.com** for specials.

All things in moderation

If your budget isn't too tight, Disney offers several moderate resort hotels, whose rooms are a bit larger (about fifty square feet larger, in fact) than the Value resorts, with expanded amenities. Not only will you have access to a hair dryer (except in Disney's Caribbean Beach Resort), television, alarm clock and telephone, you'll enjoy the extra safety and convenience of an in-room safe. Additionally, all Moderates not only have food courts for your convenience, but also table service restaurants—and at least one lounge for that end-of-

Downtown Disney Resorts

Best Western
$89-169 (rooms)
$199-399 (suites)
407-828-2424; 800-348-3765
www.orlandoresorthotel.com

Holiday Inn
$74-99
407-828-8888
www.hiorlando.com

Doubletree Guest Suites
$129-299
407-934-1000; 800-222-8733
www.doubletreeguestsuites.com

Grosvenor
$99-165 (rooms)
$345-480 (suites)

Grosvenor *(continued)*
407-828-4444; 800-624-4109
www.grosvenorresort.com

Hilton
$149-345 (rms.); 359-1500 (suites)
407-827-4000; 800-782-4414
www.hilton.com

Royal Plaza
$109-179 (rms.); 209-699 (suites)
407-828-2828; 800-248-7890
www.royalplaza.com

Wyndham Palace Resort & Spa
$129-269 (rooms)
$229-529 (suites)
407-827-2727; 800-327-2990
www.wyndham.com

the-day cocktail. And at press time, Disney had just announced its intention to include refrigerators in all Moderate and Deluxe rooms. You'll find the theming much more intricate and understated here, too, than that found at the Value resorts. Total guest capacity is also smaller at most Moderates than over at the Value resorts, which translates into a heightened sense of coziness and relaxation. Per night rates at all of Disney Moderate Resorts range from $133.00 to $219.00.

Disney's Port Orleans Resort (incorporating the French Quarter and Riverside) evokes New Orleans' jazzy French Quarter and the more rural Deep South. The newly-refurbished food court at the French Quarter is designed as a storage room for Mardi Gras floats and props—hence the name Sassagoula Floatworks and Food Factory—while Boatwright's Dining Hall is the table service eatery, located at Riverside (which also has a food court). You'll find recreational opportunities—like biking, boating, swimming, fishing—as well as a couple of shops for your convenience. Round-trip boat transportation from Disney's Port Orleans Resort takes you to Downtown Disney—a nice, relaxing, and scenic alternative to the traditional bus service. The two sections of Port Orleans are connected via walkway. "Our favorite resort is Port Orleans Riverside," say John and Lynda. "It's centrally located to all of Disney. It also has water transportation to Downtown Disney. But most of all, it's very peaceful and quiet." Crystal, Tom, and Linda are also big fans of Port Orleans, but they are partial to the French Quarter. "We always stay in Building 4, right next to the food court and real close to the alligator pool. We like it because there is only one bus stop, and everything is very conveniently located. We also enjoy the Sassagoula water transportation to Downtown Disney."

At **Disney's Caribbean Beach Resort**, five "villages" with scores of rooms surround a beautiful, 45-acre lake, and evoke the architecture of the Caribbean Islands. The landscaping is gorgeous, and the rooms are just a tad larger than rooms

---

Before You Reserve, Check Out the Discounts!

Often with a huge sigh, many travelers make that call to Disney's CRO because they know how quickly Disney's room rates can sabotage a budget. So we suggest that you always ask if there are any specials when inquiring about accommodations. Keep checking in your Sunday paper as well, since specials are sometimes announced there--either by the Company or through local travel agents. Check Internet sites that are referenced in this guide. Often, Webmasters will keep you apprised of upcoming specials. Annual Passholders and Disney Vacation Club members also receive discounts. A great Web site to help budget affordable vacations is **www.mousesavers.com**. Many Memories Team members call only after they've checked out this site.

When You Have the Urge to Concierge...

All Deluxe resorts at Walt Disney World offer concierge rooms, but at a fairly steep increase in price. However, if you can afford it, the extras you enjoy certainly make for a grand pampering. Breakfast, afternoon and evening snacks are provided, including wine, beer and other beverages. Your room is located in an area accessible only to guests who stay on the concierge floors. Separate lobby areas are provided, with TV and reading materials. Additionally, concierge staff will take care of reservations and Priority Seatings for you--as well as a number of other services.

---

in the other Moderates. One word of warning: Unlike the other Moderates, this resort charges if you open a pack of coffee. Additionally, the refillable mugs and ponchos you find on your room table will be charged to your stay if you break the shrink-wrap seal. Amenities and recreational activities parallel those found at Port Orleans, including a newly-remodeled full-service restaurant called Shutters at Old Port Royale. The unique food court is called Old Port Royale Food Court, and features hamburgers, pasta, pizza and broiled specialties.

Disney's Coronado Springs Resort rounds out Disney's Moderate Resort offerings with almost two thousand rooms surrounding a fifteen-acre lake. Once again, the amenities at this resort mirror amenities at the other Moderates — with the exception that Disney's Coronado Springs Resort offers convention facilities which, when conventions are booked here, make this resort feel a bit more upscale than the other Moderates. However, if a large convention group has booked during your stay, count on more noise in the common areas of the resort. The food court here — called the Pepper Market — is, in Dann's opinion, the best of the Moderate food courts. An unusual hybrid of counter and full service, you visit food preparation kiosks where you get your ticket punched, while drinks are refilled by cast members on the "float." You pay upon exiting. Don't be surprised by the one-dollar mandatory

The Crescent Lake-side of the BoardWalk Inn and Villas opens onto a beautiful greensward. Guests often while away the hours sitting on big rocking chairs located on the porch while looking across beautiful Crescent Lake. The Villas are part of the Disney Vacation Club (DVC).

gratuity added to your bill. Disney's Coronado Springs Resort presents a splendid Southwestern United States-Mexican theme, with a superb table service restaurant called Maya Grill (breakfast and dinner are available). Susan and John enjoy staying at Coronado Springs because of the "quiet pools, the Pepper Market, and amazingly, we actually like the convention-ish atmosphere." Jason and Lauralee credit this resort for "convincing us that we need to stay on property from now on."

When money is no object

If you're amenable to paying two hundred dollars or more for higher-quality digs, Walt Disney World is happy to oblige with its many Deluxe resort hotels. With all Deluxe resorts, the rooms are larger than rooms at the Moderate and Value resorts and more expansive in-room dining (Disney-speak for room service) is available. Your room phone has a dedicated button for pizza delivery, and ports for laptop computers (including high-speed Internet) are available—for an additional charge. Doors also open onto enclosed, carpeted hallways in most Deluxe accommodations—unlike both the Moderates and the Values whose doors open to the exterior, which often means more exterior noise coming through your door. Balconies and patios provide an extended leisure area and often, unique sights, while on-site shopping and dining opportunities are more numerous and more sophisticated. You can also expect a more intense level of service from hotel staff, and nightly room rates reflect that attentiveness. The edge that Disney's Deluxe resort hotels have over other first-class accommodations located off-property, besides location, is the

Sowing Your Oatmeal on a Sunrise Safari

If you're staying at Disney's Animal Kingdom Lodge as a concierge guest, you have the unique opportunity to participate in the Sunrise Safari Breakfast Adventure. At press time, the Adventure was available only on Tuesdays and Saturdays, limited to twenty-eight guests per tour. To participate, you must fork over $39.95 ($24.95 for children 3-11)--and be willing to start your day at 6:30 a.m.

At that ungodly hour, you and your fellow adventurers are taken to the Kilimanjaro Safaris area, where you embark on a 45-minute tour that includes many stops. And because there is plenty of time, each animal is described in great detail--unlike the quicker pace of the ride during the park's regular hours.

After the Safari, you report to the Tusker House restaurant for a superb breakfast buffet. An extra perk is a FASTPASS to Kilimanjaro Safaris--to experience the attraction once again during regular park hours.

Please note: After Sunrise Safari, if you choose to return to Disney's Animal Kingdom Lodge, you'll have to catch one of the regular Disney buses.

Company's passionate attention to theming—and often, convenient transportation options (though there are annoying exceptions).

Disney's BoardWalk Inn evokes a feeling of having stepped back in time and place to the Atlantic City at the turn of the twentieth century. BoardWalk boasts not one, but three pools—two quiet pools, and a festive main pool called Luna Park, which also features a 200-foot water slide called Keister Coaster—and a variety of restaurants from which to choose when hunger sets in. Room vistas range from pool views to Epcot views (guests' favorite) to views of the BoardWalk and Crescent Lake (around which four other Deluxe resorts are situated). In fact, BoardWalk is within walking distance of two Disney parks—Disney-MGM Studios and Epcot. Lighted footpaths are conveniently provided to both, though you can take the slower (but more relaxing) water launch. Please note that BoardWalk does not provide bus service to Disney-MGM Studios or Epcot. The buildings of BoardWalk form an arch around Crescent Lake; this resort is tops in terms of location and ambience. It's also quite the lively place, with nightclubs, shops and restaurants, open until about midnight (ESPN Club, Jellyrolls and Atlantic Dance are usually open until 2 a.m.), rounding out the BoardWalk experience. Kids particularly enjoy several games of skill—for example, the basketball toss—where the more adept can win stuffed animals, Disney-emblazoned basketballs and other prizes. Roving entertainment continues for several hours, including musicians, balancing acts, sword-swallowers, fire-eaters and fortune-tellers. One of Walt Disney World's best face painters also has a kiosk set up here. Keep in mind that BoardWalk is also marketed as a nighttime destination in its own right, so guests staying at other resorts, as well as many locals, may cause the crowds to swell until past bedtime. However, the rooms are usually insulated well enough that you'll be able to snooze without interruption. If you prefer a festive, party atmosphere, BoardWalk just might be the resort for you. The rooms at BoardWalk are spacious and appointed with casual elegance, highlighted by bright, refreshing colors of summer. The lobby, though small and intimate, is beautifully appointed, and sports two unique antique models — a miniature carousel and roller coaster. Rocking chairs are located on the verandah for relaxation or people-watching. Spoodles and the Flying Fish Café are great places to dine, and you'll have a festive time at Jellyrolls, where pianists play "dueling pianos," guests are welcome to make requests (though a tip is in order when the musicians oblige), and sing-alongs occur frequently. "I love the BoardWalk because it is definitely where all the action is," says Josh. "Even if I don't feel like going to Pleasure Island, and want to stay in my room, I can, when I'm lucky enough to snag a BoardWalk view, just sit on my balcony and enjoy the goings-on below. But even if I don't have a primo view, I still go downstairs and enjoy the atmosphere and antics along Crescent Lake. When I get tired, I'm just two minutes from my room. I also like the fact that I'm within walking distance of two parks, and don't have to rely on Disney transportation." Per night rates at Disney's BoardWalk Inn range from $289.00 to $770.00.

Also sprawling along Crescent Lake in the Epcot Resort Area, **Disney's Yacht and Beach Club Resorts** (actually two resorts situated perpendicular to one another) respectively display an austere nautical theme and a frivolous beach theme, including several volleyball courts. The Yacht Club is significantly more formal than the Beach Club, but both resorts are gorgeous and inviting. Hardwood floors and nautical antiques add to the flavor of these resort hotels, and their grounds are wonderful places to explore. Beach Club backs up to Epcot, and

If Epcot is your fave, then Disney's Beach Club may be the resort for you. It takes five minutes to arrive at the park's rear entrance.

some rooms provide glimpses into the park. Yacht Club is located just next door to Walt Disney World Swan and Walt Disney World Dolphin, with incredible views of the BoardWalk, located directly across Crescent Lake. Stormalong Bay, shared by both resorts, defies the traditional definition of a pool, with its flowing streams, waterslides and sandy beaches. It's possibly the best and most popular resort pool property-wide. It's certainly the most unique. "The Yacht Club is my favorite because the pool is so awesome," says Melanie. "We had a view of the water. Great restaurants and the closeness to Epcot can't be beat." Per night room rates at both resorts range from $289.00 to $640.00.

The remaining two Epcot area Deluxe resorts — the **Walt Disney World Swan** and the **Walt Disney World Dolphin** — are unique, imposing structures, both of which were designed by renowned architect Michael Graves. Though both hotels are located inside Walt Disney World (between Epcot and Disney-MGM Studios), the Swan is managed by Westin, while Sheraton manages the Dolphin. Still, the perks and conveniences of staying at these resorts — which cater heavily to convention and business crowds — mirror those to which you're entitled in Disney-run resorts (except that you can't use your room key to make charges outside the hotels themselves). Besides the unorthodox architecture of the hotels — the Swan has a sweeping oval roof, while the Dolphin is shaped like a great

The Walt Disney World Dolphin looms impressively beside Crescent Lake. Across a courtyard is the Walt Disney World Swan. The architectural styles are similar.

pyramid—the most outstanding exterior features are the tremendous sculptures of a pair of swans and a pair of dolphins perched on their rooftops and visible from several thoroughfares on Disney property—and from several vantage points inside Epcot. The interior appointments delight with their frivolity, and the rooms and hallways in both resorts are spacious. These two resorts complete the Crescent Lake resort picture, and offer a number of fine dining experiences. Both resorts recently received a facelift, so expect your digs to be bright and fresh. Susan and John recommend the Swan and Dolphin because of "location, location, location! Besides, we actually enjoy the adult, convention atmosphere." Chrislette and Jim have stayed numerous times at the Dolphin, which "has super access to the BoardWalk and Epcot. And we've been able to take advantage of teacher rates—so the price is right!" Both the Swan and Dolphin will discount room rates for educators, so be certain to identify yourself as such if the rates apply to you. Otherwise, you can expect nightly rates to range from $325.00 to $495.00. Bear in mind that both resorts have a distinct reservation number: **888-828-8850**. Or, visit the resorts online at **www.swandolphin.com**.

Presently, the only Deluxe resort in Disney's Animal Kingdom Resort Area is **Disney's Animal Kingdom Lodge**, a

Disney's Animal Kingdom Lodge is unique in many ways, but the opportunity to view animals from the balcony of your room is the most frequently noted quality. These rooms cost more than standard views.

magnificent, primitively elegant structure which opened its doors in April 2001. Most guest rooms (which some veterans have deemed lovely, but perhaps a bit dark) face an African savanna and afford views of actual wildlife, which often approach within fifteen feet of guest room balconies. It's not uncommon to see guests lingering on their balconies to enjoy the view of the grazing wildlife, like giraffe, zebra and antelope. (Lest you worry about your safety, know that pulsating, multi-prong sensors emit a light shock if animals get too close, though a cast member told Dann that most animals have learned to stop short of the shock.) Inside the beautifully and realistically detailed lobby—you'll have to pinch yourself as a reminder that you haven't stepped into Africa—designed to resemble (though on a larger scale) an African safari lodge, you'll delight in the numerous displays of African art pieces, artifacts and masks. Additionally, the Lodge offers several "community spaces," including an open "camp fire" surrounded by rocking chairs, and an interior fireplace which inspires a sense of introspection. Several pathways extend from the savanna-side of the Lodge out into the savanna to get you even closer to the wildlife. Because animal shifts are rotated throughout the day and night—these are *not* the same animals you see on display at Disney's Animal Kingdom—you'll be able to spot these creatures anytime (with the exception of about two hours when all animals are off-duty), and cast members are usually on hand to answer any questions you may have. The Lodge is particularly beautiful at night—with two wildly popular restaurants, and a lobby that invites exploration as well as admiration. Tours of the resort are also offered to guests as well as a Sunrise Safari. Inquire about the Lodge's free resort tours at the front desk. "I love this resort," says Becky. "The decoration is wonderful. I enjoyed the chance to try to African food, and of course, you look out your window and see giraffes eating grass out of a tree. The resort has an outdoor viewing area where you can look at the animals through the same night-vision scopes used by the Navy—a large blob became a group of sleeping wildebeests, and I could clearly see zebras and bulls. And where else would I get a chance to talk to someone from Botswana? The lobby even had the wonderful scent of burning wood from the restaurants." This resort is also Amanda's favorite. "It's the most beautiful hotel I've ever seen, and having the animals outside your balcony at dawn is something no other resort could ever top for us. The restaurants are excellent, and the hot tub is the best on property. I love the music that plays in the lobby, and the gift shop is one of the best at Walt Disney World, too. There are lots of extra activities about animals for the kids, which my son loved, and guides to talk to about the animals were available most hours." Nightly rates range from $204.00 to $595.00.

Heading toward the Magic Kingdom, you'll find four other Deluxe resorts, several of which offer stunning views of the park possessing Walt Disney's strongest touch. Located in the

Disney's Wilderness Lodge, whose lobby possesses a uniquely cozy charm, has hooked many guests, who refuse to stay anywhere else.

Stash It, Then Let the Good Times Roll!

Do you plan to arrive prior to check-in time (3:00 p.m.)--or leave several hours beyond check-out (11:00 a.m.)?

If you're staying on property, you'll find bell services willing to store your luggage when you have no access to a room.

Check-In
When your room is ready, ask the Front Desk to have your luggage sent to your room. Usually, within about ten minutes, a cast member will deliver your things. Tips are always appreciated.

Check-Out
If you need your resort hotel to hold your bags for several hours past check-out, touch the Bell Services & Valet button on your room phone. A cast member will report to your room--usually within ten minutes--to procure your luggage for safe storage until you leave for home. Again, tipping is appropriate.

Important Note: Someone must be in your room when Bell Services delivers luggage or retrieves it.

Fort Wilderness area, **Disney's Wilderness Lodge** takes you back to the Rocky Mountain lodges of the National Park Service in the early 1900s. Cast members are dressed like park rangers. A gorgeous resort among towering trees, Wilderness Lodge is situated on Bay Lake, just a stone's throw from Disney's Contemporary Resort (though you feel as though you're miles away—in a dense, lush forest). On the Bay Lake side of the resort, you'll find Disney's version of Old Faithful, with periodic eruptions to delight guests. The pool is particularly lovely, too, with a cascading stream flowing over rocks and crevasses toward the oversized pool. Both children and adults love it. The resort boasts two table service restaurants, Artist Point and Whispering Canyon Café. In the lobby, the teepee chandeliers will amuse and impress, while the magnificent fireplace will coax you into a romantic—or relaxed—

CHAPTER 11 RESORT HOTELS 235

mood. The Iron Spike Room in the Villas at Wilderness Lodge (larger Disney Vacation Club units with kitchen facilities) displays several train cars from the famous Carolwood Pacific "fair-weather train" that actually belonged to Walt Disney — he, along with his wife Lillian and friends, actually rode them in his backyard. Nightly rates at Disney's Wilderness Lodge range from $194.00 to $500.00.

Within view from the dock at Wilderness Lodge is **Disney's Contemporary Resort**, the A-framed (or toaster-shaped, depending on your point of view) "tomorrowland" hotel that Walt Disney introduced on television before his death in 1966. Because the Tower rooms open directly onto the spacious lobby, guests sometimes report a noisier stay here than at the other Disney Deluxe resorts. Garden rooms, which are somewhat more spacious and quieter, but less expensive, are accessible only by leaving the Tower; they extend along the shores of Bay Lake. If you choose the popular Tower accommodations, the higher up the room, the less likely your naps will be interrupted by laughter and conversation wafting up from the shops and restaurants below. One of the biggest draws of this resort is the fact that the monorail glides directly through the middle of it, making access to both the Magic Kingdom and Epcot easy and convenient. If you like a hotel with a cosmopolitan atmo-

A collection of stacked "modular units," the Contemporary Resort remains an impressive site—particularly when you see the lobby swallow the monorail.

sphere, this resort might be just what the doctor ordered. An appropriately-timed meal in the acclaimed California Grill, located atop Disney's Contemporary Resort, offers a glorious view of the Wishes fireworks extravaganza over the Magic Kingdom. Other restaurants are also available on the fourth-floor level of the resort. Disney's Contemporary Resort is one of three resorts that opened along with the Magic Kingdom in 1971 — so you'll be living a bit of Disney history as a guest here. While the rooms are spacious, theming is less intricate than at other Deluxe resorts. The Contemporary's pool is one of only two Olympic-size pools on Disney property. "Staying at the Contemporary meant that we could walk to the Magic Kingdom and not have to fight the monorail crowds to get back to our hotel," says Nicole. "It was great to see the

Intricately themed, Disney's Polynesian Resort beckons the traveler with its lush foliage. From the Polynesian's dock, you have excellent views of "Wishes" and King Triton's Electrical Water Pageant.

Electrical Water Pageant from our window, and to be able to hop on the monorail right in the lobby." Furthermore, the Contemporary is the only resort where you can book a parasailing experience. If interested, go to Sammy Duvall's Center at the Contemporary dock for more details. Nightly rates at this resort range from $254.00 to $525.00.

Another of Walt Disney World's original hotels is **Disney's Polynesian Resort**, also located along the monorail track, and themed with a delightful South Pacific flavor. At night, torches illuminate the landscape and the drums of a luau can be heard from the dinner show offered each evening. (A character breakfast occurs each morning at 'Ohana.) The architecture, the atmosphere and the theming are spectacular, but relaxing, and now that a volcano waterslide has been added during a recent refurbishment, this resort boasts one of the most unique pools of any property-wide. Guests also have the convenience of a short walking path to and from the Transportation and Ticket Center—meaning they do not have to transfer to another monorail once they return from Epcot to access the resort. Room furnishings are constructed of bamboo; the décor thoroughly evokes the tropics. A number of recreational activities, including small boats called Sea Raycers, are available here. The lobby is adorned with lush vegetation and a cascading waterfall, conjuring up a cool jungle paradise. Some Disney regulars refuse to stay anywhere else on

When a Bouquet is the *Only* Way

Often, guests book their vacations to celebrate a special occasion, like an anniversary, birthday or retirement. When it fits the occasion, why not call the WDW Florist, and arrange the delivery of a special gift basket to your room upon arrival? The Florist's number is 407-827-3505. These folks offer a number of standard gift baskets--or they can help you customize. To get you started, they're usually happy to fax you a listing of some of their special baskets, even before you leave home.

property. Several wonderful restaurants offer enticing meals, including Kona Café and 'Ohana. Brian calls the Polynesian the "best-themed resort by far." Nightly rates range from $299.00 to $650.00.

Walt Disney World's jewel in the crown of resort hotels is **Disney's Grand Floridian Resort & Spa**, a four-star hotel, also located along the Magic Kingdom monorail route, with exquisitely-appointed décor reminiscent of Florida's glory days of elegant hotel experiences during the Henry M. Flagler era of extravagance. You can even enjoy High Tea—a particularly appealing experience for the little princesses in your party—at the Garden View Lounge, usually from 3 p.m. until 6 p.m. (Reservations are often not accepted for High Tea; just show up, and you'll be seated shortly. Occasionally, during peak seasons, the Garden View Lounge will accept Prior-

Disney's Grand Floridian Resort & Spa is elegant enough from an exterior perspective. But wait until you step inside the grand lobby! In the afternoon, musicians play; throughout the day, you can order your favorite cocktails while relaxing in the lobby.

ity Seatings for this event. To be certain of a seating, call **1-407-WDW-DINE**.) This hotel boasts the most casually sophisticated staff who are attentive and intense. Just have a seat in the Grand Floridian's elegant lobby, and soon, someone will appear to take your beverage order, if desired. White and rose are the dominant, but relaxing, colors in the "grand" scheme of this hotel's décor, and while casual attire is fine here, you never feel as though you want to pull out that old pair of tattered jeans. During the afternoon and early evening, a jazz band and pianist alternate sets to make even lounging around the lobby both relaxing and entertaining. Disney's "hautest" restaurant is located on the second floor of the Grand Floridian—Victoria & Albert's—and though expensive, you may wish to utilize one of Disney's child care programs while indulging yourself with a fine, seven-course meal. "This hotel is absolutely breathtaking!" say Lindsey and Chuck. "The lobby itself is a sight to see, with its gorgeous chandeliers, stained glass, and Victorian style furniture. Of course, being on the monorail route is a definite plus for the Grand Floridian as well." Nightly rates range from $349.00 to $2,535.00 (for two-bedroom suites).

Home Away from Home Resorts

If you'd prefer accommodations akin to an apartment—or you're traveling with a larger group and wish to prepare some of your meals in your own kitchen (a great way to save some cash)—then Disney's Home Away from Home resorts may be just the ticket. Furthermore, this approach may allow you and your party to split the cost of accommodations while maintaining first-class comfort—thus stretching your vacation dollars for the fun stuff. Five of these Home Away from Home resorts are affiliated with the Disney Vacation Club—Disney's unique version of a timeshare program. What makes the Home Away from Home option attractive for groups and large families is the higher occupancy allowance of some of the rooms and villas, as well as the inclusion of microwave ovens, refrigerators, stoves, cookware, utensils—even a vacuum cleaner and VCR player (some units are equipped with DVD players). The one-, two-, and three-bedroom units even have washers and dryers, conveniently eliminating any need of searching for a public laundry room on property. And if you eat some of your meals in your "home away from home," you may save a king's ransom in restaurant charges. Presently, there are five Disney Vacation Club (DVC) Home Away from Home resorts: **BoardWalk Villas** ($289-$1,865), **Old Key West** ($249-$1,410), the **Villas at Wilderness Lodge** ($269-$920), **Beach Club Villas** ($289-$1,865) and **Disney's Saratoga Springs** ($259.00-$1,505). **Cabins at Fort Wilderness**, not affiliated with DVC, are also included in the Home Away from Home category, and were described earlier in this chapter. Descriptions of most resorts' public spaces appear in earlier sections within this chapter, since BoardWalk Villas, Villas at Wilderness Lodge and Beach Club Villas share common lobbies, check-in services, guest services, restaurant facilities and shopping venues with BoardWalk Inn, Wilderness Lodge and Beach Club Resort, respectively. However, Old Key West and Disney's Saratoga Springs are completely dedicated to the Disney Vacation Club; their descriptions appear below.

All DVC resorts offer Studio accommodations, which are essentially the typical double room of most resort hotels—with the added features of a sleeper sofa, a microwave oven, a small fridge, a vacuum cleaner, a small sink in the kitchenette area, and a small safe (usually). In the Studio, the bathroom facilities are basic—shower, tub, toilet, and a single sink right outside the bathroom. But you can also select a one- or two-bedroom villa, or a grand villa—which not only offers additional sleeping space, but also more living space, a full kitchen, a washer-dryer combination, a dining area, at least one DVD player or VCR to accompany the TVs, and a private Jacuzzi. Though the Studio is impressive enough, you will feel positively spoiled in one of the larger accommodations.

Disney's Old Key West is a sprawling resort located close to Downtown Disney, which evokes a feeling of stepping into the close-knit community of Key West, Florida. Unlike most Home Away from Home resorts, parking is located right outside your door—meaning that you don't have to tip a valet or bell services. Though the studios are about the same size as in the other Home Away From Home resorts, the less rectangular shape is more user-friendly and gives the illusion of more spaciousness. The resort abuts a golf course, boasts several pools, and features a gift shop, a popular restaurant called Olivia's, and boat and bike rentals. Transportation to all other Walt Disney World venues is via bus—though a twenty-minute walkway will take you to Downtown Disney. (We don't suggest using it at night.)

Disney's Saratoga Springs, named for and designed after Saratoga Springs, New York, overlooks the lakefront district of Downtown Disney. Hence, Old Key West's status of be-

Disney's Old Key West, the original Disney Vacation Club Resort, is located in a tranquil setting, adjacent to a golf course and not far from Downtown Disney.

ing most convenient to Pleasure Island has been usurped. The 184-unit development consists of four residential-style buildings with studio, one- and two-bedroom villas and Grand Villa units that sleep up to twelve guests. (In 2005, an additional 368 units will open.) Disney has captured a late-1800s look with its architecture, creating a romantic feeling reminiscent of this era in Saratoga Springs' rich history. Disney magically brings the charm of this community to life in every detail including flowers, trees, rocks, fountains and lakes. Red maples, sycamores, and river birch trees native to upstate New York as well as central Florida dot the landscape. Formal gardens, patios, and courtyards are situated close to buildings, while pastoral, forested areas are placed away from them. The rockwork draws on the granite/sedimentary slate, stone, and river rock abundant in the Adirondack region. But perhaps the most striking thing about Disney's Saratoga Springs Resort & Spa is its connection to water in various forms. To begin with, the many lakes (with their landscaped edges and dramatic, tall fountains that are lit at night) are breathtaking. The feature pool is naturally-shaped, with a bubbling spring cascading over rocks before falling gracefully toward the pool. The accompanying waterslide creates quite a splash as it weaves in and out of rockwork and passes under a stone bridge before reaching the pool.

For current and retired military personnel, a picturesque, affordable option to Disney's higher-priced accommodations is available—**Shades of Green** at Walt Disney World. The resort, which was leased in 1993 to the U.S. Army for $43 million, was formerly called The Disney Inn. The 586-room resort is located close to the Magic Kingdom, nestled between Disney's Palm and Disney's Magnolia golf courses. Though Disney still owns the land on which Shades of Green is located, the Army has leased the resort for one hundred years. Shades of Green caters exclusively to active and retired military personnel, civilian federal workers and their families. Guests are charged according to their rank. Privates pay around $72.00 per night, while high-ranking officials pay around $99.00. Considering the difficulty in finding Deluxe accommodations at Walt Disney World for under two hundred bucks per night, these rates are bargains indeed. Each room, which accommodates up to five people, has two queen beds, a day bed, television and VCR, table and chairs, a balcony or patio, and a view of either a pool, golf course or lush landscaping. Several restaurants are located at the resort, along with a couple of lounges. For reservations at Shades of Green, you must contact the resort directly. The toll-free Reservations Line is 888-593-2242; the Reservations Fax is 407-824-3665. To call the resort directly, dial 407-824-3400; the hotel's direct fax line is 407-824-3460. For even more information, point your Internet browser to www.shadesofgreen.org. "Shades of Green was great because the rooms were so big, and the price can't be beat for a Deluxe Resort," says Nicole.

Many off-property hotels offer great accommodations for generally lower rates than you'll find on Walt Disney World property. While the trade-off won't be in room quality, you'll discover fewer perks. For example, guests staying in off-property resort hotels are not eligible for Extra Magic Hours, when Disney resort guests are allowed admission to a select theme park one hour prior to the published opening time or up to three hours past closing. You'll also miss some of that great Disney theming. Still, you often save a small mint by choosing these hotels. What's more, these properties adhere to Disney's rigorous standards for quality; hence, their status as "Good Neighbors." They're not quite Disney—but still, they have Mickey's seal of approval.

Like a Good Neighbor...

Walt Disney World Good Neighbor Hotels are listed below. Notice that room rates are usually lower than those at Disney-owned resorts, but the trade-off is a lack of several perks--and location, location, location!

Lake Buena Vista Area
Comfort Inn--800-999-7300--Rates start under $100--www.comfortinnorlando.com
Radisson Inn--407-239-8400--Range from $69-139
Doubletree Club Hotel--800-521-3297--Rates start around $80-www.doubletreeclublbv.com
Sheraton Safari Hotel--407-239-0444--Rates start under $90-www.sheratonsafari.com
Holiday Inn Sunspree Resort--800-366-6299--Start around $70--www.kidsuites.com
Holiday Inn Family Suites--877-387-5437--Start around $110--www.hifamilysuites.com
Buena Vista Suites--407-239-8588--Range from $90-$150
Embassy Suites Resort--888-782-9722--Start around $130
Summerfield Suites/Wyndham--407-238-0777--Start at $70--www.wyndham.com

Celebration/Kissimmee Area
Celebration Hotel--888-499-3800--Ranges $135-$295--www.celebrationhotel.com
Howard Johnson Maingate W.--800-638-7829--$42 & up--www.orlandohojomaingate.com
Ramada Inn Resort Maingate--407-396-4466--Rates range from $49-$119
Holiday Inn Nikki Bird Resort--407-396-7300--Rates range from $60-125
La Quinta Lakeside--800-848-0801--www.laquintalakeside.com/orlando-hotel.htm
Holiday Inn Hotel/Suites Maingate E.--407-369-4488--$55-$225--www.familyfunhotel.com
Homewood Suites--888-697-8745--$70-$110--www.homewoodsuitesorlando.com
Clarion Hotel Maingate--800-568-3352--From $70-$110--www.clariondisney.com
Quality Suites Maingate East--407-396-8040--From $79-$210

International Drive Area
The Castle Doubletree--407-345-1511--Start around $80--www.doubletreecastle.com
Quality Inn International--800-825-7600--Start around $40--www.orlandoqualityinn.com
Quality Inn Plaza--800-999-8585--Start around $40--www.qualityinn-orlando.com
Rodeway Inn International--800-999-6327--Start at $33--www.rodewayinnorlando.com
Holiday Inn Express--800-365-6935--Start around $45--www.enjoyfloridahotels.com/holidayinnexpress
Hampton Inn Sandlake--407-363-7886--Start around $40
Residence Inn by Marriott--800-227-3978--Start $79--www.orlandoresinn.com/home.html
Staybridge Suites--800-866-4549--Start $74--www.lbvorlando.staybridge.com
Embassy Suites Orlando--407-352-1400--Start at $229--www.embassysuitesorlando.com

Chapter 12

When the Touring Gets Tough

The Tough Go Shopping!

Unique shopping opportunities abound at Walt Disney World—and not just venues for character souvenirs (though you'll certainly find plenty of those). While World Showcase in Epcot offers the most diversified and sophisticated shopping experience anywhere within Walt Disney World's forty-seven square miles, you'll find plenty of worthwhile treasures all over the property—from Disney martini glasses, to Mickey-embossed luggage, to dainty Disney pajamas for women and stylish golf shirts for men. "We spend tons of time shopping at Walt Disney World," says Jason. "My favorite shop is lo-

Steps to Convenient Disney Spending

If you're staying in a Disney or Downtown Disney resort hotel, Walt Disney World makes shopping about as convenient as it can get.

Don't want the responsibility of transporting your recently-acquired Disney treasures all the way back home? Fine. Just have them shipped via UPS or FedEx.

Or perhaps you'd rather keep your catches with you throughout your vacation, but you just don't feel like lugging them around the parks all day.

That's not a problem, either. Just ask the cast member who rings you up to send the package back to your resort. If you're making a purchase on the day of--or even the day before--your departure, this option is unavailable, since Disney couriers won't have enough time to make the delivery before you leave. (You *can* have them sent to the front of the park, though you must give couriers three hours to deliver them to the pick-up point.)

A great way to track your expenditures is to activate a room charge upon check-in (for guests of Disney-owned hotels only). Using cash, check or credit card, you can authorize charges to your room. Suddenly, that cute little Resort ID card becomes not only your room key but also your credit card and, if your admission medium is tied to your room, your passport to the World. Then, upon checkout, you'll be presented with an itemized bill reflecting your complete vacation spending--provided, of course, you've made all purchases on your ID card.

---

cated at the exit of Pirates of the Caribbean because it's my favorite ride. Lauralee prefers the World of Disney at Downtown Disney."

Insider's Tip: Though we'll reference specific merchandise in our shop descriptions, bear in mind that Disney shopping venues are dynamic retail enterprises. As such, stock changes frequently. Our intention is to give you an idea of the *kinds* of merchandise to be found in each shop, rather than an inventory of guaranteed discoveries. Quite simply, there's no guarantee that what's in a shop this afternoon will be there tonight. And that's no exaggeration.

Shopping at the Resort Hotels

At last count, Walt Disney World boasts twenty-three resort hotels. Within each, you'll find at least one souvenir shop which not only carries the typical character plushes, mugs, postcards, watches and shot glasses, but also resort-specific items, such as lapel pins, mugs, keychains and clothing with the requisite resort logo. Furthermore, many of the routine items — like band-aids, toothpaste, antacid tablets — that you may have forgotten can also be found here, though you'll probably have to ask the cast member at the checkout counter.

However, unless you're particularly drawn to a resort hotel because of its architectural design or sentimental value because of a previous stay, Aronda would never recommend traveling from resort to resort in search of shopping opportunities. The only unique items you're likely to find are those with embossed, stitched or engraved resort logos. Unless you're a serious collector of hotel logo items, the pay-off of resort-hop-

Establishing a Budget for Your Vacation

When trying to establish how much money to allot for your shopping excursions, a big issue is whether you're traveling with children. While adults can usually resist the inclination to go nuts over Disney merchandise, kids certainly cannot. Prices for gifts and souvenirs run a wide range. You can find Disney trinkets for as little as three or four dollars; tee-shirts cost about twenty dollars these days; nicer Disney clothing ranges from thirty-five to eighty dollars. Those popular leather jackets range from $295 to $495 (but they are gorgeous). Artwork by Disney or Disney-commissioned artists range from the hundreds to the thousands of dollars. In Josh's opinion, the prices Disney charges for the light sabers and other festive nighttime articles (which kids can't resist) are nothing short of exorbitant. He suggests going to a toy shop prior to your vacation to find something similar. At the very least, you'll probably want your children to understand that one's the limit.

"Moderate" Shopping

But only if you're shopping at the venues available at Disney's three moderate resort hotels:

CARIBBEAN BEACH
Calypso Straw Market
Calypso Trading Post

PORT ORLEANS
French Quarter
Jackson Square Gifts & Desires
Riverside
Fulton's General Store

CORONADO SPRINGS
Panchitos Gifts & Sundries

ping would never be worth the investment of time and energy such an endeavor would require. In fact, much of the merchandise found in resort shops can also be found in Marketplace shops located at Downtown Disney — a convenient one-stop shopping venue.

A caveat is in order here. Keep in mind that it's primarily in the Deluxe resorts that you'll find shops whose stock does *not* exclusively include items with Mickey Mouse silhouettes, Duck bills and Goofy ears. Within these shops, you can often find clothing and accessories by world-renowned designers, but the prices will almost always be a few dollars higher than in your local shopping mall. Of course, if you stumble on a find you can't get anywhere else — and that's certainly a possibility — you should scoop it up. Indulge yourself, if you can; after all, you're on vacation.

Let's start our shopping expedition by boarding the monorail for a circuit around the Magic Kingdom resorts. In Disney's Contemporary Resort, you'll find **Contemporary Man** and **Contemporary Woman** — both fairly upscale establishments with limited clothing and accessories for the style-conscious guy or gal. Other Contemporary Resort shops — **Fantasia**, **Concourse Sundries and Spirits**, and **Bay View Gifts** — offer magazines and books — if you have time for a vacation read — as well as toys, collectibles, snow globes, liquor and other gifts. In Aronda's opinion, the logo items — like tee-shirts, collectors' plates, keychains and so forth — are among Disney's most appealing resort products.

Down the monorail line a bit, take the Polynesian Resort stop and enjoy a different kind of shopping experience. **Trader Jack's** will beckon you inside with some unique South Seas-themed clothing, gifts and art. The colors are boldly unique here—in fact, out of all the Deluxe resorts, many guests consider the offerings here on the "edgy" side. Other shops entice with grass skirts, leis, gifts with a native touch, newspapers and magazines, and lots of pins. **Robinson Crusoe's** sells resort wear for men; **Polynesian Princess** offers brightly-colored resort fashion for women. You'll also find the amazing marine artistry of **Wyland Galleries** (another Wyland gallery is located at Disney's BoardWalk).

Next stop along the monorail route is Disney's Grand Floridian Resort & Spa, where **M. Mouse Mercantile** offers upscale character stock. Polo shirts, socks with Disney logos and Disney sunglasses are often found here—along with toys, watches and occasional imprinted office supplies. At **Bally**, Disney is only a secondary concern. Here, you'll find a wide selection of high-quality leather goods, with no sign of the Mouse, like women's purses, men's wallets and belts. You'll also find a nice selection of both men's and women's shoes—but never at a bargain. Although small, **Commander Porter's** offers a respectable stock of

Shopping "Values"

We're not talking shopping ethics here--but the Value resort hotels offer their own unique shopping opportunities.

ALL-STAR MOVIES
Donald's Double Feature
(located at Cinema Hall)

ALL-STAR SPORTS
Sport Goofy's Gifts & Sundries
(located at Stadium Hall)

ALL-STAR MUSIC
Maestro Mickey's
(located at Melody Hall)

POP CENTURY
Everything Pop
(located at Classic Hall)

men's clothing and accessories, as well as fragrances. Conversely, **Summer Lace** is a hot spot for women's apparel and accessories. **Sandy Cove**, located close to the Grand Floridian Café, looks at first glance like a typical souvenir shop—until you notice that the same Royal Albert tea service you enjoyed during High Tea at the Garden View Lounge is sold here. You'll also find scented candles, fragrant soaps and gourmet snacks.

At this point during your shopping spree, you must leave the monorail, and board a bus or boat for the short trip to Disney's Wilderness Lodge. At the **Wilderness Lodge Mercantile**, you'll find clothing with the Wilderness Lodge logo emblazoned in conspicuous places. In fact, this resort is one of the most popular spots for "logo merchandise shoppers." Because of the calming colors and the cute images of the Lodge logos, it's hard for the shop to maintain its stock of shirts with the resort logo embroidered on the breast. Other notable finds are coonskin hats—including adult sizes—Walt Disney World-exclusive toys, and pullover jackets with subtle Disney themes. This shop, with its cozy fireplace and plank floor, is a wonderful place to browse.

Now, take a boat to the Transportation and Ticket Center, where you'll either hop the Epcot monorail, or catch a bus, for a trip to the Epcot resorts. (If you take the monorail, you'll have to walk through the park to make it to the resorts; the bus is probably quicker and certainly less tiring.) Close to Epcot, treat yourself to a visit to the Walt Disney World Swan, where you'll find **Disney Cabanas**, a unique store featuring both men's and women's fashions. Across the way, at the Walt Disney World Dolphin, **Brittany's Jewels** sports a large selection of Cartier and other brand-name watches—the perfect place to spend a fortune and impress your friends. Before you leave this resort hotel, make sure you indulge your sweet tooth with some wonderful chocolates from **Indulgences**. Even a wide variety of salt water taffy flavors is available.

As much as Disney press touts Disney's BoardWalk area as a shopping and entertainment district, you'll find far more entertainment than shopping opportunities—though shopping isn't shabby, either! A cute little shop, **Character Carnival** offers little that's particularly unique—mostly the typical Disney character merchandise and other commonly found souvenirs. You may also purchase Pal Mickey here. However, **Thimbles and Threads** will provide thirty minutes or so of stimulating browsing for those interested in men's and women's apparel—including shirts, blouses, socks, golf attire, pajamas, and more. **Wyland Galleries**, also located at Disney's Polynesian Resort, is a feast for the eyes! The prices are out-of-this-world—but so is the art. This unique marine and environmental art will delight and inspire; playful dolphins and other marine life are wonderful tributes to the ocean. Even if you can't afford to make a purchase, you owe it to yourself to see these superbly unique pieces of art, with their vibrant shades of blues, grays and greens. You can peek inside the Wyland Galleries at the Polynesian Resort on this chapter's opening page (245).

At Disney's Yacht Club, **Fittings & Fairings Clothes & Notions** offers nautical fashions and character merchandise, along with jewelry, groceries and sundries. At Disney's Beach Club, **Atlantic Wear and Wardrobe Emporium** features similar items, but with a beach theme. You'll also find numerous Disney plush, and resort attire for adults. Aronda reports seeing a tee-shirt, featuring Jessica Rabbit, and a *double entendre* about surfboards ("Making Them Big Since 1950").

Next, you'll travel to Disney's newest Deluxe resort, Disney's Animal Kingdom Lodge, where you'll find temptations such as Africa-themed gifts and high-quality clothing with Disney's Animal Kingdom Lodge logo—a colorful, intricate pattern—at the **Zawadi Marketplace**, the only shop at the Lodge. You'll find African masks, pottery and wood-carved animals—as well as painted sculptures executed in this five thousand-square-foot store by the artist himself. Among the shop's treasures are beaded gourds, hand-carved chess sets, Zulu baskets and masks. You owe it to yourself to swing in for a look at this big, beautiful store.

TREASURES AT DOWNTOWN DISNEY

The next stop on your shopping expedition? Downtown Disney, a shopping and entertainment district you simply cannot miss. In fact, Downtown Disney can be considered Disney's shopping and clubbing "theme park."

Downtown Disney is divided into three sections: the Marketplace (a shopper's paradise), Pleasure Island (here, there's more drinking and dancing to be done than shopping), and West Side (a nice blend of entertainment, shopping and dining). The Marketplace offers the most voluminous shopping opportunities. The stores here are not to be missed, even if you're more into window-shopping than actually purchasing. But be forewarned. Here, more than anywhere else at the Resort, you're likely to succumb to Disney's incessant messages to spend, spend, spend!

Marketplace Shops

The Art of Disney is a spectacular store, filled with animation cels, figurines representing important Disney milestones, special commissioned art, snow globes and statues of Disney characters, as well as other artistic items with Disney themes—a delight for any Disneyana collector. You'll also find crystal—including Waterford brand with Mouse ears crafted into the design—as well as artistic household items like lamps, chairs and tables. Of late, Uncle Walt himself has been appearing on posters and canvasses with increasing frequency.

Disney's Wonderful World of Memories offers a collection of Walt Disney World-branded scrapbook supplies, including albums, pre-packaged kits, adhesive tape, pens, glue sticks, scissors and a wide assortment of Disney stickers. Also available are Disney books, stationery, pens and postcards, plus several stations where guests can create scrapbook pages and postcards.

Disney at Home is devoted exclusively to more practical

home furnishings ("practical" being a relative term), including a Mickey Mouse armchair that, once you sample its comfort, will beg to go home with you (but it costs about a grand — ottoman sold separately!). More affordable items include Disney towels, bed linens, soaps and candles, lamps, and fixtures with Disney themes, and bathroom accessories.

Disney's Days of Christmas is a year-round Christmas decoration shop with Disney characters and icons formatted into tree ornaments and other decorations. That brisk business keeps this shop — which Ed calls "just plain fun" — open all year round attests to the immense appeal Disney products have to the Christmas season. This establishment places guests beneath an oversized Christmas tree, while Disney songs and Christmas carols play on the store's soundtrack. To put you in the Christmas spirit, the aromas of pine, rosemary and cinnamon fill the air. This shop is the best place to purchase the popular Santa's red hat adorned with Mickey Mouse ears. "I love the Days of Christmas," confesses Dania. "It always gets

Legal Tender at WDW

If you're wondering what methods of payment Walt Disney World accepts, remember that Disney hasn't become a successful diversion by restricting guest choices in forking over the dough! Good old American dollars are certainly fine with the Mouse, but so are Disney Dollars (mucho fun to spend; you can purchase them at all Guest Relations), and personal checks--as long as your name and address are preprinted on the check front and match the one on your driver's license, state-issued ID, active military ID, or passport. If you find currency or checks too tedious, Disney accepts the following plastic: American Express, VISA, MasterCard, Discover Card, Carte Blanche, and Diner's Club. Spending another country's currency? Not to worry. The Mouse knows how to handle that, too. However, you must visit Guest Relations to have your currency converted into U.S. dollars.

Do You Need Another Outlet?

If you want to save a bundle on souvenirs, why not take a drive over to the three Disney outlet stores? The trips require tearing yourself away from the Mouse for awhile, but you may find a few trinkets at prices that will put even more magic into your vacation. However, shopping at these stores is often "hit-or-miss"; sometimes the stock, though always plentiful, may offer little that floats your boat. We suggest shopping the outlets first before spending a bundle in the gift shops on property. You never know when you may hit upon the same or similar items that are sold in the parks. "I love Character Premiere," says Sue. "I can't justify paying full price for anything since I'm there so often."

Orlando Premium Outlet Mall
DISNEY'S CHARACTER PREMIERE
8300 Vineland--407-238-7787
(Leaving WDW Resort on I-4, take Exit 68 into Mall area.)

Belz Factory Outlet Mall
THE CHARACTER PREMIERE
THE CHARACTER WAREHOUSE
Both stores located on International Drive. For more info, call 407-345-5285. (Leaving WDW on I-4, take Exit 30-A. At the second traffic light, which is International Drive, turn left, then go to end of street. You can't miss this outlet mall.)

me in the Christmas mood. Besides, I love the smells in there."

In **Basin**, you'll find natural bath and skin care products in a beautifully rustic setting across from the World of Disney. The shop's interior evokes the feel of a nineteenth century market where guests can browse among pin bins and metal tubs filled with fragrant soaps and lotions, or watch soap being cut by the pound from all-natural blocks.

Pooh Corner will touch every bear-lover's heart just enough to make him or her reach for the wallet. The shop's forest atmosphere enhances your shopping experience for kids' and adults' apparel, toys, accessories and decorative gifts.

At **Studio M**, you're invited to queue up for a photo-op with your favorite Mouse. If you're traveling with your family, spouse or significant other, this is a great way to have a professional photograph taken — without the tousled appearance that

CHAPTER 12 DISNEY SHOPPING 255

Need to relax, but can't afford a massage in one of Disney's great spas? Then take a trip to Basin and purchase a Bath Bomb or two. Soon, you'll transform your bathtub into heaven.

often occurs in photos taken in the parks. Photo package options vary widely in type and price.

Team Mickey's Athletic Club is a spacious shop, filled with athletic socks, jerseys, gym bags, and balls of all varieties imprinted with famous Disney characters. You can usually find Goofy baseball bats, water bottles and sports attire. Nike and ESPN are other prominent brands carried in this spacious shop.

Once Upon a Toy will appeal to the fun-loving adult and the eager child alike, since much of its stock is put on display for shoppers to enjoy before purchasing. The shop's enticing entrance sports giant Tinker Toys and Disney movie characters. Inside, you'll find modern as well as "classic" toys—such as GI Joe, Tinker Toys, Lincoln Logs, and lots, lots more. (So even if your son or daughter

can't be pleased, you're sure to be by the nostalgia.) You'll also delight in the detailed models of various Walt Disney World attractions and landmarks. The castle in the rear of the store offers the opportunity to purchase dolls and costumes of Disney's most famous princesses.

Have you developed a fetish for those cute Disney pins yet? Well, join the club! In fact, you can often encounter other pin collectors at **Disney Pin Traders**, a small (but fully stocked) shop with all the pins and accoutrements you could possibly imagine. You can even choose pin components allowing you to design and produce your own unique pin.

Don't dare bypass the crème de la crème of all Disney shopping venues — the **World of Disney**. This store has twelve rooms filled with merchandise, from pet gifts to snacks to clothing of all sorts — even luggage sporting a variety of Disney designs. One enclave overflows with nothing but toys; another is filled with various collectibles; and yet another has jewelry and enough Disney watches to allow a guest to wear a different design each day of the year. Clothing for men, women and children is available right here, with a wide variety of Disney-themed logos. This store also offers character-themed automobile accessories, including black fuzzy dice with white Mickey Mouse heads imprinted on them. If you don't find the right item for yourself — or for friends back home — in any of the Disney parks, chances are good that you'll find something at the World of Disney that will tickle your fancy. However, you won't be able to find park attraction-specific merchandise here; these items must be purchased in the parks where specific rides, shows and attractions are located. In other words, if you forget to purchase a Twilight Zone Tower of Terror hotel towel, you'll have to return to Disney-MGM Studios to find one. World of Disney is Lindsey and Chuck's favorite store. "We could literally spend hours there! There are several different rooms, each with a different theme, such as kitchen, jewelry, children and more. We love to take our time going from room to room and picking out the different souvenirs we want to take home."

Pleasure Island Shops

Though Pleasure Island caters primarily to the nightclub crowd, you'll find a few opportunities to spend your hard-earned dollars at a number of unique shops. *[Please note: Pleasure Island does not open until 7:00 p.m. While you may shop without admission, you may not enter any of the nightclubs unless you pay Pleasure Island's ticket price.]*

Suspended Animation features cels from your favorite Disney animated classics, along with commissioned ceramics. Stationery, music boxes and crystal collectibles are also available.

Changing Attitudes is a hip clothing store for both men and women, with lots of fashionable accessories, including backpacks, belts and jewelry. Stylish leather fashions are often available.

Reel Finds focuses on former possessions of your favorite celebrities—and counts on the proposition that you'll pay handsomely for the "hand-me-downs" of the famous. Examples of past items include the shirt Luke Perry wore in *8 Seconds*, a pair of Elizabeth Taylor's shoes, and signed Lauren Bacall photos.

The official Disney shop on Pleasure Island, **DTV** offers the largest selection of baseball caps around. Casual Disney fashions are available, including embroidered T-shirts, socks, watches, jewelry, and silk boxers. Disney plush and gadgets are offered for sale, too. You'll find something for everyone — young and old!

West Side Shopping

Downtown Disney West Side offers shopping venues you won't find anywhere else on property—and chances are good you won't find most of these shops back home, either.

At **Celebrity Eyeworks Studio**, check out the cool glasses

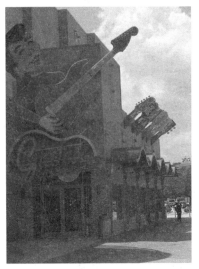

on display—reading glasses, costume glasses and sunglasses. You may not be in Hollywood, but with stylish shades purchased here, you'll certainly look (and feel) like a star.

The **Guitar Gallery** is a great place for the "strung-out" musician. You can purchase anything related to guitars—including the instruments themselves. Even if strumming someone softly with your song doesn't quite ring anyone's bell, the store's display of one-of-a-kind guitars is still worth a stop. The Gallery also offers accessories, books, guitar-themed clothing and learner packages.

In **Hoypoloi**, all sorts of decorative items good for the soul cry out for space in your place. Art work, rock gardens, incense and figurines for meditation purposes make this store a unique—and relaxing—stop. Though much of the merchandise is quite expensive, the shop is an interesting place to browse—though the temptation factor is extremely high.

Josh and Dann enjoyed shopping at **Starabilias** during a recent visit. From movie posters to movie props to autographed record albums to celebrity artwork, you'll find many delicious items begging you to take them home. Tributes to stars of film and stage appear here in the form of posters, sculptures, even limited edition collectibles. You may find an autographed record by Bette Midler, a John Waters' movie poster, a James Dean autograph, an Arnold Schwarzenegger poster, and the visages of the "glitter elite" all over the store. Expect stock

to change frequently.

Magic Masters provides magicians — and those who aspire to be magicians — not only a chance to purchase the accoutrements necessary to perform magic acts, but also an opportunity to learn from master magicians. Guests can also enter a recreation of Houdini's water torture cell for a spine-tingling "disappearance." Once you make a purchase, you're led into a secret chamber for special lessons to make your magic act work. That way, other gawking guests won't know the answer to the question: "How did she *do* that?"

And in the **Virgin Megastore**, you'll have a hard time deciding from among hundreds of CD's which ones are worthy of your investment. This store is the second largest Virgin music store on the planet. Upstairs, you'll find a generous selection of books, as well. Live concerts are occasionally performed here, and a relaxing café invites you to take a break from shopping. "I really enjoy digging through the Virgin Megastore," Ed admits. "There are none near me."

Sosa Family Cigars is a premium cigar store that features the art of hand-rolling cigars. An authentic, solid cedar humidor room keeps the cigars fresh for a primo smoking experience. You'll find cigars that aren't common back home, such as the Opus X and Fuente Hemingways. The shop will also ship all cigars except the Opus X.

Downtown Disney, like the theme parks, offers delivery to all Disney-owned resorts—as long as you're not checking out within twenty-four hours.

LET'S GO PARK-SHOPPING!

The theme parks offer plenty of shopping opportunities—if you can wrest yourself away from the attractions long enough to indulge. If you're staying in a Disney resort hotel, you can arrange to have your purchases delivered to your resort at no charge, thereby avoiding the hassle of lugging all those packages around with you. Or, if you're not staying on property (or checkout is the same or next day of your purchase date), you can have your treasures delivered to the front of the park where you can pick them up as you exit—as long as you allow at least three hours before you're ready to retrieve them. Either way, these convenient services are free to park guests; just ask the cast member who's ringing you up for the particulars.

Magic Kingdom

Arribas Brothers-sponsored **Crystal Arts** features a host of hand-blown crystal pieces that will knock your socks off!

The Main Street Emporium is one of the best shopping venues in the Magic Kingdom. If there's any complaint, it's that this shop offers the most easily accessible souvenirs Those looking for something "special" to take home may be somewhat disappointed.

You can even watch an artisan work his or her own special magic with a blow-torch. Your Main Street, U.S.A. shopping experience won't be complete without taking a gander at the hand-blown crystal Cinderella Castle, adjacent to the dining area inside the Main Street Bakery. This magnificent work of art can be yours for $25,000. If that price is a bit rich for your blood, a smaller Tinker Bell piece is available for only $975. At Walt Disney World, there's something for every budget—though at Crystal Arts, you may need to mortgage the farm!

Disney successfully attempts to heighten our fashion sense by triggering an insatiable craving for clothes which sport the images of Mickey, Goofy, Ariel, Donald, Cinderella, Grumpy—and the rest of the Disney gang. You can satisfy that craving at **Disney Clothiers**, also located on Main Street, U.S.A. More often than not, you'll be impressed by the quality of the merchandise at the Resort, and the clothing here is no exception. In fact, you may get tired of Mickey's or Minnie's smiling visage long before your shirt or hat wears out.

Main Street Emporium is a popular shopping venue which features an eclectic array of many things Disney. From battery-powered, plastic monorail sets and Main Street, U.S.A. Railroad train sets—which are coveted by kids, and also look adorable beneath your Disney-inspired Christmas tree—to Mickey, Minnie, Goofy and other character hats to postcards and tee shirts, you'll find them all here—and then some. Once the Magic Kingdom's new parade for the 100 Years of Magic Celebration—Share a Dream Come True—began, a number of collectible snow globes were added to the Emporium's stock, though that collection has dwindled of late. This shop is perhaps the Magic Kingdom's most popular store, and it remains open for about an hour past the park's official closing time. However, if you wait until the last minute to make your selection, you'll find yourself competing with dozens of other frazzled shoppers wanting to check out and return to their resorts.

Featured in several national magazines—including *Disney Magazine* and *Family Fun*—the **Harmony Barber Shop** offers the unique opportunity for a "new do." Located next to the Town Square Fire Station, you can get Michal, Maura or other stylists to coif your curls for less than twenty bucks. If you're feeling a little wild, ask them to sprinkle your locks with pixie dust. Lots of mousse keeps the dust in your hair! Barber-related gifts, such as razors, soap dishes and more, are also available.

Heading up Main Street, U.S.A. toward the park's famous icon, Cinderella Castle, you'll probably catch a whiff of one of the most delectable aromas anywhere in the World. This olfactory tease comes from the **Main Street Bakery**. While Disney actually pipes some of the aromas into the street—vanilla and cinnamon extracts are the popular sources for the enticing smells—you'll find the real thing inside. Candies, cookies, pastries—and more! The Bakery is a great place to grab a snack to nibble on during one of the Magic Kingdom's parades—or, on your way out of the park, to acquire a quick breakfast for the following morning (if you have a fridge in your room).

Before you leave Main Street, U.S.A., drop by **Uptown Jewelers**, where you'll find a wide array of silver, gold, crystal and porcelain pieces—including Disney park icons and characters. Even hand-painted, customized Disney watches may be purchased here—usually in the $250 range, and include the watch, artwork and case. Prices here range from very reasonable to "if-you-have-to-ask-you-can't-afford-it."

The various lands of the Magic Kingdom do not lack shopping opportunities, either—though Main Street, U.S.A. was specifically designed to lighten your wallet or purse. In Adventureland, you'll find several shops in the Aladdin-inspired market, Agrabah Bazaar. **Elephant Tales** features women's and men's clothing with a safari theme, along with wooden Kenyan handcrafts like letter openers, salad spoons and wind chimes. Even Aladdin-themed costumes are available for "dress-up" occasions. In **Island Supply**, a tropical surf shop, you'll find surfing attire and accessories. And in **Zanzibar Trading Company**, you'll find souvenirs related to *The Lion King*, *Jungle Book* and *Winnie the Pooh*. If Pirates of the Caribbean got you to thinking of romance and adventure on the high seas, perhaps you might like to drop by the **House of Treasure** in Caribbean Plaza. Memorabilia from Pirates of the Caribbean—as well as other, more generic pirate-related items—will beg to go home with you. You'll particularly like the high-quality rosin statues of pirates and parrots—most of which would look quite nice in your curio cabinet. Little kids can also find pirate costumes, plastic weapons and accessories—including eye patches, plastic swords and kerchiefs with skull-and-

Shopping at Celebration

If you'd like to check out Disney's classy town of Celebration, you'll notice it's a beautiful community with an intimate, unique shopping district. Celebration is easy to find. From I-4, take Exit 25A, then continue to the second traffic light, where you'll take a right onto Celebration Avenue. Just follow the signs. From Walt Disney World, take World Drive to 192 East (toward Kissimmee), then follow 192 to the second traffic light, where you'll turn right onto Celebration Avenue. You'll find a dozen or so shops and boutiques, like G.S. Winston, Fine Jewelers, Barnie's Tea & Coffee, and Lollipop Cottage. Downeast Orvis offers men's and women's clothing, fly-fishing equipment and housewares. Market Street Gallery is a designer heaven, with Boyds Bears, Disney Classics and creations from Armani and Swarovski. Many shoppers love Nottingham's, featuring old-world antiques and antique reproductions, furniture and a home design center.

crossbone images.

If you enjoyed the Country Bear Jamboree, you probably got a big kick out of the cuddly but off-key Big Al. Now you can take him home. **Big Al's** is a country store in Frontierland where you'll find the down-in-the-tooth bruin in an assortment of sizes. You can also purchase a Big Al nightshirt, making it even easier to snuggle up nightly with your very own bear.

In Liberty Square, if you're feeling patriotic after the Hall of Presidents' roll call, drop by the **Heritage House**, which has a nice selection of Early American reproductions, along with mugs, sweatshirts and kitchenware. Parents aiming to inspire a love of American history in their offspring may wish to invest in parchment copies of famous American documents, while pure nostalgia may drive you to purchase campaign

Since Stitch's Great Escape opened, this precocious little alien seems to be making appearances all over, including Tomorrowland gift shops. High fashion, after all, begins with a "Stitch."

buttons from earlier presidential elections.

Two favorite Magic Kingdom shops are located in Fantasyland. One is called **The King's Gallery**, and features "knightwear" — yes, the kind of garments knights might wear — and other collectible items (like real swords) reminiscent of the Medieval Period. You'll find some cool stuff for the next costume ball — and little girls will find beautiful princess gowns, tiaras, and even Cinderella's glass slippers. **Sir Mickey's** carries a variety of souvenirs — many of which can be found at other shops throughout the Resort — but guests speak fondly of the jackets made of leather, cotton and denim. You'll also find a variety of logo tumblers, tee-shirts and sweatshirts. The official shop of Mickey's PhilharMagic, **Fantasy Faire** features many plush Mickeys and Donalds, along with pins, tee-shirts and more. Be sure to notice the ceiling display with Donald trapped in a tuba. You can even purchase a plush Mickey dressed as "the maestro."

In Tomorrowland, the only shop where you'll find a wide selection of Stitch's Great Escape merchandise is called **Merchant of Venus**. From tee-shirts, to plush, to picture frames and keychains, Stitch has acquired his own brand. And many guests call **Mickey's Star Traders**, also in Tomorrowland, one of the Magic Kingdom's best shops because of the wide and varied selections found there. Unfortunately, because of its slightly out-of-the-way location, this shop is often overlooked. Just recently, Disney opened a shop, **Buzz Imaging**, located at the exit of Buzz Lightyear's Space Ranger Spin, where you can purchase a photograph of your experience in the attraction.

Epcot

Aronda and other Memories Team members are fully convinced that Epcot offers the best and most diverse *adult* shopping experience at Walt Disney World. In fact, some people travel periodically to Epcot just to indulge in a day or two of shopping and dining. They seldom linger long in Future World, however, because much of what you can find there is also available in the other parks, or at Downtown Disney Marketplace. However, **Mouse Gear** is a significant exception. It's a huge store in Future World, located close to the Fountain of Nations, featuring some unique Disney items and gifts, from toys to clothing to kitchenware to jewelry; it's definitely worth a visit. Susan and John like Mouse Gear because "of the way it's set up and the theming. It also seems to have a really good selection of adult items."

Just behind and to the right of Spaceship Earth is **The Art of Disney Epcot Gallery**, very similar to The Art of Disney at Downtown Disney Marketplace, and the recent Art of Disney annex in Disney's Animal Kingdom. However, what distinguishes the Epcot Gallery from the other Art of Disney locations is the frequency with which Disney artists make appearances and the expansive array of collectibles. If you're into pin-collecting, ask during your visit if any limited edition lapel pins are available. Occasionally, Disney produces a custom piece exclusively for The Art of Disney shops. (**Important Note**: Disney recently closed the Art of Disney shop in the Magic Kingdom, turning the space into Package Pick-Up.)

Once your flight to Mars is complete on Mission: SPACE, you'll exit through **Mission: SPACE Cargo Bay**, where you'll find cell phone carriers, a variety of shirts, books and videos on space exploration, backpacks, space food, pins, and even a Mission: SPACE cookie jar. Look for Hidden Mickeys as you exit the shop.

The place to find the most unique shopping experiences is World Showcase, which comprises the back half of the 300-acre park, located around World Showcase Lagoon. Take some time to wander through each World Showcase pavilion; the treasures you'll find will make your visit all the more exciting. **Important Note**: *Items specified in the shop descriptions are meant to be representative of the types of merchandise you'll find, since the shops in World Showcase change stock occasionally.*

In Canada, be sure to drop by **Northwest Mercantile**, where you'll find clothes sporting the subtle designs of the Northwest region of Canada—which means lots of attractive plaids as well as hats and shirts in a spectrum of soothing earth tones. You'll also discover hand-carved totem poles of various sizes and prices, along with maple syrup from our neighbors to the north. If your kids want coonskin hats, you'll find a stand selling them just before you reach the steps leading into the pavilion. At **La Boutique des Provinces**, Linda Edgington decoupage, pewter and more entice the serious shopper.

Moving into the United Kingdom, you'll find yourself victimized by shopping overchoice! Among the cornucopia of shops is **The Toy Soldier**, from which you may purchase toy soldiers, among many other toys imported from Great Britain, including several games involving popular British animated characters, and Winnie the Pooh items. The **Crown and Crest** features English dart boards, glasses, limited-edition chess sets, glasses that serve yards of beer (similar to those found in the Rose and Crown Restaurant and Pub), and coin and stamp sets. **The Sportsman Shoppe** offers clothing and accessories evocative of British events. Wimbledon tennis garb, gold items from Scotland's Royal and Ancient Golf Club and Saint Andres and rugby shirts are available. **The Queen's Table**, with its displays of several table settings featuring exquisite china, will show you how to serve tea, or a meal fit for royalty. The elegant Adams Room provides a lovely background for perfumes, soaps and other sweet-smelling items. **The Magic of Wales** is a small shop featuring pottery, jewelry and handcrafted gifts from Wales. **The Tea Caddy** not only offers a number of British teas for purchase, but also sweet accompaniments, like shortbreads and assorted candies. You'll also find elegant teacups and saucers, along with teapots and tea service accoutrements, crafted by famous artisans who've been "in the business" for many, many years.

France features **Plume Et Palette**, a shop which offers wares such as clothing and art, unique decorative cards, and Eiffel Tower statuettes of varying height and intricacy. **Gallerie des Halles** stocks French fragrances, like Guerlain perfumes, and soaps. Want to give your home a bit of a Parisian flavor? Then you might consider purchasing facsimiles of street signs and posters of famous Parisian landmarks. If you've had enough shopping for awhile, you're very close to a favorite place to take a break. At **La Maison du Vin**, you can sample a glass (or even better, several glasses) of French wine — and even purchase a bottle to take back to your room (prices range from about nine dollars to $290 per bottle). And at **La Patisserie**, you can snag a French pastry, then enjoy your snacks while sitting at a sidewalk table, watching the people pass by.

In Morocco, you'll find exquisite rugs — quite the accent pieces for an elegantly-appointed home — in **Casablanca Carpets**. Prayer rugs and throw pillows are also available. **Brass Bazaar** has an incredible collection of brass and glassware, including vials for rose water, bottles of which you can even purchase in the store. (Josh brought a bottle of it to the counter to

In France, even the window display entices you to sample fine French wines. The boulevard along which several shops are located will make you feel as though this pavilion is the real thing.

ask if they had any in the fridge—he thought it was a beverage! The cast member informed him that, as a sign of welcome into one's home, a Moroccan citizen pours a small amount of rose water onto the palms of a guest—a tradition she then demonstrated.) **Tangier Traders** will set you up with a stylish fez, woven belts, leather sandals, and other traditional Moroccan clothing and accessories.

Next stop? Japan, a country you simply cannot leave without visiting the newly-refurbished **Mitsukoshi Department Store**. Here, you'll find traditional Japanese women's clothing—but surprisingly, little or no men's clothing here. If you're into the bonsai scene, you can purchase both the plants and accessories—like tools, planters and books on the hobby. Children will enjoy that part of the store where the candy and other treats are located—including green tea-flavored candies and snacks con-sisting of soft milk chocolate-filled biscuits. Don't let the green pea snacks turn you off; they're actually quite tasty, particularly with beer. Of course, no Japanese shopping experience would be complete without a collection of artwork, decorative fans and origami—which are plentiful in this wonderful shop. Newly-added is a counter where you can sample saki, and if you decide you like, you can buy!

In the America pavilion, you'll enjoy stepping into **Heritage Manor**, which offers a small but inspiring selection of Americana. For example, you'll find a Mickey Mouse afghan throw in patriotic colors, pewter busts of various Presidents, and a selection of American history books.

The shops in Italy are ostentatiously up-scale; in fact, you'll feel as though you should tip-toe through them—and by all means, keep a sharp eye on the little ones. (A broken porcelain product here could mean quite the sacrifice from the piggy bank back home.) In **Il Cristallo**, the Guiseppe

Armani porcelain figurines will leave you gasping — they are *that* impressively intricate. Some of the more notable pieces include Disney classics, animal sculptures, and figures from the Jazz Age. Unfortunately, Aronda's recent visit revealed a curtailment of stock. Once you finally tear yourself away from this shop, don't leave Italy before you grab a snack from **La Bottega Italiana**, which offers pastries and other desserts, and **Delizie Italiane**, featuring great Italian chocolates and even wine-tasting opportunities.

In Germany, you'll find **Das Kaufhaus**, with limited edition steins and glassware, and **Volkskunst**, a showplace for German timepieces, including the famous cuckoo clock. **Der Teddybar** is a glorious toy shop with stuffed lambs and dolls wearing folk dresses. Be sure to have a look at the Steiff bears, even if you don't buy; you can even have a doll created to your personal specifications. For the wine connoisseur, **Weinkeller** offers 250 varieties of German wine (most of which are of the white variety). The **Glas und Porzellan** shop, in the Promenade area, features glass and porcelain items by Goebel, who makes I. M. Hummel figurines. A Goebel artist is almost always on duty to demonstrate the Hummel creative process.

The imposing China pavilion houses wonderful treasures in **Yong Feng Shangdian**. The shop offers a myriad mix of high-end Chinese imports, ranging from clothing to slippers, ancient Mahjong games to jade rings (occasionally) for both men and women. Even ornately decorated furniture, like desks and armoires, can be purchased — for quite the handsome sum. Jade sculptures, which are hard to resist, abound here, as do many styles of decorative pill boxes. Books about meditation and Eastern religions may also be found here.

In Norway, don't pass up **The Puffin's Roost**, which not only offers authentic Norwegian clothing, sweets, scents and gifts, but also the famous Ny-Form trolls, originated in 1964 by Norwegian sculptor Trygve Torgersen. These little fellows are hard to find in the United States, but their affectionate faces will tempt you to start a collection. If you're traveling with children, be sure to take their photo with the five-foot-tall troll in the center of the store. Toward the back of the store, you'll find winter parkas from the famous designer, Helly Hansen, among other cold-weather clothing items.

The last stop in World Showcase is Mexico. Disney's artistry in creating this Mexican shopping plaza beneath the stars is unbelievable. It's called **Plaza de los Amigos**—and you'll be reluctant to leave, even after you've made your purchases. Here, you'll experience "clothes encounters" for both men and women, piñatas, crystalware, art sculptures and figurines, toys and household goods. That you can find gifts for as little or as much as your budget will allow makes this shop all the more enticing.

Disney-MGM Studios

In Disney's nostalgic but delightfully frenetic tribute to Hollywood, you'll find some unique shops, most of which are flavored with the images and idiosyncrasies of the entertainment industry. More often than not, shopping itself becomes something of an attraction because of the eye-popping window displays, props that are part of the décor and the occasional Streetmosphere character who saunters in to strike up a conversation with you.

On Hollywood Boulevard, don't pass up **Celebrity 5 & 10**, which offers a wide array of Disney souvenirs, toys and confections—as well as personalized "Guest of Honor" nametags which, shaped like the official cast member badges, invite greater camaraderie with cast members and fellow guests. You'll also find a respectable stock of tee-shirts and assorted hats, as well as some attraction-specific items.

Also on Hollywood Boulevard, you'll find **Cover Story**. If you had your photo taken by a roving park photographer (a way to ensure a picture with everyone present), you'll pick it up here. These photographers are easy to spot; usually, they're wearing the traditional "Press" hats.

Keystone Clothiers offers men's clothing, watches and other accessories. Dress shirts with Disney insignias and polo shirts are frequently available. Women aren't left out, either. Blouses, both with and sans sleeves, along with pajamas and jewelry are stocked here. A variety of children's clothes adorns this shop, as well.

Just inside the park's entrance, and to your immediate left is **Sid Cahuenga's One of a Kind**, a movie collector's "junque" shop. Though Sid's stock frequently fluctuates depending on guest purchasing patterns and celebrity finds, you may find clothing someone dug out of Cher's yard sale bin ranging in price from $175 - $400. For $375, you can purchase a framed photo of film director Busby Berkeley (film credits include *The Gang's All Here*, *Dames*, *Babes on Broadway* and *Babes in Arms*), with a personal note to a friend thrown in for good measure. You'll also find movie memorabilia galore, letters actually penned by movie and television celebrities, and hundreds of vintage movie posters. Dann particularly liked the framed photo, accompanied by a signed check, of Errol Flynn — but the price was a little prohibitive at $1,250.00. Each collectible comes with a certificate of authenticity.

On Sunset Boulevard — the street where Twilight Zone Tower of Terror and Rock 'n' Roller Coaster Starring Aerosmith are located, and in whose shops you can purchase photos taken of you actually experiencing the attractions — **Mouse About Town**, with its trademark sign featuring Mickey Mouse in a tux, is one of the few stores in any of the parks to sell men's clothing exclusively. You'll find golf shirts and other attire, as well as "day planners" and desk organizers with Disney logo inscribed. It's a very cool shop.

In **Sunset Club Couture**, limited edition Mickey Mouse wrist and pocket watches entice the timepiece collector. At certain times during the day, you can even request an artist-on-duty to draw your favorite Disney character for purchase — the closest you can come to commissioning a Disney art piece for yourself.

In **Planet Hollywood**, expect to find jackets, shirts and other souvenirs with the famous Planet Hollywood logo emblazoned appropriately — similar to the kind of merchandise you find in the restaurants. You will also find prop and costume displays from several hit movies. A couple of recent displays honored several horror movies, so be sensitive to children who may be frightened.

Be sure to stop by **The Beverly Sunset**, where you can be really "bad" with Disney's famous villains. During a recent trip, we found a tee-shirt honoring the Evil Queen in *Snow White and the Seven Dwarfs*. The inscription: "Wicked Queen Anger Management Group: Not Happy With the Person You See in the Mirror? Come See Us!"

On the periphery of the Animation Courtyard, you'll find the **Animation Gallery**, where Disney animation art is both displayed and sold. You'll find some true treasures here, so even if your shopping budget is a quart low, you'll enjoy having a look at some of the exquisite pieces on display. They range from animation cels to figurines in a variety of media, as well as lithographs, posters and paintings.

In the **Studio Store**, souvenir items and clothing with the Disney Studios logo emblazoned on them appear on the racks. These items are not always souvenirs for the Orlando park per se, but rather for the production facilities located in Burbank, California. Recently, some photo reproductions of historic Disney highlights were available, including several portraits of Walt Disney. However, stock changes frequently.

If you're a *Star Wars* fan, be sure to check out **Tatooine Traders**. (You won't have a choice after you disembark from the Star Tours ride, since the exit weaves its way right through the shop.) Darth Vader masks, light sabers, various models of *Star Wars'* spacecraft and characters, and other *Star Wars* memorabilia await you there. This shop becomes a collectors' haven during Star Wars Weekends.

The **Indiana Jones Adventure Outpost**—very popular with youngsters—offers a wide array of Indiana Jones clothing and souvenirs, including the archeologist's famous hat.

Stage One Company Store, located close to Jim Henson's Muppet*Vision 3-D, features all sorts of Muppet gifts, toys and clothing. Lately, Miss Piggy seems to be the actress-du-jour

At the newly-refurbished Animation Gallery, you'll find serious artwork featuring your favorite Disney characters.

among many theme park fans—an understandable phenomenon, considering her thinly-veiled rage against those who just won't appreciate her value!

The Writer's Stop is a great place for a mug o' Joe, snacks and over-the-counter medications. You'll also find a respectable stock of various books, including many Disney publications, and compact discs. Occasionally, authors appear for signings in this shop.

Disney's Animal Kingdom

Shopping opportunities aren't as plentiful here as in the other three parks, and the famous Disney characters are downplayed somewhat. Instead, even in the shops, animals are Disney's stars.

In Safari Village, **Island Mercantile** offers a wide array of tee-shirts and animal-themed plushes. You'll also find various confections and leather carrying cases and backpacks.

In Africa, be sure to stop by **Mombasa Marketplace/Ziwani Traders**, where you'll find a small selection of clothing, wind chimes, notepads with Disney character imprints, and books about animals. Pottery, masks and musical instruments are sometimes stocked, as well.

In Dinoland U.S.A., **Chester and Hester's Dinosaur Treasures** will delight anyone who has a passionate interest in reptiles, both current and extinct. Here, you'll discover more tee-shirts, a variety of plush, pens, die cast Time Rovers (models of the ride vehicles from the attraction, Dinosaur), realistic "stuffed" dinosaurs (they can't exactly be called "plush") that younger kids really love, and the ever-popular battery-powered Magic Kingdom Main Street Railroad train set and the Walt Disney World Monorail. Now you can even expand your monorail set with the models of Disney's Contemporary Resort, Spaceship Earth, Disney's Polynesian Resort and more. Be sure to take a look to the ceiling, where you'll see more merchandising "artifacts" and a suspended electric train.

In **Creature Comforts**, clothing for infants and young children take center stage, along with a variety of Disney plush and jewelry for little girls. You can also find dresses for the little princesses in your life, and collectible key chains.

Beastly Bazaar offers a unique Mickey Mouse glitter lamp and a disco light (if you can't leave that wonderful era behind). You'll also find Mickey Mouse alarm clocks, CD cases, men's shirts, underwear and swimwear — one of the few shops at Walt Disney World to cater quite so conscientiously to men's clothing needs.

A favorite Disney's Animal Kingdom shop is **Wonders of the Wild**, located on Discovery Island, with plenty of men's and women's clothing, decorative and melodic wind chimes, and even straw hats. Artistic, hand-carved wooden animals like giraffes, elephants, and rhinos will crave domestication at your house. Several polo shirts will make you reach for your wallet, as will a framed set of Disney's Animal Kingdom trading cards for two hundred bucks (the frame is glass, both front and back). Other offerings include bonsai plants, aromatherapy kits, massage kits, necklaces and bracelets.

Chapter 13

Give Me the Soup, the Salad, & the Soufflé

And Nobody Gets Hurt!
Disney Dining

When Dann first visited Walt Disney World in 1972 — the only park open then, just one year after the Resort's grand opening, was the Magic Kingdom — it was difficult to find a decent meal anywhere on property. After Michael Eisner took over as CEO in the early eighties, Disney's culinary world changed. Not only did the counter service eateries improve the quality and variety of their menus, additional full-service restaurants opened, with innovative, delectable fares. It was no longer necessary to leave Disney property in search of a decent restaurant after your day in the parks had ended. In fact, not only had Disney's food become tasty, much of it achieved excellence, as many food critics have attested.

And so have many guests. "Nearly every dining experience we have had at Walt Disney World has been excellent," says Nicole. "Almost without exception, the food has been good and the service exceptional. I really can't pick a favorite."

Most Memories Team members indicated—if not over-

You Can't Go Wrong with These Popular Picks!

While frolicking with Mickey, you'll most certainly work up an appetite. Here are several restaurants that guests have rated above-average in terms of service and food quality.

Cinderella's Royal Table--Serves all three meals. Characters are often present. Once Upon a Breakfast can be almost impossible to book. This restaurant serves some of the best food in the Magic Kingdom.
Le Cellier--Guests rave about this Epcot eatery's cheddar cheese soup, tasty steaks and broad variety. Its pretzel bread is heavenly.
50s Prime Time--In a festive, down-home atmosphere, this Disney-MGM Studios' restaurant serves great "comfort food," and adds an element of entertainment too. Your "relatives" are your servers!
California Grill--High atop Contemporary Resort, this restaurant is one of the most highly-respected of all Orlando's dining establishments. The Memories Team ranks it #1!
Spoodles--Relaxed but tasteful, this restaurant offers a fine view of the BoardWalk, while serving savory food with a Mediterranean flair.
Beaches n Cream--This Disney's Beach Club Resort restaurant boasts the best burgers in the world--and it's not just the cast members who say so! The atmosphere is casual and entertaining. If you have kids, they'll love it here.
Boma--One mighty buffet, this Animal Kingdom Lodge restaurant serves dishes with an African flair. Conservative palates, beware!
Kona--This Polynesian Resort's cozy restaurant serves up tasty, generous portions. To fully appreciate the desserts, take the tour!

whelming enthusiasm about Disney restaurants—a high degree of satisfaction with the Resort's culinary offerings.

And sometimes, the immense dining choices available to guests make a decision difficult. "Many of my Disney vacations are restaurant-driven," says Josh. "The only problem is, I have so many favorites that I never seen to have enough time to cover them all."

> **Priority Seating Tips**
>
> ○ Decide on several dining experiences before leaving home.
> ○ Call 1-407-WDW-DINE sixty days or less before your anticipated dining date. Indicate your preferred seating time.
> ○ Jot down your Priority Seating number in a safe place. **Aronda's Prep Pad** is a good, secure location.
> ○ Report to the designated restaurant's check-in desk five minutes prior to your seating time.
> ○ If you get hungry early, show up at the restaurant and ask to be seated prior to your scheduled Priority Seating.

In this section, you'll explore dining opportunities in the theme parks first, followed by a trip to Downtown Disney. Then, you'll conclude your culinary tour at Walt Disney World's various resort hotels. Aronda will not provide an exhaustive listing or review of Disney dining experiences. In fact, counter service restaurants are listed in a convenient chart, since they're easy to spot in the parks—and the fast-food quality is essentially the same across the board. If you wish to examine an even more comprehensive listing of Walt Disney World's restaurants, try logging on to Deb Wills' All Ears Net located at **www.AllEarsNet.com**. There, you'll find not only frequently-updated menus, but also current menu prices and reviews of various restaurants.

It's always a good idea to make arrangements prior to your departure for Priority Seating at the most popular table-service restaurants. (During non-peak seasons—like October and November, up until Thanksgiving, and December prior to the Christmas holidays—you can often make Priority Seating arrangements once you arrive. This approach lends a bit

Feeding the Kids!

If you had to pay the same prices for your children's meals as you do for your own, you'd have to have the budget of royalty. However, depending on how elegant the restaurant, kids' entrees range from four dollars to about ten bucks. Kids' menus at Walt Disney World seldom soar above fifteen dollars (and that's for a mini-filet mignon at one of the most expensive eateries on property). Keep in mind, though, that Disney designates children's menu prices for kids up to the age of 12, and discourages (if not forbids) adults from ordering from those menus.

---

more spontaneity to your vacation than planning the majority of your meals before leaving home. However, if you travel during Disney's busiest times, then most of your table-service dining experiences should be pre-arranged to avoid extended wait times.)

Priority Seating (PS) is the Disney version of reservations—and may be more effective. When you call for a Priority Seating time, be flexible, if at all possible. For example, Aronda has requested a one o'clock PS, only to have the cast member at Disney Dining counter with a 1:15 offer. Jot down the time upon which you've agreed, along with your PS number, then store the information safely away until your vacation. (**Aronda's Prep Pad** is a great way to keep this information handy!) And always remember that you can make your PS arrangements sixty days or less in advance of your trip; some restaurants will allow you to make arrangements even further in advance. More than likely, you'll not encounter a glitch in the system; Disney Dining is usually very efficient at maintaining a record of your PS. However, we suggest always carrying your PS number along with you when you report to the restaurant.

Here's how Priority Seating works. PS does not hold a table for you, as reservations typically do. Instead, when you report to the restaurant for your seating, you're guaranteed the next available table for the size of your party. This way, "walk-ups" — people who have not planned for their meals, but are taking a chance for a table — are not allowed to be seated ahead of you. And someone with a later Priority Seating time will have to wait until you've been accommodated before they are escorted to their table.

You can make Priority Seating arrangements by calling 1.407.WDW.DINE. But don't give up just because Disney Dining says a Priority Seating isn't available at the time you desire. Only a certain number of tables are released to PS inventory at any given time period, while the rest are designated for walk-ups. If you don't have a PS, inquire at the front desk of the restaurant you've chosen. Often, the establishment will be able to seat you after a reasonable wait.

<u>Important Note</u>: **Our average meal prices are determined by considering recent prices on each restaurant's menu, including beverage, appetizer or salad, entree, and dessert. Of course, you can control your per-meal price by skipping the appetizer or resisting the dessert temptation. And children's menu prices are always substantially lower than adults.**

Magic Kingdom's Royal Cuisines

While most of Cinderella Castle is off-limits to guests (including an unfinished apartment for the Walt Disney family which was never used, but now provides dressing room space for Disney performers), a meal at **Cinderella's Royal Table** offers an opportunity for a peek at the interior of this majestic structure. If you're interested in breakfast here — join the crowd. Everyone else is, too. **Once Upon a Breakfast** is the most difficult meal to book at Walt Disney World, so make sure you call as soon as possible. Disney imposes a ninety-day window on PS for this meal — which seems generous — but travelers have reported that if you don't call exactly three months preceding the day on which you wish to have breakfast with the

Magic Kingdom Counter Service Restaurants

El Pirata Y el Perico
Excellent tacos, taco salads (recommended)
Pecos Bill Cafe
Burgers, hot dogs
Aunt Polly's Dockside Inn
Ham-n-cheese sandwiches (open seasonally)
Columbia Harbor House
Fish, chicken, variety of sandwiches (recommended)
Pinocchio Village Haus
Burgers, turkey sandwiches (recommended)
Cosmic Ray's Starlight Cafe
Burgers, chicken, soup--all to the accompaniment of a musically-inclined jokester of a "Lounge Lizard"
Plaza Pavilion
Pizza, fried chicken
Casey's Corner
Hot dogs, fries, beverages

Royal Court (Cinderella, her Fairy Godmother, Peter Pan, Belle and Snow White), you may find the royal table already full. Start calling no later than 7:00 a.m. Eastern Time. Additionally, for breakfast only, your request must be accompanied by a ten-dollar deposit for each adult in your party, and a five-dollar deposit for each child. (Priority Seatings for most other dining experiences do not require an advance deposit.) Cinderella's Royal Table serves lunch and dinner, as well—both are popular and delicious, albeit a bit pricey. The experience begins with your being admitted to the Castle lobby, where Cinderella herself often makes an appearance on her royal throne for photo and autograph ops with the children in attendance. Then, once you hear: "A royal table for the [your surname here] family is ready," you ascend to the restaurant via a circular elevator or winding stone stairs. The restaurant is located on the second floor of the Castle. Some tables afford wonderful views of Fantasyland. If you're not starving, request a window table when you check in for your

CHAPTER 13 MAGIC KINGDOM DINING

meal, and express your willingness to wait; cast members will try to oblige (though keep in mind that it may not be possible to honor everyone's requests). Servers are costumed as members of Cinderella's royal court, and remain in character from the moment you're escorted to your table until you pay the cheque. Remember, the Magic Kingdom is a "dry kingdom," so you won't be able to order a cocktail or wine with your meal. The food quality here is excellent; lunch focuses more on comfort foods and sandwiches, while dinner offers creative approaches to seafood, chicken, beef and pork. Characters are less likely to be roaming the restaurant during lunch and dinner as they are during breakfast—though Cinderella does make appearances in the lobby throughout the day. Kids dine at Once Upon a Breakfast for about $11.99; adult price for the meal is $21.99. The average lunch price for adults is $25.00, while dinner hovers around $35.00 per plate. "During our last visit, Hurricane Jeanne paid us a visit," explain John and Lynda. "On the day of the hurricane, we were supposed to have an anniversary breakfast at Cinderella's Royal Table to celebrate our fifteenth anniversary. Of course, everything was closed that day. We were unable to reschedule another breakfast, so we decided to schedule dinner at the Castle instead. Our waiter, Jay, found out that it was our anniversary several days before, so he

The stained-glass windows in the lower third of the photo illuminate Cinderella's Royal Table.

sprinkled Mickey confetti on us and our table, along with getting us a set of anniversary champagne glasses. We were really surprised about this. He made our anniversary celebration — even though a few days late — extremely special. Jay was wonderful!"

While the **Crystal Palace** is a beautiful restaurant (see photo page 277) located between Main Street, U.S.A. and the entrance to Adventureland, its menu is less-than-inspired. The greatest appeal of this restaurant — and the characteristic that compels many parents to take their children for a dining experience here — is its Pooh-centricity! Several Pooh characters pop by your table to pose for pictures, shake your hand, give you a hug, or engage in a little pantomime repartee. To get your food, you report to "stations" and serve yourself such selections as flank steak, barbecue chicken, black beans and rice, and various salads; you can also construct your own sandwich with a variety of breads and cold cuts. As is true of most Disney restaurants, a children's menu is available, usually consisting of fries, chicken strips, fish sticks and macaroni and cheese. The quality of the food is uneven; you're likely to find some dishes to satisfy the palate — others will leave you disappointed. Still, if you — or your kids — are Winnie the Pooh fans, then you may wish to do breakfast (it's hard to botch breakfast) or lunch here, then try another table service restaurant for dinner. Breakfast is $17.99 for adults and $9.99 for kids; lunch is $18.99 for adults, $10.99 for kids; dinner is $22.99 for adults, $10.99 for kids.

Yet another character meal in the Magic Kingdom is located at **Liberty Tree Tavern**, in Liberty Square. At this lovely restaurant adorned with antique furniture, oak plank floors and pewter ware, Chip and Dale (they'll be offended if you can't tell them apart, so do your homework), along with Minnie, Goofy and Mickey, are likely to pay your dinner table a visit (no characters appear during lunch). The restaurant, rustic, with colonial theming, is long on atmosphere — but the food service is family style, Disney's nomenclature for an "all you care to eat" situation. The servers will keep piling on the food as long as you keep ordering, all for a reasonable price. You're served platters of turkey, flank steak and fish right at your table, along with several sides. Though the food is still a couple of notches better than that served at Crystal Palace, it's still not quite up to par with table service restaurants that have a more diverse menu. Average adult price for lunch, which is a la carte, is $23.05, while you can expect to pay about $4.99 for children. The Character Dinner rings in at $22.99 for adults, and $10.99 for children.

Located on the corner of Main Street, U.S.A. and a secondary walkway to Tomorrowland, the **Plaza Restaurant** specializes in light fare, like deli sandwiches, pastas and salads. Windows adorn this lovely establishment, so you're likely to have a great view of Main Street, U.S.A. or Cinderella Castle. Unfortunately, service is occasionally slow—snail's pace, actually. Still, the food is delicious. Lately, however, some guests have found service brisk and friendly—though Josh, a.k.a. Jethro Bodine, complains of small portions. Both lunch and dinner are served here, and the average price for a full-course meal hovers around $15.74.

Located next to Exposition Hall as you enter the Magic Kingdom is the park's only other table service restaurant—**Tony's Town Square Café**, hosted by Buitoni. Lunch and dinner menus differ dramatically. (Tony's once served breakfast, but was recently discontinued. However, participants in Grand Gatherings may opt for an exclusive breakfast at Tony's.) Dinner entrees range from chicken Florentine, spaghetti and homemade meatball (the meatball is the size of a baseball!), country penne and chicken Parmesan. Seafood dishes are also available. Lunch offerings include chicken Parmesan and turkey piccata. The theming here is

delightful. The restaurant's motif comes straight from *Lady and the Tramp* — remember the scene when Lady and Tramp shared a common plate of spaghetti? — with a fountain located in the main dining room to honor the two canine lovers. Window seats afford a wonderful view of Town Square, and if you dine during SpectroMagic, you'll have a limited view of the illuminated floats. If the weather is comfortable outside, ask for a patio seat for a particularly festive time. For a full-course meal, expect to pay around $25.00 for lunch, and $34.00 for dinner.

Insider's Tip: At meal times while touring the Magic Kingdom, it's easy to break away from the crowds to catch a monorail to Disney's Grand Floridian Resort & Spa, Disney's Polynesian Resort or Disney's Contemporary Resort — or a boat to Disney's Wilderness Lodge — to sample one of the many fine restaurants located in these Deluxe resort hotels. Meals here give you a nice break from the park — as well as a chance to order a cocktail, beer or glass of wine — and you can return to play after a relaxing dining experience. Be sure to have your hand stamped when you leave the park (not necessary for Annual Passholders).

Epcot's Tasty Adventures

Epcot strikes one as a sophisticated world's fair with diverse dining opportunities. The park grows beautifully festive after dark — though adults often find it more delightful than younger children. The numerous international restaurants turn World Showcase into an exquisite culinary adventure, whether you're enjoying international cuisines, sampling a wide variety of international wines or indulging in desserts from lands far away.

In Future World, you'll find mostly counter service restaurants — which, in Aronda's opinion, are often a notch above counter service found in the other parks. Two notable table service exceptions exist — **Coral Reef** (inside the Living Seas

Chapter 13 Epcot Dining 287

pavilion) and **Garden Grill** (inside The Land pavilion). **Coral Reef** provides a spectacular environment for a meal, with windows serving as portals into panoramic vistas of the attraction's aquarium tank. The décor is redolent of a spectacular reef with green and coral colors. Even if you aren't assigned a "window" seat, the other tables are situated on tiers, so you'll still have a great view of this setting. Fresh offerings abound for both seafood lovers and landlubbers. The Coral Reef, however, can be expensive. For adults, lunch averages about $26.00, while dinner weighs in at around $33.00 per meal.

Josh and Dann enjoy a meal at the Coral Reef Restaurant. Even those who dislike seafood will find entrees to enjoy.

The **Garden Grill** offers a family-style menu for both lunch and dinner (breakfast is no longer served) — which means that the same entrees are served at every table, in an "all-you-care-to-eat" fashion. Meals here feature the likes of Minnie, Mickey, Chip and Dale who drop by to regale you while you dine. (Though often pricey, character meals are the best way to obtain great photos of your kids with characters without having to endure annoying lines.) This restaurant is "revolutionary," since it actually revolves slowly while allowing peeks at a few of the sets of the Living With the Land attraction. The "country-style" meals — the menu frequently consists of grilled chicken, flank steak and fried catfish filets — are served in platters on lazy susans for all members of your party to share. (Fried chicken strips and fries are also included for the kids.) As many guests have found at most of Walt Disney World's restaurants utilizing this approach, the food is palatable, though nothing to set your taste buds ablaze. You have

Epcot Counter Service Restaurants

Budget stretched a bit tight, or you're in a hurry? These Counter Service eateries will help conserve both bucks and time.

Electric Umbrella--Innoventions Plaza
Burgers, pizza. Breakfast during limited hours.
Sunshine Season Food Fair--The Land
Barbecue, pasta, soups, baked goods, potatoes. Expect this "food court" to be remodeled and reconceptualized during 2005.
Yorkshire County Fish Shop--United Kingdom
Fish and chips, soda and beer
Boulangerie Patisserie--France
Quiche and a variety of pastries. Recommended!
Yakitori House--Japan
Beef, chicken, noodles and sushi
Tangierine Cafe--Morocco
Mediterranean chicken, beef and lamb. Recommended!
Liberty Inn--America
Burgers, hot dogs, fries, chili and chicken
Sommerfest--Germany
Bratwurst, soft pretzels, kraut. Recommended!
Lotus Blossom Cafe--China
Egg rolls, stir-fry chicken
Kringla Bakeri og Kafe--Norway
Pastries, sandwiches and beer. Recommended!

---

to decide whether the undivided attention of Disney characters is worth compromising the quality of a meal—though if you have kids, the answer may be a resounding "yes." The price is fixed for both lunch and dinner. Lunch is $20.99 for adults, and $10.99 for children. Dinner is $22.99 for adults, and $10.99 for children.

As you leave Future World and enter World Showcase on your culinary tour, proceed in a counterclockwise direction. Soon, you'll enter the Canada pavilion, where **Le Cellier Steakhouse** is located. The trek along a narrow path toward the restaurant, designed as an underground establishment—literally—builds anticipation for a unique dining experience. You won't be disappointed—though dinner prices are a notch steep, particularly if you add wine to your meal. Beef and buffalo steaks are the specialties here. By all means, try the cheddar cheese soup; many diehard Disney diners make PS arrangements at Le Cellier Steakhouse just to sample the soup and a glass of wine. "I always get the same thing—the cheese soup," says Sue. "With wonderful breadsticks, it's a full meal for me. If I'm not eating solo, I may share the kid's chocolate mousse dessert—it looks like a moose's head and is both adorable and delicious. If I'm solo, I'll usually order a nice glass of wine so the lunch check isn't a paltry $4.00! The servers have always been great, whether I'm there solo or as part of a party of ten people." Unless you take Sue's approach to dining, you can expect adult dinner lunch checks to ring in around $25.00; average dinner prices hover around $36.00.

In the United Kingdom pavilion, you'll find the lively **Rose and Crown Pub and Dining Room**, which offers "pub grub," including fish and chips, sandwiches, meat pies and fresh salmon. The fish is cod—a mild fish, encrusted with lightly-fried batter—served with fries and English peas. The tartar sauce is a wonderful complement for the fish—in Dann's opinion, better than malt vinegar. The décor here is beautiful, as well as the view, particularly if you sit on the terrace. From there, you can watch the Friendship water taxis sail across World Showcase Lagoon, as well as experience a panoramic view of most of the international pavilions. If you're lucky enough to score a late Priority Seating, you'll have one of the best viewing locations in Epcot for **IllumiNations: Reflections of Earth**. Prices are fairly reasonable here, with lunch averaging around $18.00, and dinner around $28.00. "I love the Rose and Crown," Ed enthuses, "although their menu is a bit too limited. I recently ate dinner there when they had a piano player/singer playing all kinds of great music. After I had finished, I went up to him and asked if he'd play something I could sing along with. When I suggested Simon & Garfunkel, he immediately launched into 'Bridge Over Troubled Water,' and we sang it together—loudly!"

After crossing the bridge into France and passing International Gateway, which leads to the Epcot resort hotels including Disney's BoardWalk, you'll find two of the most delightful restaurants in Epcot. **Les Chefs de France** is a wonderful restaurant with a wide variety of superlative French food and desserts. Indeed, very few Disney diners have substandard experiences here. The menu is nouvelle cuisine, with lighter sauces using much less cream and butter than in classic French cooking. Aronda has dined here several times, and has never been disappointed—except once, when the restaurant ran out of a favored dessert. The atmosphere is lively owing to the large number of diners who can be seated at any given time, and the restaurant boasts a magnificent view of the promenade around World Showcase with its plentiful windows. (Ask for a window seat if you have time to wait; the experience will be even more delightful.) Lunch at Les Chefs de France costs around $29.00, while dinner per adult can set you back over $40.00. The menu is designed by a team of three internationally acclaimed chefs—Paul Bocuse, Roger Vergé and Gaston Lenôtre—as is the menu in **Bistro de Paris**, one flight of stairs above Les Chefs de France. The offerings here are a bit more "robust" than in its sister restaurant downstairs. Expect appetizers such as triple beef and black truffles consommé baked in a puff pastry and entrees such as a double-cut white veal chop with roasted garlic cloves, potato puree and spinach to appear on your menu. Note that the entrance to Bistro de Paris is located in back of Les Chefs de France.

While Les Chefs de France is open for both lunch and dinner, Bistro de Paris is open only for dinner—and Priority Seating is highly recommended. Both are elegant, charming restaurants; you can't go wrong with either. Expect to pay over $50.00 per dinner at the Bistro.

A few steps from France, you'll enter Morocco, where **Restaurant Marrakesh** is located. Both lunch and dinner are served here, by servers in traditional Moroccan costumes. For entertainment, a musical ensemble and a female belly dancer make appearances on a stage close to the kitchen's entrance. The restaurant, featuring beautiful tilework and an atmosphere of airiness, is elegantly understated. Authentic Moroccan fare, including couscous (semolina pasta), is served here. Aronda enjoyed a wonderful lunch consisting of chicken, fresh vegetables and couscous. The spices this restaurant utilizes are pleasantly subdued. Belly-dancing by an attractive young woman is fun to watch; she often invites guests to dance with her. Because many guests are hesitant to experiment—too bad, really, since this restaurant provides a delightfully tasty dining experience—finding available seating "on the fly" is often easy here. Note that Restaurant Marrakesh is located at the far back of the Morocco pavilion. Moroccan cast members out on the promenade in front of the pavilion will be happy to answer questions about the restaurant, or show you the menu. If you can't decide on an entrée, ask your server for a small sample to help you make up your mind. Lunch costs, on average, $28.00, while dinner weighs in around $37.00.

In Japan, you'll find two restaurants upstairs, inside the complex known as Mitsukoshi. At **Tempura Kiku**, you'll enjoy bat-

The subtle fried delicacies of Tempura Kiku in Japan.

ter-dipped, deep-fried chicken, beef, seafood and fresh vegetables that are collectively known as tempura. The flavors are subtle, yet Aronda finds the tempura-prepared vegetables even more delightful than the chicken or shrimp. The atmosphere is quiet, and seating is available around a display kitchen. For lunch, adults can expect to pay around $23.00 per meal, while dinner prices average around $31.00. **Teppanyaki Dining Rooms** is composed of five rooms, similar to those popularized by the Benihana chain. Here, you'll get to watch chefs chop, season and stir-fry on 550-degree surfaces the meats and vegetables that will constitute your meal. Aronda had a marvelous lunch of chicken, bean sprouts and vegetables, with iced green tea to drink. The chef's expertise with the knife provides amusing entertainment, even as you grow impatient to sample the results of his efforts. Note that each table seats eight—which means smaller parties may be seated together. You may expect to pay around $26.00 for lunch, and $35.00 for dinner.

In Italy, one of World Showcase's most popular restaurants, **L'Originale Alfredo di Roma Ristorante** packs 'em in, both at lunch and at dinner. Inside this crowded, but elegantly appointed, restaurant, you'll revel in the incredibly realistic trompe l'oeil murals that adorn the walls. In fact, the artistry creates the illusion that the spacious restaurant is more imposing. Be sure to let your server know if someone in your party is celebrating a birthday; the "victim" will most likely be surprised by a shower of vociferous attention from a small Italian chorus. The pasta is made on the premises—in fact, you can even watch the process as you enter—and most of the servers hail from the country this fine restaurant represents. The house specialty is fettuccine Alfredo, though many other varieties of pasta dishes are also available, as well as other less familiar, but just as authentic, Italian fare. Desserts range from ricotta cheesecake to spumoni. Don't forget to ask about the wine selection; it's a great complement to your meal. A full-course lunch will cost you around $29.00, while a full-course dinner costs around $35.00.

CHAPTER 13 EPCOT DINING 293

At the **Biergarten** in Germany, every day brings a party—called Oktoberfest. In Aronda's opinion, this restaurant is World Showcase's best-kept secret—great food at a great price. Like Teppanyaki Dining Rooms in Japan, socialization is encouraged, since each table seats up to eight guests. Aronda found both the food and the atmosphere to be delightful. At lunch, a German trio entertains, while dinner entertainment is provided by yodelers and traditional Bavarian musicians. The meal is buffet-style, with traditional German food—like bratwurst, potato salad, sauerkraut, roast chicken and pork, beets, and lots more—and Beck's beer served in 33-ounce steins. Desserts are included in the price of the meals. Despite Disney's reputation for serving less-than-stellar buffets, the food here is  of much higher quality than other Disney buffet offerings. Add a few bucks more to the posted meal price if you intend to sample German beer. The lunch buffet is priced at $14.99 for adults, and $5.99 for children. Dinner is served for $19.99 for adults, and $7.99 for children.

For Aronda, the biggest culinary disappointment of World Showcase was the meal she had at **Nine Dragons** in China. The restaurant is beautiful and austere, and gorgeously appointed with teak furnishings. But the food, in her opinion, is bland, mediocre fare. She left the restaurant with a heavy feeling in her heart and stomach—her hunger satisfied, but her appetite for a great meal—NOT. However, other guests have recently reported positive dining experiences, so perhaps staff is working toward some permanent improvements, though the most typical feedback is that the meals are mediocre at best. Food is prepared in provincial Chinese cooking styles, including Mandarin, Cantonese, Hunan, Szechuan, and Kiangche, with entrees such as stir-fried chicken, peanuts and hot peppers, and Hong Kong-style sirloin. Price of lunch will trend toward $28.00, while dinner will cost you around $30.00.

Next stop? Norway — and the not-too-stuffy, but oh-so-tasty **Restaurant Akershus**. The menu, served buffet-style, ranks in quality right up there with Germany. While Aronda doesn't usually like Disney buffets, she found herself quite delighted with Akershus. The buffet offers several fish options, but as a diner not usually drawn to morsels of the sea, she *still* found plenty of delicacies to satisfy her. The breads, cheeses and potato salad were heavenly! Both lunch and dinner are served here, and the fare is satisfying but not overbearing. If you're up for a savory meal that won't weigh you down, you'd do well to consider Akershus. Keep in mind that you'll pay extra for dessert, since it's not included in the very reasonable buffet pricing. Now, you can also enjoy the **Princess Storybook Breakfast** at Restaurant Akershus. Between the hours of 8:30 and 11:30 a.m., you can savor an audience with Disney royalty, including Belle, Jasmine, Snow White, Princess Aurora and Mary Poppins. Mulan, Esmeralda and Pocahontas may also appear. Cinderella and Ariel have other breakfast gigs. The Princess Storybook Breakfast is served family-style, and both food and accessibility of characters have met with mixed reviews. Lunch is served at a fixed price of $13.99 for adults, and $5.99 for children. Dinner costs $18.99 for adults, and $7.99 for children. Costs for desserts range from $3.75 to $6.75. The Princess Storybook Breakfast costs $19.99 for adults, and for children, $9.99.

The final stop on your culinary globe-trot through World Showcase is Mexico, where the **San Angel Inn** serves up authentic Mexican entrees. Aronda feels this restaurant is tops in atmosphere and food quality — and it's the only restaurant in World Showcase where you overlook an attraction while you dine. Both lunch and dinner are served beneath the night sky, in the shadow of a smoking volcano, while the boats of El Rio del Tiempo pass by. If you're convinced that all Mexican food is hot and spicy, you'll find a pleasant surprise here. Many Mexican spices are understated, which allows the principal flavors of chicken, beef and fish to tantalize your palate. Dann particularly enjoys the *mole poblano*, a chicken simmered in sauce with a hint of chocolate, while Josh's more conservative palate is drawn to tacos, burritos and enchiladas—also prepared to perfection. Other tasty entrees include grilled tenderloin of beef served with chicken enchilada, guacamole and refried beans, and *plato de la frontera* (a generous sampling of beef tacos, chicken burrito, rice and beans). Chips and salsa are served before your meal. Unfortunately, servers are unreasonably slow in refilling beverages. During the hot afternoons, Aronda suggests ducking into San Angel Inn for lunch. It's like experiencing a premature nightfall as you enter this pavilion, leaving the other park guests behind in the sweltering heat as you disappear into the cool darkness. Lunch costs, on average, $24.00, while dinner will set you back around $34.00.

Disney-MGM Studios Makes Food Part of the Act

Though not quite the Epicurean center that Epcot has become since that park's opening in 1982, Disney-MGM Studios has five noteworthy table service restaurants that you may wish to make part of your Walt Disney World culinary adventure. Each one takes some component of the entertainment industry, then incorporates it as a part of your overall dining experience. The results are great meals enhanced by intriguing, often hilarious entertainment.

Inside the **Hollywood Brown Derby**, located to the right of The Great Movie Ride and just outside the gateway leading into the studios section of the park, you'll find scores of framed

caricatures reproduced from the authentic ones once found inside the original Brown Derby in California. Besides an enticing variety of delectable fare from steak to chicken, you can simply feast on the Derby's landmark menu feature, a Cobb salad, just like the movie stars did in classic Hollywood. To complement the casually elegant dining atmosphere — children aren't as thrilled with this establishment as they are with most of the other table service restaurants in Disney-MGM Studios — you'll find a delightful meal in the midst of a very busy theme park. You can expect your bill to be around $28.00 at lunch. At dinner, a full-course meal costs around $34.00. Remember, wine, beer, and cocktails add more to your overall bill.

Across the park from the Hollywood Brown Derby — close to Echo Lake — you'll find **Hollywood & Vine**, with its distinctive Art Deco façade. A couple of years ago, this restaurant was set up like a typical Hollywood cafeteria on a studio lot. Hollywood & Vine offers only dinner at reasonable prices. The meal is buffet, with non-alcoholic drinks included. You'll find offerings such as sage-rubbed rotisserie turkey,

oven-baked chicken with herbs, citrus and honey, chef's catch of the day and oven-roasted prime rib of beef. Vegetables abound, along with a number of fresh salads. Assorted cakes and an ice cream bar are available for dessert. Aronda feels the food is "just okay," but it's a nice place for families to relax and get a "fill-up." "Kids absolutely adore the ice cream bar," Aronda says. The dinner buffet costs $21.99 for adults, and

$9.99 for children.

Next door to Hollywood & Vine is a guest favorite, the **50s Prime Time Café**. Here, you are seated at a dinette table right out of a 1950s-styled American kitchen, while watching some of your favorite vintage sitcoms on television sets positioned at or near your table. The food's very good—at times, excellent—and the portions are hearty; however, don't expect particularly innovative fare. Instead, you'll find comfort foods such as meatloaf, country fried steak, fried chicken, and chicken pot pie. As you might guess, this is your Mama's "stick-to-your-ribs" kind of meal—just like your sitcom Mom might prepare for you after a hard day at school. In fact, your server

---

Studios Counter Service Restaurants

Need to take a break from the heavy dining? Try these "quickie" establishments.

Rosie's All-American Cafe
Burgers, Chicken. Recommended
Backlot Express
Burgers, hot dogs, Caesar salad. Recommended.
ABC Commissary
Burgers, fish, Mediterranean & veggie entrees. Breakfast during limited hours. Recommended.
Toy Story Pizza
Pizza, salads (but only with iceberg lettuce). Passing marks only.
Min & Bill's Dockside Diner
Subs, malts
Catalina Eddie's
Pizza, salads
Toluca Legs Turkey Company
Smoked turkey legs
Dinosaur Gertie's Ice Cream of Extinction
Frozen desserts

Though not a table-service restaurant, kids love the fast-food venue, Pizza Planet, named after the restaurant that appears in the movie, **Toy Story**. *Parents must be aware, however, that this is one of the Studios' noisiest restaurants.*

acts as either your Mom, big brother or sister, aunt, uncle or cousin; they'll engage you in a lot of *schtick* and improvisation that will keep you in stitches. If you ask where the bathroom is located, your server will tell you, then remind you to scrub your hands before returning to the table. Then, upon your return, she'll ask: "Excuse me, but did you remember to wash your hands?" If you say yes, she'll want to know the color of the soap. If you say no, she'll send you back. And heaven forbid you put your elbows on the table! The act is lively, and all in good fun — and even if you're bashful about center stage for a few minutes, you've got to try this restaurant. Rather than showing you a dessert tray, your server brings a View Master to the table to pass around; inside, you'll see your scrumptious choices in 3-D. "The 50s Prime Time Café is one of the greatest dining experiences in all the parks," says Megan. "The servers have great personalities, and they really pull guests into the show. It also has the best atmosphere. I'm only twenty-two years old, but I love being surrounded by the fifties." Shelle relates an amusing anecdote about her daughter, Amanda, at the restaurant. "Amanda was slurping her shake," she says. "When our waiter-cousin heard that noise, he turned around and said to her, 'You are going to get *all* the boys like that!'" Lunch and dinner average about the same in price. You can expect each adult bill to be around $25.00.

If you choose to experience the **Sci-Fi Drive-In Dine-In**, don't make the choice because you're expecting out-of-this-world food. You won't get it. You'll find mostly ordinary sandwiches at premium prices. However, the shakes and sundaes are yummy, and many guests stop in just to sample those. Here's the set-up. A server shows you to your table, designed to look like a convertible with its top down. Your "car" is parked among hundreds of other autos facing a huge, drive-in movie screen. Similar to the Mexico pavilion in Epcot, the interior of the restaurant is designed to emulate the night sky. What flickers across the screen may seem, at first, a strange accompaniment to your meal, since Disney gives you a sampling of classic (and definitely B-grade) science fiction and horror film excerpts. But you soon realize — about the time you realize you've had better burgers back home — that the film clips are more hokey than horrifying. In the films, you'll find typical elements of camp, even some neo-Freudian imagery. In *Cat Women from Outer Space*, a man travels from earth to the moon, where only women live happily together — a sort of reverse take on misogyny. The women collude in a plot to kill him, then steal his spacecraft to travel to earth. Predictably, one woman has fallen hopelessly in love with the protagonist; she tips him off — and then, another clip begins, just when the film gets interesting. You'll also see a "Tom and Jerry" episode when Jerry is "approved" for a space flight, and Tom gets pumped into the rocket fuel chamber. Tom swims in the booster rocket fuels, and the antics continue. *Attack of the Killer Tomatoes* also makes an appearance — but not long enough to entice you to remove them from your sandwich. If children are dining with you, your server will give them a "flying saucer" after you pay the bill — actually, it's a souped-up Frisbee. The average price for both lunch and dinner here is $24.00.

Another one of Aronda's favorite restaurants at Walt Disney World is located at the Studios; it's called **Mama Melrose's Ristorante Italiano**. The fare is Italian, of course, with the restaurant's specialty being pizza from wood-burning ovens. The pastas are great here, too, as well as some of the special, customized alcoholic libations — particularly the Italian Surfer, a mixture of Amaretto, Malibu Rum and assorted fruit juices. The restaurant is set up in a warehouse containing a variety of old props, so the décor is far from classy. In fact, it's downright tacky, but in a frivolous sort of way. You'll notice Christmas decorations are strung along the wall — something you're loathe to tolerate year-round from your neighbors, but here, it works somehow. Light fixtures seldom seem to match one another, and various street signs, pictures and artwork (including a platter designed as a pizza) adorn the walls and shelves. Occasionally, Streetmosphere performers stroll among the diners, striking up conversations and involving guests at neighboring tables. Note that Mama Melrose's Ristorante Italiano sometimes adheres to rather strange dinner hours. Lunch is served at an average price of $28.00, while dinner costs about the same. If you choose to dine on Mama's famous pizzas, note that they are about $12.00 each.

Handling Your Hunger at Disney's Animal Kingdom

With two exceptions, the general rule of thumb is "don't get too hungry in Disney's Animal Kingdom." There are no table-service restaurants to speak of, other than **Rainforest Café**, which is often crowded with longer-than-necessary wait times. Generally, the food is tasty — once you get it. Each time Aronda has visited Rainforest — which is a beautiful restaurant, with tube-shaped fish tanks and Audio-Animatronics displays positioned next to many tables — she's found service to be infuriatingly slow. If you can tolerate slower-than-average service (Aronda believes this restaurant could resolve this major flaw with minor tweaking), you'll have a good time here — and the kids love it, if they haven't grown bratty because of the long wait. The restaurant is set up as a rainforest, with a thunderstorm occurring every fifteen minutes or so. The theming isn't quite Disney caliber — the restaurant is neither owned nor designed by Disney — but it makes for a nice dining atmosphere. You'll find that the most popular items are various pizzas and sandwiches; the restaurant has a number of wonderful desserts to offer. If you just want a cocktail or a beer, you can bypass the wait and head directly to the Rainforest Café's Mushroom Lounge.

Donald's Breakfastosaurus is a character breakfast — the only one on property starring Donald Duck — that lasts from park opening (often 8:00 a.m.) until about 10:30 a.m. Your servers are student paleontologists who can't seem to separate their restaurant gig from scientific issues — an ineptitude that creates funny situations involving ketchup bottles and hot chocolate cups. Once you report for your PS, your server will brief you on the controversy involving a conflict over who can rightfully claim credit for discovering the remains of a huge, duck-like skeleton. During your meal — which includes pancakes, breakfast pizza, scrambled eggs, bacon, sausage, smoked salmon, fresh fruit and lots more — Mickey, Pluto and Goofy often join Donald to roam from table to table for photo and autograph opportunities. After the breakfast buffet, the same restaurant becomes yet another fast-food counter service burger joint — with McDonald's fries and Happy Meals. Adult and children breakfasts are fixed price affairs. Adults pay $17.99, while kids' meals are priced at $9.99.

Restaurantosaurus is the setting for Donald's Breakfastosaurus, WDW's only character meal starring The Duck.

While the park, even in its seventh year of operation, closes too early to warrant even a thought about dinner, you can often get PS at **Rainforest Café** until at least 6:30 p.m., since there is a restaurant entrance outside the park. (During peak seasons, you may be able to obtain later dinner seatings.) Lunch here averages about $14.00, while dinner averages around $30.00. It is Aronda's opinion that Disney shortchanges guests with this park's paucity of dining venues, but she rec-

Disney's Animal Kingdom Counter Service

Don't want the inconvenience of waiting forever at the Rainforest Café? Then try these quick stops for meals.

Flame Tree Barbecue
Smoked chicken, ribs and pork.
Pizzafari
Pizzas, salads, and warm Italian deli sandwich. Recommended.
Restaurantosaurus
McDonald's fries, Happy Meals (for the kids), burgers and hot dogs (after Donald's Breakfastosaurus ends about 10:30 a.m.)
Tusker House
Rotisserie chicken, fried chicken sandwich, fish, vegetable fair. Breakfast during limited hours. Recommended.

---

ognizes that Disney's Animal Kingdom is still experiencing growing pains. Hopefully, we'll see additional full-service restaurants appear as the park expands. Disney's Animal Kingdom is a beautiful park, and would make an incredible setting for more fine dining.

DOWNTOWN DISNEY DINING

What happens when you're shaking your groove thang at Mannequins Dance Palace, BET Soundstage or Motion — or you're in the middle of a great purchase at the Marketplace — or you're testing your game skills at DisneyQuest — and your stomach starts to groan? No need to panic — nor to head back to your resort hotel or favorite theme park. You'll enjoy a number of options within walking distance of wherever you happen to be in Walt Disney World's most "happening" spot of all — Downtown Disney. Keep in mind, though, that as Downtown Disney heats up in the evening —

particularly after the parks close—the restaurants here can become very crowded very quickly, so don't be surprised if you have to wait awhile to be seated. To make matters even worse, some of the restaurants here—Bongos Cuban Café, for example—don't offer Priority Seating. Though it's hit or miss as to which restaurants are open, lunch at Downtown Disney is a much less pressing affair, and it's certain that your wait will almost always be short. Unfortunately, Downtown Disney isn't nearly as sexy in the sunlight as it is under the stars.

Downtown Disney Marketplace

Cap'n Jack's restaurant is a picturesque spot for fairly light meals, with an emphasis on seafood—including dishes showcasing crab, clam and shrimp. Diners whose systems are not synchronized with morsels of the sea will also find several "landlubber" specials, like chicken and roast beef sandwiches. The restaurant is located on a pier protruding into Lake Buena Vista. During a recent lunch, Aronda experienced good service, but mediocre food—though the specialty cocktails are huge and heavenly. You can have lunch for around $26.00, but dinner will set you back $37.00.

Fulton's Crab House is an elegant, traditional seafood house, operated by Levy Restaurants, located in the three-deck riverboat formerly known as the Empress Lilly (originally named for Walt Disney's wife). The lights adorning the riverboat—and the mystique of dining on such a stately vessel (actually, it's not the real thing; the restaurant is a permanent structure shaped like a floating vessel)—will draw you into one of Disney's finest culinary experiences. No seafood restaurant in the area has fresher seafood than Fulton's Crab House, which features crabs, oysters, lobster, steak, grilled

chicken and combination platters. For lunch, you can dine on a sandwich for around $12.00, but other lunch offerings will average $35.00. Dinner will cut into your cash to the tune of $43.00.

Downtown Disney's **Rainforest Café** is a derivation of the restaurant of the same name and chain in Disney's Animal Kingdom — though some guests swear that both food and service here are superior to those inside the version found at Disney's Animal Kingdom. Furthermore, this establishment features a talking tree (whose topic is ecology), along with animal experts happy to entertain your questions. Pasta, chicken and vegetarian dishes — along with a variety of pizzas — are featured. This restaurant is open for lunch and dinner; breakfast is not served here. Prices parallel those at the Animal Kingdom establishment: $14.00 for lunch, and $30.00 for dinner.

The Marketplace's newest restaurant is **Earl of Sandwich**, located in the former Gourmet Pantry shop. Earl of Sandwich is a new venture from Robert Earl, Planet Hollywood founder and CEO. The new eatery features a variety of hot, freshly prepared sandwiches served on warm fresh bread and original sauces and spreads. It also offers The Butler's Pantry, an area stocked with "grab 'n go" cold sandwiches, salads, side orders and desserts. Earl of Sandwich has a number of tasty salad dressings, and will customize your salad while you wait. This is one of the few counter-service restaurants at Walt Disney World where you can get unlimited refills of your favorite beverage (except for "specialty" drinks). You'll be hard-

pressed to find any entry more than $6.00. Earl of Sandwich is open for breakfast, lunch, and dinner.

Downtown Disney Pleasure Island

Portobello Yacht Club (a Levy restaurant) is one hot restaurant, so it's a good idea to make Priority Seating arrangements before you arrive for dinner. (Lunch is infinitely less crowded.) From gourmet pizzas baked in wood-burning ovens, to grilled meat and fish, to a wide array of pastas, you'll enjoy not only the delicacies served here but also the setting. The décor is bright and festive, and many tables have views of Lake Buena Vista. Service is prompt and attentive, with gracious servers. The restaurant itself is designed as an elegant, Bermuda-styled house that combines high gables and beamed ceilings, bright Mediterranean colors and earthy tones. The restaurant's roasted garlic spread is heavenly on the Portobello's own fresh-baked bread. Aronda recommends the individual-sized pizza with sun-dried tomatoes as a delicious appetizer. Lunch will set you back around $31.00, while dinner, a significantly more intense affair, costs around $43.00.

Downtown Disney West Side

The creation of Gloria Estefan and her husband, Emilio, **Bongos Cuban Café** offers some unique food with Cuban and Latin American flavors. You can choose a table inside, or one on the balcony which wraps around a three-story pine-

apple that serves as a West Side landmark. If you wish to have a conversation with your dining companions, you should choose a table on the balcony, since the live band inside plays Latino music at ear-shattering volume. (It's great stuff, but it *is* loud.) While Josh enjoyed his chicken entrée, Dann's beef was a bit tough—and the flavor a disappointment. Plantains are served up in several cooking styles—crunchy and salty, or sweet, like candied yams. Other guests give Bongos rave reviews. "This past September, I went to Bongos Cuban Café on the recommendation of several people," says Becky. "I am very interested in all things Cuban and have eaten Cuban food before. I found the restaurant overpriced, but with a great atmosphere. The food was very good, though." Average per-adult price for both lunch and dinner is $32.00.

With a surprisingly intricate menu, the restaurant inside the **House of Blues**—a nightclub launched by Blues Brother Dan Aykroyd—features Cajun and Creole cooking like jambalaya, etouffee and bread pudding. Appetizers range from

catfish nuggets to Voodoo Shrimp to pizza, while entrees run the gamut from unique sandwiches (like Blues Burgers and Blackened Chicken Sandwich) to New York Strip Steak and Creole Seafood Jambalaya. The lively and wildly

CHAPTER 13 DOWNTOWN DISNEY DINING 307

popular **Gospel Brunch** staged on Sundays at 10:30 a.m. and 1:00 p.m. features great entertainment along with a varied menu, including roasted garlic potatoes, bacon and sausage, omelets, Italian pasta salad, smoked salmon, marinated chicken breast and more. Lunch and dinner at the House of Blues averages around $31.00. The Gospel Brunch costs $30.00 for adults, and $15.00 for children.

Shaped like our humble planet (though the architecture is far from humble), **Planet Hollywood** is certainly unique, but the main appeal lies not in its cuisine but in its collection of movie memorabilia. In Aronda's opinion, the food, consisting mostly of sandwiches, salads, pasta and shrimp, will satisfy, but it won't impress. However,  teens will give quite a different review. Full meals at both lunch and dinner cost about $24.00.

Chef Wolfgang Puck rules at the West Side — with both a café and a dining room. In addition to Wolfgang Puck's trademark Chinois Chicken Salad, **Wolfgang Puck Café** serves up many other offerings from the famous chef, like gourmet pizzas, Thai chicken satay, pastas and rotisserie chicken. Recently, Aronda tried the butternut squash soup and spinach and five-cheese dip. Her review? Heavenly! The four-cheese pizza was great, too. Both lunch and dinner average about $30.00. **Wolfgang Puck Café – The Dining Room** is a more formal dining experience, located upstairs, and focuses on the chef's most innovative creations, like baby vegetable risotto and grilled chicken with

squash ravioli in a sage brown butter sauce. Your average cost in The Dining Room will be $45.00.

According to Rick Wetzel, his last name caused him to suffer the taunts of his schoolyard chums, who often called him by saying: "Hey, Wetzel, you pretzel." Well, now he has his revenge. **Wetzel's Pretzels**—the main restaurant is located at West Side, though there's an annex in the Marketplace—serves the perfect soft pretzel, as well as some variations on the theme. If a pretzel isn't sold in thirty minutes, then it's tossed out, assuring all diners equal chance at freshness. You'll also find flavored pretzels, including cheese, cinnamon and sugar, and garlic. Rick even serves a cheese dog, with the wiener wrapped in both pretzel and cheese. These light meals and snacks range from about $3.00 to $4.00 per item. You'll also find Häagen Dazs Ice Cream along with fresh-made lemonade.

DINING OUT INN STYLE

It's easy for Walt Disney World guests to discover excellent dining options at the resort hotels where they're staying, but they often forget to check out the many other resort restaurants available to them—and it often takes nothing more than a quick bus or monorail ride. In fact, some of the best dining opportunities Disney offers can be found within the Resort's many hotels. Unfortunately, finding time to fit even one resort dining experience into your hectic schedule can be difficult, but if you're able to book a vacation that lasts more than five days, you should be able to break away from the theme parks long enough to sample a resort restaurant or two.

In this section, you'll find a generous sampling of the most notable table-service restaurants inside Disney's uniquely-themed resorts. Also listed are counter service establishments in each of the resorts in a sidebar within this section. Like other restaurant listings, you'll find price "averages" for each dining experience. Remember that our averages include entrée, as well as appetizer, beverage and dessert; leaving either of these off will reduce your final bill. Likewise, beer, wine and cocktails can significantly increase your bill. Our average menu prices are meant to be a guide, not a guarantee.

Disney's Animal Kingdom Lodge

Here, you'll find the big, bustling **Boma – Flavors of Africa**, designed to evoke an African marketplace. It's the more relaxed of the pair of table service restaurants found at Disney's Animal Kingdom Lodge. A huge variety of palatables is served from "pods" (serving areas), buffet-style. When Josh and Dann dined at Boma, offerings included salads (like watermelon rind salad), fresh fruit, grilled chicken and pork enhanced with African spices, mahi-mahi, prime rib cut to order, soups (like pumpkin and spicy seafood gumbo) and a collection of desserts that will overwhelm you. You'll be stuffed by the time the meal ends. Dann enjoyed the meal more than Josh, who is reticent to return because he found little he liked. He also selected one of the South African wines (stocked by both restaurants at the resort), but found that it tasted too much like the "less expensive" domestics to warrant the seven dollars per glass price. Josh recommends soliciting a bit more guidance from cast members when guests are making their wine selections here. If you're willing to experiment, you'll probably find enough here to satisfy. There's also a kids' menu with chicken fingers and macaroni and cheese—though they are welcome to try the main selections, as well. Desserts here are worth the price of the meal; the décor of this restaurant—indeed, the entire resort—makes any food even more memorable. Breakfast offers more than forty-five items, including waffles and pancakes, a wide variety of juices, fresh and dried fruits, and the traditional breakfast items. Even breakfast pizza appears on the menu. Both breakfast and dinner buffets are fixed price. Breakfast costs $15.99 for adults, and $8.99 for children. Dinner prices are $24.99 for adults, and $10.99 for children.

Jiko – The Cooking Place is a more formal, sophisticated—and expensive—restaurant than Boma, featuring a wide variety of foods prepared with an African flare. Appetizers may include crispy cinnamon-spiced beef roll and foie gras dumpling. You'll feast on entrees such as horseradish-encrusted salmon on purple rice, baked chicken and mashed potatoes topped with grapefruit and various herbs, and oak-grilled beef tenderloin. South African wines are served here, as well. If you're not comfortable making a selection on your own, don't hesitate to ask your server for clarification of the menu as well as recommendations. During a recent visit, Josh enjoyed filet mignon with gourmet macaroni and cheese, while Dann indulged in a vegetarian dish that was impossible to finish in one sitting. The Pineapple, Pineapple, Pineapple dessert is topnotch. This restaurant's chef has been featured in Epcot's International Food & Wine Festival. The average price for a Jiko dinner weighs in at about $39.00.

Disney's BoardWalk

At what is arguably Disney's most festive resort, your selection widens with several excellent restaurants. If you're into sports, you'll love the **ESPN Club**, where you choose primarily from a wide variety of sandwiches, salads and other comfort foods while you watch the big game on wide-screen television monitors. (This restaurant has even installed TVs in the restrooms — to make sure you don't miss one action-packed minute!) The restaurant is most crowded for meals during popular sports events — and the atmosphere is always a bit rowdy. If you're hankering for a quiet meal, try somewhere else. Median price for both lunch and dinner is around $24.00.

Many guests rave about the **Flying Fish Café**, though landlubbers should beware there's not much on the menu for them (although steaks — and, occasionally, pastas — are also served). The décor is refreshingly appealing, with lighting fixtures depicting — you guessed it! — flying fish, but in the abstract. A very cool touch to a casually elegant restaurant. It also has a wonderful view of the BoardWalk, and changes its menu daily. Recently, Zagat rated Flying Fish Café as one of Orlando's Top Twenty restaurants. However, dining here isn't cheap. You can expect to pay around $40.00 per dinner, which is the only meal Flying Fish offers.

The **Big River Grille and Brewing Works** is a great place to have drinks — particularly its microbrew beer — but a fairly mediocre place to dine. Not that the food is bad, mind you; it is only a notch or two above food served by the Perkins restaurant chain. For appetizers, you can order crab cakes, chips and salsa and chicken quesadillas. Dann enjoyed his grilled cashew salad — but appealing names like Drunken Rib Eye and Big Brew Burger didn't help pull the entrées out of their culinary doldrums. Big River serves both lunch and dinner; either will cost you about $38.00, sans the beer.

A favorite restaurant at Disney's BoardWalk is **Spoodles**, where you'll find a wide variety of dinner selections that highlight the cooking styles of Greece, Spain, Northern Africa and Italy. Don't worry that the food is too "out there," however. You'll find plenty of very appetizing entrees, like sautéed chicken breast with couscous, spinach, tomatoes and lemon olive sauce, or medallions of filet mignon with pancetta mashed potatoes. You'll also have an excellent view of the

BoardWalk and Crescent Lake—if you request a table close to the windows. A very affordable breakfast, sans Disney characters, is available here, as well, with an international spin on traditional breakfast offerings—though plenty of the old breakfast favorites are available, too. Pizza by-the-slice is also available at a take-out window—a nice way to grab a bite on your way to the parks or back to your room, if you're staying in an Epcot resort. The average breakfast price hovers around $12.00, while dinner easily approaches $35.00.

Disney's Contemporary Resort

Named one of Zagat's Top Twenty Orlando restaurants, as well as "Restaurant of Choice" by *Orlando Magazine*, the **California Grill**, located atop the resort hotel (where a Broadway revue dinner show, "Broadway at the Top," was performed years ago when this space was home to the Top of the World restaurant), offers California pizzas, salmon, spit-roasted chicken and jumbo soufflés—all prepared in an open kitchen. The cooks are amazing to watch—if you can tear your eyes away from the endless rows of windows offering extraordinary views of the Magic Kingdom. The menu here changes frequently, so there's little way to predict with certainty what your choices will be during your visit. This restaurant tends to be among Walt Disney World's most upscale establishments, so you may wish to leave your Disney beanie and Goofy ears behind. Casual is okay, but you'll often find diners in nice resort attire. If you time your dinner just right, you'll have a wonderful view of the Magic Kingdom's Wishes fireworks display from your table—but you must be sure to request a Magic Kingdom view. Or, if you prefer, you can take the elevator to the roof for an even better vantage point. (**Note**: The elevator is no longer open for non-patrons of California Grill.) Though dinner can easily cost you around $45.00, keep in mind that pizza is significantly cheaper; most pizza offerings cost around $10.00. Desserts here are nothing short of spectacular!

Also at Disney's Contemporary Resort, you'll find **Chef**

Mickey's, another buffet-style character dining event located on the fourth floor, serving both breakfast and dinner. Characters appear during both meals. From Chef Mickey's, you'll have a dramatic view of the resort monorail passing serenely above you through the hotel. Breakfast offerings may include a fruit bar, cereal, Chef Mickey's Egg and Sausage Roulade, traditional breakfast favorites, warm bread pudding and pancakes made to order with a variety of fun toppings, including "Mickey Pancakes." At dinner, you're likely to find a premium salad bar, barbecue chicken, roast pork loin with pear demi glaze, penne pasta, broccoli au gratin, and a children's menu including macaroni and cheese, cheese pizza, hot dogs and fish nuggets. And by all means, save room for the restaurant's "fabulous sundae and dessert bar." Some Chef Mickey's veterans urge readers to try the Parmesan Mashed Potatoes. "Sitting at Chef Mickey's during the 'party' napkin-twirl thing is one of our most memorable dining experiences," say Sam and Kathy. "Watching Mickey and Minnie lead kids, including Julianne, in a conga line while monorail purple glided through the Grand Canyon Concourse next to the monorail red loading people in the background was exciting, too. We sure dig the make-your-own-cupcake feature!" Breakfast for adults costs $17.99, while you'll pay $9.99 for your kids. Dinner sets you back $26.99 for adults, and $10.99 for children.

Concourse Steakhouse is located not too far from Chef Mickey's; it serves breakfast, lunch and dinner. The food is good here, but better steaks can be found at Le Cellier and Les Chefs de France. The "smashed potatoes" are sometimes served a tad cold and dry. Lunch offerings range from soups and salads to pizzas and sandwiches. At dinner, you're likely to find many of the lunch offerings, plus the added delights of steak, seafood, and oak-roasted prime rib. Eggs Benedict are featured at breakfast, while lunch offers sandwiches as well as steaks. Dinner features a wide variety of offerings, including steaks, chicken, and fish. Breakfast costs around $12.00; lunch will set you back around $27.00, while dinner will run about $34.00.

Resort Hotel Counter Service Options

You'll find plenty of options for quick meals at Disney's numerous resort hotels. Most of them offer food quality and variety superior to that of the counter service restaurants in the theme parks.

All-Star Sports End Zone Food Court **All-Star Music** Intermission Food Court **All-Star Movies** World Premier Food Court **Pop Century** Everything Pop **Animal Kingdom Lodge** Mara **BoardWalk** BoardWalk Bakery Seashore Sweets **Caribbean Beach** Old Port Royale Food Court **Contemporary** Food & Fun Center **Coronado Springs** Pepper Market Food Court **Old Key West** Good's Food to Go	**Port Orleans Riverside** Colonel's Cotton Mill **Port Orleans French Quarter** Sassagoula Floatworks & Food Factory **Fort Wilderness** Trail's End Buffet **Grand Floridian** Gasparilla Grill and Games **Polynesian** Captain Cook's Snack Company **Saratoga Springs** Artist's Palette **Wilderness Lodge** Roaring Forks Snacks **Yacht & Beach Club** Hurricane Hannah's Grill **Swan** Splash Grill **Dolphin** Tubbi's Buffeteria

Disney's Coronado Springs Resort

In this Southwestern-themed resort, you'll find an enjoyable, all-you-care-to-eat breakfast buffet (without the characters). The restaurant, called **Maya Grill**, is quite beautiful—a surprise in a moderate resort—and the food quality ranks right up there with the best. For breakfast, you'll find all sorts of pastries and fruit, egg burritos, and hashbrowns, among other traditional breakfast items. Latin American dishes, like grilled chicken breast accentuated with Mayan salsa, and broiled beef tenderloin with chimichurri sauce, highlight the dinner menu, when the lighting is more subdued, and the atmosphere more formal than during breakfast. You'll also find steak, duck, and lamb dishes. Lunch is not served at this restaurant. Breakfast is a fixed price affair; adults pay $11.99, while the kids' price is $6.99. At dinner, expect to pay around $35.00 per full-course meal.

Port Orleans Resort—Riverside

In the resort once known as Dixie Landings, you'll find a nice restaurant serving both American and Cajun cuisine called **Boatwright's Dining Hall**. In a relaxed setting, you'll enjoy such appetizers as crab cakes, garlic cheese bites, and chicken gumbo. For the main course, a wide variety of choices avail, including Jambalaya, steaks and salmon dishes, and four-cheese ravioli. Several specialty cocktails are found on the menu, like the Bayou Bloody Mary and the Southern Belle, along with desserts such as Big River Brownie Barge, carrot cake, pecan and Key Lime pie. For breakfast, expect to see traditional offerings along with more unique choices—like banana-stuffed French toast, eggs Benedict, and the Blueprint Omelet. **Insider's Note**: Port Orleans—French Quarter no longer offers a table-service restaurant. Diners staying at the French Quarter must travel to Riverside for on-site dining. Breakfast costs around $14.00, while dinner will set you back about $32.00

Carribean Beach Resort

Shutters at Old Port Royale features American cuisine inspired by Caribbean flavors—such as citrus ginger pork chop, Calypso marinated tofu, and Mojo barbecue shrimp—not to mention its full bar with tropical specialties. The decor reflects the colors of the Caribbean and the ambience is comfortable and cozy. The restaurant renovation includes the addition of a display kitchen. Expect dinner to cost about $30.00.

Disney's Old Key West Resort

Olivia's Café has an established reputation for delectable fare among quite a few regulars. The restaurant features a variety of Key West favorites — as well as traditional southern fare — such as Key lime pie and conch fritters. For breakfast, expect traditional fare. Lunch focuses on a wide variety of sandwiches, along with chicken, pork and beef. For dinner, expect filet mignon, coconut shrimp, grilled Jamaican jerk chicken, and blue lump crab cakes. Portions here are huge. Many guests rave about the Turtle Krawl, a cocktail with coconut rum, spiced rum, and two white rums, along with pineapple, orange, and key lime juices. The wait staff is friendly and attentive. Olivia's Café occasionally serves up special holiday meals at Thanksgiving and Christmas, and on select days during the week, Winnie the Pooh and pals show up for a character breakfast. Breakfast costs around $12.00, while lunch is served for around $25.00 per meal. Expect dinner to ring up around $33.00.

Disney's Grand Floridian Resort & Spa

At Walt Disney World's "jewel in the crown" of all resort hotels, you'll find five wonderful restaurants, along with the **Garden View Lounge**, where you can enjoy High Tea each afternoon beginning at 3:00 p.m., and ending at 6:00 p.m. The experience will conjure up memories of Julie Andrews and Dick van Dyke in *Mary Poppins* as hostesses tempt you with delicacies such as dainty cucumber, egg salad, and smoked salmon sandwiches, followed by scones, Devonshire crème and jams, topped with a variety of desserts, including pastry swans. Of course, the highlight of the experience is the tea itself, which is served in Royal Albert china. "Tea for Two" allows you to sample two different teas. The elegant experience is a relaxing way to take a break from touring the parks. Though young princes characteristically get fidgety, a num-

Citricos is located on the second floor off the Grand Lobby at Disney's Grand Floridain Resort & Spa, and offers a glorious view of the Magic Kingdom.

ber of parents have reported that their little princesses really get a kick out of the experience. Attentive hostesses answer questions about the teas offered on the menu. Expect your High Tea experience to cost between $17.50 and $24.50 per person. Younger royalty will require a smaller investment.

Citricos, yet another of Walt Disney World's restaurants named by Zagat as among Orlando's Top Twenty—serves dinner only—but oh, what a dinner it is! It features market-fresh Southern French cooking—as well as breath-taking views of the Seven Seas Lagoon, and the Magic Kingdom on the opposite side. The fare here varies seasonally, but may include sautéed salmon filet, grilled swordfish, grilled loin of lamb, and braised veal shank. The restaurant's warm onion tart is a wonderful way to start your meal. To lighten your spirits, why not try a citrus-infused martini, or opt for a three-wine pair-

You'll find Narcoossee's located, not inside Disney's Grand Floridian Resort & Spa, but close to the resort dock. This casually elegant restaurant is open only for dinner.

ing with your meal courses for $25.00. It's easy to spend as much as thirty dollars or more for an entrée alone. Expect your dinner to cost around $60.00.

The **Grand Floridian Café** serves breakfast, lunch, and dinner. Breakfast is refined, and the selections are fresh and of consistently high quality. Breakfast includes salmon eggs Benedict and a traditional Japanese breakfast featuring miso soup, sticky rice, salmon, and a spinach roll. Lunch offerings range from pan-seared breast of chicken to gourmet burgers and Philly cheese steak sandwiches, which are quite memorable. The veggie burger here is the best on property. Both lunch and dinner offerings are moderately priced. Here, the food is consistently superb. Some of the fruity specialty cocktails, like the Scarlet Daiquiri, are quite refreshing, too. Expect breakfast to cost between $8.99 and $19.99, while both lunch and dinner will cost around $26.00.

Narcoossee's, located in an octagonal building on the shore of the Seven Seas Lagoon, features a variety of dinner menu options in a more casual setting than you'll find in most of the other Grand Floridian restaurants. Only dinner is served here. For pure self-indulgence, start off with Narcoossee's steamed seafood appetizer with steamed mussels, clams, and jumbo shrimp, served with garlic and herb butter, and tomato and roasted pepper coulis. Featured menu items sometimes include grilled wild salmon, grilled wahoo and rock shrimp, grilled filet mignon, and whole Maine lobster. Average price for your dinner will be around $51.00.

At **1900 Park Fare**, you'll rub elbows with Mary Poppins and friends during the most elegant character breakfast on property. Be sure to take note of Big Bertha, a band organ built in Paris almost a century ago. Dinner, which features seafood, salads, pastas, vegetables and prime rib, is also served; lunch is not. Note that both meals are served buffet-style, and that characters mingle with guests at dinner, too. Dann particularly enjoyed clowning with the Mad Hatter. When Dann insisted on getting a photograph, the Mad Hatter looked at the digital result, patted Dann's shoulder, and said: "Very professional, I say. Very professional indeed—for an amateur." "I enjoyed 1900 Park Fare for my birthday," says Toni. "They gave me a small cake. We chose not to announce it to everyone in the restaurant, but I felt important. We gave the cake to two little girls who were seated near us. They were thrilled." Breakfast price for adults is fixed at $17.99; $10.99 for children. For dinner, you'll pay $27.99 for adults, and $12.99 for children.

Though **Victoria & Albert's**—also listed among Zagat's Top Twenty Orlando restaurants—will set you back more than one hundred bucks a meal (even more if you order wine or cocktails, or reserve the Chef's Table), it is Walt Disney World's most elegant, most memorable—and most expensive—restaurant. This establishment requires appropriate attire—dresses for women, jackets for men—and provides intense, attentive service during your six-course meal. Be sure you can spare about two hours before you make reservations, which are required, along with a credit card guarantee. (Priority Seating is not accepted here.) The meal is prix fixe, so skipping a course won't save money. Furthermore, kids aren't likely to enjoy this dining experience. While the menu is customized nightly, depending on what the chef has selected from among the freshest meats and produce, you can depend on experiencing extraordinary, creative food and service. Dann and Josh sampled such dishes as poached Maine lobster over Italian couscous and Bloomsdale spinach, grilled Angus beef tenderloin with elephant garlic mash, and roulade of free range chicken with Dungeness crab. A personalized menu is presented to every guest, and women receive a long-stemmed rose. The restaurant is quiet, romantic, intimate and refined. It's such a contrast to the rest of your Disney experience that you aren't likely to forget your dinner here any time soon. The prix fixe is around $105.00 per person. Wine pairings are available for around $65.00. The Chef's Table—the ultimate in individual attention, allowing you to sample foods other diners are denied—costs between $120.00 and $170.00.

Aronda knows of no other Disney restaurant where you can actually rise from your seat to take a tour of the dessert offerings before you make up your mind. Here at Kona, you'll not want to deny yourself a dessert indulgence.

Disney's Polynesian Resort

At dinner, the relaxing, casual **'Ohana** features a sixteen-foot long open fire pit and an all-you-care-to-eat feast, which includes shrimp, poultry, pork and beef, all roasted on skewers up to three feet long. You'll also enjoy a lovely nighttime view of the Seven Seas Lagoon and Cinderella Castle. Polynesian singers and story-telling servers entertain during dinner. However, picky diners may not enjoy the platters of meat and chicken that are laid in front of them. A character breakfast, featuring Mickey, Chip and Dale, is held here every morning. The offerings, though possessing rather exotic names, are traditional breakfast fare. Both breakfast and dinner are prix fixe. Breakfast costs $17.99 for adults, and $9.99 for children. Dinner is $24.99 for adults, and $10.99 for children.

The **Kona Café** is a casual restaurant serving breakfast, lunch and dinner featuring Asian-influenced entrees. The

Teriyaki chicken salad is huge and tasty, while the desserts are not only beautiful, but also delicious. In fact, one very talented cast member concocts the desserts, and nothing else, as you'll discover if you ask your server to take you on a "dessert tour." At dinner, the coconut almond chicken is to die for. A traditional breakfast is also served here. Crystal, Tom and Linda "love Kona Café because the food is excellent." Average investments for all three meals are as follows: Breakfast, $14.00; lunch, $24.00; and dinner, $30.00.

Walt Disney World Swan & Walt Disney World Dolphin

Between the two resort hotels, you'll find that four restaurants deserve special note. The **Garden Grove Café** (Swan), situated in a five-story greenhouse, serves a full breakfast menu. For a breakfast buffet, expect to pay $17.95 for adults, $8.50 for children. You may also order a la carte. On Sundays, you may enjoy the Garden Grove's Sunday Character Breakfast, held from 7:30 a.m. until 10:30 a.m. To enjoy this event, adults will pay $16.95, while children may interact with the food and characters for $10.95. For dinner, the restaurant is transformed into **Gulliver's at The Garden Grove**. You may order from the menu items like sandwiches, pasta, and pizza. These menu items range from $13.50 to $25.00. Or, if you wish, you may enjoy the buffet; it costs $24.95 for adults, and $19.95 for children. Drinks are included. However, when Dann sampled the buffet, he admits that he quickly wished he'd ordered a la carte.

At the Swan, **Palio** is an Italian bistro noted for its focaccia, pasta and pizza. A strolling musician adds to the atmosphere. While guests have rated Palio as "Average" in terms of value, the categories of food, atmosphere and service received "Excellent" ratings. Instead of Priority Seating, you must call the Swan and Dolphin reservations line directly. That telephone number is **407-934-1609**. If you order from the menu a la carte, expect to pay around $43.00. You may also opt to sample a wide variety of Palio's delectables by choosing A Taste of Palio, which costs $42.00 without wines. Adding the wines will cost $60.00 per person.

At the Dolphin, **Shula's Steak House**, established by the legendary coach of the Miami Dolphins, serves dinner only; its specialty is certified Angus beef. The menu comes on an autographed football—which can be yours for $250. Any steak you can imagine, Shula's has it. Like Palio, Shula's does not accept Priority Seating. Reservations can be made by calling the Swan and Dolphin reservations line directly at **407-934-1609**. Expect to pay around $50.00 per dinner.

New at the Dolphin is Todd English's **bluezoo**, an incredibly beautiful restaurant just inside the entrance of the hotel. Here, you can order clam chowder or roasted beet salad, among other items, for an appetizer. Then, you can enjoy a wide variety of mostly seafood items. However, in addition to shellfish—bluezoo's specialty—you'll find pork chops, beef tenderloin, and roasted chicken on the menu. Expect your bill to hover around $45.00.

Often, Disney Vacation Club (DVC) members receive respectable discounts on various meals at some Swan and Dolphin restaurants. If you're a DVC member, refer to your *Member Update* or *Portable Perks*, provided to you at check-in, for specific details. And be prepared to show your membership card, or your Key to the World designating you as a "Member," to activate any discounts.

Disney's Wilderness Lodge

Two exquisite restaurants await you here. **Artist Point** provides a relaxing setting for dinner, featuring a creative menu that includes beef, buffalo and rabbit. Popular entrees include grilled beef tenderloin, grilled buffalo sirloin and spicy Asian-style shrimp. For dessert, try the decadent flourless chocolate whiskey cake with pecans and raspberry sorbet. Start out with mixed greens, crispy venison rolls, or smokey portobello soup.

During Epcot's International Food and Wine Festival, a number of elegant dining events are staged in The Odyssey, once a restaurant, now a special events facility. (It looks great with its recent paint job.)

Entrees to follow included grilled beef tenderloin, Hatfield pork chop, or pan-seared scallops. Desserts include a selection of Artisan cheeses, Artist Point cobbler, or a cherry cheese tart. You may also soar with the restaurant's Wine Cellar Flight, which complements dinner with a selection of fine wines from the Pacific Northwest. Wines for three courses cost $18.00; for four courses, $23.00. Otherwise, expect your bill to be around $50.00.

Whispering Canyon Café is open for all three major meals, and offers a variety of menu items, including smoked barbecue, assorted sandwiches, pastas and desserts. For dinner, Jeffro's Glazed Pork Chops are out of this world. For both lunch and dinner, you may also opt to try Whispering Canyon's all-you-care-to-eat Canyon Skillet. (Lunch price for the Skillet is $13.99 per person; for dinner, it's $21.99 per person.) Note that servers occasionally engage guests in banter that eventually becomes part of the "show." For example, birthdays often become raucous affairs, with the entire restaurant participating in honoring the celebrant, and diners who require ketchup on their steaks are publicly "ribbed." Josh and

Dann's server, Jeffro Bodeen, dished shamelessly. Several minutes after serving their bread, he stopped at their table, pointed at the bread plate, and deadpanned: "I'm sure you've heard this before, but your buns look great!" Occasionally, servers organize a horse race with the children in the restaurant. Stick ponies are distributed to the kids, who are then lined up to gallop all around the restaurant with adults waving their napkins above their heads, yelling, "Yahoo!" All but the most timid of children enjoy the activity. Aronda highly recommends this delightful dining experience. "At this restaurant, my sister dropped her fork and snuck one from another table," recalls Brian. "So, when the waiter caught her, he made a 'hat' out of a napkin and she had to wear it for the rest of the night." Average price for breakfast here is $12.00. Expect lunch to cost about $20.00. And dinner will ring in around $34.00.

Disney's Yacht & Beach Club Resorts

Three restaurants stand out at these two resort hotels in the Epcot area.

Cape May Café, located at Beach Club, offers two all-you-can-eat meals. Goofy's Beach Club Breakfast offers traditional fare with several Disney characters making their rounds. Adult cost is $17.99; children's cost is $9.99. The breakfast hours are usually 7:30 a.m. until 11:00 a.m. Though lunch is not offered here, the ever-popular Clam Bake Dinner Buffet is an All-American clam bake featuring clams, mussels, and barbecue ribs. However, if you don't like seafood, you probably

---

TIP

For economy and convenience, include both counter service and table service dining experiences. Full service dining takes significantly more time than counter service. Lunch is frequently less expensive at table service than dinner, while counter service is usually the same price throughout the day.

Though certainly not a full-service restaurant by any stretch of the imagination, Ghiradelli's, located at Downtown Disney Marketplace, is a wonderful place to sample great chocolate. The venue also boasts an exquisite ice cream shop next to the candy shop.

won't be happy with your meal. Adult pricing is $24.99; you'll pay $10.99 for your children.

At the **Yachtsman Steakhouse**, located at Disney's Yacht Club Resort, you can watch the butcher not only select your cut of meat from the glassed-in shop, but also watch the chef prepare meals in the display kitchen. For starters, try the restaurant's Stone Fruit Salad, the Oysters Rockefeller, or the Baby Spinach Salad. Then, dig in. Order a Chateaubriand for Two, filet mignon, Chilean sea bass, or the New Zealand rack of lamb. Recently, Zagat named the Yachtsman's Steakhouse as one of Orlando's Top Twenty restaurants. For this unique dining experience, expect to pay $50.00 per meal.

Also located at Disney's Yacht Club Resort, the **Yacht Club Galley** is the ideal spot for breakfast, lunch, and dinner. At breakfast, count on traditional wake up entrees, along with oatmeal brulee, omelets, steak and eggs. You'll also find a breakfast buffet for about $13.99 for adults, and $6.99 for children. At lunch, you may opt to start with chicken tenders or New England clam chowder, followed by one of a number of

Only at Disney's Animal Kingdom can you purchase a "Meal Plus Certificate," entitling you to a counter-service meal and two other refreshments over the course of the day. If you're trying to conserve meal funds, snacks in this deal may help curb hearty appetites later in the day. Aronda says that the $11.99 certificate entitles you to about $20.00 worth of food, drinks and snacks.

delicious sandwiches, like grilled chicken, crab and shrimp cake sandwich, or Galley fish and chips. Dinner is basically a repeat of lunch, with a few extra sandwiches thrown in for good measure. For dessert, enjoy Florida key lime pie, or a dessert sampler including four distinct desserts. Several refreshing tropical cocktails are available as well. Breakfast costs around $13.00 per person, while both lunch and dinner will set you back around $26.00.

Beaches & Cream, a casual restaurant themed like a fifties soda shop, features the world's best hamburgers—no, really. Aronda doubts you'll ever taste a burger quite as good as this. If you order The Kitchen Sink ice cream extravaganza, make sure you have company to help you finish it—and that you're self-confident enough to endure the stares of other amazed diners! Both lunch and dinner will cost about $19.00.

Chapter 14

Shake Your Groove Thang

Disney's Nightlife

During Aronda's first trip to Pleasure Island, she wandered around in a fog along the boulevard, encountering at every turn another cart where cocktails, wine and beer were sold. It was, she decided, a theme park devoted to booze. Shocked, she left quickly. Could it be possible that The Walt

> **Pleasure Island In Stages**
>
> Besides shows and dancing at the various Pleasure Island Clubs, you'll find plenty of "stage action" throughout the Island. Live bands perform regularly at the Rock n Roll Beach Club and the Pleasure Island Jazz Company. Not only does the outdoor West End Stage feature the evening's house band, but it's also the focal point of the New Year's Eve street party. Starting at 7:00 p.m., Pleasure Island Live begins its broadcast night. Deejays spin tunes and music videos until 2:00 a.m. The Hub Stage features a twenty-five-screen video wall. So even if the Clubs are crowded, there's plenty of action for you--outside!

Disney Company would concoct such a blatant tribute to Dionysus, the great party-god? In stereotypical fashion, Aronda thought that when Disney threw a party, it included adorable characters, lighthearted music with easy-to-remember lyrics, Mylar balloons and fireworks.

Pleasure Island represented a paradigm shift Aronda wasn't quite ready to make.

Later, however, she thought: Well, why *shouldn't* Disney break away from its image a bit and experiment with other forms of entertainment?

And so the Company has. While Pleasure Island still passes as a park whose predominant theme is hedonism (and alcohol), other features make it a wonderful place to unwind — whether you wish to drink or not. Its theme is "Carpe P.M." — and after a full day of *carpe diem* at the parks, it's a theme that works!

A caveat, however. Pleasure Island is not a place for young children, though parents are permitted to bring their offspring with them onto the Island. In fact, no one under eighteen is admitted *without* parent or guardian. But even if you decide to forego hiring a babysitting service, you'll find two clubs that won't allow anyone under twenty-one to enter — accompanied by parents or not. Occasionally Aronda encounters children on the Island—and almost invariably, they look bored, confused or unhappy. Don't let the name "Disney" mislead you into thinking the Company can't "do adult." It can—and quite well. And Pleasure Island proves it. Melanie usually goes to Pleasure Island one night of her vacation. "I love the Comedy Warehouse and the Adventurers Club," she says. "They are both a blast and interactive experiences. I don't like it when parents bring their children into the clubs and then give dirty looks to people who are drinking and having a good time. After all, that's what clubs are for."

If, as a parent, you wish to keep your children with you throughout your vacation, you can still enjoy a modified nightlife at Downtown Disney's Marketplace and BoardWalk, even with the kids in tow. Pleasure Island may constitute a premature introduction of adult amusements to your children, but Downtown Disney Marketplace after dark is certainly an appropriate diversion for them after the parks close. Positioned on Lake Buena Vista, Marketplace is quite the festive spot, with occasional outdoor live entertainment, "kiddie" carnival rides, splash fountains and many places to blow your bucks on your children's favorite toys, games, food and clothes.

However, the Marketplace closes about eleven every evening, leaving the more adult nightspots still going strong. Considering the quality and uniqueness of Disney's nighttime entertainment, parents owe it to themselves to hire a childcare service, like Kids' Nite Out, so the adults can have an evening to themselves.

Downtown Disney West Side, while primarily an array of venues adults will enjoy most, does have a virtual amusement park which can entertain children, age ten or older (younger children must be accompanied by an adult), while parents skip off to a nightclub or a lounge. And BoardWalk, wedged between Disney-MGM Studios and Epcot, not only offers several clubs catering to adults, but also entertainment out on the planks to enthrall the kids as well.

Pleasure Island

Upon entering this party complex, expect to show your ID, have your wrist banded, and the top of your hand stamped. Lately, however, Disney has been experimenting with ways of getting more guests into this party zone. For example, you may find entering Pleasure Island is free, but you must pay Island admission if you wish to visit a nightclub. But whatever method Disney is utilizing during your stay, get ready for fun! "I enjoy Pleasure Island, though I haven't been since 1997," says Becky. "I'm usually too exhausted to go out!"

Heading away from the West End Stage, traveling down the hill, past the huge television screen, take a right — and on the corner there, you'll see the entrance to **Mannequins Dance Palace**, fresh from a brand new make-over and touted as the Southeast's Number One Dance Club. The "no-exceptions" term of admission is "no one under 21," and once inside, you'll see why. (On certain nights during the week, Mannequins relaxes its 21-only age restriction to allow admission

to 18-year-olds.) The cocktails and beer flow freely; the atmosphere is over-the-edge; and there's a mix of couples dancing on the revolving dance floor—including a number of gay and lesbian couples, particularly on Thursday nights. The dance floor revolves like a turntable, a spectacular light show drenches the revelers, and a knock-your-socks-off sound system makes conversation next to impossible. The club encompasses two stories, with the huge dance floor on the bottom level. Mannequins that look as though they are costumed from a variety of Broadway shows are positioned throughout the club.

Also located on Pleasure Island is a comedy club known as the **Adventurers Club**, a two-story edifice close to the West End Stage modeled after the paneled libraries and elegant salons of similar clubs of the nineteenth century. If you take a seat at the bar, ask the bartender to work some magic—and it's quite possible your bar stool will assume a life of its own. In the drawing room, the Colonel—an irreverent and often off-color puppet operated by a hidden puppeteer—interacts with the audience and even teaches everyone a bawdy beer song. Listen carefully for the Colonel's dialog sprinkled with amusing sexual innuendo. In the library, through whose balcony a haunted organ, Fingers, has crashed (and it still plays), you'll be subjected to outrageous songs, stories and comedic *schtick*—with a fair smattering of audience participation. Be prepared for performers to single audience members out to ask semi-personal questions, and then proceed to make jokes of their responses. If you're self-conscious, you may wish to avoid the Library. You'll find several types of shows occurring periodically throughout the evening all through the Club, and plenty of private seating as well—if you and your party wish to avoid the ribald partying and enjoy a quiet conversation. But even then, there's a "talking mask" positioned on the wall; when its soliloquy turns to sex, the mask gets overheated, and actually begins to smoke. If you can, try to participate in the initiation ceremony; it's fun, irreverent, weird—and you learn a new word: "Kungaloosh!" A bit of interesting trivia: Illusionist Doug Henning served as a consultant while the Club was in the design stage. "Our favorite club is Adventurers Club," assert Jason and Lauralee. "It has that Disney feel. Everything else just feels like a club at home, only safer."

Restricted to guests who are twenty-one or older, **BET Soundstage Club**, located to the right as you face the West End Stage, features a moderate-sized dance floor and techno-pop, jazz, rhythm-and-blues, and other forms of popular music. Occasionally, BET Soundstage features live entertainment, but not when Aronda dropped in. It's still a lively, but relaxed, place; the dance floor beckons enticingly upon entry. Most evenings, a veejay shows videos by contemporary urban artists.

Probably more than any other venue on Pleasure Island, parents most frequently bring their children to the **Comedy Warehouse**. The comedy here is improv, and often, more mature than you'd like your children to hear. The Comedy Warehouse is located just to the left of West End Stage, and the line starts forming about one-half hour prior to each show, so be sure to arrive early. As they take suggestions from the audience, five comedians weave skits from audience contributions. Here's an example of some of the mildest humor: During an opening song—some of the cast have excellent voices and, well, some don't (which often adds to the comedy)—one comedian explained what NASCAR stands for: "Non-Athletic Sport Circling Around Rednecks." Then, another cast member camps it up with a "Should Have Said" scene where he was selling his Jeffrey Dahmer Smurf on eBay because it was eating his other Smurfs. Okay, so this may be over the heads of children, but the show gets a bit rougher. And the later shows tend to be less restrained than the earlier ones.

There are other treats at the Comedy Warehouse, too, as Sue relates. "This British guy named George volunteered with a story and told about the time he planned a 'romantic' evening with his wife," Sue says. "She had bought him a special pair of underwear from some sex shop. It had a zipper, and when he wore it for her, she playfully said, 'Ooh, what's in here?' and pulled down the zipper. His body parts got caught in the zipper, killing the romantic evening. The cast had a field day with this story, and in the final rhyme kept trying to set each other up by leaving them with the obvious rhyme being something they could not say. Brian ended the story with the word 'Venus,' with Jen B [one of the performers] needing to find a word relevant to the story to rhyme with that—she chose 'between us'."

You can attend multiple shows at Comedy Warehouse, and each time, the routines will be different. In fact, Comedy

All By Myself, with a Cigarette

One guest wrote Aronda, perplexed that not only was she destined to take a Walt Disney World vacation alone, but she also smokes. "And I've heard Disney is a very unfriendly place to smokers," she laments. If you're independent, and comfortable with yourself, you'll be just fine traveling solo. You might wish to avoid those restaurants catering heavily to parents and their kids. Those venues often strike a lonely chord. Otherwise, indulge yourself! You might also use your solo trips to take advantage of backstage tours--and to get lots of photos you wouldn't get with people tagging along (they wouldn't have the patience to wait while you get Spaceship Earth at just the right angle, or that unique shot through the Fountain of Nations). As for smoking--well, all the parks have smoking areas--some are quiet, beautiful spots--and you can also smoke in some bars and lounges. At Pleasure Island, the rules have changed. Once you could smoke in most clubs, except Adventurers Club and Comedy Warehouse. Now, all clubs are non-smoking. But you can always take a break to smoke outside in the street. No after-dinner cigarette, I'm afraid. Smoking is off-limits inside all WDW restaurants. And when making hotel reservations, be sure to request a smoking room.

Warehouse has a large following of "regulars." "I'm at Pleasure Island every night," says Sue, "but solely for Comedy Warehouse. Now that they've eliminated smoking in the rest of the clubs, I may venture in more often, but Comedy Warehouse is the primary reason for my visits [to Pleasure Island]. The performers are incredibly talented, and the people working outside and as servers are terrific. I'd love to see Disney ban children (younger than 15, perhaps), but realistically don't expect it to happen. My least favorite experiences are when there's a drunk in the audience saying inappropriate things, acting like a jerk, or talking loudly during the show. Luckily, that doesn't happen too often."

8TRAX is a cool club featuring music from the seventies and the disco era. The cast members working here even dress in polyester. A deejay controls the music sets—no live bands perform here. Selected nights are devoted to music from the eighties. Josh liked the music a lot—particularly when he dropped by to hear New Order's "Bizarre Love Triangle"—but the décor was more mundane than expected.

You can enjoy a laid-back atmosphere at the **Pleasure Island Jazz Company**, which hosts live entertainment nightly. With jazz from the 1930s to the present performed at less-than-ear-shattering volumes, you'll be able to *kibitz* with your party. While the dance clubs are frequently standing room only, you'll find plenty of table seating here—another feature to add to this club's relaxing atmosphere. Here, you can order a Hurricane, an original concoction by the bartenders at New Orleans' Pat O'Brien's. From time to time, couples take to the small dance floor, which is encouraged by the performers on stage. When Aronda recently dropped in, she enjoyed a performance by Felix and the Buzzcats, featuring trumpet, guitar and saxophone solos—and great vocalists. She has also become a big fan of Elliot Dyson, who plays multiple musical instruments and has a terrific voice. The bands appearing here are high caliber—and do much to heighten the speak-easy atmosphere of the Pleasure Island Jazz Company. When you're too mellow for Mannequins, try jazzing it up. You won't be

> **Bars & Lounges All Over the World**
>
> ALL-STAR RESORTS
> *All are pool bars*
> Silver Screen Spirits
> Singing Spirits
> Team Spirits
>
> DISNEY'S ANIMAL KINGDOM
> Dawa Bar
> Magic Mushroom
> *(at Rainforest Cafe)*
>
> ANIMAL KINGDOM LODGE
> Capetown Lounge & Wine Bar
> Uzima Springs *(pool bar)*
> Victoria Falls
>
> BOARDWALK
> Atlantic Dance
> Belle Vue Room
> Big River Grille
> ESPN Club
> Jelly Rolls
> Leaping Horse Libations
> *(pool bar)*
>
> BONNET CREEK GOLF COURSE
> Sand Trap Bar & Grill
>
> CARIBBEAN BEACH
> Banana Cabana *(pool bar)*
> Shutters at Old Port Royale

sorry!

Live bands entertain guests at the **Rock N Roll Beach Club**, right around the corner from Mannequins Dance Palace, where dancing and surfer-style décor abound. The music covers hits from the sixties to the present. To enter, you ascend a flight of industrial-style stairs before making your entrance on the second floor—but the dancing and the stage show occur on the first. The dance floor is fairly small, and gets crowded quickly, but the club is an energetic place to be entertained, with a lot of guest interaction with the live band.

Motion is the newest club on Pleasure Island, replacing the country music-themed Wildhorse Saloon. Here, you'll enjoy an eclectic mix of contemporary music from Top 40 to Alternative. During recent visits to this relatively new venue (it opened in 2001), crowds were moderate and the dance floor fairly empty. However, with Joan Jett and the Blackhearts' appearance in the club on New Year's Eve 2002, Motion's heightened exposure certainly earned it some new fans.

Downtown Disney West Side

In addition to a hefty selection of twenty-four screens at the AMC Theaters, and the ever-changing performance offerings at the famous House of Blues, you'll encounter one of the most sensational entertainment experiences to be found anywhere—right here in Downtown Disney West Side. It's Cirque du Soleil's ***La Nouba***. The Cirque theater is a cinch to find; it looks like a huge, white circus tent—made from steel and concrete, truly one of the most interesting pieces of architecture at Walt Disney World. Inside, you'll meet performers who "play a clown, or acrobat, or *something*." Indeed, you won't always be certain exactly what it is you are experiencing—you'll just be glad you did. The performers in this extravaganza often defy categorization. Sometimes, they even defy gender. The troupe includes acrobats, actors, dancers, clowns and musicians. There's an element of the Godfrey Reggio theme of his film *Koyaanisqatsi* (Hopi for

Bars & Lounges All Over the World

GRAND FLORIDIAN
Garden View Lounge
Mizner's
Narcoosee's
Summer House *(pool bar)*

POLYNESIAN
Barefoot Bar *(pool bar)*
Tambu Lounge

PORT ORLEANS FRENCH QUARTER
Mardi Grogs *(pool bar)*
Scat Cat's Club
PORT ORLEANS RIVERSIDE
River Roost
Muddy Rivers *(pool bar)*

SWAN/DOLPHIN
Cabana Bar *(Dolphin Pool)*
Copa Banana
Kimonos
Lobby Court
Shula's Steak House Lounge
Splash Grill *(Swan Pool)*

WILDERNESS LODGE
Territory
Trout Pass *(pool bar)*

YACHT & BEACH CLUB
Ale & Compass
Crew's Cup
Hurricane Hannah's *(pool bar)*
Martha's Vineyard
Rip Tide

Bars & Lounges
All Over the World

CONTEMPORARY RESORT
California Grill Lounge
Outer Rim
Sand Bar *(pool bar)*

CORONADO SPRINGS
Francisco's
Siesta's *(pool bar)*

DISNEY-MGM STUDIOS
Tune-In Lounge

OLD KEY WEST
Gurgling Suitcase
Turtle Shack *(pool bar)*

DOWNTOWN DISNEY
Stone Crab *(at Fulton's)*
Bongos Cuban Cafe
Portobello Yacht Club
Rainforest Cafe
Cap'n Jack's

EPCOT
Matsu No Ma *(Japan)*
Rose & Crown Pub *(UK)*
Sommerfest *(Germany)*

FORT WILDERNESS
Crockett's Tavern

POP CENTURY
Petals *(pool bar)*
Classic Concoctions

"life out of balance") in *La Nouba*, yet this show isn't as dark or as cynical as Reggio's film (though the music is just as unique as Philip Glass's music in *Koyaanisqatsi*), which depicts civilization's absence of soul or humor. *La Nouba*, performed in a permanent showplace seating 1,671 guests and constructed especially for Cirque du Soleil, celebrates life's complexities, rather than cynically disparaging them. By the way, it's fruitless to try to determine which language the voices are singing during the performance. The "words" are nonsense. The show's creator wanted everyone, regardless of their native tongue, to be equally "confused" by the lyrics. This ninety-minute performance MUST be seen! Tickets range in price from $59.00 to $82.00. Thomas and Maribeth call the show "outstanding! It is hard to describe in words how fascinating it is." Sue says it's "incredible, unbelievable, awe-inspiring! Worth twice the price—it's a don't-miss show." Shelle, Bob and daugher Amanda have seen the show twice. "And we'll continue to see it as long as it runs. It is truly enjoyable. The music is beauti-

Amanda was appalled by the ticket prices, "but once we saw La Nouba, it was the best thing we did. The live music was wonderful. The show was like an opera combined with rock concert and an exhibtion of surrealist paintings." (Photo taken shortly after hurricane damage to theater exterior.)

ful. La Nouba is much more than a show. It has music, acrobatics, and comedy all in one."

If electronic and computer games float your boat, Walt Disney World has taken them years closer to the future in West Side's **DisneyQuest**. Disney describes this complex, located next door to Cirque du Soleil, as a "self-contained, interactive theme park." The building consists of five floors—you take a unique elevator ride to the top floor where you begin your "quest"—divided into four zones: Explore, Score, Create and Replay. One of Aronda's favorite attractions in DisneyQuest is CyberSpace Mountain, where you not only design your own roller coaster, but you also ride it—courtesy of a motion simu-

lator into which your creation is programmed. Don't worry, though. If your coaster goes too high on the barf scale, just push the simulator's panic button to abort your ride. Needless to say, pre-teens and teens adore this attraction. Other computer-based and enhanced attractions include Buzz Lightyear's AstroBlaster (bumper cars whose passengers shoot balls at other drivers—younger kids love this one), Mighty Ducks Pinball Slam (this attraction transforms players into human joysticks) and Pirates of the Caribbean: Battle for Buccaneer Gold (a swashbuckling adventure). Admission to DisneyQuest—which is included on the Premium Annual Pass and other ticket options—is about $35.00 for adults, and $28.00 for children, but one ticket is good for re-entering as often as you like all day long. The attraction is open from about 10:30 a.m. until midnight—sometimes it closes at 11:00 p.m. during off-season. Please note that DisneyQuest attracts youngsters and teens by the score. Aronda stayed only a very short time, since this attraction seems more tailored to their entertainment needs—a justification for parents wondering whether to leave

You can't beat the admission price at Atlantic Dance, located on the BoardWalk. If you like driving dance music, you'll really like the classy digs inside.

---

older kids here while they enjoy other more adult entertainment at Downtown Disney. But regardless of your age, if you enjoy computerized games and gadgetry, you'll love DisneyQuest. No one can argue the creativity poured into this unique entertainment venue. Sue calls DisneyQuest "noisy, but with some really cool things to do, like CyberSpace Mountain and the virtual Pirates of the Caribbean. Video junkies will love it. I can only take it for short periods."

BoardWalk offers three club environments to entice adult revelers to heighten their Disney enjoyment. **ESPN Club** caters to the sports enthusiast, and includes a broadcasting facility, arcade, table-service restaurant, bar and more than one hundred televisions broadcasting live sports events! The Club is divided into three sections. You'll enter on The Sidelines, where you can sit at a bar or table. At Sports Central — which is the main dining area — you can watch the big game on the

Big Screen (we *meant* to use those capital letters!). And the Yard Arcade invites you to test your skills on the latest sports-themed video games.

Atlantic Dance offers a gorgeous atmosphere in which to dance to tunes spun by a deejay, or recorded music. Lately, attendance here has sagged, and Disney has been working toward making Atlantic Dance a more appealing night time destination. Aronda dropped in in October 2004, and found it a delightful nightspot. "It's really a classy place," she says. "The dance floor is huge, and a tremendous video screen has been installed above the stage. Really cool (and weird) videos were being played when I dropped in. You can also sit around the dance floor at comfortable tables, unlike some venues where you have to just stand around, looking like no one saved the last dance for you." Admission, at press time, was free!

Close by, you'll find **Jellyrolls** — another hotspot on the BoardWalk. It's a sing-along bar appropriately referred to as "home of the dueling pianos." Guests make requests of the pianists, and the musicians invite everyone to sing along. "This is the best place to tear it up in Disney," says one veteran. "Sing along, dance around and just have fun. I love this place!" This "outstanding, hippest and laid-back place features wonderfully talented piano players who always make you laugh," says another regular. Brian calls Jellyrolls his favorite nightspot. "The club has awesome piano players who are humorous and talented."

Three dinner shows round out Walt Disney World's nighttime offerings. The **Hoop-Dee-Doo Musical Revue**, performed inside Pioneer Hall at Disney's Fort Wilderness Resort and Campground, incorporates dinner with a professional saloon show. Much audience participation is expected, and indeed, makes this show more enjoyable. But if the "wild west" with its can-can girls, corny jokes, Hee-Haw style musical ditties and magic acts doesn't match your idea of a good time, you'll waste two hours better spent at Pleasure Island or a nice restaurant. However, many veteran Disney travelers adore this dinner show, for which Walt Disney World will accept reservations up to two years in advance. (Priority Seating does not work for this event; you must reserve with a credit card guarantee.) The food, unfortunately, doesn't match the quality of the performance. The menu consists of corn on the cob, baked beans, salad, barbecue ribs, fried chicken, and strawberry shortcake. If you discover you must sit upstairs, don't purchase the ticket. Josh and Dann arrived late due to a delayed backstage tour, and had to sit in the balcony, where the audience's backs "face" the stage. A ridiculous, inane and inconsiderate move on Disney's part. A ticket for the Hoop-Dee-Doo Musical Revue will set you back about $49.01 (for adults) and $24.81 (for children 3-11). The Revue, which in previous incarnations was called *Country Hoedown* and *Pioneer Hall Revue*, features the antics of Johnny Ringo, Jim Handy, Six Bits Slocum, Flora Long, Claire Delune, and Dolly Drew.

Over at Disney's Polynesian Resort, the **Spirit of Aloha Dinner Show** provides authentic music, dancing and song of the cultures of Tahiti, Samoa, Tonga, New Zealand and Hawaii. Auntie Wini serves as the night's hostess. During the show, expect "Hawaiian Roller Coaster Ride" from *Lilo & Stitch*. The food served is lanai-roasted chicken, Polynesian rice, South Seas veggies and dessert. Draft beer or white wine is included with the price of the show, which is $49.01 (for adults) and $24.81 (for children 3-11). Shows are usually scheduled Tuesday through Saturday at 5:15 and 8:00 p.m.

At Disney's Fort Wilderness, you can learn to line dance during **Mickey's Backyard Barbecue**, a favorite of youngsters. A live country band serves up the music, while Disney characters serve up plenty of smiles—though some parents have complained that access to the characters is a "bit disorganized, at best." Dinner consists of barbecued ribs and chicken, corn on the cob, and baked beans. The show, which is presented seasonally, costs $37.00 (for adults) and $25.00 (for children).

To make reservations for all dinner shows, call Disney at **407-WDW-DINE**.

Chapter 15

Enough Is Enough Is—Not Enough!
Expanding Your Disney Vacation

By now, you've done the four major Disney theme parks. You've sampled exquisite cuisine from all the restaurants you just couldn't pass up. The worms in mud (worm-shaped gummy candies in chocolate pudding) at The Land's Garden Grill were good for the kids—not so good for you. But the Cobb salad at Hollywood Brown Derby and the pumpkin-stuffed pasta at California Grill were superb. You've danced the night away at Mannequins Dance Palace, tipped the dueling pianists at the BoardWalk to play your favorite tunes, contributed to the wacky improvisation at the Comedy Warehouse, designed roller coasters and fought pirates at DisneyQuest, and splashed, floated, flirted and slid at both Blizzard Beach and Typhoon Lagoon.

Time to go home. Right?

Absolutely not!

Walt Disney World offers a number of "behind-the-scenes" tours for guests who have an insatiable lust for the Mouse—for an additional charge. A passion for Disney, as any Memories Team member will attest, is never cheap. But if you're eager to discover a few of the secrets behind the manufacture of all the pixie dust, you should consider the extra investment. Disney does an excellent job making these tours educational, entertaining and often surprising—all at once. Please note, however, that guests must be at least sixteen years old to participate in most tours. The reason, as we understand it? Disney doesn't want to spoil the show for kids who aren't yet jaded enough to separate Disney fantasy from reality (though the official line invokes "insurance considerations.")

To book Disney Adult Discoveries backstage programs or Disney's Family Magic Tour, call **407.WDW.TOUR (939.8687)**. Please bear in mind that Disney occasionally tweaks tour components, so your experiences may deviate slightly from the descriptions that follow. "I've been on Keys to the Kingdom and the all-day Backstage Magic tours," says Amanda. "I really enjoy seeing behind the scenes, but then again, there were some things I wish I hadn't seen. I was kind of crushed when I saw the reality of Splash Mountain. I really thought I was inside a mountain the whole ride. If you just have to see for yourself, take either of these tours. They're both excellent. But don't say I didn't warn you!"

Disney Vacation Club

Does a Disney Vacation infect you with an insatiable desire to spend even more time at this wonderful place?

Yet how can you fulfill that desire without bankruptcy

If you're interested in determining whether an investment in the Disney Vacation Club is right for you, just look for this sign, located in all Disney resorts and theme parks.

looming in your future?

Well, Disney offers a way to purchase your accommodations in advance for many, many years. Not only that, you'll stay in some of The World's best resort hotels — BoardWalk, Wilderness Lodge, Old Key West, Beach Club Villas and Disney's Saratoga Springs — on points, not dollars. When you make an investment in this unique timeshare concept, you actually purchase points which renew each and every year, until 2042. And with purchases at Saratoga Springs, you can invest in your vacations for fifty years. (Aronda, who is a member, imagines herself as a centenarian queuing up for a ride on the Tower of Terror.) When you call to make your reservations, you'll spend Disney points rather than money. Deluxe accommodations that ordinarily begin at $200.00 a night (at today's rate of exchange) are yours for about $85.00 per night. When you do the math on your investment, you'll figure you made the right decision.

What is this unique concept called? It's the **Disney Vacation Club** (DVC), and with membership, you'll have the ability to add enormous flexibility to your Walt Disney World vacations. Even if you grow World-weary — bite your tongue! — you have the autonomy to book vacations at hundreds of other destinations, both nationally and internationally. You can even take a voyage on the Disney Cruise Line on points. Though the DVC is a timeshare investment, its flexibility — unlike many other timeshare models — is unprecedented. Best of all, your yearly vacations are not restricted to any particular week

In a nutshell, here's how it works. After purchasing your DVC membership, determine when you're ready for another vacation. You must purchase a minumum of 150 points at about $95.00 per point; Disney will offer financing to qualified buyers. Or, if needed, you may opt to find financing on your own. Then, refer to your point charts in your Membership materials to determine how many points your vacation will cost. For example, if your Studio accommodations cost fourteen points per night during the time of your vacation, 150 points translates into more than ten nights — which, unlike other timeshares, do not have to be taken all at the same time. Once you've calculated the necessary points, pick up the phone (or open up your e-mail program) to contact Member Services for reservations. Another great perk of DVC membership is the collection of great discounts on shopping, resaurants, and ticket media. In January 2005, DVC members began saving substantially on Annual Passes and Premium Annual Passes, making frequent visits to Walt Disney World an even more affordable proposition.

Still interested? For more information, call 1-800-633-5139. Or, you can visit the DVC's official Web site at **dvcmagic.com**. Better yet, stop by a DVC Information Kiosk on your next Walt Disney World vacation, and ask for a personal tour. Cast members will happily oblige. (These Kiosks

> ### Where Did Disney Hide Mickey Mouse?
>
> Throughout Walt Disney World, you can find a number of places where Walt Disney Imagineers have planted images of Mickey Mouse concealed in the designs of attractions and resort hotels!
>
> Hidden Mickeys may contain the head and ears silhouette, the profile of Mickey's head, or an actual cartoon of the entire figure of Mickey Mouse. Start your own search with the four listed below.
>
> ○ In the Magic Kingdom's Haunted Mansion, look closely at the Ballroom Scene. Find the arrangements of plates and saucers on the banquet table--then look hard and fast as your Doom Buggy passes by.
> ○ In Epcot, look closely at the walls of the gift shop, Cargo Bay, in Mission: SPACE. You're likely to find several images of the Mouse in wall decorations.
> ○ In the Twilight Zone Tower of Terror at the Studios, the little girl in the elevator is holding a Mickey Mouse plush during the TV scene.
> ○ At Old Key West, notice the images in the balcony/patio railings.
>
> If you find your search gets too cumbersome or difficult, you can always drop by Guest Relations and ask for their comprehensive list. Or better yet, purchase Steve Barrett's excellent book called **Hidden Mickeys: A Field Guide to Walt Disney World's Best-Kept Secrets**.

may be found in all Disney resort hotels, all theme parks, and Downtown Disney.) There's no obligation—and no high pressure sales pitch. In reality, DVC sells itself. "What appeals to me about DVC is the flexibility to stay wherever, for however long or short of a stay," says Sue. (DVC operates a resort on Hilton Head Island and Vero Beach, too, and those rooms are in your inventory, as well.) "Also, I love knowing my lodging is paid for through 2042! The drawback? Once you take a DVC trip, you want more and more DVC trips. It can get expensive buying more and more points. But since that means

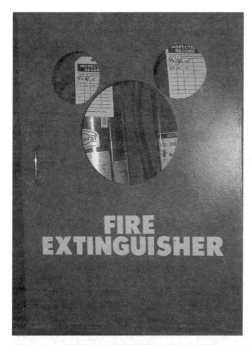

Walt Disney Imagineers plant Hidden Mickeys throughout Walt Disney World. You can add another dimension to your vacation by attempting to find them. The Fire Extinguisher Hidden Mickey is located at the exit from Who Wants to Be a Millionaire? Play It! In a number of resort hotels, you'll find Hidden Mickeys (and other characters) in the design of your bedspread.

more and more trips, it's okay with me!" And usually, members receive a DVC discount of fifteen percent on the following behind-the-scenes tours.

Backstage Magic

Backstage Magic is the crème de la crème of all backstage tours. Seven hours in duration, it includes lunch at a restaurant in one of the theme parks (when Aronda participated, she dined at Mama Melrose's in Disney-MGM Studios) where several Streetmosphere performers engage the dining tour participants in an improvised skit while they dine. Then, one of the actors—Aronda's was Constance Payne—will board your tour bus (which either Disney Cruise Line or Mears provides) under the guise of bidding you farewell. Then, suddenly, she comes out of character to tell you a bit about herself, and what it's like to work for The Walt Disney Company.

The tour actually begins at Epcot, where you'll journey backstage to the America pavilion and see the fascinating "war horse" of The American Adventure — the Audio-Animatronics-based tableaux which are "telescoped" onto stage level during the thirty-minute presentation. (These Audio-Animatronics figures are run by hydraulics, a fact that science-minded Josh found fascinating. Dann just wondered why, during pre-show tech tests, Ben Franklin twitched so erratically.) As the tour progresses, you'll visit several resort-wide backstage areas, such as the maintenance warehouse, where ride elements are repaired, refined or maintained. Aronda saw one of the Cinderella's Carrousel horses being meticulously repainted by a cast member whose sole assignment is to keep the horses beautiful. At Disney-MGM Studios, you step into the Wardrobe department where, after listening to a short presentation about the responsibilities of keeping cast members outfitted, you'll receive a small piece of fabric from a Disney character's costume. The tour ends at Magic Kingdom, where you descend beneath the park into an underground network of service tunnels called "Utilidors." (Magic Kingdom is actually constructed on the "second floor," above these service corridors.) Exits from inside these Utilidors lead into guest areas, allowing cast members in Tomorrowland costumes, for example, to enter directly onto the Tomorrowland "stage" rather than having to walk through another land — like Fantasyland — to get there. You visit the park's costume shop, the "parking" area for the floats from King Triton's Electrical Water Pageant, cast member rehearsal areas, and high-speed garbage disposal "tubes" before you enter the Main Street, U.S.A. parade production facility. You'll watch the afternoon parade on television monitors, while listening to an explanation of Disney's capacity for staging seamless transitions from unit to unit — including how parade cast members deal with problems along the route. Later, your tour guide takes you "live" through a cast member entrance into Town Square, where the "Share a Dream Come True" parade passes by. Aronda enjoyed this tour immensely, and recommends it highly. No other backstage tour will immerse you in the operations of Walt Disney World more thoroughly than this one. To take the Backstage Magic tour will set you back around $200 per person; theme park admission is not required nor included. Please note that Disney's Animal Kingdom is not included in this tour.

Backstage Safari

Backstage Safari is a three-hour tour that takes you to the backstage animal facilities at Disney's Animal Kingdom, including the nursery and the elephant barn. Cost to participate is about $65.00. A fascinating tour — and a "can't-miss" for anyone who is interested in animal care and preservation. It's amazing to see the level of compassion and care extended to the animals at Disney's Animal Kingdom. The handlers and technicians obviously love their work with the many magnificent creatures in this beautiful park. This is one of Disney's newest tours and, in Aronda's opinion, one of the Company's best. Note that you may not see actual animals during this tour — though several guests have reported encountering certain animals; one guest said his group was even allowed to touch a young rhinoceros. However, don't book Backstage Safari if an encounter with animals is necessary to your enjoyment. Instead, this tour focuses on health issues, feeding, and other animal care issues, as well as various programs Disney has instituted toward animal research and breeding. "This tour was informative about the animals, but lasted longer than stated," according to Thomas and Maribeth. "We really were not impressed. We had to leave early to make our other planned reservations. We were disappointed that it took longer, and we didn't really see a lot of animals." When Dann and Josh participated in late 2004, one of the impressive African elephants was out in its habitat, leaving only about ten feet between the tour group and the animal. Also, participants usually receive a pin for their attentive participation.

Keys to the Kingdom

Keys to the Kingdom, a 4 ½-hour tour orienting Magic Kingdom fans to the history and operation of the first Disney park that opened in Florida, takes guests into the Utilidors—allowing them to see more of these corridors than even Backstage Magic shows. You also visit an attraction—though you have to wait in the regular line—and the Production Center, where new shows are rehearsed before going live in the theme park. Cost is about $58.00; note that theme park admission is also required to participate. "We participated in the Keys to the Kingdom tour in 2003," say Lindsey and Chuck. "Having vacationed in Walt Disney World every year since birth, I didn't think there was anything I didn't know about the Magic Kingdom. I was definitely wrong! Our tour guide was excellent and was able to answer any questions the group had. He took us on different attractions and explained how they were built, how different scenes work, and he showed us some Hidden Mickeys. We also had the opportunity to go backstage and see where the parade floats are kept. Last, we were taken into the underground tunnel [Utilidors] for a look at how cast members get from place to place without being seen. This tour was definitely worthwhile."

Ed took the tour during his last trip, and "absolutely loved it. I expected it to be shorter and less informative, but it was a pleasure from end to end. I really learned a lot more about Disney and how the company does business than I ever expected."

And Crystal has yet another unique perspective. "My Mom and I went on a mother/daughter vacation in 2003 and took this tour. From that moment on, I decided I was going to be a Jungle Cruise Skipper, so in May 2004 we came down again. I interviewed with Disney, and I'm proud to say I have been around that river at least a thousand times in the last five months. I am living proof that when you wish upon a star and truly believe, your dreams really do come true."

The Magic Behind Our Steam Trains

This tour explores Walt Disney's passion for steam trains, while giving you the opportunity to join the opening crew as they prepare for the daily railroad operation at the Magic Kingdom. This tour also offers the rare opportunity to visit Disney's backstage roundhouse.

The tour highlight is the train trip back to the roundhouse with an up-close and personal look at one or more of the locomotives. But the experience is also rich in history about Walt Disney's lifelong fascination with steam trains, how Disney acquired the theme park's four locomotives, and the operating procedures cast members follow to serve their annual ridership of over three million guests. You'll receive an exclusive pin, designed by one of Walt Disney World's engineers, at the end of the tour.

Usually, the tour is offered Monday, Tuesday, Thursday and Saturday at the Magic Kingdom turnstiles at 7:30 a.m. The tour ends around 10:30 a.m. Cost is $40.00 plus tax, and theme park admission is required. Guests must be at least ten years old to participate. DVC members may request a fifteen percent discount.

DiveQuest, Dolphins in Depth, Epcot Seas Aqua Tour

In **DiveQuest**, a 2 ½-hour program where only guests with certified SCUBA experience are allowed to participate, you'll spend at least thirty minutes underwater in Epcot's Living Seas pavilion's main tank, with very impressive marine life — the same creatures, including sharks, turtles and rays, you see during the aquarium tour. Cost is $140.00, and includes all gear, the dive, refreshments, a tee-shirt, certificate, and dive log stamp; participation does not require park admission. If you're a seasoned diver, guests who have participated highly recommend this experience.

The Living Seas also hosts **Dolphins in Depth**, a 3 ½-

hour session with dolphin researchers and trainers who will allow you to actually "get physical" with these fascinating mammals, since you are encouraged to interact. Note that the dolphins are not forced to reciprocate, however; it's totally up to the animal whether to make an overture. Cost is $150.00; theme park admission is not required to participate, nor is it included. The cost includes a photo with a dolphin, refreshments, and a tee-shirt commemorating your experience. Chrislette and Jim call Dolphins in Depth "an unforgettable experience."

In **Epcot Seas Aqua Tour**, guests get an up-close look into more than sixty-five diverse species of marine life, including sharks, turtles, rays and tropical fish. This adventure takes you into the water to explore The Living Sea's marine environment using a Scuba Assisted Snorkel (SAS) unit. Before entering the water, you'll tour the aquarium, and learn about some of the marine life you'll encounter. Participants must be eight years old or older. The program begins daily at 12:30 p.m., and lasts about 2 ½ hours. Cost is $100.00, and includes all gear, refreshments, tee-shirt and a group photo.

Gardens of the World
Hidden Treasures of World Showcase

In Epcot's World Showcase, **Gardens of the World** offers you a three-hour opportunity to study plants, flowers and trees under the tutelage of a Disney horticulturalist—the best in the business. This tour is ideal for the garden enthusiast who cannot visit during Epcot's annual Flower and Garden Festival in the spring. Cost is about $60.00; park admission is also required. Note that this tour is not offered during Epcot's Flower and Garden Festival.

Hidden Treasures of World Showcase is a three-hour tour focusing on the art, architecture and traditions of world cultures as they are represented in the park. Cost is about $60.00; theme park admission is required to participate.

Supplementing Meals with Grocery Visits

Want to add a few economical snacks--or quick but nutritious breakfasts--to your great Disney meals? Try one of the Orlando area's grocery stores. Though Walt Disney World has limited supplies of grocery items at all its resort hotels, prices will be lower at these locales.

ALBERTSON'S (albertsons.com)
407-857-5666
12981 S. Orange Blossom Trail

SUPER TARGET (target.com)
407-251-5133
2155 Town Center Boulevard

GOODINGS (goodings.com)
407-827-1200
SR535 and Hotel Plaza Boulevard (Crossroads), Lake Buena Vista

PUBLIX (publix.com)
407-396-7525
2915 Vineland, Kissimmee

KASH N KARRY (kashnkarry.com)
407-847-2666
3183 W. Vine, Kissimmee

WAL-MART SUPERCENTER (walmart.com)
407-846-6611
444 West Vine (Highway 192), Kissimmee

Flower and Garden Festival

Each spring—from about mid-April until early June—Epcot bursts into full bloom during the *Flower and Garden Festival.* Hundreds of varieties of plants dominate the park, with signs providing information about the plants to interested guests. Demonstrations—like composting, examining

Epcot's Flower & Garden Festival can be hard to navigate. Look for this sign at the Festival Center, where you'll find all the answers!

how bugs keep gardens healthy, and topiary design—are also included, and special commemorative merchandise is released each year. One of the most festive components of the Festival is the Flower Power concert program; in 2003, Starship featuring Mickey Thomas, Paul Revere and the Raiders, and Arlo Guthrie appeared in the America Garden Theater. Several concerts are staged each day. Gardening demonstrations occur periodically, along with garden-themed "Streetmosphere" acts. *Epcot Garden Discoveries* are guided tours conducted by Disney horticulturists and designed especially for garden enthusiasts; cost is $59.00. Programs and exhibits for children are also featured, among many demonstrations, speakers and purchasing opportunities. Last spring, Chrislette and Jim "attended Epcot during the Flower and Garden Festival. We loved walking through the exhibits, getting new landscaping ideas, and purchasing a few souvenirs. We also heard the Buckinghams, and Paul Revere and the Raiders, at the America Garden Theater. Cool, huh?"

Undiscovered Future World

Undiscovered Future World, Epcot's newest backstage tour, leads you in a three-hour exploration of all the pavilions of Future World. This tour includes backstage and onstage areas of one of the park's most spectacular attractions — Ellen's Energy Adventure. Between shows, you're allowed to stand for about five minutes on the show floor, directly in the path of the ride vehicles. All around, Audio-Animatronics dinosaurs loom menacingly above you. It's an awesome feeling; you are close enough to touch the dinosaurs (which is not allowed). Finally, the show area fades into total darkness — Disney's effort to conserve energy while the show area isn't in use, since some of the pavilion's electricity is supplied via photovoltaic cells on the roof of the show building — and you begin to imagine that perhaps one of these large reptiles has eyes — and appetite — only for you.

Luckily, your tour guide has a large flashlight with her, and guides you safely into the sunlight. You're also treated to a backstage storage facility, and allowed to walk quickly through a cast member only area where Company D, a Disneyana shop solely for cast members who have both a job *and* a penchant for Disney, is located. Occasionally, you're treated to a special viewing area for the evening's performance of IllumiNations: Reflections of Earth, and given a special commemorative pin of the event. Participants are usually able to utilize a substantial discount for lunch at The Nine Dragons in China. Cost for the tour is about $50.00; theme park admission is required for participation. Josh participated in the tour during one of its inaugural runs. As a science "nut," "I found the explanations of the nuts and bolts of the Future World section of the park fascinating. I particularly enjoyed hearing about Alucobond, the material Spaceship Earth is made of."

Wild By Design

One of two relatively new backstage tours is the three-hour **Wild By Design**, which teaches guests some of the stories behind the conceptualization and construction of Disney's Animal Kingdom. Though you never go behind the scenes, you'll learn from knowledgeable cast members how storytelling, art, architecture and historical artifacts combine to transport guests to "exotic lands filled with wild animals." The tour takes you into the land of Anandapur in Asia, to the village of Harambe in Africa, through the colorful, relaxing world of Discovery Island. A light continental breakfast is served midway through the tour. Guests must be fourteen years old or older to participate; the tour is available only on Tuesday, Thursday and Friday. Guests report for the tour thirty minutes prior to park opening. Price is $58.00 per person; Disney's Animal Kingdom admission is required.

Disney's Welcome to the Magic Kingdom

Another new tour, **Disney's Welcome to the Magic Kingdom**, takes guests on a ninety-minute walking tour to introduce them to the seven themed lands of the Magic Kingdom. It's a perfect introductory tour for first-timers. Tour guides instruct guests on the use of park guidemaps, services available in Magic Kingdom, dining and entertainment options. Additionally, facts about Disney attractions are disclosed to guests — as well as an opportunity to experience FASTPASS. Tours are scheduled for Sunday, Monday, Tuesday, Wednesday and Friday, and are conducted in four languages:

> 8:30 – 10:00 English
> 9:00 – 10:30 Portuguese
> 9:30 – 11:00 Japanese
> 10:00 – 11:30 Spanish

Guests, who should arrive fifteen minutes prior to time of tour departure, meet by the Tour Booth near the Guest Relations Window outside the Main Entrance. There is no age requirement for this tour, but theme park admission is required. Cost is $20.00 per person, ten and older; children under ten are admitted free.

Walt Disney World Marathon

There is no shortage of special events hosted by Walt Disney World, though you must carefully plan your stay to enjoy them. **The Walt Disney World Marathon** occurs in early January of each year, and draws thirteen thousand participants from around the world. Registration, which is about $95.00, begins in the spring of each year preceding the event, and usually closes no later than October. You can choose to run or walk the course—or merely assume the less-challenging role of spectator (which requires no registration fee). If you run the entire race route, you'll put about twenty-six miles on your sneakers, but the big perk (besides your huge sense of accomplishment) is seeing backstage areas of all four parks. The 2005 Walt Disney World Marathon occurred on January 9. You may register for the 2006 event online at **disneyworldsports.com** (2005 reached its capacity months prior to the event, so don't procrastinate), or request a race application by calling 407-939-7810. Registration for the 2006 Marathon begins March 1, 2005. *Insider's Tip*: The official Walt Disney World Sports Internet site reveals a list of athletic events too numerous to list in our guide, so if you're interested, keep checking at the URL listed above.

July Fourth and New Year's Eve

Both **July Fourth** and **New Year's Eve** are monstrously crowded events at the Walt Disney World theme parks. Park admission requires the usual investment, but the parks close extra late—in 2004, all parks except Disney's Animal Kingdom closed at 1:00 a.m.—the fireworks are extra long and spectacular, and the parades are usually special editions. If you wish to stay in Walt Disney World accommodations, you'll need to book early. Otherwise, you'll have to settle for potluck off-property—which could mean no admission into the parks on the big holidays if they have already filled to capac-

During Epcot's 2004 Food & Wine Festival, Piemonte opened a "chocolate cafe" where guests could sample wines and chocolate desserts at their leisure.

ity by the time you arrive. Disney resort guests, however, are always guaranteed admission into the parks, even if they are closed to the general public because of capacity crowds. The two weeks straddling **Easter** (spring break) are also packed; the parks stay open late, but expect long waits to enjoy the attractions. Use FASTPASS whenever possible — though during these holidays, you may discover all FASTPASSes have been dispensed fairly early in the day. In our experience, Disney veterans, who have already experienced most of the gate-buster attractions during earlier visits, enjoy these holidays most since they are more inclined to look for ways to savor the Resort other than the ever-popular E-ticket rides. Unless the major attractions are high on your priority list, we suggest trying a new backstage tour, dinner show, restaurant or recreation — then going back to the parks after dinner time. You'll be surprised how favorably a unique experience will impact your vacation.

Food and Wine Festival

Epcot's *International Food and Wine Festival* extends from early October through mid-November as a result of Disney's expansion of this hugely popular event, and it's a wonderful opportunity to enjoy the cuisine of more than twenty regions around the globe. You can literally eat and drink your way around World Showcase, as Aronda did, sampling appetizer-sized portions of various foods from special kiosks set up for the event. Food samples range in price from $1.00-$4.50. Wine and beer samples range from $2.00-$7.00 per half-glass. Special meals showcasing the talents of famous chefs, including many Disney chefs, are also scheduled at selected restaurants inside Epcot. Free wine-tasting and cooking seminars are conducted daily during the Festival in special tents set up along the World Showcase promenade, as well as in the Odyssey (a former restaurant now used primarily for conventions, special events and Grand Gatherings buffets). Aronda enjoyed three wine seminars in two hours, so by the time the final one ended, she was feeling quite mellow. Special merchandise commemorating the event pops up all over the park. The crowds are usually bearable during this Festival (except on weekends), and the many available wine tastings, food samplings and cooking demonstrations can add a unique dimension to your Disney vacation. Several tantalizing reservations-only dinners are provided on weekends, showcasing the talents of some of the top chefs in the world. Disney has experimented with several distribution approaches to disseminate recipes to guests who wish to expand their culinary talents; the Festival Center can tell you whether to request e-mail recipes delivered after you return home, or procure recipe cards "on the spot." The spectacular "Eat to the Beat" music series premiered during the 2002 Festival, and has continued each year since. Aronda enjoyed listening to Mary Wilson of The Supremes (who was spectacular with her own live band), and to Sister Sledge (who would've been more spectacular if the group had not used pre-recorded music). Other musical groups have included Three Dog Night, Chic, The 5th Dimension and the amazingly talented Taylor Dayne. Disney usually announces all Food and Wine Festival details in the early summer; keep checking its official Web site at **www.disneyworld.com** for the 2005 lineup. Jason and Lauralee have traveled twice to the Food & Wine Festival. "We love to eat our way around the world," says Jason. "Or, in my case, try beer from around the world."

Mickey's Not-So-Scary Halloween Party

On ten (or twelve, depending on ticket sales) evenings preceding and including Halloween, a special, separately-ticketed event called **Mickey's Not-So-Scary Halloween Party** is staged at the Magic Kingdom. In reality, the Halloween event is a private party, when Disney closes the Magic Kingdom to the general public several hours early and allows guests who have purchased special tickets to enter. (We strongly suggest ordering these tickets as soon as possible after Disney makes them available. If you wait until you arrive, you may very well find the tickets have sold out—an almost inevitable occurrence for the Halloween Night event.) If you're feeling particularly flamboyant, you might try your hand at creative costuming and make-up. More kids than adults dress up, but you'll still be in good company if you decide to go as someone else—as long as you don't attend the party as Freddie Kruger or an equally frightening figure, since Disney wants to keep the event as kid-friendly as possible. (The horrifying version of a Halloween party happens over at Universal Studios Florida—so if you're determined to have the daylights scared out of you, the "other park" may be the best place for you.) Be sure to drop by the various Trick-or-Treat locations, marked on your special Halloween guidemap, where cast members will stuff your bag (provided by Disney) with candy, no matter how old you happen to be! Then, select your spot along the parade route to enjoy the special "not-so-scary," but ever-so-delightful Mickey's "Boo to You" Halloween parade, which features Disney's cast of famous characters dressed in their Halloween costumes, and the Headless Horseman's creepy journey through the Magic Kingdom on his spirited steed. This special edition parade features its own array of unique floats—a

The authentic and antique hearse on display in front of the Haunted Mansion is a nice prop for Mickey's Not-So-Scary Halloween Party. The cast members working the Mansion really get into their roles during this event.

---

rare treat you're sure to enjoy! A special fireworks display ignites over Cinderella Castle, then surrounds the park in a 360-degree display. Before the party ends, though, a wicked witch rides her broom high across the sky, taking over Tinker Bell's route. Advance admission for this highly-recommended event is about $32.00 for adults, and about $26.58 for children; same-day purchase is a few bucks higher. The Party lasts from 7:00 p.m. until midnight. "The Party was not what we expected," say Toni and Jim. "We were under the impression that only so many tickets were going to be sold. We were there on a Friday evening, watching the kids in lines that were much too long. Parents had their hands full because the kids got tired of waiting." Amanda, however, reports a different sort of experience. "We enjoyed going to the Magic Kingdom in costume, and seeing other guests' costumes. The best I saw were a husband as Dorothy, the wife as the Scarecrow, and their baby as Toto, all from *The Wizard of Oz*. 'Dorothy' was about 6 feet, three inches tall; it was hilarious. There were also three older ladies touring together as Flora, Fauna and Merriweather, the good fairies from *Sleeping Beauty*. The cast members all seemed to be having a really good time that night, too."

ABC Super Soap Weekend

Each November, **ABC Super Soap Weekend** is held at Disney-MGM Studios, and features stars from the ABC afternoon line-up of the network's ever-popular "stories." A very popular event indeed, Super Soap Weekend brings in actors from famous ABC soaps to pose for pictures with fans, sign autographs, participate in motorcades both in the afternoon and in the evening, and make speeches. Other festivities, also included in park admission, range from game shows to musical performances and star conversations. In 2004, soap opera stars even participated in Who Wants to Be a Millionaire? Play It! You'll also enjoy a chance to purchase one-of-a-kind memorabilia from the soaps. Crowds for this special event are enormous, so don't plan to sleep late during your stay. You'll want to rise early each morning to make sure you're able to get up close and personal with your favorite personalities. Among the more than thirty celebrities in 2004 were Susan Lucci (*All My Children*), Tyler Christopher (*General Hospital*), and Trevor St. John (*One Life to Live*). Call 407-397-6808 for current information, or visit the ABC Daytime Web site at **abc.com** (Keyword: "daytime"). In 2004, Disney's FASTPASS system was utilized for all "On Location" celebrity autograph sessions.

Disney Cruise Line

Sure, you're excited about nurturing the "child within" with a unique Walt Disney World vacation—but you also want

CHAPTER 15 VACATION EXPANSION 365

to add some maturity and sophistication to your Disney fun.

Don't fret; it can be done—with style—on one of the **Disney Cruise Line** ships. Disney Cruise Line's two luxurious vessels are christened the Disney Magic and the Disney Wonder. Both are docked at Port Canaveral, just ninety minutes away from Walt Disney World. (Both ships are very similar in design. Some venues as described may appear under a different name, depending on your vessel. The characteristic that's *not* different, however, is quality.)

Disney Cruise Line offers you a number of cruising options. Don't want to relinquish your fun days in the parks? No problem! You can combine a Walt Disney World vacation with a cruise on a "Land and Sea Vacation." After you enjoy the parks, you board the Disney Cruise Line bus for the ninety-minute trip to the ship.

A little burned out on the parks and their unavoidable crowds? Again, the Disney folks can oblige with either a Bahamian, an Eastern Caribbean, or a Western Caribbean cruise. No park hassles here—these cruises are sheer indulgence, through and through.

You're probably wondering whether Mickey and the Gang will take to the seas to entertain you. You bet! But there'll be plenty more to set your heart aflutter—and your kids' hearts, too. Because children are welcome sailors, as well, on the Disney Cruise Line—with special play and recreation areas designed just for them.

At Animator's Palate, dining becomes a unique, artistic experience as you begin your meal surrounded by a décor of black-and-white; then, as you enjoy each course, the room and the artwork displayed on the walls around you begin to glow with vibrant colors. It's like being in an animation cel while animators magically brighten the scenery around you. And while Animator's Palate caters to both adults and kids, the elegant Palo, which serves Italian cuisine, welcomes adults only.

During your play aboard the ship, you'll often see professional Disney photographers wandering around, taking guest photos. Be sure to drop by the ship's photo shop to inspect yours. If you like what you see, you can purchase any and all photos—though we don't recommend relying exclusively on ship photographers for all your vacation memories.

If you—or members of your party—are celebrating a special occasion, be sure to let Disney Cruise Line know at least three weeks prior to departure. Occasionally, cast members will conspicuously celebrate the occasion in the dining room; they'll also offer a variety of gift baskets and other merchandise that can be delivered to the appropriate cabin. The dining room celebration, if it occurs, won't cost you anything; gift baskets and merchandise will.

Disney Cruise Line provides adults and kids access to different areas of the ship which are tailored to their specific entertainment needs. Beat Street is evocative of Pleasure Island, and offers a piano bar, a dance club and a sing-along bar. Adults can also engage in activities that range from wine-tastings to guest lectures to deck parties, featuring dancing, cocktails and snacks. Teens will feel very comfortable at Common Ground, a coffee bar where young adults can listen to music and watch movies. Other teen activities occur on the

---

Night of Joy

Night of Joy, a Christian music event, occurs in September in the Magic Kingdom. A private party, Night of Joy is a three-night event held over a Thursday, Friday and Saturday. On those days, the Magic Kingdom closes early to regular park guests (usually 6 or 7 p.m.), with the event beginning at about 8:00 p.m.

If you're planning to visit in September, you may find an earlier-than-normal closing time on the weekend for Magic Kingdom, so be prepared to plan other activities for the evening if you're not interested in staying for the event. Tickets, whose prices range from $37.00 to $80.00, depending on the number of nights, can be purchased at Family Christian Stores in Florida, or by calling 1-407-W-DISNEY.

sports deck. And everyone, regardless of age, will enjoy original musical productions nightly at the Walt Disney Theater.

Besides stops at ports-of-call in the Bahamas or the Caribbean, Disney also purchased its own island called Castaway Cay (pronounced *key*), a 1,000-acre tropical island where you'll spend a full day enjoying the sun, food and surf, as well as plenty of recreational activities, like snorkeling, biking and hiking. One newer itinerary even includes a stop at Key West. Rates for Disney Cruise Line experiences vary widely — making them affordable for almost any level of income — depending on the cabin of choice and the duration of the cruise you select.

Here's what you can expect:
Seven Night E. Caribbean Cruise — $829-$4,999
Seven Night W. Caribbean Cruise — $829-$4,999
Seven Night land and Sea Vacation — $829-$4,999
(The Seven-Night Land and Sea includes 3 or 4 nights at WDW, and 3 or 4 nights aboard a Disney cruise ship, per person, based on double occupancy.)
Four-Night Bahamian Cruise — $509-$3,149
Three-Night Bahamian Cruise — $409-$2,749
Packages for kids start at $349

For more detailed information on booking, requirements, and ports of call, point your computer browser to **disney.go.com/disneycruise**. Or, call **1-800-951-3532**.

"The Rainforest Room is the bomb!" says Amanda. "Get a length-of-cruise pass and enjoy it with your spouse. It's co-ed. We weren't impressed with St. Maarten at all. I would have rather stayed on the boat. But St. Thomas was lovely. We'd try the Western Caribbean route next time. Castaway Cay was a great day, though the walk to and from the ship was a real hike. Bring everything you need for the day with you when you disembark."

Melanie calls the Disney Cruise Line "wonderful. The restaurants are great, especially Animators Palette. I like the fact that there are adult-only areas and nightlife on the ship. Castaway Cay is like heaven on earth. I would recommend it to anyone. You get character interaction and have lots of fun—just like being at Walt Disney World."

Star Wars Weekends

Each May (and sometimes extending into June), *Star Wars* fans enjoy **Star Wars Weekends**, also hosted at Disney-MGM Studios. You'll meet and greet stars from the six George Lucas movies—like Carrie Fisher (Princess Leia), Anthony Daniels (C-3PO), Peter Mayhew (Chewbacca) and Billy Dee Williams (Lando Calrissian)—and pose with some of the aliens featured in the movies. Aronda's favorite was Chewbacca, who stopped his restless pacing to pose for several pictures with her. Special collectors' lapel pins and other commemorative merchandise are available for purchase. Spontaneous theater sometimes occurs in the streets and even in a few unusual places. Storm Troopers appear on Hollywood Boulevard rooftops, poised to stave off any attacks from unfriendly extraterrestrials. The Cantina Street Party breaks into the streets every evening, when the park often stays open until 10:30 p.m. Cast from the *Star Wars* saga will autograph postcards, pictures and other collectibles, and participate in question-and-answer sessions with guests on a stage erected next to the Star Tours attraction. Last year, even Who Wants to Be a Millionaire: Play It! got in on the act by hosting entire shows devoted to *Star Wars*-based questions. Each afternoon brings a motorcade featuring a *Star Wars'* star from one of the six films. The festivities are included with regular theme park admission, though you must register for the privilege to meet the stars in person. Keep checking either **arondaparks.com** or **disneyworld.com** for updates on the 2005 Star Wars Weekends, which at press time had not been announced.

Black History Month

At Epcot, **Black History Month** is appropriately celebrated in February, with daily musical entertainment, artisans, artists, displays, storytellers, specialty foods and children's activities—all of which supplement the park's regular offerings. Usually, the celebration is headquartered at the America pavilion, though events fan out to other venues throughout Epcot. Additionally, musical and dance performances are scheduled at the America Gardens Theater throughout the month—usually with several performances daily. Aronda has attended this festive observance several times in the past, and found it uplifting and enjoyable. She particularly enjoyed her chats with various African-American artists and storytellers who've been invited to participate. Frequently, these men and women are quite candid and forthcoming about their histories, both personal and cultural. The vigorous performances on stage are not-to-be-missed—particularly the recent tribute to the great disco divas! Aronda particularly enjoyed a conversation with an artist who was originally from Charleston, SC; as an individual who migrated to the Midwest many years ago, her insights were provocative and moving. There is no additional charge for enjoying any part of the celebration.

Thanksgiving through New Year's Day

From **Thanksgiving through New Year's Day**, Walt Disney World Resort is all decked out in garland, even *more* lights than usual, and—we're *not* kidding!—snow! This is undoubtedly the most festive time of the year to visit, but keep in mind: crowds reach their peak from Christmas Day until New Year's Day. You can visit between Thanksgiving and December 25 and enjoy the same decorations, parades (with a ticket to Mickey's Very Merry Christmas Party) and festivities with far smaller crowds. Even the resort hotels are festooned with holiday decorations. Many guests celebrate the holidays at Walt Disney World yearly, and have established family traditions—like visiting all resort hotels to take in their distinctive celebrations and decorations, trying out new restaurants, and even decorating their hotel rooms for Santa. In 2004, Walt Disney World welcomed the return of the Osborne Spectacle of Lights after a year's hiatus to the newly-refurbished Streets of America Backlot at Disney-MGM Studios. They are even more impressive there than on the Residential Street (which was demolished to make room for Lights, Motors, Action! Extreme Stunt Show).

Mickey's Very Merry Christmas Party

Mickey's Very Merry Christmas Party is a separately-ticketed event at the Magic Kingdom. The private party issues an invitation to anyone spending $37.00 ($27.00 for kids) for a special ticket (on-the-spot tickets are a few dollars more; save bucks by ordering in advance).

You'll be treated to free cookies (disappointingly, not Disney's fresh-baked ones) and hot chocolate, at least five musical shows specially produced for this event and two showings of Mickey's Very Merry Christmas Parade along Main Street, U.S.A. and through Frontierland, during which snow flurries occur, courtesy of strategically placed snow-making machines. And don't forget to queue up for your special—and free, one-per-party—commemorative photograph. Later, when your print arrives, use the order blank to purchase a photo package, if desired. Most of the Magic Kingdom's rides and attractions are also open during this event. "This party is a blast!" enthuses Melanie. "It's neat to have a smaller crowd and feel like you have a private function. The shows, fireworks, and parade are wonderful. You're able to ride the attractions with very little wait. Plus, you'll experience snow on Main Street, U.S.A. It is a magical night." And Megan regards the best ending of a Magic Kingdom visit as one "when you end the night with a walk down Main Street, U.S.A., as it snows!"

Candlelight Processional

Each Christmas season, the **Candlelight Processional** at Epcot's America Gardens Theater features a chorus of four hundred singers (including Disney cast members who volunteer their time and talent), a fifty-piece orchestra, a celebrity narrator, and the Voices of Liberty. This show is a rendering of the New Testament Christmas story via narrative and music — though you need not be from a Christian faith tradition to enjoy the music. Frequently, the audience is encouraged to sing along. Celebrity narrators have included Gary Sinise, Andy Garcia, Ben Vereen and Rita Moreno. This presentation has become one of Epcot's most cherished traditions, so it draws huge crowds, with many locals among them. If you're determined to view it, be sure to arrive at least an hour (if not more) before the posted show time. ***However, to guarantee a good seat, book a Candlelight Processional Dinner Package.*** This way, you dine in an Epcot restaurant (your prepaid meal includes appetizer or salad, entrée, dessert and nonalcoholic beverage, and includes tax and tip), then use your receipt to claim a seat close to the stage for the show. In 2004, prices for the dinner package ranged from $29 to $45 for adults; children's price was always $11.99 (ages 3-11). In the past, a fifteen percent discount at select Epcot shops, good only for the day of your reservation, was awarded to all dinner package guests (though not available in 2004). Occasionally, Disney includes other perks or favors, too — like a commemorative collector's pin and lanyard — but don't expect more than the dinner and special seating. Anything else, accept as icing on your holiday cake.

Chapter 16

Fitness, Fun and Health

Disney Recreation

Even if you're not athletically endowed, and the thought of competitive sports triggers flashbacks to being the last kid on the court to be picked in your gym class, Walt Disney World still offers recreation opportunities you will enjoy. If you're a seasoned athlete, this is also the place to display your prowess, or to maintain your competitive edge.

But even more importantly, the health and fitness opportunities the Resort offers will help ensure that you don't lose the muscle tone you've worked so hard to maintain back home. All of the resort hotels have fitness rooms — some even have full-fledged gyms — where you can pump some iron, hit the treadmill, or even have a massage to better prepare you for the rigors of the Disney Dash.

Walt Disney World is a *golf* mecca in its own right. In October, the Funai Golf Classic is hosted on Disney's courses — an event that draws immense crowds. But you'll also find six major courses here with varying degrees of challenge — namely, the Palm and Magnolia, Osprey Ridge & Eagle Pines, the Oak Trail and the Lake Buena Vista courses. For the right price, Disney golfing experts will be happy to teach you the ropes. Resorts that are most convenient to the courses are Disney's Old Key West Resort, Disney's Saratoga Springs, Polynesian and Shades of Green (booking available only to guests with military affiliations). Call **407.WDW.GOLF (939.4653)** for reservations or more information. Greens fees generally range from about $109.00 to $169.00, though rates drop a bit after 3:00 p.m. Golf packages are also available. "My husband, Jim, and boys have golfed at all the courses," says Chrislette. "They are chal-

Events Sampling at Disney's Wide World of Sports

Family Fun Magazine Family Fun Run
January 8, 2005

2005 WDW Marathon
January 9, 2005

WDW Inline Marathon
April 30-May 1, 2005

Disney's Soccer Showcase Qualifer Presented by Adidas
September 3-5, 2005

Disney's Sun & Surf Baseball
May 27-30, 2005

Track & Field Showcase
March 19, 2005

MAAC Golf Championship
April 21-24, 2005

Disney's Track & Field Spring Training
February 12-April 22, 2005

Disney's Lacrosse Spring Training
February 26-April 29, 2005

Disney's Ice & Sun Hockey Classic
May 5-8, 2005

Admission
Adults: $10.75
Chidlren: $8.00

Log onto
www.disneyworldsports.com for more info!

> **Parasailing above Bay Lake**
>
> Parasailing is not Aronda's cup of tea, but she *has* talked to several people who've tried it. The anticipation, they say, is more unnerving than the actual experience. A boat takes you out on Bay Lake from the dock at the Contemporary Resort. (Look for Sammy Duvall's rental office.) Once you're into your gear (including a seat similar to a swing, and a life jacket), you stand on a platform at the back of the boat. The driver builds up to a respectable speed, then you're released from the platform, and into the sky! Veterans say the view is incredible. You see the Magic Kingdom, the Magic Kingdom resort hotels, Fort Wilderness Resort & Campgrounds, the forest surrounding the Magic Kingdom, and even some backstage areas. You're up about five hundred feet for close to ten minutes before cast members reel you back onto the boat. Honestly, you don't even get wet! No, really!

lenging and manicured beautifully. They have specials for annual passholders. It's a first-class operation."

If you prefer **miniature golf**, be sure to check out two unique miniature golf courses. Disney's Winter-Summerland, located near Disney's Blizzard Beach water park, provides a vacation retreat for Santa and his elves. While you play the two eighteen-hole courses, you'll enjoy a Christmas carol soundtrack. The second miniature golf course—Fantasia Gardens, close to the Walt Disney World Swan and Walt Disney World Dolphin—features a unique *Fantasia* film theme, with dancing hippos, leaping fountains and marching broomsticks. Both courses provide a nice solace when you're burned out from the parks. Usually, courses are open from 10:00 a.m. until 11:00 p.m. Admission is about $11.00 for adults, and $9.00 for children. Second round is half price. For more information, call **407.560.8740**. "We had lots of fun at the Fantasia Gardens Miniature Golf course," says Nicole. "We made sure to watch the film, *Fantasia*, before our trip so we were able to appreciate the detail of the theming." Crystal has also played miniature golf at Fantasia Gardens, along with her parents, Tom and Linda. "It was a good time," says Crystal. "Challenging, even for mini-golf. I almost won—twice."

If you're into **tennis**, almost every Deluxe resort hotel has tennis courts—twenty-five, to be exact. Clay courts may be found at Disney's Saratoga Springs, Disney's Grand Floridian Resort & Spa, Disney's BoardWalk, and Disney's Contemporary Resort. Peter Burwash International directs the tennis program at Walt Disney World. To reserve court time, call **407.WDW.PLAY (939.7529)** for Disney's Contemporary Resort, Disney's Yacht and Beach Club Resorts and Disney's Saratoga Springs. For Walt Disney World Swan and Walt Disney World Dolphin, call **407.934.4396**. Other courts not listed here are available on a first come, first serve basis. Note that the Contemporary, Grand Floridian, and the Swan and Dolphin charge about $15.00 an hour to play. Disney's Saratoga Springs requires a one-day health club pass—also $15.00. All other courts are free. Since rentals are not available, you must bring your own equipment.

Disney's famous Sea Raycers by Sea Ray (an upgrade from the old Water Mouse) may be rented at waterways around property.

How Much Must I Pay to Play?

Most of Disney's recreational activities require an admission charge. Here's a cross-section of those venues, with appropriate pricing.

Golf
Golf rates are per person for greens fees and electric carts.
$109-$169 per guest; $55-$70 Twilight Special
Call 407-WDW-GOLF (939-4653) to reserve or request info.

Miniature Golf
At both courses: $9.76 for adults; $7.78 for children.
Fifty percent discount applies for second round played the same day.

Fishing
Bay Lake and Lake Buena Vista--$180-$210 per group (five people or less constitutes a group). Eighty dollars for one additional hour. Price includes pontoon, guide and equipment.
Port Orleans--Cane pole fishing only at $4.00 per half hour. Four to six poles for family fishing priced at $12.50 per half hour.

For the **boating** enthusiast, several kinds of watercraft may be rented at Deluxe and Moderate resorts—as well as Downtown Disney—to sail on Disney's scenic waterways. Aronda particularly enjoyed her excursions on a Sea Ryder, a sleek two-passenger "speed boat" which travels less than twenty-five miles per hour, and costs about $22.00 per half hour. However, it gives the illusion of speed because of its small size—and the kids love it. (You must be at least twelve years old to take one out alone.) Pedalboats and pontoon boats are also available for $6.00 and $32.00 per half-hour, respectively. Few activities at Walt Disney World are more relaxing—nor more romantic, if you're with someone special—than gliding across Disney's scenic waterways. Thomas and Maribeth "enjoyed renting the [Sea Ryder] boat and seeing the Magic Kingdom and the resort areas from the Seven Seas

How Much Must I Pay to Play?

Kids Fishing--Ages 5-12: $30 per child.
All fishing may be arranged by calling 407-WDW-PLAY (939-7529).

Horseback Riding

Tours last 45 minutes, and start at Fort Wilderness Trailblaze Corral. Cost is $32 (minimum age 9 years) for a relaxing ride. Horses neither gallop nor trot, so even amateurs will enjoy. Call 407-WDW-PLAY.

Water Skiing

$80-$165 per hour for up to five persons. Call 407-939-0754.

Parasailing

Ten minutes, 450 feet: $90 single or $112.50 for 600 feet; $140 and $162.50 for tandem at same heights. Call 407-939-0754.

Wakeboarding

$80-$165--Five-person maximum. Call 407-939-0754.

Tubing

$125 for up to five persons. Call 407-939-0754.

Lagoon and Bay Lake. We were able to sit near the area where the monorail comes out from the Contemporary Resort and get some good pictures."

If *fishing* is more your speed, Disney allows it—for a fee—but don't plan a fish fry on the white sands of Seven Seas Lagoon for all your buddies. Disney's rule is that fishing is for sport only; you have to release what you catch. All you'll have to show for your efforts will be great memories and your story—embellished, of course—about the one that got away. Call **407.WDW.PLAY (939.7529)** for more information, or to make reservations. Excursions last about two hours, and depart from the Magic Kingdom resort hotels, Downtown Disney Marketplace, Port Orleans, Yacht and Beach Club Resorts. Disney also provides special fishing expeditions for kids ages six through twelve.

Let's Go Pool-Shopping!

In a nutshell, here are most of the notable pools at the various resort hotels:

All-Star Movies
The Mighty Duck, a hockey-themed pool--and Fantasia pool.

All-Star Sports
Two pools--Surfboard Bay and Grand Slam

All-Star Music
Two pools--Piano and Guitar--shaped accordingly.

Animal Kingdom Lodge
Uzima Springs Pool is the largest on property. Eleven thousand square feet of watery fun. A zero-entry pool.

Beach and Yacht Club
Stormalong Bay--a multisectioned pool with unique shipwreck slide. Three acres in size. These resorts also have several quiet pools.

BoardWalk
The major pool is Luna Park, with a 200-foot water slide called Keister Coaster. Also two quiet pools.

Caribbean Beach
A walloping nine pools--including a Spanish-themed fort main pool.

Not surprisingly, **swimming** is the most popular sport at Walt Disney World—as well as the people-watching this activity invites. Every resort hotel on property has at least one pool; many of them offer more. Though you may be tempted to try out a pool at a resort hotel other than your own, keep in mind that Disney occasionally checks resort ID cards to ensure guests aren't "pool-hopping." An added benefit of Disney pools is that they're all heated. So, if you decide on an autumn or winter vacation, you'll still be able to swim, though the Florida heat will have waned. Central Florida *does* have its cold snaps. When temperatures grow frigid—translated, that means in the mid-thirties, generally—coming out of a heated pool into the cool air can be quite a shock. Most Disney resort

Let's Go Pool-Shopping!

Coronado Springs
Major pool called The Dig Site (272,000 gallons), plus three quiet pools.

Port Orleans
In French Quarter, Doubloon Lagoon pool has statue of Alligator Band and water slide. In Riverside, Ol' Man Island is the large pool, with five quiet pools.

Grand Floridian
Florida Natural Springs Pool, with zero-entry design--plus a quiet pool.

Old Key West
Four pools total, three of which are quiet pools. New pool slide at feature pool.

Polynesian
Two pools--one quiet, and the Nanea Volcano pool, with waterfall & slide.

Pop Century
Three Pools--Hippy Dippy, Bowling Pin and Computer.

Wilderness Lodge
Park Service motif main pool begins as bubbling geyser, filled by Silver Creek Falls--plus one quiet pool.

Swan & Dolphin
Both resorts share a huge swimming complex. Two lap pools and tropical "Grotto," which features 3-acre playground with slides and more--even deejays!

---

pools are uniquely themed. Stormalong Bay, for example, is a three-acre, meandering sand-bottom pool — quite possibly the most popular at the Resort — located at the Beach and Yacht Club Resorts. Disney's Polynesian Resort recently opened a newly refurbished pool with a volcano theme — guests climb to the top of the volcano and take the water slide into the pool. Many pools are "zero entry" — meaning you (and especially the kids) don't have to jump from the concrete edge into cold water. Instead, you gradually enter the water, as though you were entering the surf.

Two **water parks** offer you daredevils high-speed waterslides, manmade waves and whitewater rides. **Typhoon Lagoon**, a 56-acre water park, is themed as a resort village

Your Mickey Mouse Health Clubs

Okay, Mouseketeers, you wanna stay in shape? Well, you can--at a number of Disney resort hotels. Here's a sampling of what you'll find during your vacation.

Contemporary Resort
Olympiad
Nautilus equipment, cardiovascular machine

Wilderness Lodge
Sturdy Branches
Spa and health club equipment

Yacht & Beach Club
Ship Shape
Whirlpool & steam room

Animal Kingdom Lodge
Zahanati
Typical health club equipment

BoardWalk
Muscles and Bustles
Steam room, tanning bed, massage

Coronado Springs
La Vida
Tanning bed and massage

Saratoga Springs
Gymnasium, Cybex machines, facials and eye-contour treatments

Swan & Dolphin
Jacuzzi, sauna, weights, massage

that was struck by a monstrous typhoon many years ago. Here, you'll find a tremendous surf pool with big waves crashing every ninety seconds—without the threats of sharks or jellyfish that come with the traditional territory. Castaway Creek, a peaceful river, circumnavigates the entire water park, enticing you to float lazily along on an inner tube, provided at no extra charge. Three whitewater rides attract thrill-seekers along with Humunga Kowabunga, consisting of three speed slides on which you can easily reach thirty miles per hour. Shark Reef, where you can obtain snorkeling equipment, allows you to swim face-to-face with sharks and other marine life. Several other attractions are also available, including Ketchakiddee Creek, a mini-park that caters to those who are four feet tall or less. A one-day ticket costs about $34.00 for adults, and about $27.00 for children (3-9). Deluxe Hopper Passes and Pre-

Though Typhoon Lagoon has historically been Walt Disney World's tamer of its two water parks, the premier of Crush 'N' Gusher may revise its reputation. Crush 'N' Gusher will feature a roller-coaster type water ride with waterjets to propel you up the inevitable hills.

---

mium Annual Passes include both water parks. Locker rooms and showers are provided, with lockers ranging from four to six dollars per day. Towels rent for about a buck, while life jackets and tubes are free. Sue says she loves "the bobbing waves at Typhoon Lagoon—and sitting by the edge of the wave pool with a book." Dann visited Typhoon Lagoon last year, after about a 10-year absence "because I always wanted to hit the more thrilling slides at Blizzard Beach. However, I must admit, the wave pool is very exciting, and overall, in my opinion, the theming is better here than at Blizzard Beach." Typhoon will heighten the thrill factor in 2005 with the new Crush 'N' Gusher, a water slide with roller-coaster-styled effects accomplished using water jets to keep you going up and down hills.

Beach boys and girls can schedule **surfing lessons** at Typhoon Lagoon three days per week, but you have to get up early. At press time, lessons were available on Tuesday, Wednesday, and Friday, and begin about 7:30 a.m. and last until 10:00 a.m. You must provide your own transportation to the park to participate. Representatives of Craig Carroll's Cocoa Beach Surfing School will show you how to master the big ones — but enroll early. Each class accommodates no more than fourteen guests, all of whom must be at least eight years old, and strong swimmers. The cost, too, is a bit restrictive — $135.00 per person — but guests who've taken these lessons report that you receive lots of individual attention from the two instructors on duty. You're also guaranteed ten to twelve waves; surfboards are provided — you don't have to bring your own. For more information, or to make reservations, call **407.WDW.PLAY (939.7529)**. A credit card number is required to hold your reservation.

Blizzard Beach, another water park somewhat similar to Typhoon Lagoon, pushes the envelope farther with several even more thrilling slides than its sister park boasts. According to the kind of fantastical theming for which Disney is famous, a strange snowstorm occurred in Central Florida, which motivated several entrepreneurs to build Florida's first ski resort. When the snow melted (who couldn't see *that* coming?), they turned it into a water park so the money, like the water, would continue to flow. Here, you'll find Melt-Away Bay, a one-acre wave pool that's a bit tamer than the one at Typhoon Lagoon; Cross Country Creek, a waterway circling the entire park, where you laze along with the current while sprawled on an inner tube (beware the dark caves, where you're likely to be victim of a brief, but cold splash); Summit Plummet, a big thrill water slide which takes you 120 feet down at about sixty miles an hour; Slush Gusher, a much tamer version of Summit Plummet, for the cautious; Teamboat Springs, a whitewater raft ride which takes five-passenger rafts down a number of waterfalls — and more. Dann tried Summit Plummet, where you're instructed to cross your ankles. Well, in his

At Disney's BoardWalk, you may rent surrey bikes, then cruise along the boards. One hill leading to the bridge connecting BoardWalk with the Epcot walkway is a killer. Surreys are a great way to relax as a family when the parks have closed for the night.

apprehension, he forgot to keep them crossed, and discovered — the hard way — what a gush of water at sixty miles per hour feels like when you don't follow instructions. "Once I recovered from that little faux pas, the ride was a breeze," he says. "It's amazingly smooth, and the anxiety preceding the trip is much worse than the actual ride." Tike's Peak provides a mini-version of the major park for the youngsters, including a snow-castle fountain play area. Admission is the same as Typhoon Lagoon. Ultimate Park Hoppers and Premium Annual Passes include admission. Like Typhoon Lagoon, lockers, showers, towels and restaurants are available. "Blizzard Beach is the greatest water park I've ever enjoyed," says Megan. "The park's main attraction is Summit Plummet; it's one of the best water slides in the world."

If team sports are your bag, you'll certainly want to pay a visit to **Disney's Wild World of Sports Complex**, home of the Amateur Athletic Union and training site for the Atlanta Braves. Activities for guests are largely hands-on, such as the NFL Experience, where you'll have an opportunity to try your hand at football in this interactive playground. The complex is a walloping two hundred acres, with a 7,500-seat ballpark, a field house with six NBA-sized courts, baseball quadraplex with three major league-sized ball fields, two Little League fields, a softball quadraplex with four lighted fields, twelve lighted Hard-Tru tennis courts, a 400-meter track and field complex, six sand beach volleyball courts, and more. Admission is $10.50 for adults and $7.75 for children under nine years of age. Tickets can be purchased at the gate, and entitle guests to watch "nonpremium" sports events and participate in the NFL Experience. If big sports events — known at Disney as "premium" — are in the works, tickets will be substantially higher. *How* much higher depends on the event. Atlanta Braves games begin in February. Orlando Rays games begin in April.

If your interest in stock car racing transcends the vicarious experience of sitting in the stands nursing a beer, then the **Richard Petty Driving Experience** is for you! Certainly, you're welcome to watch, but the fun is in the driving. Participation comes in four flavors. The "Ride-Along" allows you to be a passenger while a professional driver takes you around the track, constructed in the middle of one of the Magic Kingdom's former parking lots. For that, you'll pay about $106.00. The "Rookie Experience" includes actual instruction and eight high-speed laps on your own. The cost is about $405.00. The "King's Experience" is a five-hour excursion allowing you to experience speed over eighteen laps; it costs about $798.00 "The Experience of a Lifetime" is a thirty-lap program over three sessions, during which you work on building speed and establishing a comfortable driving line. This venue will cost you $1,330.00, but hey — if racing's your bag, what's a cool grand when you're having fun? Call **800.237.3889** for information or to make reservations. Or, you can check out the official Richard Petty Driving Experience Web site at **www.1800bepetty.com**.

Rounding out Walt Disney World's recreational offerings are jogging, spas and health clubs, bicycling and horseback trail rides. While many of the roads and highways on Disney property are much too busy to provide a safe jogging environment, your resort can provide you with a map disclosing **jogging and walking** trails close by which will keep you out of harm's way. Be careful of the Florida heat at midday, though; if you're not used to it, it's healthier and safer to run in early morning or early evening. Either way, you can expect to be inspired by clean, pleasant surroundings. Aronda's favorite walking path can be found along the canal connecting Disney's BoardWalk to Disney-MGM Studios. Add that jaunt to a couple of laps around Crescent Lake, and you've got your exercise for the day. "We seek out walking paths, or possible walking routes, and walk around talking and planning our day," say Susan and John. Diligent walkers might consider investing in a pedometer before their Walt Disney World vacation. You'll probably be surprised by the number of miles you cover daily.

Spas and health clubs are located at Disney's Contemporary Resort, Disney's Wilderness Lodge, Disney's Animal Kingdom Lodge, Disney's Coronado Springs Resort, Disney's BoardWalk Inn and Villas, Disney's Saratoga Springs, Disney's Grand Floridian Resort & Spa, and Disney's Yacht

Guests staying at the Walt Disney World Swan and Dolphin will find a huge themed swimming area that rivals any on property. An Olympic-sized lap pool is also available to guests, along with a poolside snack and cocktail bar.

For tanning amid great Disney theming, Disney's Typhoon Lagoon water park offers hundreds of beach chairs along white sand beaches and towering palm trees.

and Beach Club Resorts. While some clubs are reserved only for the specific resort hotel's guests, several have more liberal policies and allow access for all Walt Disney World guests. (If you're staying off-property, you'll have to make other arrangements in the Orlando area.) Rates are ten dollars per day, twenty dollars per length of stay or forty dollars for a family length of stay (up to five people). "Gotta love the spa at the Yacht & Beach Club," says Carrie. "I had my best massage ever there, when you exclude the fact that I was 'bumped' and had to wait nearly an hour. It was a good thing the spa was next to Beaches & Cream." And Sam's wife, Kathy, thoroughly enjoyed the Grand Floridian's spa. "She loved it, and is bugging me to send her again," says Sam.

Workout facilities are located at the Grand Floridian Spa and Health Club, Disney's Saratoga Springs, and Wyndham

Palace Resort & Spa. The Fitness Center at Disney's Saratoga Springs costs about $15 per day; $35 for length of stay access; $50 for a family of four during their length of stay. Disney's Saratoga Springs features aerobics, a gymnasium and the best line-up of Cybex machines on Disney property. The Grand Floridian Spa and Health Club features the best of all the rest — plus an ambience of sheer self-indulgence. Costs range from about $12 per day, $30 for three days, or $31.50 for your length of stay. Spa packages at Disney's Grand Floridian Resort & Spa range from $208 to $480. Couples Packages are also available. The Spa at Saratoga Springs features eye-contour treatments, facials and more.

Surrey **bicycles** are available for rental at the BoardWalk, while traditional and tandem varieties can be located at Fort Wilderness, Old Key West, Wilderness Lodge, Port Orleans, Disney Institute and Coronado Springs. Fees range from around $5.00 per hour to about $15.00 per day. Bikes with training wheels or baby seats are available. Helmets are free.

At Fort Wilderness, you can take a guided **horseback ride** on gentle horses, so expect a relaxing ride, not something out of *Blazing Saddles*. This 45-minute tour, costing $32.00 per person, which requires a cast member "cowboy" to accompany you and your party, affords some picturesque views of the Florida wilderness. Wildlife, like deer and armadillos, often cross your path, but the most memorable component of the experience will be the delightful views of the Magic Kingdom and Bay Lake. Call **407.WDW.PLAY (939.7529)** for more information or to make reservations. Please note that children under nine are not allowed to ride; there's also a weight limit of 250 pounds. (Pony rides are available for younger kids at Fort Wilderness Petting Farm.)

Disney's Magical Gatherings

Though not a recreational venue per se, Magical Gatherings — and the associated Grand Gatherings — refers to a marketing initiative, begun in October 2003, geared to heighten the enjoyment of guests who visit with a larger party in tow. Though Disney would like to make you believe that you're part of a "magical gathering" any time you step through a park's turnstiles, the truth of the matter is that the special magic doesn't begin until you bring a group of eight or more into the Resort. Then, you can enjoy a special fireworks cruise, international buffets and entertainment to accompany the meals, and even a late-afternoon safari followed by a great meal and lively entertainment.

The story started when Walt Disney World hosted a huge press event in October 2003, and began a marketing campaign to attract these Grand Gatherings. It is Aronda's contention — and there are other who will agree — that the Magical Gatherings and Grand Gatherings programs were implemented to pump up attendance in an economy that did not encourage lots of travel to the Orlando Resort. (In fact, Walt Disney World suffered significantly lower crowds, particularly from overseas guests, after the terrorist attacks of 2001. Lately, however, attendance has returned to or exceeded pre-9/11 levels.)

How did Disney arrive at the magic number of eight? Research, my dear. The Company discovered that fully 26% of all family reunion-type trips included eight or more people. Slightly over half of the survey sample identified Florida as the best destination for multi-household or extended family trips. Perhaps not surprisingly, among adults citing Florida as their preferred destination, fully 67% stated they were interested in visiting Walt Disney World.

"Whether they're friends across the street or families across the globe, the need to reconnect with each other is more important than ever — we call it 'togethering'," says Walt Disney World President Al Weiss. "We believe Walt Disney World is the most magical place there is to vacation with extended family and friends. Time together is an invaluable souvenir."

Once you decide you want to participate in Disney's unique initiative, you should visit the official Walt Disney World Web site, and before you do anything else, order the Vacation Planning Kit, complete with video or DVD. Then, download the Magical Gatherings Planner at **www.disneyworld.com/magicalgatherings**. (You must register with the site before you're allowed access to the software. Registration, along with the software, is free.) The online tools allow you to send invitations to family and friends, engage in group chats about your itinerary, create polls for consensus building, browse and share other Walt Disney World Web pages and build a complete group vacation itinerary. You can even embellish messages to group members with animations of Tinker Bell as she winks, pouts or pixie-dusts your computer monitor.

If your party includes eight or more guests (including children), you have access to other features, too. For example, a Walt Disney World team of specialists will be assigned to assist with every aspect of vacation planning — dining, tours, spa treatments, recreation, special celebration events and more. You'll also find that Disney has significantly increased the number of dining facilities that can accommodate larger parties — so you don't have to worry that your Grand Gathering will be seated at several separate tables. Other exciting options are also available, such as group souvenirs, two-way radios (to keep track of your large party) and photographic memories of your Disney vacation.

Here are four very special events available to Grand Gatherings of eight or more.

Magical Fireworks Voyage. After bidding farewell to

Tusker House is the designated site for the Safari Celebration Dinner, available only to Grand Gatherings parties.

Captain Hook and Mr. Smee on shore, your group will sail with Patch the Pirate along Seven Seas Lagoon by the Magic Kingdom. This memorable evening includes "seaward" viewing of King Triton's Electrical Water Pageant and the spectacular "Wishes Nighttime Spectacular" fireworks extravaganza over Cinderella Castle. The voyage features group trivia and song activities, and a celebration for special occasions like birthdays, reunions or anniversaries. The irrepressible Patch regales you with tales of Peter Pan on the trip back to shore. Speaking of Peter Pan, he awaits your return to pose for photos and sign autographs. Tickets for guests ten and older are $29.99; ages 3-9, $14.99.

Safari Celebration Dinner. You'll gather in the exotic African coastal city of Harambe at Disney's Animal Kingdom for high adventure on Kilimanjaro Safaris. Your group will journey through the park's authentic jungles and across the sweeping, baobab-studded savannah as you spot giraffes, elephants and other wild African creatures. The experience continues at Harambe's Tusker House Restaurant for an African-inspired dinner, Disney character appearances, up-close animal experiences and live entertainment. Ages 10 and older, $59.99; ages 3-9, $19.99.

International Storybook Dinner and IllumiNations Dessert Reception. There's no need to jet around the globe to experience dining around the world. At Epcot, international culinary favorites are on the menu for adventurous groups looking for a storybook ending to their day. Children can join in the dinner's special storytelling experience, which is punctuated with a surprise character appearance. When Aronda witnessed a demonstration of the event, Alice in Wonderland made an appearance to children sitting at the foot of the stage, where she regaled the kids with stories. A special viewing area is reserved for the evening finale, the nighttime Epcot spectacular IllumiNations: Reflections of Earth. Ages 10 and older, $59.99; ages 3-9, $19.99.

Good Morning Gatherings. Breakfast with famous characters enters a whole new dimension with this new group gathering served up with plenty of morning merriment at Tony's Town Square Restaurant in the Magic Kingdom. Your group will not only meet their favorite characters, but they will also participate in song-and-dance numbers. Mickey Mouse makes a one-on-one appearance with each guest for photo sessions. Ages 10 and up, $24.99; ages 3-9, $11.99.

And, if you have a group of twenty or more, you can work with your Grand Gatherings Travel Planner to customize a get-together at venues across property.

With the exception of custom events, it is important to understand that none of the Grand Gatherings events is a private affair for only you and your party. Other Grand Gatherings parties will share the experiences.

Currently, no Grand Gatherings events have been planned for Disney-MGM Studios.

Chapter 17

Casting Their Spell
Cast Members' Roles in Making Magical Memories

At Disney's Old Key West Resort, between the gift shop and Olivia's, you'll find a "Family Photo Album" of DVC members who send their photos to resort cast members, who then post them for other guests to see.

Few people will deny that quality is what drives the superior vacation experiences at Walt Disney World — superior entertainment, superior accommodations, superior food (usually), and superior service. But what more and more guests realize as the frequency of their Walt Disney World vacations increases is that the human factor also plays a huge role. Overall, Disney's cast members give the vacation its richness through their interactions with guests.

"Most of our magical moments have come about because of bus drivers," admit Susan and John. "Cheerful, singing, happy, smiling bus drivers are great!" They add special kudos to the cast members at Zawadi Marketplace at Disney's Animal Kingdom Lodge. "They have helped us spread pixie dust over friends' family vacations twice by arranging to have Safari Mickeys and Safari Minnies delivered to friends' rooms with notes from us."

Cast members performing character roles arguably have the highest profile positions. "Character experiences are made more fun by characters who play with you," says Melanie. "Chip stole my Minnie Mouse hat and ran away with it, then came back on put it on my friend's head. Those kinds of moments are priceless. Also, the Beast whipped his cape around me once as though he wanted a private moment with me. That was cool." And Sam credits Belle as his heroine because "she remembered my daughter, Julianne, three times during the same trip—once at Cinderella's Royal Table, inside the Exposition Hall, and during a meet-and-greet."

Because all cast members see themselves as an inherent part of the show, even retail experiences can become memorable. "A few years ago, I purchased a Mickey Mouse ring at one of the gift shops at the Grand Floridian," says Chrislette. "It was early in the morning. As the day wore on, I noticed the ring was no longer on my finger. I felt so bad. My husband, Jim, took me back to get another ring. The same cast member waited on me, and asked if I were the same guest who purchased the ring that morning. So, I told her what happened. She helped me pick out another ring, took me to the register, wrapped it up, and told me: 'Enjoy your new ring. This is *your* magical day!' No charge! I don't know her name, but I will never forget her. And I still have that ring."

"We have experienced many magical moments because of cast members, especially during our honeymoon," says Thomas. "Almost everyone we came in contact with went out of their way to make our time very special. One particular cast member was our waiter at Cinderella's Royal Table. Maribeth wanted a sugar-free, flour-free dessert. He sent someone to another restaurant to get a sugar-free cheesecake. We never expected or asked for him to go to that length, but what a wonderful treat it was. We were made to feel like the 'Prince' and 'Princess' that he called us during our meal."

As a DVC member who lives only three hours away from the Resort, Sue frequently visits Walt Disney World. "It always makes me feel good when cast members welcome me back, and comment about my absence if I've been gone for more than a month or so since the last trip. But Comedy Warehouse feels like my second home. The cast there always make me feel so welcome. Same at Old Key West. Everyone greets me and welcomes me back. It's always the little acts of kindness and caring that mean the most."

Ed says he's experienced many memorable cast member moments. "Recently, I rode out one of the hurricanes at an All-Star resort," he explains. "The 'ride-out' crew, and those who had to deal with the aftermath of dozens of guests who missed flights and had to extend their stays, were incredible! They had to deal with so many people, yet when I finally got to the front of the line, the cast member at the desk was still extremely pleasant and understanding. She went out of her way to get my stay extended at a discounted rate, and made the whole ordeal a lot more bearable." Ed also takes the occasional extra step to make certain The Walt Disney Company recognizes excellence among its cast. "When I took the Keys to the Kingdom tour, our host, Regina, was so good, I sent a note to Disney about her, stating: 'This is how Walt Disney would have wanted his cast members to be'."

Like Ed, Crystal feels there is no place like Walt Disney World, and no one like Disney cast members. "They go above and beyond the call of duty to make sure every guest has the most fabulous time of their lives," she says. "Even the little things they say and do to guests assures us that we are truly their guests, and they really strive to better our vacation, and keep us coming back."

Lindsey and Chuck were engaged at Walt Disney World. "Chuck proposed to me beneath Cinderella Castle, just after Wishes," says Lindsey. "After proposing, he surprised me even more by telling me he had booked an engagement photo shoot for the following morning. Since the entire trip to Walt Disney World was a surprise to me, I had not packed any appropriate outfits. When we returned to our hotel, the Grand Floridian, all of the clothing stores were closed." However, the couple noticed that two cast members were still inside the women's clothing store. "We banged on the window, then asked them if we could please come in and look around," Lindsey continues. "Not only did they let us in, they helped me pick out an outfit, and started up the register again so that I could purchase it that night. These two women went out of their way to make sure we were happy. And it was very much appreciated."

Toni relates a cast member kindness that involved a park attraction. "Jim and I were in a pretty long line, waiting to ride Test Track," she says. "When we finally got to the loading area, the ride broke down! And no FASTPASSes were left." In such a stressful situation, what else was there to do but shop? "One of the cast members in the shop asked how our trip had been so far. My husband told her what had happened at Test Track. The cast member told us to wait a mo-

The most thankless role is arguably that of the security officer. However, these cast members are among the first you'll encounter at each park when your bags are checked. Polite and conversant, they set the tone for the rest of your day.

ment. She went into the back, then emerged a few minutes later with a pass for us to get on Test Track at the head of the line. My husband was in heaven. She really made his day!"

Nicole relates a "magical moments" story involving Alex, her teenage son, at the Art of Disney store in Downtown Disney Marketplace. "Alex told Gene, a featured Disney artist at the store, that he would love to be a Disney animator someday," Nicole explains. "Gene spent a lot of time talking to Alex about what the job is like. As they were finishing their conversation, Gene drew a sketch of Mickey Mouse, signed it, then presented it to Alex. It was so wonderful to get that kind of one-on-one attention at a place the size of Walt Disney World. When we returned home, I wrote to Disney Guest Relations to comment on Gene and our experience with him."

A Special Invitation

Aronda would love to hear from you.

Whether you have suggestions, comments, questions—or you just want to share the memories you've made at Walt Disney World—drop her a line.

Aronda's e-mail address is:

disneyguide@arondaparks.com

Her mailing address is:

The Original Press
Attention: Aronda Parks
PO Box 3466
Summerville, SC 29484-3466

Her fax number is:

843-851-2373

Check out Aronda's companion Web site for **Making Walt Disney World Vacation Memories** by pointing your browser to:

www.arondaparks.com

Here, you'll find lots of planning tools to complement the information you've found in Aronda's book, along with printable, large-size vacation-planning worksheets.

Disney Resort Hotels Phone and FAX Numbers

Name of Resort	Phone (Area Code 407)	FAX (Area Code 407)
All-Star Movies	407-939-7000	407-939-7111
All-Star Music	939-6000	939-7222
All-Star Sports	939-5000	939-7333
Animal Kingdom Lodge	938-3000	938-4799
Beach Club & Villas	934-8000 / 934-2175	934-3850 (Both Resort & Villas)
BoardWalk & Villas	939-5100	939-5150
Caribbean Beach	934-3400	934-3288
Contemporary Resort	824-1000	824-3539
Coronado Springs	939-1000	939-1001
Fort Wilderness	824-2900	824-3508

Resort Hotel Phone and Fax List

Name of Resort	Phone *Area Code 407*	FAX *Area Code 407*
Grand Floridian	407-824-3000	407-824-3186
Old Key West	827-7700	827-7710
Polynesian	824-2000	824-3174
Pop Century	938-4000	938-4040
Port Orleans French Quarter	934-5000	934-5353
Port Orleans Riverside	934-6000	934-5777
Saratoga Spring	827-1100	827-1151
Shades of Green	824-3600	824-3460
Wilderness Lodge	824-3200	824-3232
Wilderness Lodge Villas	938-4300	824-3232
Yacht Club	934-7000	934-3450
Walt Disney World Swan	934-3000 888-625-5144	934-4499
Walt Disney World Dolphin	934-4000 888-625-5144	934-4884

Index

A

ABC Commissary 297
ABC Super Soap Weekend 364
accessibility issues 38, 45
Accordion Artiste 124
Adam's Room 267
Address (WDW) 32
Adult Discoveries, Disney 345
Advanced Training Lab 109
Adventure Begins, The 194
Adventureland 60-65
Adventurer's Club 137, 332-333
Aerosmith 159
Affection Section 180
Agrabah 263
Agrabah Bazaar 263
Akershus, Restaurant 294
Akroyd, Dan 306
Aladdin, Magic Carpets of 64-65, 134
Alberta Bound 132
Ale & Compass 337
All Ears Net 17, 49, 279
All-Star Movies 217-221
All-Star Music 217-221
All-Star Sports 217-221
Amateur Athletic Union 383
AMC-24 Theaters 37
America Gardens Theater 132
America Pavilion 124-126
American Adventure, The 124-126
American Film Institute Showcase 95
American Zoological Association 174
Anandupur 358
Animal Kingdom Dining 300-302
Animal Kingdom, Disney's 173-194
Animal Kingdom Lodge 231-233
Animal Kingdom, Disney's, shopping 274-276
Animation Gallery 273, 274
Animator's Palate 365

Annual Pass benefits (see also "tickets") 39, 51-52
Aqua Tour, Epcot Seas 354
Ariel's Grotto 79-80
Armani (porcelain) 269-270
Arribas Brothers 260
AP (see Annual Pass)
Aronda's Prep Pad 280
Art of Disney, The 252, 266
Artist Point 323-324
Artist's Palette 314
AstroBlaster, Buzz Lightyear's 340
Astro Orbiter 11, 86-87, 134
Atlanta Braves 383-384
Atlantic Dance 336, 342
Atlantic Wear and Wardrobe Emporium 251
attendance levels 46
Audio-Animatronics 60, 70, 100, 124-125, 151
Aunt Polly's Dockside Inn 282

B

Baby Care Center 205
babysitting 197-198
Backlot Express 297
Backlot Tour 148-150
Backstage Magic 349-351
backstage programs and tours 349-358
Backstage Safari 351
Bahamian cruise 365
Bakery, Main Street 262
Bally 249
Banana Cabana 336
Bank One VISA 40
Barefoot Bar 337
Barnstormer, Goofy's 80
bars and lounges 336-338
Basin 254

Battle for Buccaneer Gold: Pirates of the
    Caribbean 340
Bay Lake 11, 234
Bay View Gifts 248
Beach Club 170, 229-230
Beach Club Villas 240
Beaches n Cream 278, 327
Bear Jamboree, The Country 66
Beastly Bazaar 275
Beat Street 366
Beatniks 193-194
Beauty and the Beast--Live On Stage 156
Bedtime Stories 208
Behind the Seeds 114
Belle Vue Room 336
Belz Factory Outlet 254
Best Western 223
BET Soundstage 137, 333
Beverly Sunset, The 273
bicycling 387
Biergarten 292-293
Big Al 66
Big Al's 264
Big River Grille & Brewing Works 311, 336
Big Thunder Mountain Railroad 65-66
Bijutsu-Kau Gallery 127
Bistro de Paris 290-291
Black History Month 368-369
Blight, Priscilla 194
Blizzard Beach 382-383
bluezoo, todd english's 323
BoardWalk, Disney's 228-229, 341-342
BoardWalk Bakery 314
BoardWalk Villas 240
boating 376-377
Boatwright's Dining Hall 315
Bocuse, Paul 290
Body Wars 106-107
Boma, Flavors of Africa 278, 309-310
Bongos Cuban Café 305-306, 338
bonsai 269
"Boo to You" Halloween Parade,
    Mickey's 362
Boulangerie Patisserie 288
Bowling Pin (pool) 379
Bradbury, Ray 101
Brass Bazaar 268-269
Breathless 135
British Invasion, The 131
Brittany's Jewels 250

Brody, Pam 131
Brown Derby, Hollywood 295-296
Bruce's Shark World 117
budget, vacation 247
Buena Vista Pictures 150
Bug, It's Tough to Be a 181
Bug's Life, A 181
buses 212-213
Bush, George W. 70
Butler's Pantry 304
Buzz Imaging 265
Buzz Lightyear's AstroBlaster 340
Buzz Lightyear's Space
    Ranger Spin 83-84
Buzzy 107

C

Cabana Bar & Grill 337
Cabins at Fort Wilderness 240
California Grill 134, 278, 312
California Grill Lounge 338
Calypso Straw Market 248
Calypso Trading Post 248
Camp Dolphin 196
Camp Minnie-Mickey 182, 208-209
camping at Fort Wilderness 216-217
Canada 131-132
Candlelight Processional 371
Candlelight Processional
    dinner package 371
Cantina Street Party 368
Cape May Café 325
Capetown Lounge & Wine Bar 336
Cap'n Jack's 303, 338
Captain Cook's Snack Company 314
Carey, Drew 144
Cargo Bay, Mission: SPACE 266
Caribbean Beach Resort 224-225
Caribbean Cruise 365
Carnales, Los 119
Carolwood Pacific 235
Carousel of Progress, Walt Disney's 8,
    87-88
Carvey, Dana 108
Casablanca Carpets 268
Casey's Corner 282
Casey's Corner, pianist at 89
Castaway Cay 367
Castaway Creek 380

cast members 392-396
Catalina Eddie's 297
Celebration 7, 263
Celebrity Eyeworks Studio 257-258
Celebrity 5 & 10: 271
Central Reservations Office (CRO) 33, 215-216
Changing Attitudes 257
character appearances:
    Magic Kingdom 59
    Epcot 123
    Disney-MGM Studios 152
    Disney's Animal Kingdom 188
Character Carnival 251
Character Premiere 254
Character Warehouse 254
Charleston, SC 369
Chef Mickey's 312-313
Chefs de France, Les 138
Chester & Hester's Dinorama 188
Chester & Hester's Dinosaur Treasures 275
Chewbacca 147, 368
children's meals 280
children, traveling with 195-211
China 122-123
Chinese Theater, Grumann's 142
Christmas Party, Mickey's Very Merry 370-371
Cinderella Castle 14, 74
Cinderella's Golden Carrousel 74-75, 134
Cinderella's Royal Table 134, 278, 281-284
Cinderella's Surprise Celebration 89
Cinderellabration 89-90
Circle of Life: An Environmental Fable 115
CircleVision 360: 122
Cirque du Soleil's *La Nouba* 40, 199, 337-339
Citricos 318
Classic Concoctions 338
Cobb salad 296
Collins, Phil 191
Colonel's Cotton Mill 314
Columbia Harbor House 282
Comedy Warehouse 137, 333-335
Commander Porter's 249-250
Common Ground 366
Company D 357

Computer Pool 379
concierge service 225
Concourse Steakhouse 313
Concourse Sundries & Spirits 248
Conservation Station 179-180
Constance Payne 349
Contemporary Man 248
Contemporary Resort 10, 135, 235-237
Contemporary Woman 249
conventions 218
Copa Banana 337
Coral Reef 47, 117, 287
Coronado Springs Resort 225-226
Cosmic Ray's Starlight Café 282
counter service dining:
    Magic Kingdom 282
    Epcot 288
    Disney-MGM Studios 297
counter service dining (continued)
    Disney's Animal Kingdom 302
    hotels 314
Country Bear Jamboree, The 66
Country Bears, The 66
Country Hoedown 373
Cover Story 271
Cranium Command 107-108
Creature Comforts 275
Crescent Lake 228-229
Crew's Cup 337
CRO 33, 215-216
Crockett's Tavern 338
Cross Country Creek 382
Crown & Crest 267
Cruise Line, Disney 364-368
Crush N Gusher 381
Crystal Arts 260-261
Crystal Palace 284
Cub's Den 196
Curry, Michael 193
Curtis, Jamie Lee 104
Cyberspace Mountain 339
Cyranose de Bergerac 131

D

Daisy (Donald's Boat) 80
Dapper Dans 89
Das Kaufhaus 270
Davis, Bette 143

INDEX 403

Dawa Bar 166, 194, 336
Days of Christmas, Disney's 253-254
DeGeneres, Ellen 104
Delizie Italiane 270
Deluxe Resort Hotels 226-239
Depp, Johnny 95
Der Teddybar 270
DeVine 194
Dewey Cheatem 89
Diamond Horseshoe Saloon 68
Dig Site, The (pool) 379
DinoLand U.S.A. 175, 188, 207-208
Dinorama 188
Dinosaur 192-193
Dinosaur Gertie's Ice Cream 297
dinner shows 342-343
Disabilities, Guests with 45
discounts 224
Discovery Island 20
Disney Adult Discoveries 345
Disney at Home 252-253
Disney Cabanas 250
Disney Characters on Holiday 204
Disney Clothiers 261
Disney Cruise Line 364-368
Disney Dash 72, 93
Disney Dining 35-38, 277-327
Disney, Lillian 151
Disney-MGM Dining 295-300
Disney-MGM Studios 140-163
Disney-MGM Studios Shopping 271-274
Disneyland Park 8, 151
Disney Magic 365
Disney Pin Traders 256
DisneyQuest 339-341
Disney, Roy 9, 14
Disney Stars and Motor Cars 162-163, 205
Disney Vacation Club (DVC) 169-170, 239, 323, 345-349
Disney, Walt 8, 125
Disney Wonder 365
Disney's Animal Kingdom Shopping 274-276
Disney's Character Premiere 254
Disney's Days of Christmas 253-254
Disney's DiveQuest 253
Disney's Family Magic Tour 345
Disney's Magic Music Days 81
Disney's Wonderful World

of Memories 252
DiveQuest 353
Dolphin, Walt Disney World 230-231
Dolphins in Depth 353-354
Donald's Boat 80
Donald's Breakfastosaurus 301
Donald's Double Feature 249
doom buggy 72
Doubletree Guest Suites 223
Doubloon Lagoon (pool) 379
Downtown Disney 330-341
Downtown Disney Dining 302-308
Downtown Disney Resort Hotels 222-223
Downtown Disney Shopping 252-260
Dragon Legend Acrobats 123
Dream Chasers 111
Drew Carey's Sounds Dangerous 144
Drinking Around World Showcase 105
DTV 257
"Dude Looks Like a Lady" 160
Dumbo the Flying Elephant 5, 75, 134, 201
DVC (see Disney Vacation Club)
Dyson, Elliot 335

E

E-Ticket 53
Eagle Pines (golf) 373
Earl of Sandwich 304
Earl, Robert 304
Early Entry (See Extra Magic Hour)
Easter 360
Eastwood, Clint 143
Eat to the Beat Music Series 132
Ebsen, Buddy 151
Edgington, Linda 267
8TRAX 137, 335
Einstein, Albert 105
Eisner, Michael 49, 150, 277
El Pirato Y el Perico 282
El Rio del Tiempo 204
Electric Convenience Vehicles (ECV) 38
Electric Umbrella 288
Electrical Water Pageant 390
Elephant Tales 263
Ellen's Energy Adventure 104-106
Elvis 125

Emperor Zurg 83
Emporium, Main Street 260-261
Empress Lilly 303
Enchanted Tiki Room, The 63-64
End Zone Food Court 314
environmentalism 180
Epcot 9, 98-132
Epcot Dining 286-295
Epcot Garden Discoveries 356
Epcot Seas Aqua Tour 354
Epcot Shopping 265-271
Epcot Vybe 132
ESPN Club 310-311, 336, 341-342
Everything Pop 249, 314
Expedition: EVEREST 174
Expedition: Mars 109
Experience of a Lifetime 384
Experiment 626: 85
Express Elevator 159
Extra Magic Hours 29

F

Fabulous Five 80
Face the Darkest Fears float 90
Family Fun Magazine 208
Family Magic Tour, Disney's 345
Fantasia 248, 374
Fantasia Gardens 374
Fantasia Pool 378
Fantasmic! 136, 163, 205
Fantasmic! Dinner Package 149
Fantastic Plastic Works 103
Fantasy Faire 265
Fantasyland 74-80
FASTPASS 6, 7, 53-54, 57, 93, 115, 141, 174
fax numbers, hotel 398-399
Felix & the Buzzcats 335
Festival of the Lion King 181-182, 208-209
50s Prime Time Café 278, 296-298
Finding Nemo 116
First Aid Centers 211
fishing 376-377
Fittings & Fairings Clothing & Notions 251
Flag Retreat 89
Flagler, Henry M. 238

Flame Tree Barbecue 302
Flights of Wonder 185-187
Florida Natural Springs Pool 379
florist, Walt Disney World 237
Flower and Garden Festival 132, 355-356
Flower Power concert program 132
Flying Fish Café 311
Food & Fun Center 314
Food and Wine Festival, International 2, 360-362
Food Rocks! 114
Fort Sam Clemens 68
Fort Wilderness Petting Farm 387
Fort Wilderness Resort & Campground 10, 216-217
Fountain of Nations 102
Four for a Dollar 156
France 130-131
Francisco's 338
French Quarter, Port Orleans 223
Frontierland 65-69
Frontierland Hoedown 90
Fulton's Crab House 303-304
Fulton's General Store 248
Funai Golf Classic 373
Future World 99, 100-117
Future World Live Entertainment 110

G

G-Force Records 160
Gallerie des Halles 268
Garcia, Andy 371
Garden Grill 287-288
Garden Grove Café 322
Garden View Lounge 138, 238-239, 316-317, 337
Gardens of the World 354
Garland, Judy 125
Gasparilla Grill and Games 314
General Knowledge 107
Germany 123
Ghost Host 74
Glas und Porzellan 270
Goebel 270
Goldthwait, Bobcat 108
Good's Food to Go 314
Goofy's Barnstormer 80
golf 373-374, 376
golf, miniature 374-375, 376

In the spring, Lights, Motors, Action! Extreme Stunt Show will begin performances at Disney-MGM Studios as part of the "Happiest Celebration on Earth."

Good Morning Gatherings 391
Good Neighbor Hotels 244
gorillas 177-178
Gospel Brunch 306-307
Grand Adventures in Cooking 198
Grand Floridian Café 318-319
Grand Floridian Resort & Spa 135, 238-239
Grand Gatherings 388-391
Grandmother Willow 183
grandparents 44
Grand Slam (pool) 378
Graves, Michael 230
Great Moments with Mr. Lincoln 8
Great Movie Ride, The 142-144
Gregory, Leon 131
grocery stores, local 355
Grodin, Charles 108
Grosvenor resort 223
Guerlain perfume 268
Guest Relations 6, 48
Guitar Gallery 258
Guitar (pool) 378
Gulliver's Grill at The Garden Grove 322
Gurgling Suitcase 338

H

HAL 103
Hall of Presidents 69-70
Halloween Party, Mickey's Not-So-Scary 362-364
hand-stamping 65
Happiest Celebration on Earth 2, 89
Harambe 358
Harmony Barber Shop 210, 261-262
Haunted Mansion 72-74
Haunted Mansion (movie) 72
Headless Horseman 362-364
health clubs 385-387
height restrictions, attractions with
    Magic Kingdom 71
    Epcot 113
    Disney-MGM Studios 146
    Disney's Animal Kingdom 189
Helly Hansen 121, 270-271
Henning, Doug 333
Heritage House 264

406 MAKING MEMORIES

Heritage Manor 269
Hidden Mickeys 61, 114, 121, 142, 186, 348
Hidden Treasures of World Showcase 354
High Tea 138
Highway in the Sky 12
Hilton 223
Hippy Dippy (pool) 379
Hollywood & Vine 35, 296
Hollywood Boulevard 162
Hollywood Brown Derby 295-296
Hollywood Hills Amphitheater 163
Hollywood Pictures 150
Hollywood Tower Hotel 157
Home Automated Living 103
Home Away from Home Resorts 239-243
Honey, I Shrunk the Audience 111-112
Honey, I Shrunk the Kids Movie Set Adventure 161-162
Hoop-Dee-Doo Musical Revue 217, 342-343
horseback riding 377, 387
horticulturists 12
Housekeeping, Disney 26
House of Blues 306-307
House of Innoventions 102
House of Treasure 263
Hoypoloi 258
Hummel figurines 270
Humunga Kawabunga 380
Hurricane Hannah's Grill 314, 337
Hydrolator 116

Pocahontas admirers will find "Pochontas and Her Forest Friends" entertaining, if not inspiring. Grandmother Willow's outdoor theater offers little protection from weather of any kind, and the animal appearances offer little to assist this show out of its doldrums.

I

Iago 64
Ice Station Cool 203-204
Il Cristallo 269-270
IllumiNations 118, 132, 136, 204, 289
IllumiNations Cruise 139
Imagination pavilion 111-114
Imagineers, Walt Disney 9, 14, 71
Imaginum 124
Impressions de France 130
Incredibles, The 156
Indiana Jones Adventure Outpost 273
Indiana Jones Epic Stunt Spectacular, The 144-146
Indulgences 250
Innoventions 102-104
Intermission Food Court 314
International Storybook Dinner & IllumiNations Dessert Reception 391
Internet: Disney sites 28
Iron Spike Room 235
Irons, Jeremy 101, 87
Island Mercantile 274
Island Supply 263
Italy 123-124
it's a small world 8, 75-76
It's Tough to Be a Bug! 181

J

Jackson Square Gifts and Desires 248
Jammitors 110
Japan 127-128
Jazz Company, Pleasure Island 137, 335-336
Jelly Rolls 336, 342
Jeopardy! 104-106
Jiko--The Cooking Place 310
Jim Henson's MuppetVision 3*D 147-148, 206-207
jogging 384-385
Journey Into Imagination with Figment 113-114, 204
Judge's Tent 202
July Fourth 359-360
Jungle Cruise 60-61

K

Kali River Rapids 183-185
Karuka 194
Keister Coaster 378
Kelly, Gene 143
Kennedy, John F. 125
kennels 51
Ketchakiddee Creek 199-200, 380
Key to the World 24
Key West 367
Keys to the Kingdom 352
Keystone Clothiers 271-272
Kidcot Fun Stops 99-100, 102, 203
Kid's Night Out 197-198
Kilimanjaro Safaris 176, 177, 207
Kimonos 337
King Arthur and the Holy Grail 131
King, Martin Luther 125
King Triton's Electrical Water Pageant 91, 390
King's Experience 384
King's Gallery, The 265
Kona Cafe 278, 321-322
Kringla Bakeri og Kafe 288
Kristos 110

L

La Bottega Italiana 270
La Boutique des Provinces 267
La Maison du Vin 268
La Nouba (see Cirque du Soleil)
La Patisserie 268
La Vida 380
Lake Buena Vista (golf) 373
Land, The 114-115
Land and Sea Vacation 365
Land of Many Faces 123
Le Cellier Steakhouse 278, 288-289
Leaping Horse Libations 336
Lenôtre, Gaston 290
Leave a Legacy 112
Legend of The Lion King 78
Le Mime Roland 130
Les Chefs de France 138, 290-291
Liberty Belle 71-72
Liberty Inn 288
Liberty Square 69-74

Liberty Square Riverboat 71-72
Liberty Tree Tavern 284-285
Light Chaser 204
Lights! Camera! Action! Theater 150
Lights, Motors, Action! Extreme Stunt Show 150, 162
Lilo & Stitch 84
Lincoln, Abraham 71
Lion King, The 182
Little Mermaid 206
Little Mermaid, Voyage of The 152-154, 206
Living Seas, The 115-117
Living With The Land 114
Lobby Court 337
L'Originale Alfredo di Roma Ristorante 292
Los Carnales 119
Lotus Blossom Cafe 288
lounges (see Bars & Lounges)
Lucas, George 40, 368
luggage storage 234
Luna Park 378

M

Mad Tea Party, The 76-77
Madame Leota 74
Maelstrom 120-121
Maestro Mickey's 249
Magical Fireworks Voyage 389-390
Magical Gatherings 387-391
Magicard, Orlando 15, 17
Magic Behind Our Steam Trains 353
Magic Carpets of Aladdin, The 64-65, 134
Magic Kingdom Dining 281-286
Magic Kingdom Shopping 260-265
Magic Masters 259
Magic Mushroom 336
Magic Music Days 81
Magic of Disney Animation 155-156
Magic of Wales, The 267
Magic Skyway 8
Magic Your Way 30-31, 34-35, 50-51
Magnolia (golf) 373
Maharajah Jungle Trek 187-188, 207
mail order 53
Main Street Bakery 262
Main Street Emporium 260-261

Main Street Philharmonic 89
Main Street, U.S.A. 201-202
Making of Me, The 108
Maleficent 163
Mama Melrose's Ristorante Italiano 299-300
Mannequins Dance Palace 137, 331-332
Mara 314
Marathon, Walt Disney World 359
Mariachi Cobre 119
Mardi Grogs 337
Marketplace, Downtown Disney 199
Martha's Vineyard 337
Matsu No Ma 338
Maya Grill 314-315
Mayor Weaver 89
Meal Plus Certificate 327
Melt-Away Bay 382
merchandise phone orders 53
Merchant of Venus 265
Mexico 118-120
Michelangelo 100
Mickey Avenue 205
Mickey Mouse Club 151
Mickey's Backyard Barbecue 343
Mickey's Birthdayland 80
Mickey's Country House 80-81
Mickey's Jammin' Jungle Parade 193, 207
Mickey's Not-So-Scary Halloween Party 2, 362-364
Mickey's PhilharMagic 77-79, 201
Mickey's Star Traders 265
Mickey's Toontown Fair 6, 80-82, 202
Mickey's Very Merry Christmas Party 369-371
Mighty Duck, The (pool) 378
Mighty Ducks Pinball Slam 340
Millennium Celebration 132
Millionaire, Who Wants to Be a 152
Mime Roland, Le 130
Min & Bill's Dockside Diner 297
miniature golf 374-375, 376
Minnie's Country House 6, 81-82
Miramax Films 150
Mission: SPACE 108-110
Miss Piggy 147
Mister Toad's Wild Ride 77
Mitsukoshi Department Store 127-128, 269
Miyuki 127

Mizner's 337
M. Mouse Mercantile 249
moderate resort hotels 222-226
moderate resort shopping 248
Mombasa Marketplace and
 Ziwani Traders 274-275
monorail 12-14, 313
Moranis, Rick 112
Moreno, Rita 371
Morocco 128-130
Mo Rockin 128-129
Motion 336-337
Mouse About Town 272
MouseFest 2
Mouse Gear 266
Mouseketeer Clubhouse 196
Mozart 87
Muddy Rivers 337
Mulch, Sweat & Shears 159
MuppetVision 3-D 147-148, 206-207
Murphy, Eddie 155
Muscles and Bustles 380

N

Nanea Volcano Pool 379
Narcoossee's 319, 337
Nealson, Kevin 108
Neverland Club 196
New Year's Countdown 137-138
New Year's Day 369-370
New Year's Eve 329, 359-360
New York World's Fair 8, 88
newsletter, resort hotel 216
NFL Experience 383
Night of Joy 366
nightlife at Walt Disney World 328-343
Nine Dragons 293-294
1900 Park Fare 319-320
Norway 120-122
Northwest Mercantile 267
Notorious Banjo Brothers & Bob 90

M is for Mickey Mouse, The Walt Disney Company corporate icon whose many appearances surprise and delight.

Not-So-Scary Halloween Party, Mickey's 362-364
Ny-Form trolls 270
Nye, Bill, The Science Guy 104

O

O Canada! 131
Oak Trail (golf) 373
Odyssey 324
Off-Kilter 131
'Ohana 320-321
Oktoberfest dinner show 123
Ol' Man Island (pool) 379
Old Key West 240-241, 392
Old Port Royal Food Court 225, 314
Olivia's Cafe 316
Olympiad 380
One Man's Dream, Walt Disney: 150-152
Once Upon a Breakfast 281-282
Once Upon a Toy 255-256
100 Years of Magic Celebration 2, 150, 193
Orlando Magicard 15, 17
Orlando Premium Outlet Mall 254
Orlando Rays 384
Osborne Spectacle of Lights 369-370
Osprey Ridge (golf) 373
Outer Rim 338
outlet malls 254

P

package delivery 246
packages, vacation 43
Palio 322
Pal Mickey 18-19, 21
Palm (golf) 373
Pam Brody 131
Palo 365
Panchito's Gifts & Sundries 248
Pangani Forest Exploration Trail 175, 177-178
PAP (see Annual Pass)
parasailing 374, 377
parent-swapping 69
Park-Hopper Option 34
park-hopping 65

payment methods, Walt Disney World 253
Payne, Constance 349
Pecos Bill Cafe 282
Penelope Prose 89
Pepper Market Food Court 225, 314
Perlman, Rhea 87
Petals Pool Bar 338
Peter Burwash International 375
Peter Pan's Flight 77
PhilharMagic Concert Hall 78
Philharmonic, Main Street 89
phone numbers, Disney 44-45
phone numbers, hotels 398-399
PhotoPass, Disney's 52
photo spots:
    Magic Kingdom 70
    Epcot 104
    Disney-MGM Studios 145
    Disney's Animal Kingdom 184
pianist at Casey's Corner 89
Piano (pool) 378
Piccoli, Michael 87
pin-collecting 171
Pinocchio Village Haus 282
Pin Traders, Disney 256
Pioneer Hall 342
Pioneer Hall Revue 343
Pipa, the Talking Trashcan 180
Pirate Adventure, Disney's 197
Pirates of the Caribbean 61-62
Pirates of the Caribbean: Battle for Buccaneer Gold 340
Pizzafari 302
Planet Hollywood 272-273, 307
Playhouse Disney: Live On Stage! 5, 154-155, 206-207
Plaza de los Amigos 271
Plaza Pavilion 282
Plaza Restaurant 285
Pleasure Island 136, 168, 198-199, 328-337
Pleasure Island Jazz Company 137, 335-336
Plume et Palette 268
Pocahontas and Her Forest Friends 182-183
Poet Laureate Penelope Prose 89
Polynesian Princess 249
Polynesian Resort 135, 237-238
Polynesian Village Resort 101
Pooh Corner 254

pool-hopping 378
pools, list of 378-379
Pop Century Resort 23, 221
Port Canaveral 365
Port Orleans Resort 223-224
Portobello Yacht Club 305, 338
Prep Pad, Aronda's 280
Primeval Whirl 190
Princess Storybook Breakfast 294
Priority Seating 279-281
Project X 8-9
Prose, Penelope 89
Prospector "Gold Dust" Gus 90
Puffin's Roost, The 121, 270-271

Q

Queen's Table 267

R

Rafiki's Planet Watch 175, 178-181
railroad:
    Walt Disney World
    Railroad 69, 82
    Wildlife Express 179
Rainforest Café 300-302, 304, 338
Rashad, Phylicia 192
RCID 9
recreation 372-387
Reedy Creek Improvement District 9
Reel Finds 257
Reflections of China 122-123
Reflections of Earth, IllumiNations 118, 132, 136
Research, Disney 6
resort hopping 23
resort hotels 214-244

I is for Imagination, the Epcot pavilion where water falls toward the sky, Figment appears when you least expect him, and a 3-D movie audience escapes by the skin of its teeth!

resort hotel shopping 247-251
Restaurant Akershus 294
Restaurant Marrakesh 129, 138, 291
Restaurantosaurus 302
restroom locators
    Magic Kingdom 60
    Epcot 117
    Disney-MGM Studios 147
    Disney's Animal Kingdom 183
Richard Petty Driving Experience 384

Ride-Along 384
Rip Tide 337
River Roost 337
Rivers of America 68
Roaring Forks Snacks 314
Robinson Crusoe's 249
Robot 110
Rock n Roll Beach Club 137, 336
Rock n Roller Coaster
    Starring Aerosmith 5, 159-161

Rolodex, Disney 44-45

Romance at Walt Disney World 133-139
Rookie Experience 384
room charge 246
Roosevelt, Eleanor 125
Rose & Crown Pub & Dining
    Room 289-290, 338
Rosie's All-American Cafe 297
Royal Albert china 250
Royal Plaza 223

S

Safari Celebration Dinner 390
Safari Village Island Mercantile 274
Safari Village Trails 181
Sam Clemens, Fort 68
San Angel Inn 119, 138, 294-295
Sand Bar 338
Sand Castle Club 196
Sand Trap Bar & Grill 336
Sandy Cove 250
Saratoga Springs Resort &
    Spa, Disney's 240-242

The beautiful okapi graze along the Pangani Forest Exploration Trail in Africa at Disney's Animal Kingdom.

Sassagoula Floatworks &
    Food Factory 314
Scat Cat's Club 337
Sci-Fi Drive-In Dine-In 138, 298-299
scrapbooks 252
SCUBA diving 353
Sea Base Alpha 115
Sea Raycers 375
Seashore Sweets 314
seasons at the parks 46, 215
Security, Walt Disney World 395
Segway 103
Serling, Rod 157
Serveur Amusant 130
Seven Seas Lagoon 11
Shades of Green 242-243
Share a Dream Come True 90, 202
Shark Reef 380
Ship Shape 380
shipping packages 246
shopping 245-276
Short, Martin 108
Shula's Steak House 322-323
Shula's Steak House Lounge 337
Shutters at Old Port Royale 315, 336
Sid Cahuenga's One of a Kind 272
Siesta's 338
Silver Creek Falls 379
Silver Screen Spirits 336
silverback gorillas 177-178
Simba's Cub House 196
Singing Spirits 336
Sinise, Gary 109, 371
Sir Mickey's 265
Si Xian 123
skeptics about Disney 164-172
Slush Gusher 382
Smith, Dave 151
smoking at Walt Disney World 334
snow in Florida 369
Snow White's Scary Adventures 79
Soares, Steve 28
Soarin' 114
Sommerfest 288, 338
Sorcerer Mickey's Hat 142
Sosa Family Cigars 259-260
Sounds Dangerous 144
SPACE: Mission 108-110
Space Mountain 82-83
Space Base 109
Space Race 109

Spaceship Earth 100-102
spas 385-387
special needs 109
SpectroMagic 91, 202
Spelmann's Gledje 121-122
Spirit of Aloha Dinner Show 343
Spirit of America Fife & Drum Corps 126
Spirit of Epcot, The 98
Splash Grill 314, 337
Splash Mountain 66-68
Spoodles 278, 311-312
Sport Goofy's Gifts & Sundries 249
Sports, Disney's Wide World of 373,
    383-384
Sportsman Shoppe, The 267
spring break 360
Stage One Company Store 273-274
Stand-By Line 54
Starabilias 258
Star Tours 146-147, 368
Star Wars 146-147, 368
Star Wars Weekends 147, 368
Statler & Waldorf 148
Stave Church 121
Steiff bears 270
Stitch's Great Escape 84-85
Stone Crab 338
Storm Troopers 368
Stormalong Bay 378
Streetmosphere 19, 141-142
Streets of America Backlot 370
Studio M 254-255
Studio Store 273
Sturdy Branches 380
Summer House 337
Summer Lace 250
Summit Plummet 382
Sunrise Safari Breakfast Adventure 227
Sunset Boulevard 156
Sunset Boulevard Glee Club 141
Sunset Club Couture 272
Sunshine Season Food Fair 288
supermarkets, local 355
Super Soap Weekend, ABC 364
Superstar Television 21
Surfboard Bay (pool) 378
surfing lessons 382
surrey bicycles 383, 387
Suspended Animation 257
Swan, Walt Disney World 230-231

414 Making Memories

swimming 378-379
Swiss Family Treehouse 62-63

T

Taiko Drums 127
Tambu Lounge 337
Tangier Traders 269
Tangierine Café 288
Tarzan Rocks! 191-192, 208
Tatooine Traders 273
Tea Caddy, The 267-268
Teamboat Springs 382
Team Mickey's Athletic Club 255
Team Spirits 336
Temple of Heaven 122
Tempura Kiku 291-292
tennis 375
Teppanyaki Dining Rooms 292
Territory 337
Test Track 110-111
Thanksgiving 369-370
Thimbles and Threads 251
tickets and passes 30-32, 50-51
Tike's Peak 200
Tiki Bird Room, The Enchanted 63-64
Tilly, Jennifer 72
Timekeeper, The 87
Timeline, Walt Disney World 10-11
Time machine 100
Tinker Bell 202
Toluca Legs Turkey Company 297
Toad's Wild Ride, Mr. 77
Tom Morrow 167
Tom Morrow 2.0's Playground 103
Tom Sawyer Island 68
Tomorrowland 82-89
Tomorrowland Indy Speedway 85, 86
Tomorrowland Transit Authority 11, 88-89
Tony's Town Square Cafe 285-286
Toontown Fair, Mickey's 6, 80-82, 202
Toontown Hall of Fame 81
Torgersen, Trygve 270
Touchstone Pictures 149
Tower of Terror, Twilight Zone 156-158
Town Square 89
Toy Soldier, The 267
Toy Story Pizza 297
Trader Jack's 249
Trailblaze Corral, Ft. Wilderness 377
Trail's End Buffet 314
transportation 212-213
Transportation and Ticket Center 237
Trebeck, Alex 104
Treasures of Morocco 129
Tree of Life, The 174, 181
Triceratop Spin 5, 190-191
Trout Pass 337
Tubbi's Buffeteria 314
tubing 377
Tumble Monkeys 182
Tune-In Lounge 338
Turtle Shack 338
Turtle Talk with Crush 117, 203
Tusker House 302, 390
20,000 Leagues Under the Sea 79-80
Twilight Zone Tower of Terror 156-158
Typhoon Lagoon 379-381

U

Ultimate Home Theater 103
Ultimate Park Hopper 32
Undiscovered Future World 356-357
United Kingdom pavilion 131
Universe of Energy 104-106
Uptown Jewelers 262
Utilidors 14, 350-352
Uzima Springs (pool) 378
Uzima Springs Bar 336

V

VABS 92
vacation packages 43
vacation planning:
    budgeting 41-42, 46-55
    Internet resources 28
    mistakes to avoid 13
value resorts 217-222
value resort shopping 249
Vereen, Ben 371
Vergé, Roger 290
Verne, Jules 87
Victoria & Albert's 320
Victoria Falls 336
video, vacation planning 33
View Master 298
Villas at Wilderness Lodge 240

Virgin Megastore 259
VISA, Disney 40
Voices of Liberty 126
Volkskunst 123, 270
Voyage of The Little Mermaid 152-154

W

wakeboarding 377
walking 384-385
Walt Disney: One Man's Dream 150-152
Walt Disney Pictures 150
Walt Disney Theater 367
Walt Disney World Florist 237
Walt Disney World Marathon 359
Walt Disney World Railroad 69, 82
Walt Disney's Carousel of Progress 8, 87-88
"war horse" 350
Wassalou 194
water parks 379-383
water skiing 377
Waterford crystal 252
Wayne, John 143
Weaver, Sigourney 142
Web sites, Unofficial Disney 28
Weddings, Disney 34, 36
WEDway People Mover 88
"We Go On" 132
Weinkeller 270
Weiss, Al 7, 389
Welcome to the Magic Kingdom, Disney's 358
Wells, H.G. 87
Wendt, George 108
West Side, Downtown Disney 136, 199
West Side Shopping 257-260, 337-341
Wetzel's Pretzels 307-308
Wetzel, Rick 307
Where's the Fire? 103
Whispering Canyon Café 324-325
Who Wants to Be a Millionaire: Play It! 152
Wide World of Sports, Disney's 373, 383-384
Wild By Design 357-358
Wilderness Lodge 33, 233-235
Wilderness Lodge, Villas at 240
Wildernss Lodge Mercantile 250

Wildhorse Saloon 336
Wildlife Conservation Fund 180
Wildlife Express 179
Williams, Robin 87
Wills, Deb 17, 49, 279
wine-tasting seminars 361
Winnie the Pooh, The Many Adventures of 77, 201
Winter-Summerland, Disney's 374
Wishes Nighttime Spectacular 72, 90-91, 134, 202
Wizard of Oz 143
Wolfgang Puck Café 307
Wonderful World of Memories, Disney's 252
Wonderland Tea Party, The 198
Wonders of Life 106-108
Wonders of the Wild 275-276
Woody & Friends 68
World of Disney 256
World Premier Food Court 314
World Showcase 99, 117-132
World Showcase Lagoon 132
World Showcase Players 130
World Update 216
Writer's Stop, The 274
Wyland Galleries 249, 251
Wyndham Palace Resort & Spa 223

Y

Yacht Club 229-230
Yacht Club Galley 326-327
Yachtsman's Steakhouse 325-326
Yakitori House 288
Yard Arcade 342
Yong Feng Shangdian 270
Yorkshire County Fish Shop 288

Z

Zahanati 380
Zanzibar Trading Company 263
Zawadi Marketplace 251
Zazu 64
Zip-a-Dee-Doo-Dah 67
Ziwani Traders 274-275

ARONDA'S WDW VACATION PREP PAD

Need a vacation planner that's big enough to hold all your plans, but small enough to go all over the World with you?

The Original Press is pleased to offer **Aronda's Walt Disney World Vacation Prep Pad**, the quintessential vacation organizer whose small size makes it easy to carry around in the parks, whether in your fanny pack, your pocket, purse or backpack. **Prep Pad** pockets safely store your FASTPASSes, tickets, receipts, PhotoPass cards and more.

As a **Making Walt Disney World Vacation Memories** reader, you're entitled to more than 30% off the original price of $7.95. Just complete the coupon below — or write your name and address on a slip of paper — and enclose a check or money order (payable to The Original Press) for $5.49 for each **Prep Pad**. For all orders in the U.S., please add $1.00 for the first Prep Pad, then add fifty cents for each additional one. For all orders outside the U.S., please write Aronda at disneyguide@arondaparks.com for a shipping quote.

The Original Press
Prep Pad Offer
PO Box 3466
Summerville, SC 29484-3466

Name
Address
City, State, Zip
E-Mail
Pads Ordered_____   Total Enclosed_____